Stephen Neale is Assistant Professor of
Philosophy at Princeton University.

Descriptions

Descriptions

Stephen Neale

A Bradford Book
The MIT Press
Cambridge, Massachusetts
London, England

Library of Congress Cataloging-in-Publication Data

Neale, Stephen.
    Descriptions / Stephen Neale.
        p. cm.
    "A Bradford book."
    Includes bibliographical references.
    ISBN 0-262-14045-4
    1. Languages—Philosophy. 2. Description (Philosophy)
3. Anaphora (Linguistics) I. Title.
P106.N36   1990
121'.68—dc20   90-34300
                                                                 CIP

For my mother and father

Contents

Preface

In *Mind* for 1905, Bertrand Russell published a fourteen-page paper entitled "On Denoting" in which he presented his famous *Theory of Descriptions*. The present work is, in part, an attempt to explicate, defend, and extend the central theses of that notoriously difficult and controversial paper, and to explain why these theses should be taken very seriously by contemporary philosophers, logicians, and linguists.

Unlike Russell's paper, it is not the purpose of the present work to present any fundamentally new ideas; its purpose is to fuse a variety of existing ideas in a coherent and productive way, and to present the results in a form that will be useful to both philosophers and linguists. There have been many innovative moves and technical accomplishments in the philosophy of language, philosophical logic, and theoretical linguistics since the beginning of the century; and in light of some of these developments, a strong case can be made for giving the Theory of Descriptions a prominent position in contemporary work on the semantics of natural language. Not only does Russell's theory interact in elegant and productive ways with contemporary accounts of quantification, variable-binding, anaphora, syntactical structure, and indexicality, it also forces the philosopher of language to think hard about important methodological issues concerning the so-called "division of linguistic labor."

The present essay is a thoroughly overhauled and expanded version of my doctoral thesis, written under the supervision of John Perry at Stanford University and submitted in August 1988. Two factors jointly conspired to steer me toward a thesis on descriptions. In the spring of 1985, I attended a graduate seminar on the philosophy of language taught by John Perry and Jon Barwise. I was a staunch advocate of broadly Gricean accounts of speaker's meaning and the semantics-pragmatics distinction; since Barwise and Perry saw things rather differently, there was a great deal to argue about. Much of their seminar was devoted to the interpretation of "singular terms," and since I had already made up my mind to write on the semantics-pragmatics distinction, I began to think that detailed work on definite descriptions would provide the basis of a valuable case study. A lengthy conversation with Paul Grice, a close reading of Saul Kripke's openly Gricean characterization of the debate surrounding so-called "referential" uses of descriptions, and a couple of off-hand remarks by Stuart Hampshire all reinforced my belief that a critical examination of the Gricean defense of Russell would make a good chapter. An entire dissertation on descriptions seemed out of the question—especially after Stuart's comment that the only surer way to unemployment in the humanities was a dissertation on Virginia Woolf.

The second route to definite descriptions was a graduate seminar on events taught by Julius Moravcsik and Ed Zalta in the autumn of 1985. It seemed to me that some important metaphysical issues were turning on delicate semantical matters concerning the interpretation of various modal operators and definite descriptions of actions and events. The problems here seemed both more pressing and more exciting than those surrounding the semantics-pragmatics distinction, and a rather different dissertation started to come into focus. It would be easy enough, I thought, to spell out and defend Russell's theory in a single chapter using the material on descriptions from the earlier project. I could then move on to descriptions of actions and events, and finally to the metaphysical issues that had bothered me in the first place. I never got past stage one. The Theory of Descriptions seemed to be under attack from all sides, and I decided that a thorough defense was in order.

Many people have influenced this work over the last few years. A chronological tour seems to me to be both the most pleasurable way to record one's debt and the easiest way to avoid oversight. My earliest and greatest debt is to John Perry, who began his supervision by overseeing the conversion of an early paper into a rough draft of Chapter 3 in the summer of 1986. Discussions with Trip McCrossin were invaluable at this stage. Autumn of 1986 was spent at Corpus Christi College, Oxford, rewriting Chapter 3 and putting together a first draft of Chapter 2. Thanks go to Martin Davies, Kathinka Evers, Jennifer Hornsby, Peter Strawson, David Wiggins, and Deirdre Wilson for valuable discussion and hospitality. I am particularly indebted to Martin, who by way of written comments, conversation, and the discussion of descriptions in his underutilized book *Meaning, Quantification, Necessity*, has left his mark on every chapter of the present work.

Versions of Chapter 3 were presented in talks at CNRS in November 1986, at University College London in December 1986, and back at Stanford in January 1987. I am especially grateful to François Recanati and Dan Sperber for valuable discussions while I was in Paris. I'm not sure how many long afternoons François and I spent discussing descriptions and the semantics-pragmatics distinction, but I *do* know that our discussions played an important role in the subsequent restructuring of Chapter 3—although François disagrees with the main conclusions drawn there.

On returning to Stanford in January of 1987, I began to worry about various problems concerning the interpretation of pronouns anaphoric on definite and indefinite descriptions, and I found myself drawn to Gareth Evans' pioneering work on pronominal anaphora. At the same time as I began jotting down notes for Chapter 5, I began work on a joint paper with Peter Ludlow on Russell's theory of *indefinite* descriptions. We gave two talks on indefinite descriptions and anaphora at Stanford later that spring and I presented a summary of our position at a summer meeting of the ASL in Granada, Spain. Ever since, there has been a two-way flow of ideas and examples between parts of our joint paper and several sections of the present work (3.5, 4.2, 5.4, 5.5, and 5.7). This is not to say that Peter agrees with everything in *this* essay.

Work on Chapters 5 and 6 continued throughout the academic year 1987-88, and some of the material was presented at a meeting of the ASL in New York in December 1987, a talk at the University of Pittsburgh in January 1988, a talk at Linacre College, Oxford in February 1988, and an APA Pacific Division meeting in Portland in March 1988. I am grateful to Nick Asher, George Bealer, Nuel Belnap, Joe Camp, Richard Gale, James Garson, Dan Isaacson, Jeffrey King, John McDowell, and John Perry for asking searching questions and making many useful suggestions.

The first version of Chapter 4 was dashed off in the autumn of 1987. I had never really thought that nonextensional contexts created any problem for the Russellian; but Dagfinn Føllesdal and John Perry convinced me that it would be rash to just assume this and that it was important to spell out in detail why I was not afraid to join those who permit quantification into modal contexts and those who have faith in the Russellian account of *de re–de dicto* ambiguities as the products of scope permutations. Parts of this chapter were presented in talks on modality and events given at MIT, Stanford, and Berkeley in the fall of 1989.

While at Stanford I received valuable advice and much-needed support from a number of people, including John Barwise, Johann van

Benthem, Paddy Blanchette, Joan Bresnan, Sylvain Bromberger, Mark Crimmins, Adrian Cussins, John Etchemendy, Dagfinn Føllesdal, Jonathan Franklin, Paul Grice, Stuart Hampshire, David Israel, Martin Jones, Trip McCrossin, David Magnus, Julius Moravcsik, John Perry, Justine Rosenheck, Stanley Peters, Jamie Rucker, Ivan Sag, Nicola Stronach, Leora Weitzman, Tom Wasow, and Ed Zalta.

I have spent much of the last year and a half rewriting the dissertation as a book. Three points about my writing should be mentioned. The first point is relatively minor: I have not been especially careful about use and mention (except where necessary) and for the most part I have used single quotes where others might have been tempted to use corner quotes.

Second, despite the conceptual and technical complexity of some of the issues addressed, I have attempted to present all of the material in a form that might be useful to upper-level undergraduate students in philosophy. Writing in this way has forced me to clarify certain issues in my own mind and has (to some extent) prevented me from proceeding too quickly and making several nontrivial assumptions. It has also given me the chance to produce a book I could use at certain points in a first course on the philosophy of language. Drafts of Chapters 2, 3, and 4 were, in fact, used in such a course at Princeton in the spring of 1989, and I am very grateful to a number of students who gave me tips for improving the presentation. Inevitably, the result of writing in this way is a work that may drag in places for the professional philosopher.

The third point about my writing concerns the possibly excessive number of notes and references. With an eye to readability, I have relegated a fair number of historical, technical, and linguistic remarks and other clutter to the notes gathered at the end of each chapter. Some of the notes are self-contained; others expand upon points in the main text, entertain alternative hypotheses, or point to other parts of the text or to other notes; still others contain only references; *all* of them can be ignored on a first pass.

I have gone to some lengths to trace ideas where appropriate, and this has led to several amusing episodes with colleagues. I was pleased when I found a distinction between quantificational and referential interpretations of descriptions in Rundle (1965), published a year before Donnellan's (1966) influential paper. Martin Davies then drew my attention to a similar distinction in Mitchell (1962). Several weeks later, John Perry directed me to a related distinction in Marcus (1961). I then discovered that Geach (1962) and Hampshire (1959) had both anticipated and responded to a potential referential challenge. But then François Recanati undercut my efforts by tracing the distinction to the theological writings of the seventeenth-century French philosopher Antoine Arnauld.

I had assumed for some time that the earliest mention of the idea that descriptions might be treated as restricted quantifiers (or that the determiner 'the' might be treated as a binary quantifier) was due to Grice (1969). David Lewis pointed out to me that the same point was made by Sharvy (1969). An excursion into David's filing system unearthed several unpublished papers and some lecture notes from the mid-to-late 1960s that made use of the same idea. References in these papers and notes finally led me to Prior (1963), which, as far as I have been able to ascertain, is the earliest published source.

In response to a question from Johann van Benthem at a summer meeting of the ASL in Granada, I came up with what I thought was an interesting and novel solution to one of the main problems involving so-called "donkey" anaphora. Modifying Gareth Evans's theory of "E-type" anaphora, I suggested that unbound pronouns anaphoric on indefinite descriptions and universally quantified phrases might go proxy for number-neutral definite descriptions. In the autumn, I wrote a paper in which I explored this idea. I sent a copy to Martin Davies and received a letter back inviting me to look at p. 175 of his book, where, in passing, he had made the same suggestion (for indefinite descriptions). Later Jim Higginbotham traced the same idea to a circulated but unpublished paper by Terry Parsons (1978). (No doubt Recanati is at this moment wading through musty theological manuscripts. . . .)

At Princeton I have received valuable comments and suggestions from Jeremy Butterfield, Bob Freidin, Gil Harman, Richard Holton, David Lewis, Saul Kripke, Michaelis Michael, Scott Soames, Dan Sperber, and Nancy Worman. I am also grateful to Princeton University for granting me a leave for the academic year 1989-90, the first semester of which was used, in part, to put the finishing touches to this project.

A graduate seminar on anaphora that I taught with Scott Soames had a significant impact on the rewriting of Chapters 5 and 6. Very special thanks must go to Scott and to Peter Ludlow and Martin Davies for helping me to work out some of the details of the account of descriptive anaphora examined in those chapters, and for taking the trouble to read through the entire manuscript and provide me with detailed written comments. I am also indebted to Irene Heim, James Higginbotham, Jeffrey King, and Richard Larson for written comments on various portions of the manuscript.

Finally, I want to thank the people who have saved me so much time, labor, and anxiety: Ingrid Deiwiks, Dawn Hyde, and Trip McCrossin at Stanford, Alice Devlin, Richard Holton, Bunny Romano, and Nancy Worman at Princeton, and Joanna Poole and Lorrie LeJeune at the MIT Press.

Parts of Chapters 5 and 6 are based on "Descriptive pronouns and donkey anaphora," *Journal of Philosophy*, 1987. Material reprinted by permission.

S.N.

Descriptions

. . . in this chapter we shall consider the word *the* in the singular, and in the next chapter we shall consider the word *the* in the plural. It may be thought excessive to devote two chapters to one word, but to the philosophical mathematician it is a word of very great importance: like Browning's grammarian with the enclitic δε, I would give the doctrine of this word if I were "dead from the waist down" and not merely in prison.

BERTRAND RUSSELL

. . . that paradigm of philosophy, Russell's theory of descriptions.

FRANK RAMSEY

Chapter 1

Introduction

It seems clear that we are capable of entertaining thoughts about particular objects or individuals. It seems equally clear that on various occasions, and for a variety of reasons, we desire to express some of these thoughts, and that we are capable of doing so by uttering sentences of subject-predicate form, such as the following:

(1) Lisa is asleep
(2) Modena is less than one hundred miles from Bologna
(3) I'm tired
(4) You don't look well
(5) This vase is chipped
(6) That's a spider.

On the face of it, the following sentences also look like good candidates, but as we shall see, appearances can be deceptive:

(7) My mother is British
(8) The man in the gabardine suit is a spy
(9) A man I met in the pub last night gave me a hundred pounds
(10) Lisa's departure caused me great distress.

The particular thought (or thoughts) I can be said to have expressed on a given occasion will be a function of the words I have used and their syntactical organization. In each of sentences 1–10, there seems to be a natural division between the grammatical *subject* and the grammatical *predicate*. Abstracting away from indexical and other context-dependent features of language for the moment, we might paint the following picture: For a sentence 'b is G', where 'b' is a singular noun phrase and '— is G' a monadic predicate phrase, 'b' refers to an individual b, and '— is G' predicates something of b. In the parlance of truth-conditional semantics, 'b' refers to b, and 'b is G' is true if and only if b is G. On this account, we might say that the thought (or proposition) expressed by an utterance of 'b is G' is *about b*, i.e., about the referent of 'b'.

But there are sentences of grammatically subject-predicate form that do not function in this way. Anselm worried about *Nihil me docuit volare* ('Nothing taught me to fly'); Lewis Carroll worried about 'Nobody walks faster than I do'. Related worries surface with 'Some politicians will lie to get elected' and 'All men are mortal'. Since there is no clear sense in which the grammatical subjects of any of these sentences refers to a particular individual (of which a certain thing is predicated), there would appear to be no prospect of providing a uniform semantical treatment of noun phrases in natural language. This was something that Frege saw, and he invented a theory—quantification theory—that enabled him to treat these *grammatically* subject-predicate sentences as having no *logical* subjects. In effect, Frege's *quantificational* analyses of such sentences was the inauguration of the modern tradition of distinguishing between *grammatical* and *logical* form.

Frege handed us an intuitive, semantically significant distinction between two classes of noun phrases: the class of singular referring expressions and the class of quantifiers. (For the purposes of this chapter, we can pass over the fact that Frege's quantifiers are unrestricted and that a distinction must therefore be drawn between *quantifiers* and *quantified noun phrases*; see 2.5.) But how, exactly, are we to decide to which category any particular noun phrase belongs? In English, the morphological and syntactical differences between singular and plural are imperfect guides. First, there is the annoying fact that 'all men', 'some men', and 'no men' are syntactically plural, whereas 'every man', 'some man', and 'no man' are syntactically singular; yet it is obvious that the latter are just as much quantifiers as the former. Having granted ourselves the discretionary power (in such "obvious" cases) to classify certain syntactically singular noun phrases as quantifiers, it might be thought that all other singular noun phrases are referring expressions: proper names ('Lisa', 'Bologna'), personal and impersonal pronouns ('she', 'her', 'herself', 'you', 'it'), demonstrative pronouns ('this', 'that'), definite descriptions ('the man in the gabardine suit', 'the table'), indefinite descriptions ('a man I met in the pub last night', 'a friend of mine'), demonstrative descriptions ('that man in the corner', 'this vase'), and nominalizations of one form or another ('Lisa's departure', 'Nixon's resigning'). However, there are some important philosophical and linguistic differences between these categories, and when they are explored, compared, and refined, difficult choices have to be made concerning the nature of the relation between certain expressions belonging to one or other grouping, and those objects to which they are taken to refer.

Russell's analyses of definite descriptions (phrases of the form 'the so-and-so') and indefinite descriptions (phrases of the form 'a so-and-so') mark the modern beginnings of this sort of concern.[1] For it was Russell who first took exception to viewing this intuitive class of singular noun phrases as a unified *semantical* category. According to Russell, where '*b*' is a genuine referring expression (a "logically proper name"), the picture presented above is correct. The sole function of a referring expression is to pick out an object. If that object satisfies the predicate of the sentence, then the sentence is true; or rather the *thought* or *proposition*—I shall use these terms interchangeably—expressed by an utterance of the sentence is true. If the referent of '*b*' does not satisfy the predicate, then it is false.

But how are we to treat definite descriptions like 'the largest prime number', 'the present King of France', and 'the Fountain of Youth', to which nothing answers? We can certainly make meaningful assertions by employing sentences containing such expressions:

(11)   There is no such thing as the largest prime number
(12)   The largest prime number is greater than 10^{29}
(13)   Ralph thinks the largest prime number is greater than 10^{29}
(14)   Jane wants to marry the present King of France
(15)   John has never seen the present King of France
(16)   The King of France does not exist
(17)   Ponce de Leon searched for the Fountain of Youth.

One approach to these sentences would be to posit a realm of nonexistent entities to serve as the referents of the descriptions they contain; indeed, this is an approach that Russell once took.[2] But by 1905 he felt that this position was "intolerable," and the Theory of Descriptions emerged, in part, as part of Russell's desire to purify his ontology. According to Russell, if a putative referring expression '*b*' can be supposed not to refer, yet a sentence containing '*b*' still be supposed to express a determinate thought, then '*b*' cannot be a genuine referring expression.[3] Whenever we encounter such a situation, the *Theory of Descriptions* is to be wheeled out and the sentence given a logical parsing in which there is no genuine "subject." For the whole purpose of the Theory of Descriptions is to make available a special class of *object-independent* thoughts. A genuine referring expression '*b*' may be combined with a (monadic) predicate expression to express an *object-dependent* thought, a thought that simply could not be expressed or even entertained if the object referred to by '*b*' did not exist. A definite description 'the *F*', by contrast, although it *may* in fact be satisfied by a unique object x, can be combined with a (monadic) predicate to express a thought that is not contingent upon the existence of x.[4] For descriptions, on Russell's account, belong with the quantifiers—what he calls *denoting* phrases—and not with the referring expressions.[5]

Informally, we may state the main thesis of the Theory of Descriptions thus: If 'the F' is a definite description and '— is G' a monadic predicate phrase, then the proposition expressed by an utterance of 'the F is G' is logically equivalent to the proposition expressed by an utterance of 'there is one and only one F, and everything that is F is G'.[6] And this proposition is object-independent, in the sense that there is no object for which 'the F' stands, upon which the existence of the proposition depends.

What, then, is the philosophical significance of this theory? Of course it can be seen as a contribution to a purely semantical project, that of constructing an empirically adequate theory of meaning for natural language. Indeed, one of my aims in this essay is to provide a clear characterization of this contribution. I want to suggest that the Theory of Descriptions has application well beyond the sorts of phrases and constructions Russell dealt with. Indeed, if (*i*) all descriptions are quantifiers, and (*ii*) the domain of application of the Theory of Descriptions is as broad as I suggest it is, then it is at least arguable that every natural language noun phrase is either a quantifier or a referring expression.

While the semantical project is undoubtedly an important and interesting one, it should be emphasized that Russell's primary concerns lay elsewhere. The Theory of Descriptions was originally conceived as a contribution to metaphysical and psychological projects, and to that extent it was a tool with which to dissolve certain philosophical puzzles. For instance, the theory is supposed to give us a way of characterizing the thoughts expressed by sentences like (11)–(17). It is plain that perfectly determinate thoughts may be expressed by utterances of these sentences despite the fact that they contain nondenoting descriptions. Because it treats descriptions as complex existential quantifiers rather than referring expressions, the Theory of Descriptions gave Russell the power to explain this fact without positing a realm of nonexistent objects. (Russell also considered the Theory of Descriptions to be the first important breakthrough in his quest to solve the set-theoretic paradoxes.)

The Theory of Descriptions also played an important role in Russell's epistemology. Russell was so committed to the view that there could be no illusion of entertaining an object-dependent thought when, in reality, there was no actual object that the purported thought was about, that he was led to the thesis that only a sense-datum could be trusted as the "subject" of such a thought. Because of the close connection between his theory of thought and his semantics, this led Russell to the view that the proposition expressed by an utterance of a sentence consisting of an ordinary proper name combined with a monadic predicate could not be object-dependent. And by treating names as "disguised" descriptions, he was able to provide an analysis of such sentences as expressing object-independent propositions.

Russell was not the last philosopher to wield the Theory of Descriptions as a philosophical tool. It has been appealed to many times by philosophical logicians, particularly those defending the coherence of quantified modal and epistemic logics. Arthur Smullyan (1948), for example, has argued that Quine's (1943, 1953) attacks on quantified modal logic turn on a failure to see that, *qua* quantifiers, definite descriptions lie beyond the domain of application of the *Principle of Substitutivity*. In my opinion Smullyan thoroughly discredits Quine's attempts to demonstrate the incoherence of quantified modal logic. However, the debate continues to the present day because Quine and others have misunderstood Russell and failed to appreciate the main points of Smullyan's paper. This matter is addressed in detail in Chapter 4. Attention to the scope of descriptions in nonextensional contexts and to matters of substitutivity is often crucial in metaphysics and in the philosophy of mind and action where definite and indefinite descriptions of events and actions are common currency. In Chapter 4, I shall also indicate why I think that some confusion in recent discussions of event identity has arisen through inattention to the logical forms of sentences containing descriptions of events. The Theory of Descriptions is, then, of interest not only to the project of constructing a semantical theory for natural language but also as a useful tool with which to investigate the logical structures of certain philosophical claims.

Many of the popular objections to the Theory of Descriptions have their roots in Strawson's (1950) "On Referring." Underlying each of Strawson's objections is the belief that descriptions are genuine referring expressions and that to insist otherwise is just to misunderstand the function of singular noun phrases in communication. Now it is surely not open to dispute that a sentence of the form 'the F is G' may be used to *communicate* an object-dependent thought to someone to the effect that some particular individual b is G. This might be because a particular description is associated in some way with a particular *proper name*, or because it could be associated, in the context in question, with a particular *demonstrative*. On the first count, Marcus (1961) has pointed out that over a period of time a description may actually come to be used as a proper name—as "an identifying tag"—its descriptive meaning "lost or ignored" ('The evening star' and 'the Prince of Denmark' are two of her examples). On the second count, Donnellan (1966) has exploited examples like the following. Suppose you and I are at a party together and both notice a man standing alone in the far corner; I also notice that he is trying to attract your attention, so I say to you, "The man in the far corner is trying to attract your attention." Here I might be said to be using the definite description 'the man in the far corner' *referentially*, in the sense that I intend to *communicate* an object-dependent thought (about that very man) rather than (or rather than *just*) an object-independent thought to the effect that the unique satisfier of a certain descriptive condition also satisfies some other condition. (Similar cases can be constructed involving *in*definite descriptions.)

No one, I take it, contests the phenomenon of referential usage. But there is considerable disagreement as to the *significance* of this phenomenon when it comes to the construction of a semantical theory. A number of philosophers have argued that where a description is used referentially, we must reject Russell's object-independent truth conditions. On Russell's account, an utterance of 'the F is G', is true just in case there is some entity x such that x is uniquely F and x is G. But according to Russell's opponent, when 'the F' is being used referentially, the truth-conditions make no mention of any uniquely descriptive condition. In such a case 'the F' is functioning as a singular referring expression: it is being used to refer to some particular individual b; and the utterance is therefore true just in case b is G. It is suggested, in short, that descriptions are *semantically ambiguous* between quantificational and referential *interpretations*.

The ambiguity theory has been spelled out and endorsed in one form or another by Rundle, Donnellan, Stalnaker, Partee, Peacocke, Hornsby, Kaplan, Devitt, Wettstein, Recanati, Fodor and Sag, and Barwise and Perry.[7] Although there are a variety of theoretical differences in the way these philosophers have accommodated referential usage, there are two theses most of them seem to hold (or to have held): (*i*) Russell's analysis does not provide a correct account of the proposition expressed by an utterance of a sentence containing a description used referentially; and (*ii*) a correct account will be stated in terms of an object-dependent proposition, the character of which will depend upon the identity of the 'referent' of the description, as used on that occasion (in the simplest cases, this will just be the unique object satisfying the description).

The typical response from those sympathetic to Russell appeals to an intuitive but tricky distinction between *semantics* and *pragmatics*.

In our daily talk we very often convey things indirectly, relying on what we take to be our interlocutors' abilities (innate or learned) to grasp (see, deduce) what *we* mean by our utterances. But this does not force the semanticist to build the range of messages it is possible to convey by using a given sentence into the semantics of the sentence itself. This point of view has been most clearly articulated by people like Grice and Searle.[8] Indeed, the first published defence of a unitary Russellian analysis of descriptions in the face of the referential challenge was, I believe, the one sketched by Grice towards the end of his 1969 paper "Vacuous Names."[9] Grice's idea is to appeal to an antecedently motivated distinction between what a speaker *says* (the proposition expressed) and what the speaker *means* (what the speaker seeks to communicate to the hearer). According to Grice, the truth-conditions of an utterance of a sentence of the form 'the *F* is *G*' are strictly Russellian, even if 'the *F*' is used referentially. The speaker may, however, wish to get it across to the hearer that a particular individual *b* is *G*, and may succeed in doing this by (e.g.) exploiting the fact that both speaker and hearer take *b* to be the *F*. While the proposition that *b* is *G* may well be part of what is *meant*, Grice suggests, it is not the proposition actually expressed (what is *said*, as he puts it), nor is it a consequence of that proposition.

This strategy has been articulated and defended by Kripke, Searle, Klein, and Davies.[10] These philosophers hold (or have held) something like the following two theses: (*i*) Russell's analysis gives a (more or less) correct account of the proposition expressed by an utterance of a sentence containing a description, even when the description is used referentially; and (*ii*) the fact that we may communicate object-dependent propositions by using description-containing sentences is to be accounted for by a theory of communication, speaker's meaning, or speech acts, not by a semantical theory. Let's call this the *pragmatic* account of referential usage.

One of my aims in this essay is to defend the Theory of Descriptions as a genuine contribution to the semantics of natural language. This will involve deflecting several distinct arguments against the unitary Russellian analysis that have gained some currency over the years. In my opinion, none of these arguments has any real force; indeed, I shall attempt to show that each involves substantial confusion and outright error. I shall also attempt to undercut the ambiguity theory by presenting a clear and explicit statement of the pragmatic account of referential usage and explaining its advantages and strengths.

A second aim is to delimit the domain of application of the Theory of Descriptions. I shall suggest that the theory can (and should) be extended to: (*i*) *plural* descriptions like 'the men in the corner', (*ii*) *numberless* descriptions like 'whoever shot John F. Kennedy', (*iii*) *possessives* like 'Smith's murderer' and 'his dog', (*iv*) *indexical* descriptions like 'my mother' and 'that man's bicycle', (*v*) *relativized* descriptions like 'the father of each girl' and 'each girl's father', (*vi*) *derived nominal* constructions like 'Mary's departure', and (*vii*) *gerundive nominal* constructions like 'my leaving in such a hurry'. All of these will be pulled into the descriptive camp and provided with plausible Russellian analyses.[11]

A complete semantical theory for a language like English will undoubtedly be composed of various interacting subtheories, such as theories of reference (subsuming theories of names and demonstratives), quantification, mass terms, indexicality, anaphora, conditionals, nominalization, adverbial modification, tense, aspect, ellipsis, modality, attitude reports, nonassertive speech acts, and so on. From a methodological standpoint we have no alternative to proceeding in a modular fashion, attempting to find a phenomenon that is to some suitable extent isolable, open to investigation in abstraction from various other phenomena. We can then construct a theory of the phenomenon we are interested in and begin to look at its predictive power, particularly as it interacts with theories of other isolable phenomena.

I am going to take this methodological strategy very seriously. Indeed, one underlying theme will be that many of the alleged difficulties for the Theory of Descriptions are not really difficulties that concern descriptions *per se*. They are either reflexes of more general issues in the theory of quantification, or else the products of the inevitable complexities that emerge when one takes into account descriptions in constructions (or linguistic contexts) that have their own semantical or syntactical problems (and hence fall under their own semantical subtheories), or some combination of both. The moral that will (I hope) emerge is that the Theory of Descriptions interacts in a variety of interesting and powerful ways with theories of (e.g.) indexicality, ellipsis, syntactical structure, anaphora, modality, tense, and attitude reports. (I shall not, of course, attempt to work out the precise details of the various theories with which the Theory of Descriptions must interact.)

A third aim is to push to its limits one plausible way of thinking about the semantical content of anaphoric pronouns, and to explain the role of the Theory of Descriptions within a general theory of anaphora. It is plausible to suppose that both nonanaphoric (e.g., *deictic*) pronouns and pronouns anaphoric on referring expressions are themselves referring expressions. Following Geach (1962) and Quine (1960), philosophers have tended to treat pronouns with quantified antecedents ('every man', 'few Englishmen', and so on) as the natural language analogues of the variables of quantification theory. However, Evans (1977, 1980) has demonstrated conclusively that a very natural class of pronouns anaphoric on quantifiers cannot be interpreted as bound variables. With the help of some elementary ideas from contemporary grammatical theory, Evans provided a syntactical characterization of a semantically necessary distinction between bound and unbound anaphoric pronouns; he then argued that unbound pronouns anaphoric on quantifiers are interpreted via definite descriptions recoverable from the clauses containing their antecedents. This theory certainly has a lot to recommend it. However, as several philosophers and linguists have pointed out, it has some major defects, and in Chapters 5 and 6 I shall argue for a derivative theory that is, I believe, both technically superior and of greater explanatory value. *En route*, the derivative theory will be used to defuse some influential arguments against Russellian interpretations of certain occurrences of descriptions. The theory will also be tested on a variety of anaphoric puzzles that have been widely discussed by philosophers, logicians, and linguists.

A fourth aim is to use the Theory of Descriptions as a philosophical tool for dealing with certain problems concerning events, although most of what I would like to say on this topic will have to wait for another occasion.

The essay is organized as follows.

Chapter 2 concerns the philosophical and formal foundations of the Theory of Descriptions. Particular emphasis is placed on the distinction between object-dependent and object-independent thoughts that lies at the heart of Russell's psychology in the period with which I am concerned (1905–1919). The formal statement of Russell's theory is then located within a general account of natural language quantification that treats descriptions as restricted quantifiers. The theory is then extended to nonsingular descriptions and more complex types of descriptions.

Chapter 3 concerns context. The Theory of Descriptions is first supplemented with a theory of indexicality. A broadly Gricean distinction between the proposition expressed and those propositions the speaker seeks to convey is defended. Following Grice and Kripke, this work is then used to account for various ways in which descriptions may be used in different communicative settings. In particular, two influential arguments for a semantically distinct referential interpretation of descriptions are disarmed.

In Chapter 4, I turn to matters of scope, substitutivity, and opacity. Typically, Russellians have accounted for the *de re–de dicto* distinction, as it occurs in sentences containing descriptions and nonextensional operators, in terms of scope permutations. But this means quantifying into nonextensional contexts, and Quine has argued that such "unbridled" quantification leads to incoherence. After examining a common misunderstanding about descriptions and the Principle of Substitutivity, I examine Quine's argument against quantifying into modal contexts and conclude, with Smullyan, that the argument turns on an illegitimate technical move that is intimately connected to the aforementioned misunderstanding about descriptions and substitutivity. I then defend Smullyan from objections raised by Quine and others before turning briefly to attitude contexts. Finally, the Theory of Descriptions is extended to cover descriptions of events and used to examine certain claims about event identity.

Chapters 5 and 6 concern the semantics of anaphoric pronouns, particularly those whose antecedents are quantifiers, such as definite and indefinite descriptions. It might be thought excessive to devote two chapters to anaphoric pronouns, but to the philosopher, the linguist, the logician, and even the native speaker they are words of very great importance. Several philosophers have presented arguments designed to show that definite and indefinite descriptions functioning as the antecedents of certain occurrences of pronouns cannot be treated quantificationally. I explore a quite general theory of the semantics of anaphoric pronouns that seems to cover all of the relevant data as well as some long-standing anaphoric puzzles.

Notes

1. See Russell (1905, 1919). The pretense that all definite descriptions begin with the word 'the' will be dropped in due course.

2. See Russell (1903). See also Meinong (1904).

3. See Whitehead and Russell (1927), p. 66.

4. This particular way of thinking about the distinction between definite de-scriptions and genuine referring expressions is clearly articulated in the works of Gareth Evans and John McDowell. See, in particular, Evans (1982), chaps. 2 and 9, and McDowell (1986). See also Blackburn (1984).

5. Russell (1905), p. 41. The word 'denote' has been used by philosophers, linguists, and logicians to express a variety of relations that hold between linguistic and nonlinguistic objects. For Russell, 'denotes' is best under-stood as 'describes', 'is satisfied by', or 'is true of'. Thus 'the present

Queen of England' denotes/is satisfied by/is true of Elizabeth Windsor. For Russell, it is the *descriptive condition* rather than the denotation that does the semantical work. (I am here grateful to David Wiggins for discussion.)

6. This is somewhat simplified; the Theory of Descriptions is not just offered as providing analyses of sentences with descriptions in subject position. Russell's formal statement makes it clear that the theory has a much broader application. For discussion, see 2.3 and 2.6.

7. See Rundle (1965), Donnellan (1966, 1968, 1978), Stalnaker (1972), Partee (1972), Peacocke (1975), Hornsby (1977), Kaplan (1978), Devitt (1981), Wettstein (1981, 1982), Recanati (1981, 1986, 1989), Fodor and Sag (1982), and Barwise and Perry (1983).

8. See especially Grice (1967) and Searle (1975).

9. The general form of the Gricean response to a potential referential challenge seems to have been anticipated by Hampshire (1959, pp. 201–4) and by Geach (1962, p. 8).

10. See Kripke (1977), Searle (1979), Klein (1980), and Davies (1981). This general approach is also endorsed by Wiggins (1975), Castañeda (1977), Sainsbury (1979), Evans (1982), Salmon (1982), Blackburn (1984), Davidson (1986), and Soames (1986).

11. I had originally planned to include an appendix on the prospects of unifying the account of (i)–(vi) with an account of the interpretation of *mass noun* descriptions (like 'the water') and so-called "collective" interpretations of plural descriptions (as in 'the men pushed the VW up the hill'), an idea first presented by Sharvy (1980). It soon became clear, however, that within the confines of the present work it would not be possible to do justice either to the semantical and metaphysical subtleties involved in spelling out such a unified theory or to the burgeoning literature on these topics. The proper place for such a discussion is in a sequel rather than an appendix.

Chapter 2

The Theory of Descriptions

2.1 Introductory Remarks

It is virtually impossible to do justice to the semantical and logical insights of Russell's Theory of Descriptions without a proper grasp of its philosophical foundations; and this requires a sensitivity to, and an awareness of Russell's sensitivity to, issues that are at least as much psychological as they are semantical (or logical). Of course any final evaluation of the theory, construed as a contribution to semantics and logic will depend upon its predictive power in the face of problems concerning identity, substitutivity, propositional attitude reports, the logical (and other) modalities, nondenoting noun phrases, quantifier scope, pronominal anaphora, and so on. But semantical problems cannot be addressed in a vacuum. There is an important respect in which semantical questions cannot be detached from questions about *understanding*; this is something Russell saw, and nowhere is it more in evidence than in his distinction between names and descriptions. Indeed, if one ignores his theory of thought, one runs the very grave risk of failing to understand and appreciate his Theory of Descriptions.

I have three main aims in this chapter. The first is to lay out the philosophical and psychological underpinnings of Russell's theory. The second is to locate the semantical side of the theory within a general account of quantified noun phrases in natural language. The third is to explore and extend the range and application of the theory. Although the initial discussion will, of necessity, have a definite exegetical character, I shall not shy away from rejecting what I perceive to be inessential features of Russell's overall proposal. For example, his sense-datum epistemology and his consequent desire to treat ordinary proper names as disguised descriptions, his talk of objects as constituents of singular propositions, and his use of the formalism of *Principia Mathematica*, even if they are not objectionable in themselves, seem to me to be features that can be dispensed with without compromising either the general appeal of the Theory of Descriptions or the distinction between object-dependent and object-independent propositions that lies behind it.

After discussion of the philosophical foundations of the theory (2.2), I turn to its formal statement (2.3) and a preliminary appraisal of its value when applied to sentences of natural language (2.4). A general discussion of quantification in natural language (2.5) then gives us a syntactical and semantical framework within which to locate the Theory of Descriptions, extend it to nonsingular and more complex descriptions, and dispense with the formalism of *Principia Mathematica* (2.6). The chapter ends with a brief discussion of what one need *not* be committed to when one endorses the Theory of Descriptions (2.7).

2.2 Philosophical Foundations

Let us take as a point of departure the idea that a particular dated utterance u of a sentence ϕ by a speaker S expresses a *proposition*. For convenience, let us treat as interchangeable the locutions "the proposition expressed by S's utterance u of ϕ," "the proposition S expressed by his or her utterance u of ϕ," and "the proposition S expressed by uttering ϕ." (In an investigation into the conceptual relations between semantical notions, these locutions would undoubtedly have to be separated, but for present purposes this will not be necessary.)

The propositions we express using sentences of natural language are determined, at least in part, by the words these sentences contain and their syntactical organization. Russell was concerned with both of these aspects of meaning. In the period with which I am concerned, he held what might be called a "realist" theory of meaning: every meaningful item of language stands for something real. The meaning of an expression is simply that entity for which it stands. In the case of an utterance of a sentence ϕ this entity is a *proposition*. In the case of an utterance of a genuine referring expression, it is the expression's *referent*. An utterance of a sentence 'b is G', where 'b' is a referring expression and '— is G' is a monadic predicate phrase, expresses an *object-dependent* (or *singular*) proposition, the identity of which is dependent upon the identity of b.[1] And this proposition is *true* if and only if b is G.

With respect to natural language, I shall use 'genuine referring expression' (or 'genuine singular term') to cover ordinary proper names, demonstratives, and (some occurrences) of pronouns. (For the purposes of the present chapter, proper names will serve as model referring expressions; demonstratives and pronouns will be officially introduced in Chapters 3 and 5.) This taxonomy is somewhat stipulative, but it has a basis in intuition and a rationale that will unfold as we proceed.[2]

For Russell, there is an important connection between meaning and understanding: one understands an expression just in case one *knows* its meaning. Since the meaning of a referring expression is just its referent, understanding such an expression consists in knowing what the expression refers to. But what is it to know such a thing? Russell offers us the following:

> To understand a name you must be acquainted with the particular of which it is a name, and you must know that it is the name of that particular (1918, p. 205).[3]

To make sense of this claim, let's back up a little and turn to the principle at the heart of Russell's theory of thought, to what Evans (1982) calls *Russell's Principle*:

> It is not possible for a subject to think about (e.g. have a belief about, make a judgment about) something unless he knows which particular individual he is thinking about (Russell, 1911, p. 159).

As Evans points out, the difficulty with this principle is interpreting it in such a way that it says something useful. If *knowing which* is interpreted in accord with colloquial usage, the principle is surely too restrictive (someone might make a judgement about something he is looking at (or about himself) even when it would be natural for us to say that he does not know what he is looking at (or who he is)). But if *knowing which* is interpreted in a looser spirit, we run the risk of trivializing the principle. The detective will *know who* murdered Smith: "Smith's murderer," he will declare, even though he does not know the identity of the killer.

Russell held that there are two very different ways of cashing out *knowing which*. One may be directly acquainted with (or have a memory of being directly acquainted with) the individual in question; or one may think of the individual as the unique satisfier of some definite description or other.[4] Intuitively, we feel there are some entities with which we can be directly acquainted: ourselves, objects in our perceptual fields, and objects with which we have recently had epistemic contact, for instance. This intuitive notion of acquaintance seems to be the one Russell had in mind in "On Denoting."[5]

But we may have knowledge of a rather different sort. The center of mass of the solar system at the first instant of the twentieth century, the candidate who gets the most votes at the next general election, the first person born in the twenty-first century, the man with the iron mask, and so on are all examples of things known to us by *description*. Knowledge of something by description is not really knowledge *about* an individual at all:

> I shall say that an object is "known by description" when we know that it is "the so-and-so," i.e. when we know that there is one object, and no more, having a certain property (1911, p. 156).

The point of this remark is to emphasize that knowing something by description is a species of knowing *that* rather than knowing *which*. It is sufficient for knowledge of something by description that one know a purely *general* proposition, a proposition that is not dependent upon the existence of any individual in particular.[6] In other words, to know something by description it is not necessary to have had any sort of epistemic contact with the object that, in fact, satisfies the description one knows it under.[7] Where we have a thought about a particular individual to the effect that it has some property G, we entertain a *singular* proposition, a proposition that has that individual as a "constituent." Where we have just a thought to the effect that the unique satisfier of some description, whoever or whatever it may be, has G, we entertain a purely general proposition, a proposition that does not have the satisfier of the description as a constituent. Let us call this type of general (object-*in*dependent) proposition a *descriptive* proposition.

We now have the material necessary to start piecing together Russell's account of the relationship between thought and meaning. If we take a referring expression 'b' and a one-place predicate '— is G', the proposition expressed by an utterance of 'b is G' is dependent upon the identity of the referent of 'b': the utterance expresses a true proposition just in case the referent of 'b' is G. This, of course, still leaves us with the question of what to say if 'b' has no referent). The intuitively correct result we want is that no proposition is expressed, in the sense that there is nothing that has been said to be G.

On Russell's account, this result is guaranteed by the Principle of Acquaintance, which requires us to be acquainted with every constituent of any proposition we understand (see note 5). If 'b' is an empty referring expression, then there is nothing acquaintance with which would constitute being acquainted with the referent of 'b', and hence nothing which constitutes understanding the proposition expressed by 'b is G'. But if nothing constitutes understanding the proposition expressed by 'b is G', then it makes no sense to say that a proposition was expressed. The net result is that in order to entertain an object-dependent proposition about a particular individual, one must be acquainted with that individual.

Russell finally came to place a very severe constraint on knowledge by acquaintance. Bent on exorcising the possibility of someone entertaining an object-dependent proposition when, in reality, there is no object which the purported proposition is about, Russell maintained that only a sense-datum could be trusted to be the "subject" of such a proposition. It is by now pretty generally agreed that this position is untenable, and I shall not spend any time addressing any of the familiar objections to it. But if it is easy to reject Russell's final notion of acquaintance, it is not easy to articulate a common-sense alternative of the sort he seems to have had in mind in 1905. It will not do to just list the sorts of things (e.g., material objects) with which we can be acquainted. We are now confronted with the question "In what does acquaintance with an object consist?" (or "What conditions must obtain for a subject S to entertain an object-dependent thought about an object?"), a question that simply does not arise (or is at least trivially answered) if the object is a sense-datum. One's inclination is to say that a subject S can entertain an object-dependent thought about b if S has had epistemic contact with b, for instance, if b is an object S is currently perceiving, or an object that S has perceived in the past, but this may well make acquaintance too easy. For present purposes, I propose to adopt a convenient partial specification drawn up by Davies (1981). For cases in which b is a medium-sized material object,

> [t]he negative partial answer is that if a person is totally causally isolated from the object then he can have no singular beliefs concerning it. The positive partial answer is that if a person has had frequent perceptual (particularly visual) contact with the object and is able reliably (although perhaps not infallibly) to recognize the object as the same object again then he can have singular beliefs concerning it (p. 97).[8]

On this sort of account, understanding the proposition expressed by an utterance of 'b is G' will involve not only having had some sort of epistemic contact with the referent of 'b', but also seeing that it is that object to which 'b' refers.[9] When these two conditions obtain, let us say that the subject *identifies* the referent of 'b'.[10]

Having detached Russell from his sense-datum epistemology, we can ascribe to him the following principle:

(R1) If 'b' is a genuine referring expression (singular term), then for a (monadic) predicate '— is G', it is necessary to identify the referent of 'b' in order to understand the proposition expressed by an utterance u of 'b is G'.[11]

If 'b' were to have no referent, then there would be nothing identification of which would constitute identifying the referent of 'b', and hence nothing that would constitute *understanding* the proposition expressed by an utterance of 'b is G'. But if nothing were to constitute understanding the proposition expressed, what sense would it make to say that a proposition *was* expressed? None whatsoever. We are forced to conclude that

(R2) If 'b' has no referent, then for a (monadic) predicate '— is G', no proposition is expressed by an utterance u of 'b is G'.

By way of shorthand, let's say that for a given utterance u of 'b is G', one understands u if and only if one grasps the object-dependent proposition that b is G and realizes that it is this proposition that is expressed by u.[12] Let's briefly take stock. For a referring expression 'b' and a monadic predicate '— is G', an utterance of 'b is G' expresses a true proposition if and only if the referent of 'b' is G. The two additions Russell makes to this (essentially Fregean) picture are captured by (R1) and (R2). Russell would, at times, have us believe that (R1) and (R2) are best accommodated by construing the referent of 'b' as a *constituent* of the proposition expressed. But it is not obvious that this is the only way, or even the best way, of achieving the desired result. (R1) and (R2) require only that the identity of the individual referred to by 'b' be a determinant of the identity of the proposition expressed by 'b is G'.[13] We can parcel all this up by saying that if 'b' is a genuine referring expression, then for any monadic predicate '— is G', the proposition expressed by an utterance of 'b is G' is *object-dependent*. An object-dependent proposition is a proposition about a particular individual (or particular individuals) that would simply not be available to be entertained or expressed if that individual (or those individuals) failed to exist. (No object? No proposition. Failure to identify the object? Failure to understand the proposition.)

This is a good point at which to note an important feature of referring expressions that has aroused a good deal of attention since the appearance of Kripke's 'Naming and Necessity'. Consider the following sentence:

(1)   Aristotle was fond of dogs.

Kripke points out that understanding the proposition expressed by an utterance of (1) involves not only a grasp of "the (extensionally correct) conditions under which it is in fact true" but also of "the conditions under which a counterfactual course of history, resembling the actual course of history in some respects but not in others, would be correctly (partially) described by (1)" (1980, p. 6). The generalized version of this claim Kripke calls the thesis of *rigid designation*. A proper name like 'Aristotle' is a *rigid designator*:

> Presumably everyone agrees that there is a certain man—the philosopher we call 'Aristotle'—such that, as a matter of fact, (1) is true if and only if *he* was fond of dogs. [*Footnote*: That is everyone, even Russell, would agree that this is a true material equivalence, given that there really was an Aristotle.] The thesis of rigid designation is simply—subtle points aside [*footnote*: In particular, we ignore the question of what to say about counterfactual situations in which Aristotle would not have existed]—that the same paradigm applies to the truth conditions of (1) as it describes *counterfactual* situations. That is, (1) truly describes a counterfactual situation if and only if the same aforementioned man would have been fond of dogs, had that situation obtained (*ibid.*).

From Kripke's observation, let's draw up the following:

(R3) If '*b*' is a genuine referring expression that refers to *x*, then '*b*' is a rigid designator; i.e., *x* enters into a specification of the truth conditions of (the proposition expressed by) an utterance *u* of '*b* is *G*' with respect to actual and counterfactual situations.[14]

(This is not a statement about languages spoken in counterfactual situations; it is a statement about the expression '*b*' as used in *our* actual language. If '*b*' is a rigid designator of *x*, then whether or not the proposition expressed by an utterance of the sentence '*b* is *G*'—a sentence of our actual language—is true at a counterfactual situation depends only upon how things are with *x*.

The importance of (R3) will become clear when we compare referring expressions with definite descriptions, and again when we examine modal contexts in Chapter 4.

We are now in a position to state the main claim and the main purpose of Russell's Theory of Descriptions. The main claim is that that a phrase of the form 'the *F*' is not a genuine referring expression; or, to put it another way, the proposition expressed by an utterance *u* of 'the *F* is *G*' is object-*independent*. The purpose of the theory is to make available a class of propositions to serve as the meanings of (utterances of) sentences of the form 'the *F* is *G*', whether or not anything answers to 'the *F*'.

Russell realized that phrases of the form 'the *F*' are no more referring expressions than are quantified noun phrases of the forms 'an *F*', 'some *F*', 'no *F*' and 'every *F*'. Frege had provided an intuitive distinction between referring expressions ("names" as he called them) and quantified noun phrases; but according to Russell, Frege's classification was in need of one important and far-reaching revision: definite descriptions belong with the quantified phrases not with the referring expressions. The propositions expressed by utterances of, e.g., 'some F is G', 'every F is G', 'no F is G', and 'the F is G' are object-independent. For example, to say that *some F is G* is to express a proposition the truth conditions of which are given by

$$(\exists x)(Fx \ \& \ Gx).$$

To say that every F is G is to express a proposition the truth conditions of which are given by

$$(\forall x)(Fx \supset Gx).$$

To say that *the F is G*, Russell argues, is to express a proposition the truth conditions of which are given by

$$(\exists x)(Fx \ \& \ (\forall y)(Fy \supset y=x) \ \& \ Gx)).$$

That is, 'the F is G' is true if and only if the conjunction of the following three clauses is true:

(a)   There is at least one F
(b)   There is at most one F
(c)   Everything that is F is G.[15]

The formal details of this proposal can wait until 2.3. Right now, I want to emphasize the nontechnical differences between descriptions and referring expressions. In contrast with (R1) and (R2), we get the following:

(D1)   If 'the F' is a definite description, then for a (monadic) predicate phrase '— is G', the proposition expressed by an utterance of 'the F is G' can be perfectly well understood by a person who does not know who or what is denoted by 'the F' (indeed, even if nothing satisfies 'the F', and even if that person knows that nothing satisfies 'the F').[16]

(D2)   If 'the F' is a definite description, then for a (monadic) predicate phrase '— is G', an utterance of 'the F is G' expresses a perfectly determinate proposition whether or not there is any individual that satisfies 'the F'.

The conclusion we are to draw from (D1) and (D2) is that the proposition expressed by an utterance of 'the F is G' is not *about* who or what actually satisfies 'the F'; the proposition is *object-*

independent. Unlike names, definite descriptions are not genuine referring expressions.[17]

In its essential respects (D1) is just an explicitly linguistic version of the claim that we can have knowledge by description, and it can be found as early as the second paragraph of "On Denoting":

> It often happens that we know that a certain phrase denotes unambiguously, although we have no acquaintance with what it denotes; this occurs in the above case of the centre of mass [of the solar system at the first instant of the twentieth century] . . . [I]n thought . . . we do not necessarily have acquaintance with the objects denoted by phrases composed of words with whose meanings we are acquainted (1905, p. 41).

From today's perspective, and reading between the lines somewhat, we might put Russell's point thus: Since the meaning of a complex phrase depends only on the meanings of each of its parts and their modes of combination, it is sufficient for understanding a complex phrase that one understand each of its parts and be able to project from the meanings of the parts to the meaning of the whole on the basis of syntactical structure. Applied to definite descriptions this means that one can perfectly well grasp the proposition expressed by a sentence without knowing who or what is described by any descriptions it may contain. It is, of course, necessary to grasp the meanings of each of the *parts* of a description; but knowing who or what happens to be described by the description as a whole is something that lies well beyond that. Ignorance of the denotation of a description is, then, not only of no psychological significance (when it comes to entertaining a descriptive thought), it is of no *semantical* significance.

This point can be driven home by consideration of counterfactual situations. Right now, as I write, David Wiggins is the Honorary Librarian of the Oxford Philosophy Library. Suppose I utter (2):

(2)   The current Honorary Librarian is very interested in questions about identity.

What I say, given the way things are, is true. But *in virtue of what, exactly*? It is tempting to answer that my utterance is true in virtue of facts concerning *David Wiggins*. But we should not be misled by such talk. To echo Kripke (1980, p. 6), understanding the proposition expressed by (2) involves not only a grasp of "the (extensionally correct) conditions under which it is in fact true" but also "the conditions under which a counterfactual course of history, resembling the actual course of history in some respects but not in others, would be correctly (partially) described by (2)," Now suppose, counterfactually, that it is not David Wiggins but, say, John Perry who is the Honorary Librarian. Since Perry is very interested in questions about identity, the proposition expressed (what I *actually* say) would still be true. But it is plain that there is now no sense in which its truth conditions depend upon how things are with David Wiggins, as he is not (in the counterfactual circumstances) the Honorary Librarian. It is clear, then, that David Wiggins does not enter into a proper specification of the truth-conditions of (2). (This is not, of course, to say that the *truth* of my utterance in the actual world does not depend on how things are with David Wiggins. It does, since *he* is the Honorary Librarian.) In short, since (*a*) David Wiggins does not enter into a specification of the truth conditions of (2) in certain counterfactual situations, and (*b*) no one else enters the truth conditions in the actual situation, by (R3) the proposition expressed by my original utterance is neither Wiggins-dependent nor anybody-else-dependent.[18] Thus:

(D3) The individual *x* that actually satisfies a definite description 'the *F*' does not enter into a specification of the truth conditions of 'the *F* is *G*' in either actual or counterfactual situations.

In view of the important difference in the logical behavior of genuine referring expressions and definite descriptions that is encoded in (R3) and (D3), we must certainly follow Kripke (1972) in rejecting the view that ordinary proper names are disguised definite descriptions (a view that Russell came to hold). To rehearse one of Kripke's examples, if 'Aristotle' is cashed out as, say, 'the last great philosopher of antiquity', then (1) will come out as something like (1'):

(1)   Aristotle was fond of dogs

(1')   Exactly one person was last among the great philosophers of antiquity, and any such person was fond of dogs.

On the assumption that Aristotle was, in fact, the last great philosopher of antiquity, then the actual truth conditions of (1') agree extensionally with those of (1). But what Kripke so rightly emphasizes is that in counterfactual situations the truth conditions can come apart: "With respect to a counterfactual situation where someone other than Aristotle would have been the last great philosopher of antiquity" an account of (1) as (1') "would make that other person's fondness for dogs the relevant issue for the correctness of (1)!" (1980, p. 7).[19]

I should stress that endorsing the Theory of Descriptions *qua* theory of *descriptions* does *not* commit one to a treatment of proper names as disguised descriptions. Indeed, Kripke himself is a good example of someone who is sympathetic to Russell's analysis of descriptions but not to his descriptive analysis of names (see Kripke, 1977).[20]

Let us now return to Russell's rationale for a quantificational analysis of descriptions. Although the truth of (D1) is quite sufficient to falsify the view that descriptions are genuine referring expressions, it is the stronger thesis (D2) upon which Russell chooses to focus when arguing for the Theory of Descriptions.[21] First, the rhetoric: The sentence 'The king of France is bald', is "not nonsense," Russell (1905, p. 46) insists, "since it is plainly false." The proposition expressed by an utterance of 'The king of France is bald' is true, according to Russell, just in case there is exactly one thing that is king of France and that one thing is bald. Consequently, on Russell's account, if someone were to assert, 'The king of France is bald' right now, the fact that there is no king of France would be no barrier to understanding the speaker's remark. A perfectly determinate proposition would be expressed, viz., the *descriptive* proposition that there is exactly one king of France, and that one thing is bald. And as there is no king of France, this proposition would not be true; therefore, says Russell, it would be untrue, i.e., false.

Now Strawson has contested this claim, insisting that if nothing satisfies the description then the question of the truth or falsity of the proposition expressed "simply does not arise." As he puts it, the speaker would *"fail to say anything true or false"* (1950, p. 13) because the *presupposition* that there is a unique king of France is false.[22] This is a curious claim that we should pause to consider.

Russell's first mistake, says Strawson, is his failure to distinguish the meaning of a particular sentence-type from the proposition expressed by a particular dated utterance of that sentence.[23] The same sentence (e.g., 'the king of France is bald') may be used on one occasion to say something true, on another occasion to say something false. During the reign of Louis XIV it may have been used to say something true; during the reign of Louis XV, to say something false. Thus sentences are not the sorts of things that are true-or-false; utterances are.[24] The *sentence* 'The king of France is bald', is not devoid of meaning, says Strawson; but it does not follow from this that a given *utterance* of that sentence expresses a true or false proposition. On the contrary, if there is no king of France then no one has been referred to, and hence no true or false proposition expressed. There are several points we should take up here.

(*i*) Strawson is quite right to distinguish between the linguistic meaning of a particular sentence and the proposition expressed by a particular dated utterance of that sentence, if only because of indexical expressions like 'I', 'this', 'present', 'here', and so on, which can be used to refer to different things on different occasions. But as Russell (1959) points out in his response to Strawson, the question of how to treat indexicals is, in the first instance, quite distinct from the question of how to treat descriptions. Of course definite descriptions may contain indexical components ('the *present* king of France', 'the man who gave me *this*', etc.); but all this means is that there are descriptions to which the Theory of Descriptions *and* a theory of indexicality apply (see 3.3 for discussion). Indeed, as Grice (1970) points out, Russell seems to have been aware of this back in "On Denoting": one of his original examples of a definite description was 'my son', which contains an indexical element 'my'. We must, I think, concur with Grice that

> . . . Russell would have been prepared to say that one and the same denoting phrase might, on the face of it, have one denotation when used by one speaker, and another when used by another speaker, and perhaps none when used by a third speaker. Russell did not regard the denotation of a phrase as invariant between occasions of the use of the phrase, which may make one think that he did not make the mistake Strawson attributed to him (p. 39).

No substantive issue turns on Russell's failure to separate sentences from utterances when talking about descriptions. Russell is so very obviously concerned with the proposition expressed by a particular utterance—rather than the more abstract notion of the linguistic meaning of sentence-types—that it is very difficult to lend any sort of sympathetic ear to Strawson on this point. If Russell were being more precise, he would say not that the *sentence* 'The king of France is bald' is equivalent to the sentence obtained by conjoining sentences (*a*), (*b*), and (*c*) above, but that the proposition expressed by a particular utterance of 'the king of France is bald' is equivalent to the proposition that would be expressed, in the same context, by a particular utterance of the sentence obtained by conjoining sentences (*a*), (*b*), and (*c*). To say all this is not to undermine Strawson's own position. For Strawson, the intuition that a proposition is expressed by a sentence of the form 'the *F* is *G*' is, in some cases at least, weaker than the intuition that the sentence-type is meaningful. And his own theory is based on the undeniable fact that the more robust intuition is compatible with the view that descriptions are genuine referring expressions.

(*ii*) There is an ambiguity in Strawson's original statement of the view that if there is no king of France then someone who utters 'the king of France is bald' "fails to say anything true or false." It can be understood as meaning that no proposition is expressed or that a proposition that is neither true nor false is expressed.[25] But on reflection, the ambiguity appears to resolve itself. The idea that an utterance of a sentence containing a nondenoting description expresses a determinate proposition, but one that lacks a truth-value, conflicts with Strawson's view that descriptions are devices used for *referring*. Strawson's position, then, is that *no proposition is expressed*. This is made clear in Strawson (1974).[26]

(*iii*) Within the general semantical picture we have assembled so far, there are good reasons to reject any theory that predicts that the presence of a vacuous description in a sentence means that no proposition is expressed by an utterance of that sentence. First, Strawson concedes that the Theory of Descriptions provides a perfectly good specification of the conditions that would have to be satisfied for an utterance of 'the king of France is bald' to express a *true* proposition. (1950, p. 5.) But since Russell's specification does this without mentioning any particular individual, *ipso facto* it provides an equally good specification of the conditions under which an utterance of this sentence expresses an *un*true proposition. Rather more transparently, since no particular individual plays a role in the specification of Russell's truth conditions, a change in (or lack of) denotation cannot bring about a change in these conditions, which concern not an individual but the relationship between two (possibly complex) properties. The relationship either does or does not hold, so the proposition expressed either fits or fails to fit the facts. If it fits the facts, it is true; if it fails to fit them, it is untrue i.e., false. (See Russell, 1959, pp. 243–44.)

Second, the general Strawsonian position view runs into serious trouble as soon as we move away from the simplest sentences. Consider the following sort of example that Russell was interested in accounting for:

(3)   The king of France does not exist.

An utterance of (3) made today would be true precisely because there is no king of France. But on Strawson's account, since the presupposition that there *is* a unique king of France is false, no proposition is expressed. If the Strawsonian objects to the example on the grounds that a solution to the more general problem of negative existentials will carry over to (3), or on the grounds that 'exists' is not a genuine predicate, the Russellian can switch to an example like (4):

(4)   The king of France is not bald since there is no king of France.

Again, an utterance of (4) would be true because there is no king of France.[27] The Strawsonian might now protest the use of examples involving negation. But negation is not essential to the point as we can see by considering (5):

(5)   This morning my father had breakfast with the king of France.

If I uttered (5) now, I would unquestionably say something false. But on Strawson's account, I will have expressed no proposition because the presupposition that there is a unique king of France is false. Therefore I will not have said something false. The Strawsonian might respond to this type of example by postulating some sort of semantical asymmetry between descriptions in subject position and those which form part of a predicate phrase. But this will not help. Consider (6):

(6)   The king of France was interviewed on *the Tonight Show* last night.

An utterance of (6) made today would be plainly false. The fact that the example involves the passive is also irrelevant; consider (7):

(7)   The king of France shot my cat last night.

Again, clearly false. And the fact that example (7) contains a direct object that *does* succeed in denoting is also irrelevant; consider (8):

(8)   The king of France shot himself last night.

Descriptions occurring in the contexts of psychological verbs create the same sort of problem for the Strawsonian. For instance, I may make a perfectly intelligible statement by uttering (9):

(9)   Ponce de Leon thought the fountain of youth was in Florida.

Indeed, I may do so even though I know that there has never been a fountain of youth.[28]

At the very least, then, we must reject the view that the presence of an empty description *always* results in a failed speech act. Indeed, this is something Strawson (1964) came to concede. In an attempt to reduce the number of incorrect predictions made by his earlier theory, he suggests that sometimes the presence of a nondenoting description renders the proposition expressed false and at other times it prevents a proposition from being expressed at all (sometimes 'the *F* is *G*' *entails* the existence of a unique *F*, and at other times it (only) *presupposes* it). Since nothing appears to turn on structural or logical facts about the sentence used, Strawson suggests restricting the "truth-value gap" result by appealing to the *topic of discourse*.[29] But surely the truth value of what one says depends upon whether the world is as one has said it is; to let the decision as to whether one has said something false or said nothing at all depend upon such things as what is the primary or overriding focus of the discourse at any given moment—to the extent that such a notion is even theoretically manageable—is to give up this idea. Indeed, it is to give up doing serious semantical work altogether, or else to give up the idea that presupposition is a semantical phenomenon. As Sellars (1954) and others have emphasized, all sorts of factors may conspire deter the native speaker from *saying* that a given utterance is true or false, but that is hardly enough to show that the utterance lacks a truth-value.[30]

Russell, as we shall see in the next section, has no problem with sentences like (3)-(9). Without yet looking at the formal statement of his semantics for descriptions, the considerations adduced thus far show that he was at least right to dislodge descriptions from the class of genuine referring expressions: a perfectly determinate thought is expressed by an utterance of 'the *F* is *G*' independently of what is denoted by, or whether anything is denoted by, 'the *F*'.

2.3 The Formal Theory

Only through its formal statement can the full domain of application of the Theory of Descriptions be made explicit. In particular, the formal statement extends to descriptions that are not the grammatical subjects of sentences, and makes it clear that descriptions may contain variables bound by exterior operators—something that will be very important when we look at anaphora on descriptions in Chapters 5 and 6. Moreover, when the formal statement is seen in the light of more recent work on natural language quantification, it becomes clear how nonsingular descriptions should be handled. The exact place of the Theory of Descriptions within an account of natural language quantification will be addressed in 2.6. In this section, I shall just be concerned with its original statement as presented in *14 of *Principia Mathematica*.

From the point of view of grammar, descriptions are *bona fide* singular noun phrases with more or less the same distributional properties as referring expressions (viz., names and demonstratives).[31] But from a semantical perspective, an important difference has emerged:

sentences with referring expressions as grammatical subjects express object-dependent propositions; sentences with descriptions as grammatical subjects express object-*in*dependent propositions. *Qua* denoting phrase, a description has no 'meaning' in and of itself in the sense that there is no entity for which it stands, upon which the identity of the proposition expressed depends. To this extent, at least, there is an important mismatch between our syntactical and semantical taxonomies.

The formal statement of the Theory of Descriptions aims to reconcile (in part) these syntactical and semantical observations by making explicit the logical structure of sentences containing descriptions. On Russell's account, to say that the proposition expressed by 'the F is G' is object-independent is, from a logical perspective, just to say that it possesses the characteristics of the proposition expressed by a sentence with an overt *quantifier phrase* in subject position. Descriptions are to be assimilated to the class of quantified noun phrases, what Russell calls "denoting phrases."[32]

We can begin by noting that counterparts of (D1) and (D2) hold for the denoting phrases 'every F', 'an F', and 'some F'.[33] Suppose $a, b,..., z$ are all of the physicists who attended a certain conference. One day a friend, who has been reading the newspaper, says to me,

(1)   Every physicist who attended that conference was arrested immediately afterwards.

It is perfectly clear that I can grasp the proposition expressed by this utterance and indeed come to have the belief that every physicist who attended that conference was arrested immediately afterwards, without knowing *of* any of $a, b,..., z$, that they are physicists who attended that conference. In short, not knowing who is denoted by 'every physicist who attended that conference', is no obstacle to understanding the proposition expressed by my friend's utterance of (1). And, of course, even if *no* physicists attended that conference, my friend would still have expressed a perfectly determinate proposition with perfectly determinate truth-conditions. The proposition expressed is object-independent. Again, the counterfactual case is instructive. My friend's utterance could still be true if none of $a, b,...,$ z were arrested, i.e., where, *in the counterfactual situation*, none of $a,$ $b,..., z$ are physicists who attended that conference but all those physicists who *did* attend that conference were arrested immediately afterwards.

It is standard procedure to capture the object-independence of the proposition expressed by an utterance of a sentence of the form 'every F is G' by treating the subject noun phrase 'Every F' as a device of universal quantification in the manner familiar from first order logic. The "logical form" of 'every F is G' is given by $(\forall x)(Fx \supset Gx)$, which is true if and only if everything (in the domain of discourse) that is is F is also G.

If the universally quantified noun phrase 'every physicist who attended that conference' in (1) is replaced by the indefinite description 'a physicist who attended that conference', the situation is virtually the same:

(2)   A physicist who attended that conference was arrested immediately afterwards.

It is perfectly clear that I can grasp the proposition expressed by my friend's utterance of (2) and indeed come to have the belief that a physicist who attended that conference was arrested immediately afterwards, without knowing *of* any of $a, b, \ldots, z$, that they are physicists who attended that conference, and without knowing of any one of them that he or she was arrested immediately afterwards. Such ignorance is no obstacle to understanding the proposition expressed by my friend's utterance. And, of course, even if *no* physicists attended that conference, my friend would still have expressed a perfectly determinate proposition with perfectly determinate truth-conditions. The proposition expressed is object-independent. Again, the counterfactual case is instructive. My friend's utterance could still be true if none of $a, b, \ldots, z$ were arrested, i.e., where, *in the counterfactual situation*, some physicist other than one of $a, b, \ldots, z$ who attended that conference was arrested afterwards.[34]

Following Russell, it has long been customary to capture the object-independence of the proposition expressed by an utterance of a sentence of the form 'an F is G' by treating the indefinite description 'an F' as a device of existential quantification.[35] The "logical form" of 'an F is G' is given by $(\exists x)(Fx \,\&\, Gx)$, which is true if and only if at least one thing (in the domain of discourse) is both F and G.

Russell captures the object-independence of the proposition expressed by an utterance of 'the F is G' by treating the definite description 'the F' as a device of complex quantification analysable in terms of 'an F' and 'every F'. This involves treating definite descriptions rather like the nonprimitive logical connectives in *Principia Mathematica*. These symbols are provided with what Russell calls "contextual definitions." To define an expression ζ contextually is not to provide a stipulative or explicative definition of ζ; rather, it is to provide a procedure for converting any sentence containing occurrences of ζ into an equivalent sentence containing no occurrences of ζ. For instance, in *Principia Mathematica* material implication is "defined" as follows:[36]

*1.01 $p \supset q$ $=_{df}$ $\neg p \lor q$

The equality sign and subscript together signify that the formula on the left "is defined to mean the same as" the formula on the right. So it is not $\supset$ itself that is defined, but rather every formula in which it occurs. To say that a symbol is contextually defined is just to say that every well-formed formula in which it occurs abbreviates (in a uniform way) a formula in which it does not occur.

The method of contextual definition is applied by Russell to descriptions, as they are "incomplete" symbols, by which he means that they too are symbols having "no meaning in isolation," in the sense of not being expressions that stand for things. In *Principia Mathematica (PM)*, a description is represented by a term of the form $(\iota x)(Fx)$, which can be read as "the unique x satisfying (Fx)." On the face of it, then, the *iota*-operator is a variable-binding device for forming a term from a formula. A predicate symbol G may be prefixed to a description $(\iota x)(Fx)$ to form a formula $G(\iota x)(Fx)$, which can then be unpacked in accordance with a suitable contextual definition. As we saw earlier, on Russell's account the proposition expressed by an utterance of 'the F is G' is logically equivalent to the proposition expressed by the conjunction of the following three clauses:

(*a*)   There is at least one F
(*b*)   There is at most one F
(*c*)   Everything that is F is G.

Matters of scope aside for the moment, on Russell's formal account a sentence of the form $G(\iota x)(Fx)$ is, defined as "meaning the same as"

(*d*) $(\exists x)((\forall y)(Fy \equiv y=x) \,\&\, Gx)$

or, equivalently, and perhaps more perspicuously,

(*e*) $(\exists x)(Fx \,\&\, (\forall y)(Fy \supset y=x) \,\&\, Gx)$.

(*d*) and (*e*) are just first-order renderings of the conjunction of (*a*), (*b*), and (*c*). (It is clear then, that introducing definite descriptions into the language of *PM* does not add to its expressive power. Descriptions are abbreviatory devices that enable Russell to simplify his formulae and (as we shall see in 4.3) shorten his proofs.) But neither (*d*) nor (*e*) constitutes a final contextual definition because of the possibility of ambiguity where a formula containing a description is itself a constituent of some larger formula.

This is conveniently illustrated with negation. For a genuine referring expression 'b', there is simply no difference between wide and narrow scope negation: b is not-F just in case it is not the case that b is F. For a denoting phrase, however, there is a formal ambiguity with respect to a sentential connective or operator. Let 'Kx' represent 'x is king of France' and 'Bx' represent 'x is bald'. Then the formula '$\neg B(\iota x)(Kx)$' is ambiguous as there is not a unique formula for which it is an abbreviation. The formula containing the description might express a true proposition because, for instance, the king of France exists but is not bald, [viz., $(\exists x)((\forall y)(Ky \equiv y=x) \ \& \ \neg Bx)$], or because it is false that the king of France exists and is bald [viz. $\neg(\exists x)((\forall y)(Ky \equiv y=x) \ \& \ Bx)$].[37] Whitehead and Russell adopt a rather cumbersome device for representing what they call the "scope" of a description. Basically, the description is recopied within square brackets and placed immediately to the left of anything that is within its scope, suitable delimiters indicating the extent of that scope, as is customary with quantifiers.[38] Thus the two possibilities for 'The king of France is bald' can be represented as (I) and (II) respectively:

(I) $[(\iota x)(Kx)]\neg\{B(\iota x)(Kx)\}$ [i.e., $(\exists x)((\forall y)(Ky \equiv y=x) \ \& \ \neg Bx)$]

(II) $\neg\{[(\iota x)(Kx)]B(\iota x)(Kx)\}$ [i.e., $\neg(\exists x)((\forall y)(Ky \equiv y=x) \ \& \ Bx)$].

In (I) the description has what Russell calls a "primary occurrence" by virtue of having scope over the negation; in (II) the description has a "secondary occurrence" by virtue of lying within the scope of the negation.[39]

The distinction between primary and secondary occurrences of descriptions allows Russell (1905, p. 48) to address a problem he states more or less as follows. By the law of the excluded middle, either 'b is G' or 'b is not G' must be true. In particular, the proposition expressed by either (i) 'the present king of France is bald' or (ii) 'the present king of France is not bald' must be true. Yet if one enumerated the things that are bald, and then the things that are not bald, one would not find the present king of France in either list.

On Russell's account the proposition expressed by (i) is false, as there is nothing that is king of France. Therefore the proposition expressed by (ii) must be true. The law of excluded middle is not violated as the proposition expressed by (ii) where 'the king of France' has a secondary occurrence ((II) above) is true. Whenever a nondenoting description has a primary occurrence, however, the proposition will be false because the first clause of the three-clause analysis will be false.

The main proposition of the Theory of Descriptions can now be stated:

*14.01 $[(\iota x)(Fx)]G(\iota x)(Fx) =_{df} (\exists x)((\forall y)(Fy \equiv y=x) \, \& \, Gx)$.

Since there is no possibility of a genuine referring expression failing to refer, no predicate letter in the language of *PM* stands for 'exists'. However, since Russell wants to make sense of sentences like 'The king of France does not exist', he introduces a symbol 'E!' that may be combined with a description to create a well-formed formula with existential import:

*14.02 $E!(\iota x)(Fx) =_{df} (\exists x)(\forall y)(Fy \equiv y=x)$.

By successive applications of *14.01 and *14.02, any well-formed formula containing a definite description (no matter how complex the material that occupies the position occupied by 'G' in *14.01) can be replaced by a logically equivalent formula that is description-free (for further discussion, see Chapter 4).

2.4 Descriptions in Natural Language

Our task now is to spell out exactly how and when the formal statement of the Theory of Descriptions is to be applied to sentences of natural language. But before we can do that we shall have to say what we mean by 'definite description' once we step outside the language of *Principia Mathematica*.

Russell's formal theory can be applied to *every* sentence containing a definite description that can be formulated in the syntax of *PM*, whatever the surrounding context. As Mates (1973) emphasizes, this includes sentences containing "open" descriptions such as $(\iota x)(Fxz)$. Since this is a perfectly well-formed term, it is plain that a description may contain a variable bound by a higher operator. For instance,

(1) $(\forall z)(G(\iota x)(Fxz))$

is a well-formed sentence that, when expanded, will come out as

(2) $(\forall z)(\exists x)((\forall y)(Fyz \equiv y = x) \, \& \, Gx)$.

Carried over to the analysis of descriptions in natural language, this means that the Theory of Descriptions will be applicable not only to sentences containing simple descriptions but also to a sentence like (3):

(3)   Every man loves the woman that raised him

in which the pronoun 'him', inside the description 'the woman that raised him', functions as a variable bound by 'every man'. We can represent the logical form of this sentence as

(4) $(\forall x)(Mx \supset Lx(\imath y)(Wy \ \& \ Ryx))$

in which the description $(\imath y)(Wy \ \& \ Ryx)$ contains the variable x bound by the universal quantifier. This does not, of course, conflict with the idea of an implication of uniqueness. In both the English sentence and in the formal counterpart, uniqueness is relative to men. I shall call descriptions containing (internally) free variables *relativized definite descriptions*. As will become clear, the possibility of relativized descriptions gives the Theory of Descriptions enormous expressive power.[40]

Following Russell, discussion of definite descriptions typically centers on phrases of the form 'the so-and-so'. This fact, coupled with the success we just had in applying the Theory of Descriptions to a complex phrase of that form, suggests that, applied to natural language, the domain of the theory is all and only those sentences containing singular noun phrases beginning with the word 'the'. As to whether *only* expressions of this form are definite descriptions, it is reasonable to suppose that Russell would have been quite happy to apply the theory to sentences containing genitive noun phrases like 'Smith's murderer', 'that man's wife', 'my parrot', and so on, even though, strictly speaking, these are not of the favored superficial form. (After all, as Grice (1970) observes, on p. 47 of "On Denoting," Russell says that 'my only son' is "a denoting phrase which, on the face of it, has a denotation when, and only when, I have exactly one son.") So, following friends and foes of Russell's theory alike, I shall henceforth take genitive noun phrases of this form to be definite descriptions. (Of course, with a little work, (and a definite degree of unnaturalness) we can transform genitive noun phrases into expressions beginning with 'the': 'the murderer of Smith', 'the wife of that man' (cf. French, 'la femme de cet homme'), 'the parrot that is mine'. (There is, of course, nothing illegitimate about a description of the form '$(\imath x)(Fxb)$' where 'b' is referential.)

Following the practice of many linguists, let's take a noun phrase (NP) the first element of which is a determiner (like 'some', 'the', 'a', 'every', 'no', etc.) to be of the syntactical form Det + N', where N' ("N-bar") is a simple or complex nominal expression (like 'man', 'tall man', 'very tall man', 'man who owns a donkey', etc.). We can gloss over most of the internal structure of N', as it is not relevant to the issue at hand. Thus definite descriptions in English may be of the syntactical form Det + N'.

But from the point of view of semantics, we also want to count 'Smith's murderer', 'that woman's husband', and 'my wife', as descriptions. Each of these is of the form (NP + *poss*) + N', where *poss* is the possessive (or genitive) marker. 'Smith' + *poss* becomes 'Smith's; 'that woman' + *poss* becomes 'that woman's'; 'I' + *poss* becomes 'my'. Now we can say that a definite description in English may be of either of the following forms:

(I)   'the' + N'   (e.g., 'The king')
(II) (NP + *poss*) + N´   (e.g., 'Smith's murderer').

Since definite descriptions themselves are NPs we can have ever more complicated descriptions. For example, 'the king's father' is of the form of (I) and 'Bill's father's dog's basket' is of the form of (II). And, of course, such descriptions are perfectly good ones in *Principia* notation:

(5) $(\imath x)(Fx(\imath y)(Ky))$
(6) $(\imath x)(Bx(\imath y)(Dy(\imath z)(Fzb)))$.[41]

The Theory of Descriptions has enormous expressive power. It enables us to represent and characterize the truth conditions of sentences containing simple descriptions, as in, 'The king is wise'; relativized descriptions, as in, 'every man loves the woman who raised him'; and recursively generated descriptions, as in, 'Bill's father's dog's basket is brown.' And if we use an NP like 'each girl' in the NP slot in a description of the form (II), we can class a phrase like 'each girl's father' (or 'the father of each girl', see notes 40 and 41) as a relativized description (or at least as *containing* a relativized description). In the notation of *Principia*, (7) will come out as (8):

(7)   Each girl's father cheered her
(8) $(\forall x)(Gx \supset C(\imath y)(Fyx)x)$

in which $(\imath y)(Fyx)$ contains a variable x bound by the universal quantifier. (Relativized descriptions will play an important role when we look at anaphora on descriptions in Chapters 5 and 6.) Again, it is simply unclear how Strawson's theory is supposed to deal with such examples.

As for the question whether *all* phrases of the form 'the so-and-so' are definite descriptions, G. E. Moore (1944) points out that such phrases are often used in ways that, at least on the surface, appear to resist analysis in terms of the Theory of Descriptions. Russell has given "a true, and most important, account" of perhaps "far the commonest" use of "*the* in the singular" says Moore (p. 215), but the assertions typically made by using sentences such as 'the whale is a mammal', or 'the heart pumps blood through the arteries', will fall outside its scope. Characteristically, Moore is bringing up an important terminological issue. He points out that it is not clear from Russell's own writings whether uses of such sentences typically involve different uses of *descriptions*, or different uses of the word 'the'. In "On Denoting," descriptions are said to be denoting phrases, and a phrase is said to be denoting "solely in virtue of its *form*" (p. 41). And Russell (1919, p. 172) says he is out to provide a "definition of the word *the* (in the singular)." But it is not clear whether we are to conclude from such talk that all expressions of the *form* 'the so-and-so' are descriptions. In response to Moore, Russell (1944) says,

> Mr. Moore points out, quite correctly, that the Theory of Descriptions does not apply to such sentences as 'the whale is a mammal'. For this the blame lies on the English language, in which the word 'the' is capable of various different meanings (p. 690).

Russell seems anxious to concede that the word 'the' can be used in English in a way that has nothing to do with a unique satisfier of some descriptive condition or other. As he puts it in *Principia Mathematica* (p. 30), he is concerned with 'the' used "strictly, so as to imply uniqueness." Here Strawson (1950, pp. 1–2) is in agreement with Russell: the sort of "generic" use of a description one would normally associate with an utterance of 'The whale is a mammal', is something to be put to one side; what is at issue is the "uniquely referring use," of a description, what Russell might call the "uniquely denoting use."[42]

Although I shall not address Moore's example further, I think Russell is doing himself an injustice here. The sort of generic or tenseless flavor of the example is not something determined by the phrase 'the whale' itself. First, as Strawson points out one can use the same phrase in the uniquely denoting way, for instance in an utterance of 'the whale hit the side of the ship'. Second, we find the same phenomenon with sentences like 'a whale is a mammal' or 'whales are mammals'. Part of the task of the philosopher of language is to explain what is going on in these cases quite generally, a problem that is nothing to do with descriptive phrases *per se*. (Perhaps we need to quantify over species or think more about the relationship between universal and existential quantifiers in Russell's analysis of definite and indefinite descriptions.)

We are in a similar situation when it comes to descriptions whose heads are *mass* rather than *count* nouns. It is sometimes argued that phrases like 'the water', 'the sugar', and so on resist Russell's analysis. However, Sharvy (1980) has pointed out that where 'F' is a mass noun, and '$\leq$' represents 'is a part of', replacing '$=$' by '$\leq$' in *14.01 seems to get the right result:

*14.01' $[(\imath x)(Fx)]G(\imath x)(Fx) =_{\mathrm{df}} (\exists x)((\forall y)(Fy \equiv y \leq x) \ \& \ Gx)$.

So if it is possible to construe the *identity* relation as a special sort of *part of* relation, it may well be possible to adopt *14.01' in place of *14.01.[43] Of course, before such a suggestion can be converted into a serious theory, a barrage of important metaphysical questions must be faced; but the very possibility of exploring this sort of option should at least indicate that the Theory of Descriptions should not be written off at the first sign of danger.

Indeed, one of the things I hope to show in this essay is that several purported objections to the Theory of Descriptions really have nothing to do with descriptions *per se*. Since it is virtually impossible to tackle one philosophical problem without getting completely embroiled in several others, the most plausible and insightful thesis may be greeted by a barrage of apparent counterexamples. But very often an objection may be defused by making legitimate abstractions and idealizations from other philosophical problems. What initially looks like a counterexample may, upon reflection, turn out to be a quite irrelevant point that arises only because one problem interacts with another. With this methodological outlook in mind, I suggest we begin on a more optimistic note than Russell did when he replied to Moore. Until we encounter knock-down evidence to the contrary, all occurrences of phrases of the form 'the so-and-so' in the singular are to be treated as definite descriptions, i.e., as analyzable in terms of the Theory of Descriptions.

Such a stance immediately invites objections from those philosophers who, while they may reject Strawson's claim that descriptions are *by their very nature* a subclass of referring expressions, argue that *some* occurrences are referential. The most influential statement of such a view has come from Keith Donnellan, who argues for what he calls a *referential use* of definite descriptions.[44] Suppose you and I are at a gathering and we both notice a man standing alone in the far corner; I notice that he is trying to attract your attention, so I say to you,

(9)   The man in the far corner is trying to get your attention.

Here I might be said to be using the definite description 'the man in the far corner' *referentially*, in the sense that I intend to communicate an object-dependent thought (about that very man) rather than (or rather than *just*) an object-independent thought to the effect that the unique satisfier of a certain descriptive condition is trying to attract your attention.

Now as Grice (1969) and Kripke (1977) have pointed out, there is no challenge to Russell here unless Donnellan is claiming that the man I intend to communicate information about enters into a specification of the *truth conditions* of my utterance, i.e., unless Donnellan is claiming that the *proposition expressed* is object-dependent. In his earliest writing on this topic, Donnellan seemed to be uncertain whether he wanted to go this far. However, in subsequent literature a very clear challenge to a unitary Russellian analysis of descriptions has emerged: A definite description 'the *F*' may, as it occurs in a particular utterance of 'the *F* is *G*', function as a genuine referring expression, thus rendering the proposition expressed on such an occasion *object-dependent* rather than descriptive.[45] I shall take this claim (or pair of claims) to embody the thesis that there is a semantically distinct referential interpretation of definite descriptions.

I believe this thesis is quite mistaken, but I am going to postpone discussion until Chapter 3. There are three reasons for this. First, there is still quite a lot of work to do on Russell's positive proposals and the way they can be implemented in contemporary theories of quantification. Second, it is virtually impossible to grasp many of the issues involved without putting together, at least in broad outline, some sort of framework within which one can clearly separate genuinely semantical characteristics of an expression ζ from features of the use of ζ that derive from nonsemantical considerations impinging upon communicative activity. Third, there are several distinct arguments in the literature that are claimed to establish beyond doubt the existence of a referential interpretation. These arguments bring into play a variety of subtle issues concerning quantifier scope, variable-binding, opacity, and anaphora, and a lot of ground must be covered before the arguments can be evaluated properly. However, by the time we reach the middle of Chapter 5, each of the arguments will have been deflected, and the Theory of Descriptions extended to territory Russell himself never covered.

2.5 Quantifiers in Natural Language

It is sometimes argued that Russell's analysis does such violence to surface syntax that it simply cannot be construed as playing a role in a compositional semantical theory. This claim is misguided. Recent work on determiners and quantifiers in natural language points the way to a uniform theory in which the Theory of Descriptions has a natural resting place. As we shall soon see, the formalism of *Principia Mathematica* is no more essential to the Theory of Descriptions than is Russell's sense-datum epistemology or his consequent desire to treat proper names as truncated descriptions.

An endorsement of the Theory of Descriptions as providing the correct truth conditions for (utterances of) sentences containing definite descriptions is perfectly consistent with a rejection of the view that prior to semantical interpretation, such sentences (or any others for that matter) must be mapped onto sentences of the language of *Principia Mathematica* (or a related first-order language incorporating the unary quantifiers $\forall$ and $\exists$). It is the purpose of the next two sections to disengage the Theory of Descriptions from standard first-order notation by locating it within a more general quantificational framework that will help us in several ways as we proceed.

In the language of *PM*, quantified sentences of the form 'all *F*s are *G*s' and 'some *F*s are *G*s' are represented by means of the standard unary quantifiers devised by Frege (1879). But these English sentence-types are very obviously *binary* in structure: the determiners 'all' and 'some' are devices for expressing *relations* between *two* universals, in these particular examples *F*-ness and *G*-ness. (This is essentially the way Aristotle treated quantified sentences in his syllogistic.) Let **F** be the set of things that are *F*. We can now say that 'all *F*s are *G*s' is true if and only if $\mathbf{F} = \mathbf{F} \cap \mathbf{G}$; and 'some *F*s are *G*s' is true if and only if $\mathbf{F} \cap \mathbf{G} \neq \varnothing$.

It was Frege who first discovered that these binary structures could be expressed in a formal system containing just the *unary* quantifiers $\forall$ and $\exists$—or indeed just one of these devices, as long as we have negation. But despite their enormous power, when it comes to representing the truth conditions of quantified sentences of natural language, these "standard" quantifiers are inadequate in several respects. We can represent the English sentences 'Everything is mortal' and 'Something is mortal' as (1) and (2) respectively:

(1) $(\forall x)(\text{mortal}(x))$

(2) $(\exists x)(\text{mortal}(x))$.

But as soon as we attempt to capture the force of genuinely *binary* structures like 'All men are mortal' or 'Some men are mortal', we have to introduce sentential connectives if we wish to continue using the standard quantificational notation:

(3) $(\forall x)(\text{man } x \supset \text{mortal } x)$

(4) $(\exists x)(\text{man } x \text{ \& mortal } x)$.

As Wiggins (1980) and Barwise and Cooper (1981) have pointed out, this presents two related problems. The first concerns the relationship between the superficial syntactical structures of English sentences and the syntactical structures of their logical representations. There is nothing in the quantificational formulae corresponding to the subject noun phrases in the original sentences. Moreover, each quantificational formula contains, as a proper constituent, two open sentences joined by a sentential connective, yet there is no constituent of either English sentence corresponding to such an expression. It is, of course, possible to come up with synonymous sentences of English, or at least logician's English, that to some extent reflect the use of these connectives:

(5)   Everything is if a man then mortal

(6)   Something is both a man and mortal.

But to claim that the logical forms of the original sentences are to be characterized via *these sentences* is just to push the problem back to explaining the relationship between the original sentences and the sentences of logician's English.

The second problem concerns generality. As is well-known, there are plurality quantifiers that simply resist the unary mold. Suppose we wished to add a unary quantifier MOST to represent 'most'. The idea would be that (MOST $x)(Fx)$ is true if and only if most things in the domain of quantification (i.e., more than half of them) are F. This is fine for representing sentences like 'Most things are mortal', but as soon we encounter a genuine binary structure, we get stuck. For instance, suppose we wish to represent (7):

(7)   Most men are immortal.

What we require is a formula of the form of (8):

(8)   (MOST x) (man x © immortal x)

where '©' is a binary, truth-functional connective. Clearly '©' cannot be '&' for then (7) would mean that most things are men-and-immortal. Nor can '©' be '⊃' for then it would mean that most things are if-men-then-immortal. But since nearly everything is not a man, nearly everything is if-man-then-immortal; therefore the sentence will come out true whether or not most men are immortal (here I borrow heavily from Wiggins' succinct discussion). In fact, there is no sentential connective that captures what we require of '©'; indeed, it is not possible to define 'most Fs' in first order logic at all, even if attention is restricted to finite domains.[46]

The problem is that in (8) the "quantifier" *most* is ranging over the entire domain of quantification rather than just those things that are men. Intuitively, we want something like the following result:

'most Fs are Gs' is true if and only if $|F \cap G| > |F - G|$.[47]

(F = the set of things that are F. $F \cap G$ = the set of things that are both F and G. $F - G$ = the set of things that are F and not-G. $|F \cap G|$ is the cardinality of $F \cap G$.) This suggests that we should treat 'most' and other natural language determiners ('some', 'every', 'all', 'no', and so on) as exactly what they appear to be: devices that combine with *two* simple or complex formulae (or predicates, depending upon how one views matters) to form a formula.

There are two standard ways of formalizing this idea, what I shall call *BQ* and *RQ*. According to *RQ*, a determiner is an expression that combines with a formula (or predicate) to form a restricted quantifier.[48] So, for instance, 'most' combines with, say, 'men' to form the restricted quantifier 'most men'. Let's represent this as

[most x: men x].

This quantifier combines with a second formula '— are mortal' to form a formula 'Most men are mortal', which we can represent as

(9)   [most x: men x] (mortal x).

Satisfaction can then be defined in the usual way.[49]

According to *BQ*, a determiner is a *binary* quantifier, a device that combines with a pair of formulae (or predicates) to form a formula (the quantifier is "binary" not in the standard sense that it simultaneously binds two distinct variables (see Mostowski, 1957), but in the sense that it combines with two formulae (or predicates).[50] On this account, 'Most men are mortal' can be represented as

(10)   [most x] (men x : mortal x)

where the colon is just a syntactical device for separating the first from the second formula.

A sentence containing a quantified noun phrase like 'most men who know Greek', which itself contains a restrictive relative clause, can be represented in either system. For instance, 'Most men who know Greek are mortal' will come out as either (11) or (12):

(11)   [most x: men x & x know Greek] (mortal x)

(12) [most x] (men x & x know Greek : mortal x).[51]

It has been argued by Gareth Evans that sentences like the following

(13) Most men who own *a car* wash *it* on Sunday

(14) The only man who owns *a donkey* beats *it*

where there is some sort of anaphoric relation between the italicized indefinite description and the pronoun 'it', tell against treating quantified noun phrases as restricted quantifiers and in favor of treating determiners as binary quantifiers.[52] However, for reasons we cannot go into until Chapter 6, Evans is just mistaken on this point; the two systems have the same expressive power and capacity for encoding antecedent anaphor relations.[53] The only significant difference between the systems is that the first allows us to view quantified noun phrases like 'most men', 'most men who know Greek', 'some tigers', and so on, as syntactical and semantical units, and consequently its formulae tend to be much easier to parse. For these reasons, it is the system I shall adopt.

For the sake of having some clear and unambiguous notation to work with, let's informally modify the formation rules of a standard first-order language. We can replace the rules that specify that if ϕ is a well-formed formula then so are $(\forall x)\phi$ and $(\exists x)\phi$ with the following:

(Q1) If ϕ is a well-formed formula with x free, and
       if D is one of 'some', 'no', 'every', 'all', 'a', 'the', 'most', etc.,
       then '$[Dx: \phi]$' is a well-formed quantifier phrase.

(Q2) If ψ is a well-formed formula with x free, and
       if '$[Dx: \phi]$' is a well-formed quantifier phrase,
       then '$[Dx: \phi](\psi)$' is a well-formed formula.[54]

The notion of variable binding operative in (Q1) and (Q2) is very simple. We have two types of variable-binding operator: determiners and quantifiers. A determiner Dx binds any free occurrences of x in the formula with which it combines to form a unary quantifier. And a unary quantifier $[Dx: \phi]$ binds any free occurrences of x in the formula with which it combines to form a formula. (For syntactical details, see 5.6.)

We can now write some sample truth clauses:

(∗1) '[every x: Fx] (Gx)' is true iff $|\mathbf{F} - \mathbf{G}| = 0$

(∗2) '[no x: Fx] (Gx)'   is true iff $|\mathbf{F} \cap \mathbf{G}| = 0$

(*3) '[some x: Fx] (Gx)' is true iff $|F \cap G| \geq 1$

(*4) '[an x: Fx] (Gx) is true iff $|F \cap G| \geq 1$

(*5) '[most x: Fx] (Gx)' is true iff $|F \cap G| > |F - G|$.

(I have not attributed existential import to 'every F'. If it is wanted, add "and $|F| \geq 1$" to the right hand side of (*1). This matter is unimportant for present concerns.)

Using this notation, we can perspicuously and unambiguously represent the quantificational structures of sentences with more than one operator, the scope of such devices being understood exactly as in first-order logic. For instance, the negation sign '¬' can be prefixed either to the entire sentence, as in (15_1), or to the open sentence that contains the predicate, as in (15_2):

(15_1) ¬ [Dx: Fx] (Gx)

(15_2) [Dx: Fx] ¬ (Gx).

Quantifications on nonsubject positions and multiple quantifications can also be represented. For instance, the alleged scope ambiguity in

(16) Every boy loves some girl

is captured as follows:

(16_1) [every x: boy x] ([some y: girl y] (x loves y))

(16_2) [some y: girl y] ([every x: boy x] (x loves y)).[55]

In these formulae a quantifier combines with an open sentence that is itself the product of combining a quantifier with an open sentence.

Since we can represent both multiple quantifications and restrictive relative clauses, we can also handle a sentence like (17), which will come out as (18):

(17) Every man who owns a donkey is happy

(18) [every x: man x & [a y: donkey y] (x owns y)] (happy x).[56]

We can also represent sentences containing pronouns bound by quantifiers. For instance, (19) will come out as (20):

(19) *Every man* saw a woman *he* knew

(20) [every x: man x] ([a y: woman y & x knew y] (x saw y)).

In a similar fashion we can also represent a sentence like (21), which raises some interesting syntactical issues that are discussed in 5.6:

(21) An F.B.I. agent in *each C.I.A. division* is keeping tabs on *it*.

The subject noun phrase in (21) contains two determiners, 'an' and 'each', the linear order of which is misleading as to relative scope. And as May (1977, 1985) observes, in order that we do not get a free variable, the logical form of (21) must be

(22) [each y: C.I.A. division y] ([an x: F.B.I. agent x & x in y]
      (x is keeping tabs on y)).[57]

As we shall see in 6.3 and 6.5, once we have the means of distinguishing bound from unbound pronouns, we shall also be able to represent sentences like the following:

(13) Most men who own *a car* wash *it* on Sunday

(14) The only man who owns *a donkey* beats *it*

(23) If John buys a donkey, he vaccinates it

which have been much discussed in the literature.[58]

2.6 Descriptions as Quantifiers

As I mentioned earlier, it is sometimes suggested that the Theory of Descriptions is too cumbersome and unwieldly to merit a place in a serious compositional semantics.[59] Such a charge puts too much weight on the particular formalism of *Principia Mathematica* and not enough on the psychological and semantical insights behind the theory itself. There is indeed a measure of inelegance involved in spelling out the logical form of a sentence of the form 'the F is G' as

$$(\exists x)((\forall y)(Fy \equiv y = x) \ \& \ Gx).$$

And this inelegance is clearly exacerbated when sentences containing more than one description are unpacked. A sentence of the form 'The F R-ed the G' will come out as

$$(\exists x)(\exists u)((\forall y)(Fy \equiv y=x) \ \& \ (\forall v)(Gv \equiv v=u) \ \& \ Rxu)$$

which truly obliterates the relationship between semantical structure and surface syntax.

But of course the formalism of *Principia Mathematica* is not an essential feature of the Theory of Descriptions. If we wanted, we could use the language of 2.5 to characterize the logical structure of 'the F is G' as

[some x: Fx] ([every y: Fy] ($y=x$ & Gx)).

To do this would *not* be to present an *alternative* to the Theory of Descriptions; it would be to choose a language other than that of *Principia Mathematica* in which to state and apply the theory.

But of course there is no need to use such an indirect method of incorporating the Theory of Descriptions into a semantical theory. As Russell points out, on his account definite descriptions are really complex *in*definite descriptions, i.e., existentially quantified noun phrases with a uniqueness condition built in. But we should not become preoccupied with the existential character of the analysis. As *14.01 makes clear, it is by introducing *universal* quantification that the implication of uniqueness is captured. And to this extent, definite descriptions are just as much *universally* quantified noun phrases as they are existentially quantified noun phrases. 'The F is G' is true iff (*i*) all Fs are Gs and (*ii*) there is exactly one F. Since the word 'the' is a one-place quantificational determiner just like 'some', 'most', 'every', etc., we can treat it as combining with a formula to form a restricted quantifier of the form [The x: Fx].[60] We can then provide the following truth clause:

'[the x: Fx] (Gx)'   is true iff $|F - G| = 0$ and $|F| = 1$.

Again, this is not to propose an alternative to Russell's theory; it is just to find a more congenial method of stating it. [the x: Fx] (Gx) is *definitionally equivalent to* $(\exists x)((\forall y)(Fy \equiv y=x) \mathbin{\&} Gx)$.

As Chomsky (1975) has pointed out, one useful consequence of focusing on the universal rather than the existential character of Russell's analysis is that the relationship between singular and plural descriptions comes clearly into view. Intuitively, there is a just a cardinality difference between the truth conditions of a sentence containing a singular description and those of the corresponding sentence containing the description in its plural form. Whereas 'the F is G' is true if and only if all Fs are Gs and there is *exactly one* F, 'the Fs are Gs' is true if and only if all Fs are Gs and there is *more than one* F.[61] It would be a simple matter to add plural descriptions to the language of *Principia Mathematica*. Using $(\pi x)(Fx)$ to represent a plural description 'the Fs', we could formulate the following contextual definition:

$[(\pi x)(Fx)]G(\pi x)(Fx) =_{df}$
$(\exists x)(\exists z)(Fx \mathbin{\&} Fz \mathbin{\&} x \neq z) \mathbin{\&} (\forall y)(Fy \supset Gy)$.

This faithfully captures the truth conditions of 'the Fs are Gs'; but it certainly does not illuminate the relationship between singular and plural descriptions. By contrast, Chomsky's truth clauses make the relationship very clear:

(∗6) Where 'F' is singular,

   '[the x: Fx] (Gx)' is true iff $|F - G| = 0$ and $|F| = 1$

(∗7) Where 'F' is plural,

   '[the x: Fx] (Gx)' is true iff $|F - G| = 0$ and $|F| > 1$.

We can, if we want, add a further truth clause for sentences containing what I earlier called *numberless* descriptions such as 'whoever shot John F. Kennedy' and 'whatever I say'. Let 'whe' represent the number-neutral descriptive determiner:

(∗8) '[whe x: Fx] (Gx)'   is true iff $|F - G| = 0$ and $|F| \geq 1$.

The determiner 'both' creates what we might call *dual* descriptions:

(∗9) '[both x: Fx] (Gx)'   is true iff $|F - G| = 0$ and $|F| = 2$.

Let me reiterate: using this framework to represent the quantificational structures of sentences containing definite descriptions in no way conflicts with the Theory of Descriptions construed as an account of the semantics of certain English sentences. We are not, by virtue of being Russellians about descriptions, committed to the view that the sentences in question must be beaten into sentences in the language of *Principia Mathematica* or something very similar. From the point of view of explicating the logical structure of sentences containing descriptions, treating them as restricted unary quantifiers (or treating the definite article as a binary quantifier) results not in a clash with Russell but in an explanation of where the Theory of Descriptions fits into a more general theory of natural language quantification, a theory that treats determiners like 'every', 'some', 'all', 'most', 'a', 'the', 'which', and so on, as members of a unified syntactical and semantical category.[62]

The particular formalism we have adopted allows us to capture this syntactical and semantical uniformity in a perspicuous way. This extends well beyond sentences containing simple descriptions. In particular, it allows us to characterize sentences containing

(a) *Descriptions containing relative clauses.* For example, (1) will come out as (1₁), and (2) will come out as (2₁):

(1)   The man who loves Mary is insane

(1₁)   [the x: man x & x loves Mary] (x is insane)

(2)   The man whom Mary loves is insane

(2_1)   [the x: man x & Mary loves x] (x is insane)

(*b*) *Relativized descriptions.* For example, (3) will come out as (3_1), and (4) as (4_1), and (5) as (5_1):

(3)   *Every man* loves the woman who raised *him*

(3_1)   [every x: man x] ([the y: woman y & y raised x] (x loves y))

(4)   The father of *each girl* (each girl's father) is good to *her*

(4_1)   [each x: girl x] ([the y: y father-of x] (y is good to x))

(5)   The man who bought *each donkey* fed *it*

(5_1)   [each x: donkey x] ([the y: man y & y bought x] (y fed x)).

(*c*) *Descriptions of the form* (NP + *poss*) + N'. For example, (6) will come out as (6_1), and (7) will come out as (7_1):

(6)   Smith's murderer is insane

(6_1)   [the x: x murdered Smith] (insane x)

(7)   Smith loves his wife

(7_1)   [the x: x wife-of-Smith] (Smith loves x).

(*d*) *Pronouns bound by descriptions.* For example, (8) will come out as (8_1), and (9) will come out as (9_1):

(8)   The President likes himself

(8_1)   [the x: President x] (x likes x)

(9)   The President married a woman he loved

(9_1)   [the x: President x] ([a y: woman y & x loved y] (x married y)).

The domain of the Theory of Descriptions is really quite vast. Indeed, as we shall see, once it is recognized just how many types of phrases the theory applies to, a variety of syntactical and semantical puzzles simply evaporate. In Chapters 4, 5, and 6, I shall discuss some important examples. But before that, various arguments deemed to invalidate or restrict the application of the theory need to be addressed.

2.7 Concluding Remarks

We have seen that the purpose of the Theory of Descriptions is to make available a class of descriptive propositions. A descriptive proposition can be expressed by an utterance of a sentence containing a description whether or not anything satisfies the description; and even if the description is satisfied, the proposition expressed can be grasped without knowledge of who or what satisfies it.

Let me conclude this chapter with a list of some important features of the Theory of Descriptions.

(*i*) The theory is logically independent of Russell's sense-datum epistemology (2.2). Hence one can endorse the theory *qua* theory of *descriptions* without being committed to the restricted notion of acquaintance Russell finally adopts.

(*ii*) Consequently, one is not obliged to extend the application of the theory beyond what we would ordinarily regard as definite descriptions. Indeed, considerations such as those adduced by Kripke (1972, 1980) concerning truth conditions with respect to counterfactual situations demonstrate that Russell was certainly wrong to treat ordinary proper names as disguised descriptions (2.2). (One could still, perhaps, treat *some* alleged names as disguised descriptions, for instance the names of fictional characters or deities, if one so desired, but there may well be problems there too.)

(*iii*) The distinction between genuine referring expressions and descriptions is quite independent of Russell's views about the constituents of propositions. Although Russell talks of object-dependent propositions containing objectual constituents, this is a quite inessential feature of his proposal. The crucial difference between an object-dependent (i.e., singular) thought and a descriptive thought is that the former is contingent upon the existence of some particular individual (2.2). A descriptive thought is object-independent.

(*iv*) The theory does *not* (contrary to some opinion) ride roughshod over the distinction between sentences and utterances (2.2). Russell was clearly concerned with the propositions expressed by utterances of sentences rather than the more abstract notion of linguistic meaning. There is nothing to prevent us from grafting on a suitable theory of indexicality when the time comes, and thereby extending the theory to indexical descriptions (3.3).

(*v*) The formalism of *Principia Mathematica* is dispensible. The Theory of descriptions has a natural place within a general theory of natural language quantification in which determiners like 'some', 'all', 'a', 'the', etc. are treated as members of a unified syntactical and semantical category (2.5, 2.6).

(*vi*) With a little thought, the theory can be extended to nonsingular descriptions like 'the students in Bill's class', 'whoever shot J. F. Kennedy', and so on (2.6).

(*vii*) Relational descriptions (like 'Bill's mother'), relativized descriptions (like 'the woman who raised him', as it occurs in 'Every man loves the woman that raised him'), and inverted descriptions (like 'each girl's father'), present no special problems (2.4, 2.6).

(*viii*) Since descriptions are treated as quantifiers—ultimately restricted quantifiers when the position is thought through—all sorts of interesting scope interactions are predicted; not just with negation and other quantified noun phrases, but also with various types of nonextensional operators (Chapter 4).

(*ix*) The fact that descriptions are not treated as referring expressions does not preclude them from functioning as the antecedents of anaphoric pronouns. First, *qua* quantifiers they may bind pronouns functioning as the natural language counterparts of the logician's bound variables (Chapter 5). And second, there are good syntactical and semantical reasons for thinking that a very natural class of pronouns that are anaphoric on quantifiers are not actually bound by them but rather go proxy for definite descriptions (Chapters 5 and 6).

(*x*) Although we have so far considered only descriptions of persons and material objects, the Theory of Descriptions may also be applicable to definite descriptions of *events* such as 'the sinking of the *Titanic*', 'Mary's departure', and so on (4.6).

Notes

1. The terms of art 'singular' and 'object-dependent' can both be misleading. Talk of *singular* propositions is liable to mislead because if '*b*' and '*c*' are referring expressions, then the proposition expressed by '*b* and *c* are *G*', is still singular in the intended sense, despite the fact that the subject noun phrase '*b* and *c* is plural. Talk of *object-dependent* propositions might mislead because a predicate may contain a referring expression as a constituent (i.e., it may express a relational property). So even if '*b*' is not a referring expression, the proposition expressed by '*b* is *G*' might still be object-dependent, but not in the intended sense. For convenience, and following standard practice, when I talk of object-dependent (singular) propositions, I shall mean propositions that are object-dependent with respect to the subject position of the sentences used to express them. (This is still, of course, problematic because of the possibility of descriptions containing referring expressions and the existence of synonymous active/passive pairs of the form '*b* R-ed *c*'/'*c* was R-ed by *b*', but there should be no confusion in what follows.)

    Russell sometimes cashes out object-dependence in terms of propositions containing objects as constituents. (See e.g., Russell (1904), p. 169; (1905), p. 56; (1918), pp. 245 and 275. This particular view of singular propositions has been revived by Kaplan (1975, 1978). It has been argued by McDowell (1977, 1982, 1986), Davies (1981), and Evans (1982) that objectual constituency is a quite inessential feature of Russell's picture of the relationship between referring expressions and singular propositions. What *is* essential is that the existence of the proposition depend upon the existence of the object, and on their account this can be captured without taking the object to be a constituent of the proposition.

Russell actually used the word 'proposition' in a variety of ways from 1903 onwards, at times appearing to have given up altogether on the notion behind it. In *The Principles of Mathematics* (1903) propositions are said to have objectual constituents. By 1905, this is less clear. In his first statement of the Principle of Acquaintance ("On Denoting," p. 56), Russell says that the constituents of any proposition we can entertain are "entities with which we have immediate acquaintance"; but elsewhere in that paper he seems to talk of propositions as logico-linguistic objects—in fact, several times he uses 'proposition' where one would expect to find 'sentence' (or 'utterance'). In "The Philosophy of Logical Atomism" (1918) and *An Introduction to Mathematical Philosophy* (1919) there is overt talk of propositions having *logical* constituents, as when it is said that the referent of a logically proper name '*b*' will be the "logical subject" of the proposition expressed by (an utterance of) '*b* is *G*'. This way of putting things plays a central role in his exposition of the Theory of Descriptions. A sentence of the grammatically subject-predicate form 'the *F* is *G*' is said to have a logical form quite different from a sentence of the form '*b* is *G*' (where '*b*' is a referring expression) in that it has no *logical* subject. (As we shall see in 2.6, however, one can endorse the Theory of Descriptions and still treat a description 'the *F*' as a semantical unit.)

2. Names introduced by description ("Let's call whoever invented the wheel *Julius*") are not *genuine* referring expressions but quasi-referring expressions. Again this is stipulative at present, but the rationale will emerge in due course. See in particular, note 20.

    It is arguable that the taxonomy adopted in the main text covers all and only those expressions that Russell regarded as "names" in 1905, or at least all those he would have regarded as such if he had extended his views to cover pronominal anaphora. For reasons that were mainly epistemological, by 1911 Russell came to think of most names and demonstratives as only "masquerading" as referring expressions. For discussion, see note 5.

3. John Perry has pointed out to me that the first conjunct of Russell's requirement would appear to be redundant. If I am not acquainted with *b*, then on Russell's account, strictly speaking I cannot know that '*b*' is a name of *b*. (Until we get to Russell's restricted notion of acquaintance, the difference between what Russell calls *logically proper names* and what I am calling *genuine referring expressions* (*genuine singular terms*) is immaterial.)

4. Russell (1911, 1912). See also Russell (1905), pp. 41–42, 55–56.

5. By the time of "Knowledge by Acquaintance and Knowledge by Description" (1911), Russell had come to hold the notorious restricted view, according to which we are acquainted only with sense-data, universals, and, perhaps, ourselves. It was this epistemological shift that led Russell to extend the Theory of Descriptions not only to names of fictional objects—something he had already done in "On Denoting" to liberate himself from the ontological extravagances of *The Principles of Mathematics*—but

also to what we would ordinarily regard as proper names for existents. The semanticist can perfectly coherently endorse the Theory of Descriptions *qua* theory of *descriptions* without extending it in this way and without commitment to Russell's restricted view of acquaintance. The restricted notion of acquaintance is an obvious target for those sympathetic to Wittgenstein's so-called "private language argument." For a clear and engaging discussion of these points, see Sainsbury (1979).

6. It does not, of course, follow that on Russell's account one can have knowledge of something without knowing *anything* by acquaintance. Indeed, this possibility is explicitly excluded by the Principle of Acquaintance: "Every proposition which we can understand must be composed wholly of constituents with which we are acquainted" (1912, p. 32). This principle is first stated in Russell (1905) at p. 56. See also Russell (1911) on p. 159.

7. This is not, of course, to preclude the possibility that something that is the unique satisfier of some definite description or other is also known to us by acquaintance: "We shall say that we have 'merely descriptive knowledge' of the so-and-so when, although we know that the so-and-so exists, and although we may possibly be acquainted with the object which is, in fact, the so-and-so, yet we do not know any proposition '*a* is the so-and-so', where *a* is something with which we are acquainted" (1911, p. 156).

8. It is, of course, the in-between cases that are problematic. One view that has been explored in some detail by Evans (1973, 1982) is that perceptual contact between *S* and *b* is a central kind of informational transaction, and that a subsequent informational exchange between *S* and some other subject *S'* who has not had direct perceptual contact with *b* may still preserve information from *b*. In this connection, see also McDowell (1977, 1986), Sainsbury (1979), and Peacocke (1982).

9. This addition is the second half of Russell's condition (see above): "To understand a name you must be acquainted with the particular of which it is a name, and you must know that it is the name of that particular."

10. The terminology in this context is due to Evans (1982).

11. See note 20.

12. Understanding an utterance of a sentence is thus very different from understanding the sentence uttered; I may understand the sentence 'This is broken' without understanding a particular utterance of this sentence. For extended discussion, see 3.3.

13. In this connection, see Evans (1982) and McDowell (1986).

14. This way of characterizing rigidity is explicit in Peacocke (1975). For relevant discussion of (R3) with respect to "rigid descriptions," see note 18.

15. Stating (c) as 'Everything that is *F* is *G*', rather than 'Whatever (or whoever) is *F* is *G*', eliminates a potential confusion. As G. E. Moore (1944, pp. 179–81) points out, it is at least arguable that the latter entails

the existence of at least one F, in which case clause (a) is redundant. Moore's observation raises an interesting question, about the status of phrases of the form 'whoever is F' or 'whatever is F'. I am inclined to view such phrases as descriptions that are, from the point of view of semantical interpretation, *numberless* or *number-neutral* (i.e., neither singular nor plural). Even if it gives rise to an implication of existence, 'Whoever is F is G' does not give rise to a semantical implication of uniqueness (of course, in certain circumstances it may be clear that the speaker believes there is only one F, but that's not the issue). 'Whoever is F is G' might be paraphrased as 'the person (or persons) who is (or are) F is (or are) G', which makes clear its neutrality with respect to number. (The encumbrance of such paraphrases might explain the existence of numberless descriptions.) *Syntactically*, 'whoever' is singular, at least if verb agreement is anything to go by, witness the third person singular inflections on 'buy' and 'be' in (e.g.) 'Whoever buys one of these is getting a bargain'. The possibility of numberless descriptions will be investigated in more detail when we have covered plural descriptions (2.6) and when we have decided exactly which phrases to count as descriptions (2.4). For discussion of numberless pronouns, see 6.3.

16. This aspect of Russell's theory has been stressed by (e.g.) Evans (1982), Blackburn (1984) and McDowell (1986).

17. This aspect of Russell's theory is stressed by Kaplan (1971, 1978); the theory is about logical form, i.e., it is about the *kind* of proposition expressed by an utterance of 'the F is G'.

This is a good point to make the following note for future reference: One who holds the thesis that descriptions may, on occasion, be interpreted as genuine referring expressions has an obligation to show that on such occasions, if there is no object that can be construed as the "referent" of the description, then no proposition (*a fortiori* no general proposition) is expressed, and hence that nothing constitutes understanding the utterance in question.

18. The point is made very clearly by Peacocke (1975, p. 117):

> [Suppose] two school inspectors [are] visiting an institution for the first time: one may say to the other, on the basis of the activities around him, "The headmaster doesn't have much control of the pupils." Here there is no object such that the school inspector has said of it that it doesn't have much control over the pupils. One cannot say that the headmaster is such an object, since what the inspector (*actually*) said would be true even if someone else were headmaster.

Two minor points. First, one might be tempted to think of the definite description 'the smallest prime number' as a rigid designator because it *denotes* the same object (the number two) in both actual and counterfactual situations. To distinguish such examples from those that he was particularly interested in, Kripke (1980) distinguishes between *de jure* and *de facto* rigidity. A proper name is rigid *de jure* in that it is part of the way a name functions that is is a rigid designator (it is in the nature of a name—even a "descriptive name," see note 20—to be rigid). A definite description 'the F' is said to be rigid *de facto* if it happens to contain a predicate 'F' that in each actual and counterfactual situation is true of one and the same unique object. My own (slight) preference—and I see this is built into the way I have worded (R3)—is to say that no definite description is rigid: an expression ζ is a rigid designator just in case an utterance of a sentence 'ζ is G' expresses an object-dependent proposition.

This brings me to the second point. To claim that the proposition expressed by an utterance u of 'the F is G' is not object-dependent is not to say that it is *impossible* to construct a consistent semantical theory in which definite descriptions are treated as *nonrigid* referring expressions (Thomason and Stalnaker (1968) have constructed such a theory). But as Evans (1979, 1982) points out, the fact that we can provide a perfectly good account of the semantics of descriptions by treating them as *quantifiers* imposes a substantial methodological burden on those who would complicate the semantics with an additional class of referring expressions that do not satisfy any of (R1)–(R3). For discussion, see Chapter 4.

19. This is just one of a battery of arguments that Kripke (1971, 1972, 1979, 1980) provides against the view that names are disguised descriptions.

20. At this point, it seems appropriate to say a little more about my use of 'genuine' as it occurs in 'genuine referring expression' (and 'genuine singular term'). As I mentioned earlier, ordinary proper names, demonstratives, and pronouns (on some of their uses) are to be treated as genuine referring expressions (singular terms). In the light of the discussions in Kripke (1972) and Evans (1979, 1982), it is plausible to suppose that so-called "descriptive names" are also referring expressions of some sort—a descriptive name is a name introduced by descriptive stipulation: "Let's call whoever invented the zipper *Julius*." Of course, descriptive names will typically not satisfy (R1) and (R2), and to this extent they do not qualify as *genuine* referring expressions in the intended sense. They *do* appear to satisfy (R3), however; and to this extent I propose to call them *quasi*-referring expressions. (Cf. Evans' (1982) distinction between Russellian and non-Russellian referring expressions. Evans (1977) claims that certain anaphoric pronouns ("E-type" pronouns) also satisfy (R3). For reasons that will emerge in Chapter 5, it is clear that E-type pronouns do *not* satisfy (R3), and to this extent they are not even *quasi*-referring expressions.)

21. It should be clear that, given certain plausible assumptions, (D1) follows from (D2), parenthetical clauses and all. Three other arguments against the view that descriptions are referring expressions are presented in "On Denoting," but I shall not focus on them here as the point can, I believe, be made quite persuasively without grappling with problems raised by identity statements, negative existentials, and attitude reports. For discussion, see Chapter 4.

22. Strawson (1950) does not actually use the term 'presupposition' to label the phenomenon in question—he first uses it in this connection in Strawson (1952). Furthermore, he appears to vacillate between viewing (what he later calls) presupposition as an epistemological or pragmatic

relation between a person and a statement, and a logical relation between two statements. As pointed out by Sellars (1954), an epistemological or pragmatic notion of presupposition appears to have no bearing on the semantical issues Strawson took himself to be addressing when he took on Russell. In response to Sellars, Strawson (1954) explicitly claims that it is the logical notion he is interested in: a statement S presupposes a statement S' just in case the truth of S' is a precondition for the truth or falsity of S. The initial ambiguity in Strawson's position (to the extent it is present in the 1950 paper) interacts with a far more important ambiguity discussed in the main text: Is it Strawson's view that *no statement* is made (when there is no king of France)? or that a statement is made, but one that is neither true nor false?

There are important relationships between these two ambiguities that make it exceedingly difficult to construct any sort of consistent position from Strawson's various writings on definite descriptions and presupposition (Strawson, 1950, 1952, 1954, 1964, 1974, 1986). I shall certainly not attempt to provide any sort of detailed examination of Strawson's discussions of presupposition here—that would be quite an undertaking. In fact, I feel rather uneasy about criticizing Strawson's positive proposals for dealing with definite descriptions without providing, at least in some sort of preliminary way, a clear statement of his general position, and for that reason, I shall confine most of my remarks to his criticisms of Russell, although at many places it is not easy to discern the precise nature of the criticism without attributing to Strawson this or that position. On some of the problems Strawson must face, see Nerlich (1965), Gale (1970), Grice (1970, 1981), Mates (1973), Kempson (1975), and (in rather truncated form) notes 23–29 below.

Both logical and pragmatic notions of presupposition have surfaced in more recent work by linguists and philosophers, and following (e.g.) Stalnaker (1972) it is now common practice to distinguish between "semantic" and "pragmatic" presupposition, and to do so along more or less the lines that emerge, upon reasonable reflection, from the debate between Sellars and Strawson. A great range of disparate and unrelated phenomena has been dubbed "presuppositional" over the years, but as argued in considerable detail by Wilson (1975), Kempson (1975), Boer and Lycan (1976), and Lycan (1984), it seems highly implausible that any theoretically important notion will do justice to the full range of data that semanticists professing an interest in "presupposition" seek to explain, even if the distinction between "semantic" and "pragmatic" presupposition can be made sufficiently clear to be useful. Indeed, in the light of Grice's (1961, 1967) pioneering work on the nature of rational discourse and on the distinction between the proposition the speaker expresses by his or her utterance ("what is said") and those propositions he or she (only) "conversationally implicates" (see 3.4), it is plausible to suppose that there is precious little remaining for a theoretically interesting notion of presupposition to be about.

(Frege and Grice both point out that words like 'but', 'still', 'yet', 'even', and others contribute to the literal meanings of sentences in ways that are not truth-conditional, but as Grice (1961) points out, such items do not give rise to *presuppositions* in Strawson's sense. For discussion see Chapter 3, note 19.)

23. Strawson usually talks about *the statement made* or about *what is said*, but seems to acknowledge that such talk is equivalent to talk about *the proposition expressed* (1950, p. 7). Indeed, if it were not, we could hardly take him to be engaging *Russell*. To facilitate the discussion, henceforth I shall use 'proposition' rather than 'statement' throughout.

24. Actually, Strawson takes *uses* of sentences to be true or false, and in this he appears to be making a mistake on his own terms. If someone uttered the sentence 'The king of France is bald' during the reign of Louis XIV, and if at that time Louis XIV was not bald, then the speaker would have said something false; now if the same speaker uttered the very same sentence a few years later when, in fact, Louis XIV was bald, he would, on this second occasion, have said something true. Yet on Strawson's account he will have made the *same use* of the sentence, viz., to refer to Louis XIV and say something about him. Thus Strawson is wrong to take uses of sentences to be true or false. In order to equip him with some sort of defensible position, I shall take it that he thinks that *utterances* (or *particular dated uses*) of sentences are true or false.

25. The ambiguity in question is examined in detail by Nerlich (1965) and Grice (1970).

26. In conversation, Strawson has informed me that this is what he had in mind at the time he wrote "On Referring." As Nerlich (1965) points out, however, there are passages in later works—Strawson (1952) and Strawson (1954)—which suggest that sentences containing nondenoting descriptions express propositions lacking a truth value, or at least propositions lacking one of the *standard* truth values, i.e., true or false. In both of these places Strawson explicitly adopts the view that presupposing is a *logical* relation between propositions—rather than a pragmatic relation between speakers and propositions, see note 22—and it as least arguable that this was one reason he was led to countenance propositions lacking a standard truth value. For as Grice (1970) observes, if it is true (*a*) that no proposition is expressed by an utterance of 'The king of France is bald', (*b*) that when it is neither true nor false that the king of France is bald, this is because of the falsity of what is presupposed—viz., that there is a king of France, and (*c*) that presupposing is a logical relation between propositions, then there is an immediate difficulty. What is it, Grice asks, in the case of 'The king of France is bald' that presupposes the existence of a king of France? Not the proposition that the king of France is bald since, by hypothesis, there is no such proposition. Strawson (1952, 1954) avoids this problem by allowing an utterance of 'The king of France is bald' to express a proposition that is neither true nor false, whereas Strawson (1964) appears to want to avoid it by dropping the line that presupposition is a genuinely logical relation between propositions. It is unclear, to me at least, how a theory that allowed for the possibility of propositions that are neither true nor false could fail to be construed as a theory that posited some third truth-

value—call it "neither true nor false." In which case, I am not at all sure that such a theory can avoid paradox, when applied to sentences like 'It is true that the king of France is bald', 'It is false that the king of France is bald', and so on. (Though see van Fraassen 1968, 1969, 1970.) In any event, it seems to me rather unwise to rush into the realm of three-valued logics *just* to handle the problems raised by nondenoting descriptions—there may well be other reasons—without first examining both the alternatives and the ramifications of a departure from bivalence.

27. As pointed out by Bar-Hillel (1954), Strawson's (1950) position on nondenoting descriptions seems to conflict with his own usage, witness the last sentence of "On Referring": "Neither Aristotelian nor Russellian rules give the exact logic of any expression of ordinary language; for ordinary language has no exact logic."

28. Mates (1973) points out that Strawson's theory faces further problems in connection with examples like the following,

    (i)   *Every man* danced with the woman *he* loved
    (ii)   The million pound fortune of every Englishman is in jeopardy
    (iii) The man who bought *each donkey* vaccinated *it*

in which the descriptions contain variables bound by exterior operators. (Italics will be used throughout the present work to indicate relevant anaphoric connections.) Russell's theory has no problems with these sentences (see 2.4, 2.6), but it is not at all clear how the presuppositional theory is supposed to handle them (nor is it clear how Hornstein's (1984) theory can cope with them, since on his account definite descriptions *by their very nature* must take wide scope over regular quantifiers. For discussion of Hornstein's views on descriptions, see the notes to Chapter 4.)

29. General difficulties for this proposal are pointed out by Gale (1970), Kempson (1975), Donnellan (1981), and Lycan (1984).

30. See (e.g.) Gale (1970), Blackburn (1984), and Lycan (1984).

31. It is not clear that any qualification is necessary here. It is sometimes claimed that descriptions can, and names cannot, be modified by restrictive relative clauses. For instance, (i) is grammatical but (ii) is not:

    (i)   The man who boarded my boat was a pirate
    (ii)   * John Silver who boarded my boat was a pirate.

But the apparent description 'the man' as it occurs in (i) is really just a linear sequence 'the' + 'man' and not a genuine constituent of (i). Rather, as Quine (1960, p. 111) suggests, 'the' combines with the complex common noun 'man who boarded my boat' to form the noun phrase 'the man who boarded my boat', which *is* a genuine definite description. The position occupied by this description may, of course, be occupied by a name. Similarly for 'every man who boarded my boat', 'most men who boarded my boat', etc. (for details, see 2.5, 2.6, and 5.6).

32. Of course, it is still open to argue that descriptions belong in some *third* category distinct from the referring expressions and the quantifiers (or to a category of nonrigid referring expressions; see note 18). I have not seen any good argument to this effect, however. Indeed, it seems to me that a

good case can be made for the view that there are just these two semantical classes of noun phrases in natural language. (See Chapter 5 for a discussion of the place of pronouns within this simple semantical taxonomy.)

33. The discussion in this paragraph borrows from Davies (1981) and (to a lesser extent) from Blackburn (1984).

34. Russell's official arguments against the view that indefinite descriptions are referring expressions are most clearly stated in Chapter XVI of his *Introduction to Mathematical Philosophy*. For discussion, see Ludlow and Neale (forthcoming).

35. In recent years Russell's existential analysis of indefinite descriptions has come under as much attack as his analysis of definite descriptions, and for the same sorts of reasons, viz., worries about referential usage, scope, opacity, anaphora, and so on. At appropriate places in this essay I will mention one or two of the arguments employed against the existential analysis of indefinite descriptions, but I shall not go into any detail as the main issues are taken up in Ludlow and Neale (forthcoming). One influential argument I will address, however, is due to Kamp (1981) and Heim (1982) and concerns the anaphoric relation in a sentence like 'Every man who bought *a donkey* vaccinated *it*.' For discussion of this argument, see 6.3.

36. *Principia Mathematica*, p. 94. I have taken the liberty of putting the equality sign and subscript together rather than putting "Df" to the far right as Russell and Whitehead do.

37. For the purposes of this chapter, I shall avoid the vexed question of whether or not sentences of English that contain both descriptions and negation are genuinely ambiguous in the way Russell suggests; all I want to do right now is illustrate Russell's method of representing scope. For discussion, see Grice (1981) and the final note to Chapter 4.

38. For discussion of Whitehead and Russell's notion of scope in relation to the notion familiar to much recent work in syntactical theory, see 5.6.

39. There is nothing strained about Russellian descriptions taking scope. In the pure language of *Principia Mathematica*, descriptions are not terms at all but devices for abbreviating interactive quantification. Consequently, it does not violate the spirit of Russell's theory to treat descriptions as genuinely quantified expressions within a system that contains (e.g.) restricted quantifiers. In this connection, see 2.6.

40. Consider the following examples from Mates (1973) and Evans (1979), respectively:

   (i)   The million pound fortune of every Englishman is in jeopardy
   (ii)   The father of *each girl* is good to *her*.

   If we spell out the logical forms of these examples, again we find universal quantifiers binding variables inside definite descriptions. For example, (ii) can be rendered as

   (iii) $(\forall x)(Gx \supset P(\iota y)(Fyx)x)$

(where P stands for 'is good to'). But notice that as far as surface grammar is concerned, the universal quantifier is a constituent of the description in subject position. This fact has been used by May (1977, 1985) as evidence for a level of syntactical representation ("Logical Form" or "LF") at which scope relations are made explicit. In particular, May observes that the pronoun 'her' in (ii) seems to function as a variable bound by 'each girl', and suggests that this is explicable on the assumption that in the LF representation of (ii) 'each girl' has been "moved" (in a syntactically principled way) from the position it occupies in its surface structure (more precisely, its S-Structure) representation. For discussion, see note 57 and 5.6.

41. I do not mean to be understood as claiming that (I) and (II) capture two very distinct syntactical analyses of descriptions that need to be built into a grammar. Rather, (I) and (II) serve to characterize the sorts of superficial noun phrases that I think the Theory of Descriptions applies to. It may well be the case that an adequate grammar of English specifies that, at some level of linguistic representation, all descriptions are of the form of (I), some minor stylistic rule converting some of them into the form of (II). For instance, a description 'The F of H' might become 'H's F'. For insightful remarks on the syntactical and semantical relationships between phrases of class (I) and phrases of class (II) see Higginbotham (1983). Translated into Russell's *iota* notation, Higginbotham's proposal is (very roughly) that a phrase like (i) is interpreted as (ii):

    (i) $(NP + poss) + N'$
    (ii) $(\iota x)(Nx \ \& \ Rxb)$

where N is the property expressed by N', b is the referent of the NP (where the NP is a referring expression), and R is some contextually determined relation. For instance, 'John's cat' might come out as

    (iii) $(\iota x)(\text{cat } x \ \& \ \text{John owns } x)$.

In many cases there will be no need to specify a relation R, as it is given by the N' in question. For example, 'John's father' will come out as

    (iv) $(\iota x)(x \text{ father-of John})$.

I shall more or less assume Higginbotham's proposal in what follows. I am here indebted to Sylvain Bromberger for discussion.

42. A caveat is still in order because of the possibility of names beginning with 'the'. Kripke (1972) suggests that 'The Holy Roman Empire' and 'The United Nations' fall into this category. Marcus (1962) suggests that over a period of time a description may actually come to be used as a proper name. 'The evening star' and 'the Prince of Denmark' are two of her examples.

43. In the paper cited, Sharvy attempts to provide a unified theory of singular definite descriptions, plural definite descriptions, and mass noun descriptions. I have not made any attempt to utilize Sharvy's very interesting proposals here because of (*a*) semantic problems concerning distributive readings of plurals that Sharvy fails to address, (*b*) the fact that the problems raised by collective readings and mass nouns are not

specific to definite descriptions, and (c) general metaphysical problems concerning parts and wholes that cannot be addressed in this essay.

44. See Donnellan (1966, 1978). For detailed discussion, see 3.2 and 3.5.

45. See (e.g.) Peacocke (1975), Hornsby (1977), and Kaplan (1978).

46. On the first count, see Rescher (1962); on the second, see Barwise and Cooper (1981). It should be stressed that neither of these points tells against truth-conditional semantics. For discussion, see Evans (1977, 1977a), Wiggins (1980), and Davies (1981). See also notes 47 and 49.

47. My use of set-theoretic notation on the right-hand side of the biconditional is just meant to bring out the binary nature of the quantification. It is certainly not meant to suggest that we cannot handle 'most Fs' within a standard truth-theoretic semantics that defines truth in terms of satisfaction. On the contrary, it is a routine matter to provide the relevant axiom; see note 49.

It is sometimes suggested that 'most Fs are Gs' can only be true if *substantially* more things are both F and G than F and not-G, where the correct interpretation of 'substantially' is determined contextually. The point made in the main text is unaffected.

48. This approach is taken by, e.g., Sharvy (1969), Barwise and Cooper (1981) and Higginbotham and May (1981).

49. A sequence s satisfies '[most v_i, ϕ] (ψ)' iff most sequences satisfying ϕ and differing from s at most in the ith place also satisfy ψ. (The nature of the restricted quantification comes through very clearly in the metalanguage; similarly in parallel axioms for the other determiners. For discussion, See Davies (1981).)

50. This approach is taken by, e.g., Evans (1977), Wiggins (1980), and Davies (1981).

51. In either case, although not strictly accurate, we can think of the relative pronoun 'who' as a bound variable. For elaboration, see 5.6.

52. See Evans (1982) p. 59 for an explicit statement of this claim, and see Evans (1977) pp. 136–9 for the formal argument.

53. Evans' argument is discussed in 6.3.

54. More precisely:

(Q1') If ϕ is a well-formed formula that contains at least one occurrence of b, and if D is one of 'some', 'no', 'every', 'all', 'a', 'the', 'most', etc., then '[Dx: $\phi(b/x)$]' is a well-formed quantifier phrase, where '$\phi(b/x)$' is the result of replacing at least one occurrence of b in ϕ by x.

(Q2') If ψ is a well-formed formula that contains at least one occurrence of b, and if '[Dx: ϕ]' is a well-formed quantifier phrase, then '[Dx: ϕ]($\psi(b/x)$)' is a is a is a well-formed formula, where '$\psi(b/x)$' is the result of replacing at least one occurrence of b in ψ by x

55. We shall allow the first argument of a two-place predicate to precede that predicate. Thus I write 'x loves y' rather than 'loves $x\,y$'.

56. For details, see 5.6, where relative clauses and variable-binding are discussed at length.

57. For similar examples involving definite descriptions, see note 40.

58. I should, at this point, say something about the formulae I have been using to represent the quantificational structure of English sentences. By using the resources of a semantically well-understood and perspicuous notation, I do not think the working semanticist is committed to a notion of "Logical Form," construed as a level of syntactical representation. However, the work of (e.g.) Chomsky (1981), Higginbotham (1980, 1983, 1983a, 1987), Higginbotham and May (1981, 1981a), Huang (1982), Ludlow (1985), and May (1977, 1985) suggests very strongly that a variety of subtle facts about quantifier scope and bound anaphora can be elegantly explained on the assumption that there is such a level of syntactical representation. For reasons outlined in 5.6, I am largely sympathetic to the genuinely linguistic side of this proposal. However, for the purposes of the present chapter, I would like to keep well clear of the sorts of philosophical and technical issues that emerge as soon as one begins to talk of logical form in this way.

     For the purposes of this chapter, the logical forms I am employing can be viewed as formulae of a well-understood metalanguage; but no harm will be done if they are thought of as related in a fairly transparent way to, say, LF ("Logical Form") representations of the sort derived from S-Structure representations in Chomsky's (1981) Government-Binding (GB) framework. (For fuller discussion, see 5.6.) In retrospect, Russell's claim that the superficial grammatical form of a sentence is not always a reliable guide to its logical form is really just the claim that surface syntax alone will not tell us whether a noun phrase is a *referring expression* or a *quantifier*. We must be careful not to assimilate this or that expression to one or other group on the basis of superficial characteristics. According to Russell, this is what Frege did with descriptions: he observed that when all is well with a definite description it denotes exactly one object, and went on to treat descriptions as names (referring expressions) instead of quantifiers.

59. See (e.g.) Strawson (1952) and Thomason (1969).

60. As far as I am aware, the first explicit mention of this possibility in print is is due to Prior (1963). See also Grice (1969, 1970, 1981), Sharvy (1969), Montague (1970), Evans (1977a, 1979, 1982), Wiggins (1980), Barwise and Cooper (1981), Davies (1981), and Higginbotham and May (1981a, 1981b). Attempts to incorporate this idea into a general syntactical and semantical account of quantifiers in natural language can be found in Montague (1970), and, in a more recent syntactical setting, in Higginbotham and May (1981a, 1981b). I am grateful to James Higginbotham and David Lewis for help in compiling the references in this note.

61. As Vendler (1967, p. 51) so aptly puts it, the relation between singular and plural descriptions lies in the fact that a use of the definite article 'the' signals the speaker's intention to exhaust the range of a certain predicate. Of course, as with any other quantifier a precise specification of the

predicate involved may have to take into account various contextual factors (see 3.3 and 3.7).

It is well known that some sentences containing plural noun phrases like 'this man and that woman', 'a man and a woman', 'Russell and Whitehead', 'the men', 'three women', 'John and a man I met in the pub', and so on admit of (or require) *collective* or *group* readings. The existence of such readings raises a variety of interesting semantical and ontological issues; but to the extent that providing an adequate semantics for sentences containing plural noun phrases on their collective readings is a very general task that has nothing to do with descriptions *per se*, I have not attempted to say anything substantial about collective readings of descriptions in this essay. For recent work on collective readings see Link (1987) and Lønning (1987).

62. Two points concerning the uniformity of this category. First, I have not, in the main text, discussed the interrogative determiner 'which', but there does not seem to be any good reason for not treating the so-called *wh*-phrases it creates as interrogative quantifiers of the same general type as those discussed above (see Evans, (1977) and Higginbotham and May (1981).) For instance, we can represent 'Which man saw Bill?' as:

    (i)   [which x: man x](x saw Bill)

and 'Who murdered Smith?' as:

    (ii)   [which x: person x](x murdered Smith).

Second, it is widely (though not universally) held that certain determiners—most notably 'a certain', and 'any'—create quantifiers that are, in some contexts at least, resistant to taking narrow scope with respect to certain operators. If it is true that such quantifiers do not exhibit the full range of scope interactions, a degree of caution is, perhaps, in order when we say that determiners form a *uniform* semantical category. On the other hand, it would be quite wrong to follow Hornstein (1984), who goes so far as to claim (*i*) that quantifiers of the form 'a certain F' and 'any F' take widest possible scope and hence differ in fundamental syntactical and semantical ways from those of the form 'every F', and 'an F', and (*ii*) that quantifiers of the form 'the F' pattern with 'a certain F' and 'any F'. For discussion, see Chapter 4, note 4.

Chapter 3

Context and Communication

3.1 Introductory Remarks

As we saw in the last chapter, *prima facie* there is a case to be made for the view that descriptions may, on occasion, function more like referring expressions than quantifiers. Consequently, if Russell's theory is to serve as a *general* account of the semantics of descriptive phrases, an explanation of what is going on in such cases must be provided. And this means taking into account the powerful effects of *context* on the interpretation of utterances.

This breaks down into two distinct tasks. First, we need to graft onto the framework presented in Chapter 2 an account of context-sensitive expressions like indexicals and demonstratives, if only for the reason that definite descriptions—indeed quantifiers quite generally—may contain such expressions as *constituents*. Second, we need, at least in broad outline, a general framework within which to discuss the relationship between the genuinely semantical features of an expression ζ and those features of the use of ζ that issue, at least in part, from nonsemantical facts about the context of utterance and from constraints governing rational discourse. In particular, we need a framework within which we can provide a reasonably clear and precise characterization of the intuitive Gricean distinction between the *proposition expressed* by an utterance and the proposition (or propositions) the speaker seeks to communicate by it, what we might call *the proposition(s) meant* by the speaker.

In 3.2, I shall make some preliminary remarks about the history and nature of the referential challenge to the Theory of Descriptions. In 3.3, I begin the examination of the effects of context on the interpretation of descriptions with the aid of a standard theory of indexicality. Section 3.4 is primarily an exegetical discussion of various strands of Grice's work on meaning and implicature, which will be put to use in 3.5 and again in later chapters. (Grice's own machinery and terminology will be modified slightly to suit the present discussion, but this section can still be skipped by those familiar with Grice's program.) In 3.5, I attempt to spell out the details of the Gricean response to the referential challenge. In 3.6, I turn to the problems apparently raised by so-called "incomplete" descriptions like 'the table'.

3.2 The Referential Challenge

In the 1960s, several philosophers published papers in which they pointed to apparently *referential* "uses" or "functions" of definite descriptions. Marcus (1961), for example, noted a namelike use of descriptions. As she puts it, over a period of time a description may come to be used rather like a proper name (as "an identifying tag") its descriptive meaning "lost or ignored." Marcus suggests that 'the evening star' and 'the Prince of Denmark' are examples of this sort. Similarly, Mitchell (1962) distinguished between two "functions" of descriptions, one of which is to *identify* an individual in much the same way as a name does.[1] And Rundle (1965) argued for a genuinely referential interpretation of descriptions that could be put to use in modal contexts. According to Rundle, the *prima facie* ambiguity in a sentence like

(1)   The first person in space might not have been Gagarin

should be seen as the product of an ambiguity in the definite article: the definite description 'the first man in space' is ambiguous between Russellian and referential interpretations.[2]

In 1966, Keith Donnellan published an influential paper in which he distinguished between what he called *attributive* and *referential* uses of descriptions; he then argued that Russell's theory did not provide an accurate account of sentences containing descriptions used referentially. To illustrate his distinction, Donnellan asks us to consider a sentence like

(2)   Smith's murderer is insane

as used in the following two scenarios:

(*i*)   A detective discovers Smith's mutilated body and has no idea who has killed him. Looking at the body, the detective exclaims, "Smith's murderer is insane."

(*ii*)   Jones is on trial for Smith's murder, and you and I are convinced of his guilt. Seeing Jones rant and rave in court, I say to you, "Smith's murderer is insane."

On Donnellan's account, in case (*i*) the description 'Smith's murderer' is being used attributively; in case (*ii*) it is being used referentially. In the attributive case, Russell's analysis may well provide an accurate account of the proposition expressed. That is, in this situation the detective plausibly expresses the descriptive proposition that whoever it was that uniquely murdered Smith is insane. But in the referential case, Donnellan urges, the description functions like a referring expression not a quantifier phrase, and the proposition expressed is not faithfully captured by Russell's quantificational analysis. According to Donnellan, I will, by my use of 'Smith's murderer', be *referring to* Jones, and hence I will be saying something *about him*, viz., that he (Jones, that man in the dock) is insane.[3]

Grice (1969) noted a similar distinction:

> (1) A group of men is discussing the situation arising from the death of a business acquaintance, of whose private life they know nothing, except that (as they think) he lived extravagantly, with a household staff that included a butler. One of them says "Well, Jones' butler will be seeking a new position."
> (2) Earlier, another group has just attended a party at Jones' house, at which their hats and coats were looked after by a dignified individual in dark clothes with a wing-collar, a portly man with protruding ears, whom they heard Jones addressing as "Old Boy," and who at one point was discussing with an old lady the cultivation of vegetable marrows. One of the group says "Jones' butler got the hats and coats mixed up" (p. 141).

Grice points to two important features of case (2) that are not shared by case (1). First, only in case (2) has some particular individual been "'described as', 'referred to as', or 'called', Jones butler by the speaker" (p. 141). Second, in case (2), someone who knew that Jones had no butler and who knew that the man with the protruding ears, etc. was actually Jones' gardener "would also be in a position to claim that the speaker had *mis*described that individual as Jones butler" (p. 142).[4] As a preliminary convenience, let us take the first of these features to be characteristic of *referential* usage (a more useful and precise characterization will be provided in 3.5).

Unlike Donnellan, Grice did *not* feel that there was a problem for Russell here. On Grice's account, the intuitive distinction between case (1) and case (2) is quite consistent with the view that "descriptive phrases have no relevant systematic duplicity of meaning; their meaning is given by a Russellian account" (1969, p. 143). If one is to understand what is going on in case (2), Grice suggests, one needs to invoke an independently motivated distinction between what a speaker *says* (in a certain technical sense) and what he or she *means* (also in a technical sense)—or, as I shall put it in 3.4 and 3.5, between the *proposition expressed* and the *proposition(s) meant*.[5]

Those influenced by Donnellan have tended to see things rather differently. Despite some early equivocation, in the 1970s a very simple and exact claim emerged:

> (A1) If a speaker *S* uses a definite description 'the *F*' referentially in an utterance *u* of 'the *F* is *G*', then 'the *F*' functions as a referring expression and the proposition expressed by *u* is *object-dependent* (rather than descriptive).[6]

As I mentioned in Chapter 2, I shall take this claim (or pair of claims) to entail the view that there is a semantically distinct referential interpretation of definite descriptions. On this view, descriptions are *semantically ambiguous* between Russellian and "referential" interpretations, i.e., the definite article is lexically ambiguous.[7] One of the main aims of the present chapter is to compare the view that definite descriptions are ambiguous with the Gricean view that referential usage is a nonsemantical phenomenon.

For convenience, let us continue with the policy (adopted in 2.2) of treating as interchangeable the locutions (*a*) "the proposition expressed by *S*'s utterance *u* of ϕ," (*b*) "the proposition *S* expressed by *S*'s utterance *u* of ϕ," and (*c*) "the proposition *S* expressed by uttering ϕ," where *S* is the speaker, *u* is a particular dated utterance, and ϕ is a sentence of English. Let's now define what we might call *a basic case* of a referential use of a definite description 'the *F*' as it occurs in a particular utterance *u* of 'the *F* is *G*' made by a sincere speaker *S*. In the basic case four conditions obtain:

(*a*)   There is an object *b* such that *S* knows that *b* is uniquely *F*;
(*b*)   It is *b* that *S* wishes to communicate something about;
(*c*)   'The *F*' occurs in an extensional context;[8]
(*d*)   There are no pronouns anaphoric on this occurrence of 'the *F*'.

According to the "referentialist," if these four conditions are satisfied, the proposition expressed by *u* is true if and only if *b* is *G*. Thus the proposition expressed by *u* will be true on the referential interpretation if and only if it is true on the Russellian interpretation. So unless the referentialist can provide an argument that demonstrates beyond any doubt that one must entertain an object-dependent proposition about *b* in order to grasp the proposition expressed by *u*, he or she is forced to move away from the basic case in order to provide a convincing case for an ambiguity. (There is still, of course, an onus on the Russellian to explain how a referential use of a description can arise from general pragmatic principles.)

To the best of my knowledge, no one has ever provided the requisite argument for an ambiguity in the basic case. However, there are, in the literature, four quite distinct arguments for a non-Russellian interpretation that involve departing from the basic case in one way or another. The first such argument I shall call the "Argument from Misdescription." This argument involves toying around with conditions (a) and (b) in order to produce cases in which the Russellian and referential analyses yield propositions that differ in truth-value. The referentialist then urges that our ordinary intuitions favor the referential interpretation.

The second argument for a non-Russellian interpretation I shall call the "Argument from Incompleteness." This involves relaxing condition (a) in order that 'the F' may be an "incomplete" definite description like 'the table', which seems to resist Russell's analysis on account of not being uniquely-denoting. Again, an interpretation of such descriptions as referring expressions is supposed to get things right.

The third type of argument involves dispensing with condition (c) in order to examine sentences in which definite descriptions occur in nonextensional contexts, such as those created by modal and temporal operators and psychological verbs. Here a variety of interconnected considerations about scope, variable-binding, and opacity seem to have convinced some philosophers that the postulation of a referential (or otherwise non-Russellian) interpretation of descriptions will circumvent technical difficulties that arise for a unitary quantificational analysis. For example, it is sometimes claimed that so-called *de re* readings of sentences containing definite descriptions and nonextensional operators either lie beyond (or else stretch the plausibility of) Russell's theory because of semantical or syntactical constraints on quantification into nonextensional contexts. Arguments that are based on such considerations I shall call versions of the "Argument from Opacity."

The fourth type of argument for an ambiguity involves dispensing with condition (d) in order to allow for pronouns that are anaphoric on 'the F'. It is then argued that certain anaphoric relations cannot be accounted for if the description is analyzed in accordance with Russell's theory. This argument comes in several different forms, some of which interact in interesting ways with versions of some of the other arguments. I shall call the general form of the argument the "Argument from Anaphora."

In this chapter, I shall address only the Arguments from Misdescription and Incompleteness. The Arguments from Opacity and

Anaphora bring up questions about necessity, opacity, quantifier scope, syntactical structure, and variable-binding that we will not have the machinery to address until we get to Chapters 4 and 5. Before looking at *any* of the arguments, however, we need to say a little about the role of context in the interpretation of utterances.

3.3 Context and the Propositions Expressed

Russell rarely invokes the intuitive distinction between sentences and *utterances* of sentences. However, we saw in 2.2 that once the philosophical underpinnings of the Theory of Descriptions are in focus, it is clear that Russell is concerned with the propositions expressed by particular utterances of sentences containing descriptive phrases; he is *not* primarily concerned with the more abstract notion of the linguistic meaning of sentence-*types*.

To facilitate discussion, let's distinguish between what we can call *meaning* and *value*; that is, between the *linguistic meaning of an expression* ζ, and the *semantical value of a particular dated utterance u of* ζ. Expressions have meanings; utterances of expressions have values.[9] In keeping with the discussion in Chapter 2, the semantical value of an utterance of a sentence ϕ is a *proposition*. The semantical value of an utterance of a subsentential expression α is whatever the utterance of α contributes to the identity of the proposition expressed by the utterance of the sentence ϕ of which α is a constituent. For the purposes of this chapter, it will be convenient to adopt Russell's talk of object-dependent propositions containing their "subjects" as constituents. (The reason is that this way of characterizing object-dependent propositions is utilized by several philosophers who have argued for a semantically distinct referential interpretation of definite descriptions. I will be addressing two of their official arguments later in this chapter, and working with the same conception of a proposition will make it easier to focus on the relevant issues and avoid orthogonal engagements. My use of this notion of a proposition should not be confused with any sort of commitment to its overall philosophical utility.)

On this account, the semantical value of an utterance of a *referring* expression is just the expression's *referent*. The characteristic property of an utterance of an *indexical* expression is that its semantical value depends, in a systematic way, upon the *context of utterance*. Thus the characteristic property of an utterance of an *indexical referring* expression is that its referent depends, in a systematic way, upon the context of utterance.

Consider the first person singular pronoun 'I', as it occurs in the sentence 'I am cold'. If I utter this sentence right now, I will be the referent of my utterance of 'I'. But if you utter the very same sentence right now, you will be the referent of your utterance of 'I'. It is clear, then, that distinct utterances of 'I' may receive distinct individuals as their respective semantical values. But this does not mean that the *linguistic meaning* of the expression-type 'I' changes from occasion to occasion, or person to person. To know the linguistic meaning of the word 'I' is to know something constant across utterances, roughly that the referent is the individual using the word. Similarly for 'you': the referent is the addressee (or addressees).

The same distinction needs to be made for demonstrative noun phrases such as 'this', 'that', 'that man', etc. Although different utterances of such expressions may have different *semantical values*, we are not forced to conclude that they have variable *linguistic meanings*. This is something that Russell apparently saw:

> The word 'this' appears to have the character of a proper name, in the sense that it merely designates an object without in any degree describing it . . . the word 'this' is one word, which has, *in some sense*, a constant meaning. But if we treat it as a mere name, it cannot have in any sense a constant meaning, for a name means merely what it designates, and the designatum of 'this' is continually changing . . . (Russell 1948, pp. 103–4).

Although Russell was close to distinguishing between meaning and value here, he does not seem to be guided by any general considerations reflecting the distinction between expression-types and particular utterances of expressions. Rather, he isconcerned with the fact that demonstratives seem to be a bit like ordinary names (they refer without describing) and a bit like descriptions (they may be associated with different individuals on different occasions of utterance), but are really neither.[10] However, from the perspective I am adopting, the distinction should be seen as a reflex of the distinction between expression-types and particular utterances of expressions.

In simple formal languages like the first-order predicate calculus, there is neither room nor need to distinguish between meaning and value. Not until we introduce context-dependent expressions does the relevant gap open up. Following Strawson (1950), we might say that mastery of the linguistic meaning of an indexical referring expression consists in the mastery of some sort of *rule* or *recipe for referring* that takes into account the situation of utterance. The linguistic meaning of such an expression might be *identified* with this rule. For instance, since the referent of an utterance of 'I' is simply whoever is speaking, the rule for 'I' might be characterized as: *the referent is the individual speaking*. (To characterize the linguistic meaning of 'I' in this way is not, of course, to say that 'I' and 'the individual speaking' have the same linguistic meaning.) And since the referent of an utterance of 'you' is whoever is being addressed by the speaker, the rule for 'you' might say something like: *the referent is whoever is being addressed.*

Such proposals have been implemented by taking the linguistic meaning of an indexical expression to be a function from contexts to semantical values.[11] On this account, a context C can be represented as an ordered n-tuple, the elements of which are features of the situation of utterance relevant to determining semantical value. For example, on a simple model, C might be represented as a quadruple $<s, a, t, p>$, where s = the speaker, a = the addressee, t = the time of utterance, and p = the place of utterance. Following Lewis (1972), let's call the particular features that make up C "contextual coordinates." Using $[\![\zeta]\!]$ to represent the function that is the linguistic meaning of an expression ζ, we can formulate some elementary rules:

$$[\![I]\!] (<s, a, t, p>) = s$$
$$[\![you]\!] (<s, a, t, p>) = a$$
$$[\![now]\!] (<s, a, t, p>) = t$$
$$[\![here]\!] (<s, a, t, p>) = p.$$

In contrast to these "pure indexicals," Kaplan (1977) has suggested that genuinely demonstrative uses of the demonstrative pronouns 'this' and 'that', the personal pronouns 'he', 'she', 'him', 'his', and 'her', and demonstrative descriptions like 'this man', and 'that woman', require accompanying "demonstrations," and that the rule for a genuine demonstrative specify that *the referent is the object of that demonstration.* To capture this we can construe a context as an ordered quintuple

$$<s, a, <d_1,..., d_n>, t, p>$$

where $d_1,..., d_n$ are the objects of any demonstrations $\delta_1,...,\delta_n$ in the utterance.[12]

It is important to see that indexical pronouns like 'I' and 'you', demonstrative expressions like 'this', 'that', 'this vase', and 'that man', and demonstrative occurrences of personal pronouns like 'he' and 'she' are genuine referring expressions and hence subject to (R3), a fact that is sometimes overlooked because of their context-sensitivity. As Kaplan (1977) has emphasized, once we distinguish the situation of utterance from the actual or counterfactual situation at which the proposition expressed is to be evaluated for truth or falsity, the intrinsically rigid nature of demonstratives is plain to see. Suppose I point to someone and say to you

(1)   That man is a spy.

The referent of my utterance of the demonstrative 'that man' is the person I am demonstrating in the situation of utterance. However, we do not want to say that the definite description 'the man I am demonstrating' determines the referent of (this particular utterance of) 'that man'. The proposition expressed by my (actual) utterance of (1) is true at some worlds in which I fail to point during my lifetime. And descriptions such as 'the man I am talking about' or 'the man I have in mind' will not do because the proposition expressed by my (actual) utterance of (1) is true at some worlds in which (e.g.) I never utter a word or think about anyone. It is clear, then, that a sentence of the form 'that F is G' is semantically very different from a sentence of the form 'the F is G'. An utterance of the former expresses an object-dependent proposition; an utterance of the latter expresses an object-independent proposition.

Under certain reasonable assumptions to do with compositionality, a corollary of the distinction between the meaning of a referring expression b and the value (i.e., referent) of a particular utterance of b is a distinction between the meaning of a sentence 'b is G' and the value of (i.e., the proposition expressed by) an utterance of 'b is G'. This comes out clearly when we turn to *understanding*. Suppose I have a room in which I keep nothing but a private vase collection. One day, I let a friend into the room and leave him there to browse. After a few minutes he calls out to me

(2)   This vase is broken.

There is a clear sense in which I cannot grasp the proposition expressed by his utterance unless I establish the referent of "this vase." (This, of course follows from (R1), on the assumption that the demonstrative phrase 'this vase' is a genuine referring expression; see above.) But there is an equally clear sense in which I know the *meaning* of the sentence uttered, simply by virtue of my knowledge of English—that is, by virtue of my knowledge of the meanings of the words of which the sentence is composed, and my ability to project the meanings of phrases on the basis of the meanings of their parts and their syntactical organization. We might say that although I do not know *which* proposition my friend has expressed, I know the *sort of* proposition he has expressed. He has said *of* some particular vase or other—which I have yet to identify—that it is broken. Another way of putting this is to say that although I do not come to entertain an object-dependent proposition concerning any particular vase, I come to entertain an object-independent proposition to the effect that one of my vases is broken.

(Consider the following nonlinguistic analogy. My friend says nothing while he is in the room, but after a few minutes I hear a crash. I deduce that he has broken one of my vases. It is in virtue of the fact that some particular vase broke that I heard what I heard, and that I came to believe what I came to believe. However, I only came to have an object-*in*dependent belief to the effect that one of my vases was broken, not an object-dependent belief concerning any particular vase.)

Precisely the same considerations apply in the case of pure indexicals. Suppose I return home at 7:30 P.M. and find the following message on my answering machine: "Guess what? I just flew in from London and I want to take you out for dinner tonight. I'll pick you up at eight." The voice is female and sounds familiar, but owing to the poor quality of the machine I cannot recognize it. Since I fail to establish the referent of "I," I fail to establish the proposition expressed. But I know the *sort of* proposition expressed: that's why I take a shower rather than start cooking.

It is important to see that quantifiers, including descriptions, may contain indexical expressions as constituents:

> every *currently* registered Democrat
> the *present* king of France
> the first person *I* saw this morning
> a woman who came to see *you*
> the men who delivered *your* sofa
> the girl who made *this vase*
> most philosophers *I* have met
> *my* mother
> *that woman*'s car.

Now it would be quite inappropriate to object to the Theory of Descriptions on the grounds that the implication of uniqueness is not honored by a sentence containing an indexical description. It is worth running through an example just to see how an indexical description like 'my mother' works. We saw earlier (2.2) that for Russell the semantical value—what he would call the "meaning"—of an utterance of a referring expression '*b*' is just its referent; and the semantical value of an utterance of a sentence '*b* is *G*' is an object-dependent proposition. An utterance of a definite description, by contrast, will not take an object as its semantical value, because a description is a quantifier not a referring expression. The semantical value of an utterance of 'the *F* is *G*' is a descriptive proposition to the effect that there is one and only one thing that is F and that one thing is G. There is no object for which the grammatical subject 'the F' stands that is a genuine constituent of that proposition. Before looking at 'my mother', let's look at 'Stephen Neale's mother'. An utterance of

(3)   Stephen Neale's mother is English

expresses the proposition we can represent as

(4)   [the x: x mother-of Stephen Neale] (x is English)

which invokes the relational property *being mother of Stephen Neale*, i.e., $(\lambda x)(x$ mother-of Stephen Neale).[13] But what property gets into the proposition expressed by an utterance of

(5)   My mother is English

made by me? The same relational property. This does not mean that the relational description 'Stephen Neale's mother', and the indexical description 'my mother', have the same linguistic meaning. On the contrary, they have quite different rules of use. Only I can use the latter to invoke the property of being mother of *me*. However, you may use 'My mother' to invoke the property of being mother of *you*. The fact that the denotation of 'my mother' changes from speaker to speaker poses no threat to the Russellian implication of uniqueness. When I utter 'My mother is English', unique motherhood is relative to *me*; when you utter it, it is relative to you.[14]

It is not, then, the *sentence* 'the F is G' that carries any *particular* implication of uniqueness, but particular dated utterances of that sentence. The linguistic meaning of the sentence is just a rule for use that, among other things, specifies that the description is being used correctly only if there is, relative to the particular context $<s, a, <d_1, \ldots, d_n>, t, p>$, just one object satisfying the description in question. It is clear, then, that the Theory of Descriptions is not threatened by the existence of descriptions containing indexical components. Rather, this gives the Theory of Descriptions yet more expressive power (the importance of indexical descriptions will come out in 3.5 and 3.7).

In this section, I have made the common assumption that the proposition expressed by an utterance u of a sentence ϕ bears a tight relationship to the linguistic meaning of ϕ. To the extent that this relationship *is* tight, there is also a tight connection between understanding ϕ and understanding an utterance u of ϕ. But as we saw, there are several respects in which the linguistic meaning of ϕ may underdetermine the proposition expressed by u because of the various parameters left open by indexical expressions, parameters that must be pinned down by u's contextual coordinates.

Notice that knowledge of the language to which ϕ belongs together with knowledge of the relevant contextual coordinates will not necessarily put a hearer H in position to grasp the proposition expressed by u. The existence of lexical and structural ambiguity means that a particular string of sounds may satisfy the phonological criteria for being a tokening of sentence ϕ or of sentence ϕ^* ("Visiting relatives can be a nuisance"). Then there are the interpretive problems raised by (e.g.) names and pronouns. Consider an utterance of

(6)   Nicola thinks she should become a banker.

H will need to assign referents to 'Nicola' and to the pronoun 'she', which may or may not be anaphoric on 'Nicola'.[15] H is surely seeking the reading that S *intended*. Indeed, if H assigns to 'Nicola' a referent other than the one S had in mind, it is clear that H has not grasped the proposition expressed.[16]

For a referring expression 'b' and a monadic predicate '( ) is G', the identity of the proposition expressed by a particular utterance of 'b is G' is dependent upon the identity of the object b referred to by 'b'. The utterance expresses a true proposition just in case b is G. The proposition in question is object-dependent in the sense that it simply could not be expressed, or even entertained, if b did not exist.

The connection with contemporary talk of *truth conditions* can be made explicit by focusing on what it means to understand a proposition. To understand an object-dependent proposition, one must have identifying knowledge (2.3) of the thing the proposition is about. In addition, one must know what property is being ascribed to that object. Thus we reach the position advanced by Wittgenstein, in the *Tractatus*, that understanding a proposition involves knowing what is the case if it is true.[17] And by extension we might therefore say that understanding an utterance (of a sentence) involves knowing its truth conditions—indeed its truth conditions in actual and counterfactual situations (2.2)—and that a specification of the semantical value of an utterance (of a sentence) consists, at least in part, in a specification of its truth-conditions.

3.4 Propositions Expressed and Propositions Meant

It is clear that a hearer H may gather a lot more from an utterance than the proposition it expresses. Quite different thoughts may come to H's mind. Let's begin with some trivial examples of the sort we shall *not* be concerned with. I am in a restaurant in San Francisco; the waitress asks me if I'd like an aperitif and I reply,

(1)   I'd like a gin and tonic, please.

On the basis of certain acoustic properties of my utterance, the waitress may come to believe that I am English, or that I have a cold or hay fever. Such propositions are irrelevant to the communicative act performed, as are other propositions that are, in some sense, *made available* by my speech act but that may not spring immediately to mind, such as the proposition that I can speak English or the proposition that I am not dead.

Of considerably more importance for current concerns is the fact, emphasized by Grice (1961, 1967), that there are speech acts involving, in some communicatively *relevant* way, propositions other than the proposition strictly and literally expressed. A speaker may express a particular proposition by means of an utterance yet at the same time *communicate* something beyond this. Consider the following example due to Grice (1961). You are writing a letter of recommendation for one of your students who has applied for a position teaching philosophy at another institution. You write

(2)   Jones has beautiful handwriting and is always very punctual.

The people who read this letter will surely conclude that you do not rate Jones very highly as a philosopher. And if so, you have succeeded in communicating a proposition to that effect. There is an intuitive distinction here between the proposition you expressed by the utterance and the proposition (or propositions) you sought to *convey* by it, what we might call the *proposition(s) meant*.

There is no temptation to say that the proposition that you do not rate Jones very highly as a philosopher is (or is a consequence of) the proposition expressed by your utterance. There is no specifiable method of correlating this proposition with the proposition determined by the linguistic meaning of (2) together with the contextual coordinates of the utterance. The sentence has a clear linguistic meaning based on the meanings of its parts and their syntactical arrangement, a meaning that has nothing to do with your assessment of Jones' philosophical abilities, even when the relevant contextual coordinates are plugged in. On the other hand, we might say that *you mean*, by your utterance of (2), that you do not rate Jones very highly. This is something that *you* have implied or suggested by uttering (2) in this particular context.

It is clear, then, that there may, on occasion, be a divergence between the proposition (or propositions) strictly and literally expressed by an utterance and the proposition(s) meant. (In the case we just considered, they might well be disjoint; in other cases they might not be; see below.) Indeed, there seems little doubt that any plausible account of the way language works in communication will have to appeal to a distinction of this sort.

We have reached the familiar Gricean view, then, that at least three different notions need to be distinguished when talking about the "meaning" of a sentence ϕ as uttered by a speaker S on a given occasion: (*i*) the linguistic meaning of the sentence ϕ; (*ii*) the semantical value of ϕ relative to the context of utterance (the proposition expressed); and (*iii*) what S meant by uttering ϕ (the proposition(s) meant). But we need to get a lot clearer about the notion in (*iii*) and its relation to the notion in (*ii*) before we can use either with any confidence in our investigation.

In the simplest cases we might say that the proposition *expressed* is meant, and that in many such cases the proposition expressed *exhausts* the proposition(s) meant. But, of course, in Grice's letter of recommendation example this is not the case at all. How, then, might we characterize when a proposition is meant? One constraint that comes to mind is the following: For a particular utterance u of ϕ made by a speaker S to a hearer H, a proposition P is meant only if, on the basis of uttering ϕ, S *intends* H to entertain P. But we can go further than this. Borrowing from Grice's (1957, 1967) seminal work in this area, we might impose the following constraint on what it is for S to mean that p by uttering ϕ:

(G1)   By uttering ϕ, S means that p only if for some audience H, S utters ϕ intending:

   (1) H to actively entertain the thought that p, and
   (2) H to recognize that S intends (1).

Consider the restaurant scene again, where the waitress learns from certain acoustic properties of my utterance of

(1)   I'd like a gin and tonic, please

that I am English (or that I have a cold or hay fever). All *I mean* by my utterance is that I'd like a gin and tonic; I do *not* mean that I am English (or that I have a cold or hay fever). The first intention mentioned in (1) prevents such communicatively irrelevant propositions from being classed as part of what I mean because I do not *intend* the waitress to entertain the thought that I am English (or the thought that I have a cold or hay fever).

A modification of the same example will explain the role of the intention mentioned in (2). Suppose I do actually intend the waitress to realize that I have a cold (in order to get sympathy), or to realize that I am English (because I think I will get better service as a tourist), but I don't want her to realize that this is my intention. Intuitively, we don't want to say that *I mean* that I have a cold (or that I am English). The intention in (1) allows these propositions through. But I do not intend the waitress to *realize* that I intend her to think that I have a cold (or that I am English), so the intention in (2) prevents these propositions from being classed as a part of what I mean by my utterance.[18]

With the aid of this tentative constraint on when a proposition is meant, let's now turn to Grice's theory of *conversational implicature*. As Kripke (1977) and others have emphasized, several of Grice's proposals have a direct bearing on how we might characterize the uses of descriptions in various types of communicative settings. I shall therefore spend a little time going over certain features of Grice's general picture before putting it to use in the area of main interest.

On Grice's (1967) account, conversation is a characteristically purposeful and cooperative enterprise governed by what he calls the *Cooperative Principle*:

(CP) Make your conversational contribution such as is required, at the stage at which it occurs, by the accepted purpose or direction of the talk exchange in which you are engaged.

Subsumed under this general principle, Grice distinguishes four categories of more specific maxims and submaxims enjoining truthfulness, informativeness, relevance, and clarity.

Maxim of Quantity: Make your contribution as informative as is required (for the current purposes of the exchange). Do not make your contribution more informative than is required.

Maxim of Quality: Try to make your contribution one that is true. Specifically: Do not say what you believe to be false; do not say that for which you lack adequate evidence.

Maxim of Relation: Be relevant.

Maxim of Manner: Be perspicuous. Specifically: Be brief and orderly; avoid ambiguity and obscurity.

Of central concern to us is Grice's claim that there is a systematic correspondence between the assumptions required in order to preserve the supposition that the Cooperative Principle and attendant maxims are being observed and a certain class of propositions meant, what Grice calls *conversational implicatures*. The letter of recommendation case discussed earlier is a good example of a case that seems to involve a deliberate and flagrant violation of the Cooperative Principle, or at least one or more of the maxims. On Grice's account, by writing "Jones has wonderful handwriting and is always very punctual," (in this context) you appear to have violated the maxim enjoining relevance—since Jones is one of your students, you must know more of relevance than *this*. Furthermore, you know that more information than this is required in this particular context. Not surprisingly, the reader is naturally led to believe that you are attempting to convey something else, perhaps something you are reluctant to express explicitly. This supposition is plausible only on the assumption that you think Jones is no good at philosophy. And this is what you have *conversationally implicated*. In general, a speaker S conversationally implicates that which S must be assumed to believe in order to preserve the assumption that S is adhering to the CP and maxims.[19]

Grice contrasts this case with one in which there is supposed to be "no obvious violation" of the Cooperative Principle. Suppose H is standing by an obviously immobilized car and is approached by S. H says to S, "Where can I buy some gas?" S replies, "There is a gas station around the next corner." If S did not think, or think it possible, that the gas station was open and had gas for sale, his remark would not be properly relevant; thus he may be said to conversationally *implicate* that it is open and has gas for sale. That is, S implicates that which he must be assumed to believe in order to preserve the assumption that he is adhering to the CP, in particular, the maxim enjoining relevance.

On Grice's account, a necessary condition for an implication to count as a conversational implicature is that it be *cancellable*, either explicitly or contextually, without literal contradiction, or at least without linguistic transgression.[20] For instance, in the letter case you might have continued with "Moreover, in my opinion he is the brightest student we have ever had here." This addition might be odd, but it would not give rise to any literal contradiction. Notice that it might well be the case that in this example only what is implicated is meant (i.e., backed by your communicative intentions). You may have no idea what Jones' handwriting is like because he has only shown you typed manuscripts of his work (or because he has never shown you anything), and you may have no opinion as to whether or not he is punctual. Here the proposition implicated *supplants* the proposition expressed with respect to being meant.[21] The truth-values of the proposition expressed and the proposition(s) implicated may of course differ. Jones may have quite atrocious handwriting, and you may know this; but given the relevance of the proposition implicated, you may care very little whether the proposition expressed is true. That is, the primary message (what you *meant*) may not be calculable at the level of the proposition expressed but only at the level of the proposition implicated, in the sense that it is the latter that has the backing of your communicative intentions. (In the stranded motorist case, the propositions implicated seem to *supplement* (rather than supplant) the proposition expressed.)

Although cancellability is taken by Grice to be a necessary condition of an implication's being classed as a conversational implicature, rather more importance is attached to derivability:[22]

> . . . the final test for the presence of a conversational implicature ha[s] to be, as far as I [can] see, a derivation of it. One has to produce an account of how it could have arisen and why it is there. And I am very much opposed to any kind of sloppy use of this philosophical tool, in which one does not fulfil this condition (Grice 1981, p. 187).

Let's call this the *Justification Requirement*. On Grice's account, whenever there is a conversational implicature, one should be able to reason somewhat as follows:

(*a*)   S has expressed the proposition that *p*.

(*b*)   There is no reason to suppose that S is not observing the CP and maxims.

(*c*)   S could not be doing this unless he thought that *q*.

(*d*)   S knows (and knows that I know that he knows) that I can see that he thinks the supposition that he thinks that *q* is required.

(*e*)   S has done nothing to stop me thinking that *q*.

(*f*)   S intends me to think, or is at least willing to allow me to think, that *q*.

(*g*)   And so, S has implicated that *q*.

In each of the cases we have considered, it is possible to justify the existence of the implicature in question in this sort of way.[23]

So far, we have only looked at cases involving what Grice calls *particularized* conversational implicature. The presence and content of a particularized conversational implicature depend in a very transparent way upon facts about the particular context of utterance. Of rather more philosophical interest are those implicatures the presence and general form of which seem to have very little to do with the particular details of a given context of utterance, so-called "generalized" conversational implicatures. It is tempting to characterize the syntactician as that philosopher of language whose job it is to provide a finite, systematic characterization of a proprietary body of intuitions concerning such things as syntactical well-formedness, i.e., grammaticality. Analogously, we might view the semanticist as that philosopher of language who does the same thing for intuitions of truth, falsity, entailment, contradiction, and so on. In effect, the semanticist's aim is to construct a theory that will, among other things, yield predictions in accord with these intuitions. But great care must be taken when appealing to semantical intuitions. An initial judgment of truth or falsity, or of entailment or contradiction, might have to be reevaluated in the light of further considerations or a little tutoring of one form or another. For instance, what at first sight may seem like a semantical entailment may, upon further reflection, turn out to be something quite different.[24]

Grice (1961, 1967) argues that there has been a tendency among some linguistically oriented philosophers to overcharacterize the linguistic meanings of certain linguistic expressions. Let ζ be such an expression. According to Grice, certain conversational implicatures that typically attach to uses of ζ have been treated, mistakenly, as part of ζ's meaning. Semantical claims about certain "intentional" verbs (e.g., 'seem', 'try', 'intend', 'know', and 'remember') and about the linguistic counterparts to some of the formal devices of quantification theory (e.g., 'and', 'or', 'if...then...', 'the', and 'a') were some of Grice's philosophically important targets. Indeed, for Grice, conversational implicature is a powerful philosophical tool with which to investigate the logical forms of certain philosophical claims and also clarify the relationship between formulae of quantification theory and sentences of natural language.

For example, *pace* Strawson (1952, p. 79ff.), it is at least arguable that many of the apparently divergent implications that seem to be present when the English word 'and' is used to conjoin sentences are not attributable to any sort of lexical ambiguity in the word but can be understood as conversational implicatures of one form or another, there being no difference in meaning between 'and' and the & of classical logic.[25] Compare the following sentences:

(1) The moon goes around the earth and the earth goes around the sun

(2) Jack and Jill got married and Jill gave birth to twins

(3) The President walked in and the troops jumped to attention.

One feature of & is that it is commutative (p & q is equivalent to q & p). This does not seem to create a problem for the view that the occurrence of 'and' in (1) has the force of &. But in (2) the conjuncts describe events and, in the normal course of things, someone who uttered this sentence would be taken to imply that Jack and Jill got married *before* Jill gave birth to twins. Indeed, if the order of the conjuncts is reversed, so is the implication. And in (3) there seems to be an implication not just of temporal priority but of causal connection.

On the basis of facts like these, one might be led to the view that 'and' is at least three ways ambiguous. Now the fact that the truth of 'p and$_{(3)}$ q' guarantees the truth of 'p and$_{(2)}$ q', which guarantees the truth of 'p and$_{(1)}$ q' might well make one wonder whether the postulation of such ambiguity is not a little extravagant. Indeed, on Grice's account, there is another, perhaps preferable avenue that might be explored. It is good methodological practice, Grice (1967) suggests, to subscribe to what he calls *Modified Occam's Razor*: *Senses are not to be multiplied beyond necessity*. Given the viability of a broadly Gricean distinction between the proposition expressed and the proposition(s) meant, if a pragmatic explanation is available of why a particular expression appears to diverge in meaning in different linguistic environments (or in different conversational settings) then *ceteris paribus* the pragmatic explanation is preferable to the postulation of a semantical ambiguity.

As Grice observes, pragmatic explanations of what is going on in (2) and (3) do seem to be available. The implication of temporal sequence might be explicable in terms of the fact that each of the conjuncts describes an event (rather than a state) and the presumption that the speaker is observing the Maxim of Manner, in particular the submaxim enjoining an orderly delivery.[26] And the implication of causal connection in (3) might be explicable in terms of the presumption that the speaker is being relevant. Again the conjuncts describe events and it is natural to seek some sort of connection between them since the speaker has mentioned them both in the same breath. The idea, then, is that these implications are cases of *generalized* conversational implicature. I am not going to present a serious defense of the view that 'and' *always* means & (even if restricted to cases where it conjoins pairs of sentences rather than pairs of noun phrases or pairs of verb phrases); I just want to outline the form a pragmatic explanation of the alleged ambiguity is supposed to take.[27]

The reasons for preferring pragmatic explanations over the postulation of semantical ambiguities are, of course, economy and generality. A pragmatic explanation is, in some sense, *free*: the machinery that is appealed to is needed anyway. In any particular case, this may not in itself constitute an overwhelming objection to a theory that posits an ambiguity; but in the case of 'and' the generality lost by positing several readings is considerable. Grice makes three relevant observations here. First, there is the fact that implications of (e.g.) temporal priority and causal connection attach to uses of the counterparts of 'and' across unrelated languages. One could, of course, posit parallel ambiguities in these languages; but the phenomenon is more readily explained as the product of general pragmatic considerations. Second, it is not unreasonable to assume that implications of the same sorts would arise even for speakers of a language containing an explicitly truth-functional connective &. Third, the same implications that attach to a particular utterance of p & q would attach to an utterance of the two sentence sequence $p. q.$ It seems clear, then, that on *methodological* grounds the pragmatic account of the temporal and causal implications in (2) and (3) is preferable to an account that makes essential use of a semantical ambiguity. Of course, there may well be uses of the English word 'and' that resist a truth-functional semantics, but I do not take myself to arguing for the view that the word has just one meaning; my purpose is to illustrate Grice's point that where semantical and pragmatic accounts handle *the same range of data*, the pragmatic account is preferable.

It will be convenient now to focus on an example of generalized conversational implicature that involves the use of the determiner 'some'. (This will put us on course for a detailed discussion of the determiner 'the' in the next section.) Suppose two journalists S and H are discussing a recent demonstration in a notoriously repressive country. There was some violence at the demonstration and several of the demonstrators were killed, allegedly by the police. S was present at the demonstration and he knows that some of the deaths were accidental because he saw two demonstrators accidentally run over by a car full of other demonstrators. H knows that S dislikes the repressive regime, but he also knows that S is a very honest reporter. When H quizzes S about the deaths, S says,

(4)   Some of the deaths were accidental.

In this situation, S would very likely be taken to endorse the truth of, or at least entertain the possibility of the truth of (5):

(5)   Some of the deaths were not accidental.

But we don't want to say that 'some Fs are Gs' entails 'some Fs are not Gs', or even that (4) entails (5). Nor do we want to say that 'some' is ambiguous, that on one reading 'some Fs are Gs' entails 'some Fs are not Gs' and that on another it does not. At least, not if a pragmatic explanation is available of how (4) may be used to convey a proposition that differs from the proposition it would be taken to express on its standard quantificational reading.

And of course a pragmatic explanation *is* available. Intuitively, the proposition expressed by (4) is "weaker" than the one expressed by

(6)   All of the deaths were accidental.

And since in a typical communicative setting it would be more appropriate (informative, straightforward, relevant) to make the stronger claim (if it were believed true), a speaker who makes the weaker claim (in such a setting) will, *ceteris paribus*, conversationally implicate that he or she does not subscribe to the stronger claim. Now if S does not subscribe to the view that all of the deaths were accidental, S must be willing to entertain the possibility that some of the deaths were not accidental.[28] Using a Gricean justification schema,

(a)   S has expressed the proposition that some of the deaths were accidental.

(b)   There is no reason to suppose that S is not observing the CP and maxims.

(c)   S could not be doing this unless he were willing to entertain the possibility that some of the deaths were *not* accidental. (Gloss: On the assumption that S is adhering to the Maxim of Quantity, if he thought that *all* of the deaths were accidental he would have said so. Therefore S is willing to entertain the possibility that some of the deaths were not accidental. (On the assumption that S is adhering to the Maxim of Quality, he does not think that *none* of the deaths were accidental, since he has said that some of them *were*.))

(d)   S knows (and knows that I know that he knows) that I can see that he thinks the supposition that he is willing to entertain the possibility that some of the deaths were not accidental is required.

(e)   S has done nothing to stop me thinking that he is willing to entertain the possibility that some of the deaths were not accidental.

(f)   S intends me to think, or is at least willing to allow me to think, that he is willing to entertain the possibility that some of the deaths were not accidental.

(*g*)   And so, *S* has implicated that he is willing to entertain the
possibility that some of the deaths were not accidental.

It seems to me that we should resist the temptation to formulate
pragmatic rules with which to derive certain standard cases of generalized conversational implicature. For instance, it might be suggested
that a pragmatic theory contain a rule like the following:

(7)   [some *x*: *Fx*] (*Gx*) » *Ψ* [some *x*: *Fx*] ¬ (*Gx*)

where » stands for something like 'conversationally implicates unless
there is good evidence to the contrary', and *Ψ* stands for something
like 'the speaker is willing to entertain the possibility that'. In one
very important respect, nothing could be further from the spirit of
Grice's theory than the construction of such an avowedly singular
pragmatic rule. For Grice, the conversational implicatures that attach to a particular utterance must be justifiable given the CP and
maxims, construed as quite *general* antecedent assumptions about the
rational nature of conversational practice. It is important not to be
misled by Grice's intuitive distinction between particularized and
generalized implicatures into thinking that instances of the latter do
not have to satisfy the Justification Requirement. To label a certain
range of implicatures "generalized" is not to bestow upon them some
special status, it is simply to acknowledge the fact that the presence
of the implicatures is relatively independent of the details of the
particular conversational context.

We now have enough of a framework in place to begin addressing
the issues raised by so-called referential uses of descriptions.

3.5 The Referential Challenge Revisited

As I mentioned in 3.2, we can, I believe, ascribe to those who see the
need for a semantically distinct referential interpretation of definite
descriptions the following thesis:

(A1)   If a speaker *S* uses a definite description 'the *F*' referentially
in an utterance *u* of 'the *F* is *G*', then 'the *F*' functions as a referring expression and the proposition expressed by *u* is *object-
dependent* (rather than descriptive).

But what does it mean to say that a definite description is being used
referentially on a given occasion? (Or, to use the alternative
terminology of Kripke (1977) and Donnellan (1978), what does it
mean to say that a particular use of a definite description is
accompanied by speaker reference?).

This question is addressed by Donnellan (1978). Consider S's utterance u of the sentence 'The strongest man in the world can lift at least 450lbs.' Donnellan claims, quite rightly in my opinion, that it is not enough for S's use of 'the strongest man in the world' to be classified as referential that there exist some object b such that S knows (or believes) that b is the strongest man in the world. On such an account, the referentialist would be committed to the fantastic view that whenever S knows (or thinks he or she knows) who or what satisfies some description or other, S can no longer use that description nonreferentially. This would, indeed, be a peculiar consequence: the existence or nonexistence of a particular semantical ambiguity in a speaker's idiolect would be based solely on the speaker's epistemological history.[29]

Donnellan also claims, again correctly in my opinion, that it is not enough for S's use of 'the strongest man in the world' to be classified as referential that there exist some object b such that the grounds for S's utterance are furnished by the object-dependent belief that b is the strongest man in the world and the object-dependent belief that b can lift 450lbs.[30] What is characteristic of a referential use, Donnellan suggests, is the nature of "the intentions of the speaker toward his audience" (p. 50).

In the light of the discussions in 3.2 and 3.4, we might suggest that a speaker S uses a definite description 'the F' referentially in an utterance u of 'the F is G' if and only if there is some object b such that S means by u that b is G. But this is not quite strong enough. Suppose it is common knowledge between S and H that the tallest man in the world, whoever he is, is spending the weekend with Nicola. Suppose that there is no individual b such that either S or H believes of b that b is the tallest man in the world; however, it is common knowledge between S and H that the tallest man in the world (whoever he is) is very shy and that Nicola will take him with her wherever she goes this weekend. S and H are at a party on Saturday and it is a matter of some interest to S and H whether Nicola is present. S overhears a conversation during which someone says "The tallest man in the world is here." S goes over to H and says "The tallest man in the world is here" intending to communicate that *Nicola* is here. In this example there clearly is some object b (viz., Nicola) such that S means by u that b is here; but equally clearly, S's utterance does not involve a referential use of 'the tallest man in the world'. We seem to need something more like this:

(A2) A speaker S uses a definite description 'the F' referentially in an utterance u of 'the F is G' iff there is some object b such that S means by u that b is the F and that b is G.[31]

The debate between the Russellian-Gricean and the referentialist can now be summarized as follows. The referentialist endorses (A1) and (A2); the Russellian (to the extent that he or she believes that it is possible to provide a clear account of referential usage) endorses (A2) and (A3):

(A3) If a speaker S uses a definite description 'the F' referentially in an utterance u of 'the F is G', 'the F' still functions as a quantifier and the proposition expressed by u is the object-independent proposition given by [the x: Fx](Gx).

In short, then, the Russellian-Gricean sees referential usage as an important fact about *communication* to be explained by general pragmatic principles not something of *semantical* import. Let us now examine this position.

As Evans (1982) observes, there are two rather different cases of referential usage to take into account, according as the putative referential description is supposed to be functioning like a *name* or like a *demonstrative*. Suppose that you and I both know Harry Smith and it is common knowledge between us that Harry is the present Chairman of the Flat Earth Society. Harry calls me up and informs me that he will be arriving in San Francisco next Saturday. Later that day I see you in the street and I say,

(1)   The Chairman of the Flat Earth Society is coming to San Francisco next Saturday

fully intending to communicate to you the object-dependent proposition that Harry Smith is coming to San Francisco next Saturday, rather than (or rather than *just*) a descriptive proposition concerning the unique satisfier of a certain descriptive condition. I utter (1) intending you (*a*) to actively entertain the (object-dependent) proposition that Harry Smith is coming to San Francisco next Saturday, and (*b*) to recognize that I intend you to actively entertain that proposition (see (G1)). And I feel confident that these intentions can be fulfilled because I believe (*i*) that you have identifying knowledge of Harry Smith, (*ii*) that you take Harry Smith to uniquely satisfy the description 'the Chairman of the Flat Earth Society', and (*iii*) that you can infer from the fact that I have used this description that I wish to convey something to you about Harry Smith. There would appear to be no barrier, then, to saying that (part of) what *I mean* by my utterance of (1) is that Harry Smith is coming to San Francisco next Saturday; the object-dependent proposition that Harry Smith is coming to San Francisco next Saturday is (one of) the *proposition(s) meant*.

Now it is clear that I might have conveyed to you that Harry Smith is coming to San Francisco next Saturday by uttering (2) instead of (1):

(2)   Harry Smith is coming to San Francisco next Saturday.

Consequently, one might consider interpreting the description (as it occurs in this utterance) as something akin to a proper name. Let's say that in this case the description is used *referentially$_N$* ('N' for 'name').

Let's now turn to a rather different example of the sort exploited by Donnellan (1966). We are at a party together; in one corner of the room is a man, x, wearing a top hat; I notice that x is trying to attract your attention, so I say to you,

(3)   The man wearing a top hat is trying to attract your attention

fully intending to communicate to you an object-dependent proposition (about x), rather than (or rather than *just*) a descriptive proposition concerning the unique satisfier of the descriptive condition. I utter (3) intending you (*a*) to actively entertain the (object-dependent) proposition that x is trying to attract your attention, and (*b*) to recognize that I intend you to actively entertain proposition that proposition. And I feel confident that these intentions can be fulfilled because I believe (*i*) that you have identifying knowledge of x, (*ii*) that you take x to uniquely satisfy the description 'the man wearing a top hat', and (*iii*) that you can infer from the fact that I have used this description that I wish to convey something to you about x. There would appear to be no barrier, then, to saying that (part of) what *I mean* by my utterance of (3) is that x is trying to attract your attention; the object-dependent proposition that x is trying to attract your attention is (one of) the *proposition(s) meant*.

Now it is clear that I might have conveyed to you the same object-dependent proposition by uttering

(4)   That man is trying to attract your attention

accompanied by some sort of demonstration or gesture. Consequently, one might consider interpreting the description (as it occurs in this utterance) as something akin to a demonstrative. Let's call this a *referential$_D$* use of a description ('D' for 'demonstrative').[32]

The question for the semanticist here is whether we need semantically distinct non-Russellian interpretations of the descriptions in (1) and (3) in order to make sense of the scenarios just constructed.

There are good methodological reasons to resist a complication of the semantics of the definite article in this way. The first thing to remember is that the phenomenon of referential usage is not something peculiar to definite descriptions. Consider the following example adapted from Wilson (1978). You and I both see Harris lurking around at the party; we both know (and know that the other knows) that Harris is a convicted embezzler; later in the evening I see Harris flirting with your sister so I come up to you and say,

(5)   A convicted embezzler is flirting with your sister

fully intending to communicate to you the object-dependent proposition that Harris is flirting with your sister. I utter (5) intending you (*a*) to actively entertain the (object-dependent) proposition that Harris is is flirting with your sister, and (*b*) to recognize that I intend you to actively entertain that proposition. There would appear to be no barrier, then, to saying that (part of) what *I mean* by my utterance of (5) is that Harris is flirting with your sister; the object-dependent proposition that Harris is flirting with your sister is (one of) the *proposition(s) meant*.

It is clear that I might have conveyed to you that Harris is flirting with your sister by uttering (6) instead of (5):

(6)   Harris is flirting with your sister.

We appear to have here something approximating a referential$_N$ use of an *indefinite description* (modifications to (A2) would capture this).

It is, of course, open to the referentialist to claim that indefinite descriptions are also ambiguous between Russellian and referential *interpretations*.[33] But the Gricean-Russellian will claim that some sort of important communicative generalization is being missed by proceeding in this way. Indeed, as Sainsbury (1979) emphasizes, the case for an ambiguity in the definite article weakens considerably once it is realized that sentences containing all sorts of quantifiers may be used to convey object-dependent propositions. Suppose it is common knowledge that Smith is the only person taking Jones' seminar. One evening, Jones throws a party and Smith is the only person who turns up. A despondent Jones, when asked the next morning whether his party was well attended, says,

(7)   Well, everyone taking my seminar turned up

fully intending to inform me that only Smith attended. The possibility of such a scenario, would not lead us to complicate the semantics of 'every' with an ambiguity; i.e., it would not lead us to posit semantically distinct quantificational and referential interpretations of 'everyone taking my seminar'.

We find a similar situation with plural quantifiers.[34] Suppose that Scott Soames, David Lewis, and I are the only three people in Lewis's office. Soames has never played cricket and knows that I know this. In addition, Soames wants to know whether Lewis and I have ever played cricket, so I say

(8)   Most people in this room have played cricket

fully intending to communicate to Soames that Lewis and I have both played cricket. There is surely no temptation to complicate the semantics of 'most' with an ambiguity, no temptation to posit a semantically distinct referential interpretation of 'most people in this room'. The natural thing to say is that given his background beliefs and given the quantificational proposition expressed by my utterance in the context in question, Soames was able to *infer* the truth of a particular object-dependent proposition (or two object-dependent propositions). I was thus able to convey an object-dependent proposition by uttering a sentence of the form 'most Fs are Gs'. (Similar cases can be constructed using 'all senators', 'many Americans', 'few Stanford women', 'five of us', 'a convicted embezzler', 'some politicians', 'the man wearing a top hat', 'the women who work for Martha', and so on.)

Thus the Gricean-Russellian views the referential use of definite descriptions as an instance of a more general phenomenon associated with the use of quantified noun phrases. Of course, definite descriptions are particularly susceptible to referential usage because of their own particular semantics. As Klein (1980) points out, if S is observing the Maxim of Quality, S will typically believe that one and only one object satisfies the description used. (The complications introduced by so-called *incomplete* descriptions like 'the table', 'the cat' and so on are discussed in 3.7.) And quite often S will believe this because S knows of some particular object b that b is uniquely F. The beginnings of an explanation of the quite general phenomenon of communicating object-dependent propositions using quantified sentences surely lie in the fact that the grounds for a quantificational assertion are very often object-dependent beliefs of one form or another. (By (A1), object-dependent grounds do not suffice for referential usage, of course.) I know that some Britons are currently residing in the U.S.A. One reason I know this is that I know that I am British and that I am currently residing here, and I know that John McDowell is British and that he is currently residing here. Thus the grounds for my asserting

(9)   Some Britons are currently residing in the U.S.A.

are furnished by object-dependent beliefs about John McDowell and about me. Similar remarks apply to the cricket case discussed a moment ago. Add to this the context of utterance, shared background assumptions, the sorts of inferential abilities we all possess, and the sorts of Gricean considerations that appear to govern rational discourse, and the way is open for a quite general explanation of how it is that we manage to convey object-dependent propositions using quantificational sentences, including, of course, sentences containing descriptions.

Consider the referential$_N$ use of 'the Chairman of the Flat Earth society' in (1) again. Echoing Grice, we might say that

(a)   S has expressed the proposition that [the x: Fx](Gx).

(b)   There is no reason to suppose that S is not observing the CP and maxims.

(c)   S could not be doing this unless he thought that Gb (where 'b' is a name). Gloss: On the assumption that S is observing the Maxim of Relation, he must be attempting to convey something beyond the general proposition that whoever is uniquely F is G. On the assumption that S is adhering to the Maxim of Quality, he must have adequate evidence for thinking that the F is G. I know S knows that b is the F, therefore S thinks that Gb.

(d)   S knows (and knows that I know that he knows) that I know that b is the F, that I know that S knows that b is the F, and that I can see that S thinks the supposition that he thinks that Gb is required.

(e)   S has done nothing to stop me thinking that Gb.

(f)   S intends me to think, or is at least willing to allow me to think, that Gb.

(g)   And so, S has implicated that Gb.

On a referential$_D$ use of 'the F', (c) might be replaced by

(c')   S could not be doing this unless he thought that Gb (where 'b' is a demonstrative.) Gloss: On the assumption that S is observing the Maxim of Relation, he must be attempting to convey something over and above the general proposition that whoever is uniquely F is G. On the assumption that S is adhering to the Maxim of Quality, he must have adequate evidence for thinking that the F is G. It is not plausible to suppose that he has just general grounds for this belief; therefore he must have object-dependent grounds. I can see that there is someone b in the perceptual environment who could be taken to satisfy the description 'the F', and I can see that S can see this. Therefore the grounds for his assertion that the F is G are plausibly furnished by the belief that Gb.[35]

Although a description 'the F' does not itself refer to any individual, following Kripke (1977) let us say that in situations like those just discussed *the speaker S refers* to an individual, the individual S is interested in communicating a proposition about.

We have reached the situation, then, in which we appear to have a perfectly good explanation of referential uses of definite descriptions that does not appeal to any sort of semantical ambiguity. The Russellian and the ambiguity theorist agree that when a description is used referentially, (one of) the proposition(s) *meant* is object-dependent; they just provide different explanations of this fact. The referentialist complicates the semantics of 'the'; the Russellian appeals to antecedently motivated principles governing the nature of rational discourse and ordinary inference. As far as accounting for the data we have considered, a stalemate appears to have been reached.

But general methodological considerations lend support to the Russellian. Modified Occam's Razor enjoins us not to multiply senses beyond necessity, i.e., to opt for a theory that (*ceteris paribus*) does not have to appeal to a semantical ambiguity. The similarity with the case of 'and' (discussed in 3.4) is striking. First, the phenomenon of referential usage is not something specific to English, nor even to Indo-European languages. Second, as already noted, the phenomenon is not even specific to definite descriptions, it arises with quantifiers quite generally. Third, as Kripke (1977) has pointed out, there is no good reason to suppose that speakers of a language who are taught explicitly Russellian truth conditions for sentences containing definite and indefinite descriptions would not come to use such phrases referentially. Furthermore, speakers of a version of first-order logic without descriptions might still succeed in referring to particular individuals by using existential quantifications of the form 'there is exactly one F and whatever is F is G.' Indeed, as Kripke (1977, p. 17) observes, on occasion one can even get away with this sort of thing in English:

(10)   Exactly one person is drinking champagne in that corner and I
       hear he is romantically linked with Jane Smith.

On methodological grounds, then, if attention is restricted to basic
cases (3.2), a unitary Russellian theory seems to be preferable to a
theory that posits a semantical ambiguity.[36]

3.6 The Argument from Misdescription

Up to now, discussion of referential usage has been restricted to what
I earlier called the *basic case*. I want now to turn to the first of
several arguments that are often appealed to by some of those who
reject (A3) in favor of (A2), the Argument from Misdescription. This
argument comes in two forms. What I shall call the "standard" form
of the argument is due to Donnellan (1966) and goes something like
this. Consider a referential$_D$ use of 'Smith's murderer'. Now suppose
Smith was not in fact murdered but died of natural causes. On
Russell's account, the definite description 'Smith's murderer' will be
nondenoting, therefore the proposition expressed will be false (it is
not the case that there exists some unique x such that x murdered
Smith). But this, Donnellan claims, is just incorrect. For suppose the
man *S meant*, viz., Jones, *is* insane. Then, surely *S* will have said
something true of that man. The moral we are supposed to draw is
that ". . . using a definite description referentially, a speaker may
say something true even though the description applies to nothing"
(p. 207). And the conclusion we are encouraged to accept is that when
a description is used referentially, it is the object *S* wishes to convey
something about rather than the descriptive condition used to get at
this object that is of semantical relevance. The proposition expressed
is therefore object-dependent rather than descriptive.[37]

The problem with this argument is that it relies on the existence of
a clear intuition that the proposition expressed is still true despite
the fact that neither Jones nor anyone else satisfies the description
'Smith's murderer'. But this is simply not so. We feel an uneasy
tension when we are presented with such cases. As several authors
have noted, we want to say that *S* did something right but *also* that
S did something *wrong*. After all, the description he used *failed to fit*
the person *S* wanted to "talk about," and to that extent the speech
act was defective.[38]

The referentialist can say nothing useful here, but the Russellian
can provide a theoretical explanation of the aforementioned tension:
What has been left out by the referentialist is the Gricean distinction between the proposition expressed and the proposition(s) meant.
Indeed, one of the earliest overt defenses of the Theory of Descrip-

tions in the face of the Argument from Misdescription was the one sketched by Grice (1969) himself. According to Grice, "what, in such a case, a speaker has *said* may be false, what he *meant* may be true" (p. 142). The proposition expressed by an utterance of 'the F is G' is still descriptive, but the speaker may exploit the fact that both speaker and hearer are willing to entertain the idea that some particular individual *b* is uniquely F in order to communicate an object-dependent proposition about *b*. Again, the proposition that *b* is G may well be part of what is *meant* but it is not the proposition expressed, nor is it implied by it.[39] Applied to Donnellan's example, the proposition expressed by my utterance of 'Smith's murderer is insane' is false; but the proposition I intended to communicate is true (if Jones is indeed insane). Thus the Russellian-Gricean has, if only in a rudimentary way, an account of the conflicting pretheoretic intuitions we typically have when presented with cases involving misdescription. The possibility of misdescription does not advance the case for a semantically referential interpretation in the least; indeed, the unitary Russellian analysis has the edge here.

More or less the same is true with what we can call the *inverted* form of the Argument from Misdescription, due to Hornsby (1977). Consider again a referential$_D$ use of 'Smith's murderer is insane'. Now suppose that the man I *meant* was not insane, and moreover that he did not murder Smith. But suppose that the man who did murder Smith is insane. On Russell's account, the proposition expressed is true, since the unique individual who murdered Smith is insane. But according to Hornsby this is a mistake. I was talking about that man there in the dock, and since he is not insane my utterance cannot be true. We should conclude, Hornsby suggests, that on this occasion, 'Smith's murderer' functions as a genuine referring expression.

The problem with this form of the argument is that it relies on the existence of a clear intuition that the proposition expressed is false, despite the fact that the unique individual that does in fact satisfy 'Smith's murderer' is insane. But this is simply not so. As with the standard form of the argument, we feel an uneasy tension when we are presented with such cases, a tension the Russellian-Gricean can explain.[40]

I doubt these sorts of considerations can be worked up into knock-down arguments against a semantically distinct referential interpretation. However, Salmon (1982) argues that related counterfactual considerations cast serious doubt on the viability of a referential interpretation. Occurrences of 'Smith's murderer' that are semantically referential will be rigid designators. Consequently, if I utter the sentence 'Smith's murderer is insane' in a context C, with the intention that 'Smith's murderer' refer to Jones, then the proposition expressed by my utterance is true with respect to any counterfactual situation in which Jones is insane, even those in which Jones does not murder Smith, those in which Smith is not murdered, those in which Smith does not exist, and those in which there are no murders. And this, Salmon maintains, is quite unacceptable.

Salmon's argument can also be inverted. If I utter the sentence 'Smith's murderer is insane' in a context C, with the intention that 'Smith's murderer' refer to Jones, then the proposition expressed by my utterance is false with respect to any counterfactual situation in which Jones exists but is not insane, even those in which Smith is murdered and the person who murdered him is insane. I must admit I am sympathetic to Salmon's reaction to such results, but I doubt that it is possible to arrive at judgments of truth or falsity that are not to some extent clouded by either one's initial position on the debate or one's views about the bearers of truth or falsity.[41] My own conclusion—a conclusion I am perfectly happy with—is that cases involving misdescription simply provide no evidence for a semantically referential interpretation of descriptions.

3.7   The Argument from Incompleteness

In 3.3, we established that the propositions expressed by utterances containing indexical descriptions like 'my mother' or 'the philosopher I most admire' are partially determined by context. But it is not just overtly indexical descriptions that are context-sensitive. This can be illustrated with the help of the following passage from Strawson's "On Referring":

> Consider the sentence, 'The table is covered with books'. It is quite certain that in any normal use of this sentence, the expression 'the table' would be used to make a unique reference, i.e. to refer to some one table. It is a quite strict use of the definite article, in the sense in which Russell talks on p. 30 of *Principia Mathematica*, of using the article "strictly, so as to imply uniqueness." On the same page Russell says that a phrase of the form "the so-and-so," used strictly, "will only have an application in the event of there being one so-and-so and no more." Now it is obviously quite false that the phrase 'the table' in the sentence 'the table is covered with books', used normally, will "only have an application in the event of there being one table and no more" (1950, pp. 14–15).

There is an important truth in this passage. A speaker may use a definite description when, strictly speaking, it is quite clear that there is no object that uniquely satisfies it. And, on the face of it, this seems to pose a problem for Russell. If I say to you right now

(1)   The table is covered with books

I would not normally be understood as committing myself to the existence of one and only one table. But a naïve application of the Theory of Descriptions appears to have precisely this unwelcome consequence. And since there does not seem to be any good reason for doubting that a determinate proposition is expressed by an utterance of (1), *prima facie* the Russellian is under some obligation to specify its content. By contrast, a theory that postulates a semantically distinct referential interpretation of descriptions seems to provide a natural account of what is going on in (1): the description functions as a referring expression.

Let's call a description 'the *F*' that appears to have a legitimate application even if there is more than one *F* an *incomplete* or *improper* description.[42]

The first thing to notice about incompleteness is that it is neither a necessary nor a sufficient condition for referential usage, an observation made explicit by Peacocke. That incompleteness is not necessary:

> If you and I visited the Casino at Monte Carlo yesterday, and saw a man break the bank . . . and it is common knowledge that this is so, then the description
>
> > "The man who broke the bank at Monte Carlo yesterday"
>
> as it occurs in a particular utterance *today* of
>
> > "The man who broke the bank at Monte Carlo yesterday had holes in his shoes"
>
> may well be satisfied by just one object in the universe, but it is here [referential] (1975, p. 117).

That incompleteness is not sufficient:

> [Suppose] two school inspectors [are] visiting an institution for the first time: one may say to the other, on the basis of the activities around him, "The headmaster doesn't have much control of the pupils." Here there is no object such that the school inspector has said of it that it doesn't have much control over the pupils. One cannot say that the headmaster is such an object, since what the inspector (*actually*) said would be true even if someone else were headmaster (*ibid.*).[43]

Whenever we find some phenomenon associated with the use of definite descriptions, we should look for corresponding phenomena associated with the uses of other quantifiers. This tactic served us well in 3.5 when we examined how someone might convey an object-dependent proposition while expressing (only) an object-independent proposition, and it serves us equally well here. Suppose I had a dinner party last night. In response to a question as to how it went, I say to you

(2)   Everyone was sick.

Clearly I do not mean to be asserting that everyone in existence was sick, just that everyone *at the dinner party I had last night* was. In some fashion or other, this is discernible from the context of utterance.[44] Similar examples can be constructed using 'no', 'most', 'just one', 'exactly eight', and, of course, 'the' (as it occurs with both singular and plural complements). Indeed, the problem of incompleteness has nothing to do with the use of definite descriptions *per se*; it is a quite general fact about the use of quantifiers in natural language.[45] What is needed, then, is not just an account of incomplete descriptions, but a quite general account incomplete quantifiers. It seems unlikely, therefore, that incompleteness raise any special problems for a quantificational analysis of descriptions that do not have to be faced in any event by quantificational analyses of other quantifiers.[46]

There are two main approaches to incompleteness in the literature, what we might call the *explicit* and the *implicit* approaches. According to the explicit approach, incomplete quantifiers are *elliptical* for proper quantifiers. As Sellars puts it, the descriptive content is "completed" by context. According to the implicit approach, the context of utterance delimits the domain of quantification and leaves the descriptive content untouched.[47] Consider sentence (2) again. On the explicit approach, the quantifier 'everybody' (as it is used on this occasion) is elliptical for 'everybody at the dinner party I had last night', or some such "narrower" quantifier. On the implicit approach, the domain of quantification is understood as restricted to some favored class of individuals (or to some favored part of the world).[48]

On the assumption that one (or both) of these approaches (or something very similar to one or other of them) will play a role in any complete theory of natural language quantification, any theory that treats definite descriptions as quantifiers is at liberty to appeal to either when incompleteness arises. Consider again Strawson's example

(1)   The table is covered with books.

On the explicit approach (taken by, e.g., Sellars 1954), a particular utterance of 'the table' might be elliptical for (e.g.) 'the table *over there*'.[49] On the implicit approach, the domain of quantification might be restricted to (e.g.) objects in the immediate shared perceptual environment. The mere fact that we find incomplete descriptions in discourse does not *by itself*, then, give us any reason to abandon Russell's quantificational analysis of descriptions.[50]

Nonetheless, some philosophers have argued that there are intrinsic problems with one or other of these approaches to incompleteness, and that instead of being contextually completed, some occurrences of incomplete descriptions simply have to be provided with semantically referential interpretations.

Let's suppose that an incomplete description is elliptical for a proper (i.e., uniquely-denoting) description recoverable from the context of utterance. As a general account of incomplete descriptions, this type of proposal has come under fire from Donnellan (1968), Hornsby (1977), Wettstein (1981), and Recanati (1986).[51] In his brief discussion of incomplete descriptions, Donnellan is quite willing to accept the elliptical proposal for descriptions used nonreferentially:

> Without considering the two uses of descriptions, the reply [to Strawson's comments cited above] one is inclined to make on Russell's behalf is that in the loose way of everyday speech the context is relied upon to supply further qualifications on the description to make it unique. This seems a plausible reply when considering attributive uses. Suppose someone says, "The next President will be a dove on Viet Nam," and the context easily supplies the implicit "of the United States" (1968, p. 204, note 5).

But Donnellan does not think that this will work for incomplete descriptions used referentially:

> But where one has a very "indefinite" [i.e., incomplete] definite description, with many things in the world satisfying the actual description, the reply is not so plausible. These are commonly, I believe, referential uses. A speaker wants to refer to some object and uses an "indefinite" definite description. Asked to make his description more precise, he may have to think about how best to do it. Several further descriptions may come to mind, not all of which are actually correct. Which, then, shall we say is the full but implicit one? Once we see the function of a referential description, however, we need not suppose that there is any one description recoverable from the speech act that is supposed uniquely to apply to the object referred to. The audience may through the partial description and various clues and cues know to what the speaker refers without being in possession of a description that uniquely fits it and which was implicit all along in the speaker's speech act (ibid).

Donnellan is not, then, arguing *from* incompleteness *to* referentiality; rather he seems to be claiming that the method of contextual supplementation is implausible *if the description in question is being used referentially*. Wettstein (1981) suggests that we have here the basis of a knock-down argument for a semantically distinct referential interpretation of descriptions. For according to Wettstein, in many cases where an incomplete description is used there will simply be *no* adequate way of contextually deriving a complete description. And the only plausible way out, he suggests, is to concede that in such a case the description is functioning as a *demonstrative* referring expression and that consequently the proposition expressed is object-dependent rather than descriptive. On this account, then, the description takes as its semantical value the object the speaker intended to communicate something about (in the sense of 3.5).

To fix ideas, let's consider Wettstein's argument as applied to one of his own examples. Suppose, on a particular occasion of utterance, 'the table' is taken to be elliptical for 'the table in room 209 of Camden Hall at [time] t_1.' According to Wettstein, this proposal is unworkable because there are a number of nonequivalent ways of filling out the descriptive condition to make it uniquely applicable and no principled way to choose between the resulting descriptions. For instance, 'the table on which Wettstein carved his name at [time] t_2' might well be satisfied by, and only by, the unique object that satisfies the descriptive condition 'table in room 209 of Camden Hall at t_1'. Since it is the descriptive condition rather than the denotation that makes it into the proposition expressed, on Russell's account the particular choice of uniquely-denoting description seems to be crucial: a different description means a different proposition. And this apparently leaves the Russellian with the embarrassing task of deciding which of these nonequivalent descriptions is the correct one.

According to Wettstein, it is "implausible in the extreme" to suppose that the situation of utterance somehow enables the hearer to recover the correctly completed description, viz., the one the speaker intended. In many cases, there will simply be no such indication. Moreover, in many cases it doesn't even make sense to ask which of a batch of nonequivalent, codenoting descriptions is *the correct one*. What criterion would one use in deciding which description is the correct one? The one that figures in the speaker's intentions?

> In many cases . . . the speaker will have no such determinate intention. If the speaker is asked which Russellian description(s) was implicit in his utterance of 'the table' he will not ordinarily be able to answer. 'Although I meant to refer to that table' our speaker may well reply, 'I don't think I meant to refer to it *as* the table in in room 209 of Camden Hall at t_1 as opposed to, say, *as* the table at which the author of *The Persistence of Objects* is sitting at t_1. Nor did I intend to refer to it *as* the table in 209 *and* the table at which the author . . . as opposed to, say, just *as* the table in 209' (1981, p. 247).

If we can't, even by enlisting the help of the speaker, determine which complete description the incomplete description is elliptical for, Wettstein argues, it doesn't make sense to say that there *is* some such correct, complete description.

According to Wettstein, the entire problem can be sidestepped by endorsing the neo-Russellian conception of an object-dependent proposition and treating the description as a referring expression that contributes just an object to the proposition expressed. In short, the description is to be viewed as a device of *demonstrative reference.* Embarrassing questions about the complete descriptive content are then circumvented, as it is the *object itself,* rather than any particular descriptive condition, that makes it into the proposition expressed. We can call this the Argument from Incompleteness for a referential interpretation of descriptions.

The first sign that something is amiss here is the fact that the argument seems to go through just as well with other quantifiers and with descriptions used *non*referentially. Consider again the sentence

(2)   Everyone was sick

uttered in response to a question about last night's dinner party. On the explicit approach, the quantifier 'everyone' (as it is used on this occasion) might be viewed as elliptical for 'everyone at my dinner party last night', 'everyone who ate at my house last night', or some other quantifier of the form 'every *F*' that denotes everyone who came to to the dinner party I had last night. Since the descriptive content is different in each case, the precise character of the proposition expressed depends upon which of these codenoting quantifiers is selected. It is clear, then, that Wettstein has put his finger on a very important fact about elliptical analyses of incomplete quantifiers (and perhaps ellipsis quite generally); but it is beginning to look as though no real support for a referential interpretation of descriptions is going to come out of this.

Ironically, this becomes much clearer when we take into account Wettstein's own remarks on incomplete descriptions used *non*referentially. Consider the case of the detective who comes across Smith's body and has no idea who killed him. Rather than uttering 'Smith's murderer is insane' or 'The man who murdered Smith is insane', the detective simply says,

(3)   The murderer is insane.

According to Wettstein,

> As in the cases of referential uses . . . there will be any number of ways to fill out the description so as to yield a Russellian description (e.g., 'Harry Smith's murderer', 'the murderer of Joan Smith's husband', 'the murderer of the junior senator from New Jersey in 1975') and in many cases there will be nothing about the circumstances of utterance or the intentions of the

speaker which would indicate that any of these Russellian descriptions is the correct one (1981, p. 250–1).

As Wettstein observes, here he is in conflict with Donnellan, who suggests that the elliptical proposal *will* work for descriptions used nonreferentially. Indeed, Wettstein concedes, on Russellian grounds, that the objection he has raised cannot be overcome by treating *this* occurrence of 'the murderer' as a device of demonstrative reference: "One fully understands the proposition without having any idea who murdered Smith" (p. 251). We seem to be stuck:

> [1] 'the murderer' is not elliptical for some Russellian description, and [2] no appeal to the referent of 'the murderer' will account for propositional determinacy (1981, p. 251).

Given his endorsement of [1], Wettstein then makes a very odd suggestion. Although this occurrence of the description 'the murderer' is not referential, Wettstein suggests that demonstrative reference still plays a role in a proper characterization of its content:

> For in uttering, 'the murderer is insane' in the presence of the mutilated body, the speaker relies on the context to reveal *whose* murder is in question. The speaker, that is, makes an *implicit* reference to the victim (*ibid.*).

Recall that Wettstein's own account of descriptions used referentially is supposed to be immune to the problem of codenoting, nonequivalent descriptions that he has raised for the Russellian. The reason, of course, is that Wettstein explicitly endorses the neo-Russellian conception of an object-dependent proposition: it is the object itself (rather than any descriptive condition or sense) that gets into the proposition expressed. But on this conception of an object-dependent proposition, in the example we are considering there is simply no difference between saying that there is an "implicit reference" to the victim and saying that the incomplete description 'the murderer' is elliptical for a uniquely denoting description, such as 'the murderer of *that man*' (where 'that man' refers to the victim), or 'the murderer of *him*' (where 'him' refers to the victim), or '*his* murderer' (where 'his' refers to the victim), all of which contribute the same thing to the proposition expressed, viz., the descriptive condition *murderer-of-b* where *b* is the victim himself rather than some description of *b*. Wettstein is just mistaken in claiming that 'the murderer' is "not elliptical for some Russellian description" (*ibid*); the proposition expressed by (3) is given by (4):

(4)   [the x: x murdered b] (x is insane).

It is unclear why Wettstein thinks the description in (4) is non-Russellian. One possibility is that he has conflated (*a*) the notion of a *referential description* (i.e., a description that is interpreted referentially), and (*b*) the notion of *a description containing a referential component*. An alternative diagnosis is that he is unwilling to countenance descriptions containing relational predicates like 'murderer-of-*b*', where '*b*' is a referential term. But this is certainly not a constraint the *Russellian* is obliged to work under.[52] If '*R*' is a binary relational predicate, '*b*' is a name, and '*x*' is a variable, then '*Rbx*' is an open sentence, and '[the *x*: *Rbx*]' is a perfectly good definite description (2.6). Perhaps Wettstein is just unwilling to allow the Russellian access to descriptions containing context-sensitive elements such as demonstratives or indexicals. But again, there is no reason to constrain the Russellian in this way (3.3). (As Grice (1970) observes, one of Russell's (1905) own examples of a definite description is 'my son'.) To the extent that one countenances indexical and demonstrative referring expressions—and Wettstein certainly does—if '*b*' is an indexical or demonstrative, then '[the *x*: *Rbx*]' is a perfectly good Russellian description, albeit one with an indexical or demonstrative component. I submit, then, that if descriptions may contain overtly referential components (including indexical and demonstrative components), then there is nothing to prevent the ellipsed elements of incomplete descriptions from being referential. And this is very different from saying that the *description* is interpreted referentially.[53]

The completion of incomplete descriptions with referential components is implicit in Evans' discussion of incompleteness:

> . . . travelling in a car through the United states, I might pass through a town whose roads are particularly bumpy, and in consequence say "They ought to impeach the mayor." I do not intend my audience to identify the object spoken about as one of which he has information; I intend merely that he take me to be saying that the mayor of this town, through which we are passing, ought to be impeached, and this statement is adequately represented quantificationally (1982, p. 324).

Evans is surely right to claim that in his example there is no intention to identify any individual—and hence no temptation to regard this particular utterance of the incomplete description 'the mayor' as referential. Moreover, Evans suggests that he (the speaker) *would* be able to complete the description in a uniquely appropriate way, and supplies a plausible completion using referential rather than descriptive material. As the neo-Russellian would put it, it is the *town itself* rather than some descriptive characterization of the town that gets into the descriptive condition and thereby into the proposition expressed.

There is no reason, of course, why descriptions used referentially should not also be completed using referential material, thus avoiding the problem raised by nonequivalent codenoting descriptions. As Soames (1986) remarks, this suggestion is very natural for descriptions such as 'the Mayor' or 'the murderer', where an additional argument place can be made available for a particular individual specified by the context of utterance. But with examples like 'the table' (which Strawson originally used to attack Russell, and upon which Wettstein fastens in mounting his own attack) it is true that there is no natural argument position to be made available. However, the contextual coordinates (3.3) of an utterance provide further nondescriptive material. One way of construing Sellars's (1954) original proposal for dealing with 'the table' is that reference is made to the spatial coordinate. On Sellars's account, an utterance of 'the table' is treated as elliptical for (e.g.) 'the table *over here*', or 'the table *over there*', both which of course contain indexicals sensitive to the spatial coordinate p rather than additional descriptive material.[54] Wettstein's own list of complete descriptions for which 'the table' might be viewed as elliptical includes only sentences containing descriptions completed with additional *descriptive* material ('the table in room 209 of Camden Hall at t_1', 'the table at which the author of *The Persistence of Objects* is sitting at t_1', and so on). This is the weak point in his discussion. The semanticist who regards (utterances of) incomplete quantifiers—including incomplete descriptions—as elliptical for complete quantifiers is under no obligation to treat the ellipsed material as free of referring expressions and indexicals.

An account of how incomplete descriptions are to be treated is not required solely to ward off the Argument from Incompleteness. First, incompleteness affects descriptions used *non*referentially, so a general account of the phenomenon cannot be based on a referential interpretation. Second, incompleteness affects quantifiers more generally, not just definite descriptions. And to that extent, appeals to contextual coordinates and ellipsed material are independently required by any adequate theory of natural language quantification.[55]

It should be noted that the problem of incompleteness can also emerge with descriptions used *anaphorically*, as in (5) and (6):

(5)   I bought *a donkey* and a horse last week. For some reason *the donkey* will not eat anything.

(6) *Three women* and *a man* arrived in a large truck. *The women* got out and began dancing in the road while *the man* played the accordian.

In these cases, it is plausible to suppose (as Evans (1977) has argued) that the descriptions in question are completed using material from the clause containing their antecedents. For discussion, see 5.5.

3.8 Concluding Remarks

We have seen in this chapter that the Theory of Descriptions is not threatened by the fact that context plays important and complex roles in the way sentences containing descriptions are understood. First, indexicality is a pervasive feature of natural language, and the fact that quantifiers, including definite descriptions, may contain indexical components does nothing to undermine either the schematic theory of quantification presented in 2.5 or the place of the Theory of Descriptions within that theory. Second, the fact that a speaker may use a definite description to convey an object-dependent proposition poses no threat to this picture; in particular it provides no support for the view that descriptions are ambiguous between Russellian and referential interpretations. Again, the phenomenon is one that is not specific to descriptions but something we find with quantifiers quite generally. Once one takes into account (*a*) a very natural distinction between the proposition expressed and the proposition(s) meant, (*b*) the nature and role of context, (*c*) communicative aims or goals, and (*d*) our abilities to make certain elementary inferences, the general form of an explanation of this phenomenon comes clearly into view. Finally, no support for a referential interpretation of descriptions can be derived from the fact that quantifiers may be superficially incomplete.

Notes

1. Mitchell (1962, pp. 84–85) writes:

    Definite descriptions occurring as the subjects of sentences, have at least two distinct functions, which may be illustrated by two sets of examples:

    1. a. 'The Prime Minister presides at Cabinet meetings'
        b. 'The Sovereign of Great Britain is the head of the Commonwealth'
        c. 'The man who wrote this unsigned letter had a bad pen'

    2. a. 'The Prime Minister has invited me to lunch'
        b. 'The Queen made a tour of the Commonwealth'
        c. 'The author of *Waverley* limped'.

It is not difficult to see that the grammatical subjects of the sentences quoted in List 1 are not used—as proper names, for instance, are used—to refer uniquely. For 'The Prime Minister' and 'the Sovereign' we can substitute, without change of meaning, 'Whoever is Prime Minister' and 'Whoever is Sovereign'. . . . With the sentences in List 2 the case is different. The subject phrases serve to identify individuals, and what is predicated in each case is predicated of the individuals so identified.

2. Construed as a general account of such readings, this position has been falsified by Cartwright (1968) and Kripke (1977), both of whom produce examples whose *de re* readings are not correctly captured by referential interpretations. For discussion, see 4.2 and 4.3.

3. It is tempting to think of Donnellan as simply labeling Mitchell's distinction (see, e.g., Davies, 1981). However, I do not think this is quite right. First, Mitchell seems to think that his two "functions" of descriptions are tied to the particular sentences used, whereas Donnellan argues that the same sentence may be used with either an attributive or a referential "reading" of the description it contains. Second, Mitchell's (1c)—see note 1—is very like the sorts of examples Donnellan uses to illustrate his attributive use in that the proposition expressed seems to be "about" an individual only under a description. However, (1a) and (1b) seem to be "about" a particular role or position that may be filled by different individuals on different occasions. Thus I am not much inclined to see Mitchell's nonidentificatory function as a genuine precursor of Donnellan's attributive use. In particular, it seems to me that an utterance of (1b) could be true even if there were not, at the time of utterance, a Sovereign of Great Britain. Suppose the Queen dies and for various complex reasons a constitutional crisis ensues that somehow prevents Prince Charles or anyone else from taking the throne. A true utterance of (1b) might still be made.

François Recanati has pointed out to me that something very close to Donnellan's distinction can be found in the work of the seventeenth-century French philosopher Antoine Arnauld, author of the *Port-Royal Logic*. See Dominicy (1984), pp. 123–27.

4. Grice also echoes the point, made by Mitchell (1962) and Donnellan (1966), that in case (1), one may legitimately insert 'whoever he may be' after the definite description. In view of of certain worries pointed out by Searle (1979), I have not emphasized this characteristic of case (1).

5. This is also the view of Hampshire (1959), Geach (1962), Kripke (1972, 1977), Wiggins (1975, 1980), Castañeda (1977), Sainsbury (1979), Searle (1979), Klein (1980), Davies (1981), Evans (1982), Salmon (1982), Davidson (1986), and Soames (1986). There are important differences of detail in these proposals, but at the same time there is a consensus that the phenomenon of referential usage does not warrant the postulation of a semantical ambiguity in the definite article. (My indebtedness to the detailed discussions by Kripke, Sainsbury, Searle, and Davies will become clear as this chapter unfolds.)

6. This way of characterizing the alleged semantical significance of referential usage is explicit in (e.g.) Peacocke (1975), Hornsby (1977), and Kaplan (1978); it also seems to be what Donnellan (1978) has in mind. As both Kripke (1977) and Searle (1979) emphasize, for those who advocate a *semantical* distinction between Russellian and referential descriptions, there is still the problem of providing an account of *when*, exactly, a definite description *is* referential (see 3.5). The importance of this fact seems to be recognized by Donnellan (1978).

7. The argument implicit in this remark is unpacked in note 36. In places, Donnellan (1966) suggests that he is highlighting a "pragmatic" rather than a semantical ambiguity. But as Searle (1979) quite rightly points out, it is quite unclear what a "pragmatic ambiguity" is supposed to be:

> "I went to the bank" is semantically ambiguous. "Flying planes can be dangerous" is syntactically ambiguous. But what is a pragmatic ambiguity? Is "You are standing on my foot" supposed to be pragmatically ambiguous because in some contexts its utterance can be more then just a statement of fact? If so, then every sentence is indefinitely "pragmatically ambiguous." If we had a notion of "pragmatic ambiguity" we would also have a notion of "pragmatic univocality" but in fact neither notion has any clear sense at all (Searle, 1979, p. 150, note 3).

All things considered, it seems to me that the (semantical) ambiguity thesis is held by Rundle (1965), Donnellan (1966, 1968, 1978), Stalnaker (1972), Partee (1972), Peacocke (1975), Hornsby (1977), Kaplan (1978), Devitt (1981), Wettstein (1981, 1982), Recanati (1981, 1986, 1989), Fodor and Sag (1982), and Barwise and Perry (1983), among others. Recanati (1989) explicitly denies that his view entails a semantical ambiguity; I disagree. For discussion, see note 36.

A parallel semantical thesis for *indefinite* descriptions appears to be held by (e.g.) Partee (1972), Chastain (1975), Donnellan (1978), Wilson (1978), Fodor and Sag (1982), Barwise and Perry (1983), and Stich (1986), among others For discussion, see King (1988) and Ludlow and Neale (forthcoming).

8. An expression ζ occurs occurs in a nonextensional context just in case ζ is within the scope of a nonextensional operator. The notion of a nonextensional operator will be characterized in detail in 4.3. For present concerns, we can just say that a unary, sentential, sentence-forming operator O is extensional just in case the truth-value of '$O(\phi)$' depends only upon the truth-value of the embedded sentence ϕ. Thus, the contexts created by modal operators and attitude verb frames are nonextensional.

9. I was tempted to borrow Kaplan's (1977) technical terms "character" and "content." However, any suggestion of commitment to Kaplan's intensional machinery is best be avoided by using different terminology. I have, however, drawn on Kaplan's informal remarks on indexicals and demonstratives in which his character-content distinction is introduced.

10. In the period with which I am primarily concerned (1905–1919) Russell came to view the class of genuine names as restricted to just (e.g.) 'this'

and 'that', which makes his (albeit later) talk of demonstratives as not "mere" names rather misleading in the present context.

11. See (e.g.) Montague (1968), Lewis (1975), and Kaplan (1977).

12. Further contextual coordinates may be required to capture other essential features of context. For discussion, see Lewis, (1975) p. 175.

13. $(\lambda X)\zeta$ represents a function from objects of the type over which X ranges to objects of the same type as ζ. The Russellian could take the semantical value of a description [the $x: Fx$] to be the function denoted by (λP) ([the $x: Fx$] (Px)), i.e., as a function from properties to propositions. See Montague (1970, 1973).

14. We can construct analogous cases for a description such as 'your mother', which contains an element sensitive to the addressee coordinate a; 'that man's mother', which is sensitive to the demonstration coordinate d; 'the current U.S. President', sensitive to the temporal coordinate t; and 'the woman who was just sitting here', sensitive to the temporal and spatial coordinates t and p.

15. It is open to argue that (6) is actually ambiguous according as the pronoun is to be given an anaphoric or nonanaphoric (e.g., demonstrative) reading (see Evans (1977, 1980) for discussion). The general form of the problem the hearer is faced with is the same.

16. As argued by Sperber and Wilson (1986), even if we anchor indexicals, assign referents, and fully disambiguate an utterance, very often H will *still* not be able to properly characterize the proposition expressed because of vagueness, ellipsis, and so on. As they put it, sentence meaning *radically* underdetermines the proposition expressed.

17. Wittgenstein, *Tractatus Logico-Philosophicus*, 4.024.

18. Part of Grice's project involves providing an analysis of meaning that does not presuppose any linguistic or otherwise semantical concepts, so (G1) is not a genuine Gricean condition because ϕ is implicitly understood to be a *sentence*. More appropriate would be the following:

(G2)   By producing u, S means that p only if for some audience H, S produced u intending:

(1) H to actively entertain the thought that p, and
(2) H to recognize that S intends (1)

where u is any piece of behavior the production of which is a candidate for meaning something. For the purposes of this essay, (G1) will suffice because (*a*) I am not attempting any sort of reductive analysis, and (*b*) the examples I am most concerned with all involve linguistic utterances. In cases where u is an utterance of the sentence ϕ, I see no harm (for present purposes) in treating as interchangeable the locutions "by producing u, S means that p" and "by uttering ϕ, S means that p."

Grice's attempts to provide necessary and sufficient conditions for utterer's meaning make use of a third intention designed to rule out cases where some feature of the utterance in question makes it completely obvious that p. Grice was worried by cases like the following: (*i*) Herod presents Salome with the head of St. John the Baptist on a charger; (*ii*) in response to an invitation to play squash, Bill displays his bandaged leg. According to Grice, we do not want to say that Herod *meant* that St. John the Baptist was dead. Nor do we want to say that Bill *meant* that his leg was bandaged. (We may well want to say that he meant that he could not play squash, or even that he had a bad leg, but not that his leg was bandaged.) Thus Grice suggests the addition of a third clause, the rough import of which is that S intend H's recognition of S's second intention to function as a reason for H to actively entertain the thought that *p*. Candidate conditions of the form of (G2) are therefore superseded by conditions of the form of (G3):

(G3)   By producing *u*, S means that *p* only if for some audience H, S produced *u* intending:

(1)   H to actively entertain the thought that *p*,
(2)   H to recognize that S intends (1), and
(3)   H's recognition that S intends (2) to function, at least in part, as a reason for (1).

It is not clear to me that the additional constraint in (3) is necessary. The same degree of manifestness seems to be present in certain cases involving properly linguistic utterances. Consider an utterance of, e.g., 'I can speak English', or an utterance of 'I can speak in squeaky voice' said in a squeaky voice (I owe this example to Neil Smith), or an utterance of 'I am over here' bawled across a crowded room at someone known to be looking for the utterer (this example is due to Schiffer (1972)). In none of these cases is there a temptation to say that the speaker did not *mean* what he or she said. As I have stated it, I am not sure whether clause (3) really blocks such cases, but in any event, in the light of the similarities between these cases and those that worried Grice, I do not feel the need for an additional constraint on utterer's meaning, such as (3), that is supposed to prevent (e.g.) Herod from meaning that St. John the Baptist was dead, or Bill from meaning that his leg was bandaged. On this matter, see also Schiffer (1972) and Sperber and Wilson (1986).

19.   Grice's wording suggests that a particular maxim or submaxim concerns only what is said (e.g., 'Do not say what you believe to be false') while another concerns, perhaps, what is *meant* (e.g., 'Be relevant'). (I owe this observation to Deirdre Wilson.) However, except for those submaxims under Manner (perhaps) that apply only to what is said, I think we must interpret Grice as allowing a violation of a maxim at the level of what is said to be over-ridden by adherence to that maxim at the level of what is implicated. This seems to me to be the only way to make sense of his account of flouting; i.e., blatantly violating a maxim at the level of what is said but adhering to it at the level of what is implicated does not involve a violation of the CP.

A variety of complications for Grice's theory are discussed by Sperber and Wilson (1981, 1982, 1986) and Wilson and Sperber (1981, 1986), who utilize some of Grice's insights in their *relevance*-based approach to utterance interpretation. Since writing the body of this chapter, I have come to believe (mostly through conversations with Dan Sperber) that my own discussion might well have been facilitated had I made use of Sperber and Wilson's theory rather than Grice's.

20. Consider an utterance of 'She is poor and she is honest. Moreover, I don't think she's honest'. The linguistic transgression here is not of the order of an outright contradiction; rather it is more like an instance of Moore's paradox. Nor will contradiction ensue in cases involving an attempted cancellation of what Grice calls *conventional* implicature. Unlike conversational implicatures, conventional implicatures arise regardless of context and are (at least in part) attributable to linguistic convention. To borrow one of Grice's (1961) examples, there is no truth-conditional difference between 'She is poor and honest' and 'She is poor but honest', but we are still inclined to say that these sentences differ in meaning. On Grice's account, an assertion of the latter would involve an additional "non-central" speech act indicating the speaker's (or perhaps someone else's) attitude towards the propositional content of the central speech act (i.e., the assertion that she is poor and honest), an attitude of unexpectedness or contrast. This Grice calls a *conventional* implicature.

There are complex issues involved in spelling out Grice's remarks on this topic, in particular the extent to which the precise content of a given conventional implicature is conversationally determined, i.e., established by recourse to the maxims of conversation and not just to linguistic meaning. As Grice (1961, p. 127) observes, in the example just discussed there is no prospect of characterizing the conventional implicature as a "presupposition" in any interesting sense of this much-abused term: even if the implicature were false, i.e., even if there were no reason on Earth to suppose that poverty and honesty contrasted in any way, what is asserted could still be false, say if she were *rich* and honest. I am here indebted to discussion with Paul Grice.

21. In such a case, Grice would say that you "made as if to say" that p, and implicated that q, as long as you had no intention of inducing (or activating) in your interlocutor the thought that p.

22. Cancellability cannot be a sufficient condition because of ambiguity. Consider the following exchange. A and B meet in the street:

A: Where are you going?
B: I am going down to the bank to get some money.
A: Who do you bank with?
B: I'm sorry, I don't understand.
A: You said you were going down to the bank to get some money.
B: And so I am; I keep my money buried in a chest down by the river.

One might be tempted to argue that B's first utterance carries with it the implication that B is about to visit some sort of financial institution, and that his third utterance succeeds in cancelling this implication. Of course, no one would be tempted to argue that 'bank' is unambiguous in English; but since Grice wanted to account for certain alleged ambiguities of philosophical importance in terms of conversational implicature rather than lexical (or syntactical) ambiguity, he cannot (and does not) take cancellability as a sufficient condition for implicature.

23. As pointed out by (e.g.) Sperber and Wilson (1986), since q is simply introduced without explanation in step (c), this schema cannot be con-

strued as a characterization of any sort of method for actually *calculating* implicatures, but only as a method for establishing whether or not a particular implication qualifies as a conversational implicature.

24. As Chomsky has emphasized, the syntactician is in a very similar position with respect to intuitions concerning well-formedness (grammaticality). And as Rawls (1971) has pointed out, more or less the same considerations carry over from syntax to ethics.

25. I shall restrict attention to cases where 'and' conjoins sentences for the simple reason that it seems unlikely, to me at least, that all occurrences of 'and' that conjoin (e.g.) noun phrases can be analysed in terms of logical conjunction. While a sentence like

(i)   Russell and Whitehead lived in Cambridge

might be analysable in terms of the conjunction of (ii) and (iii),

(ii)   Russell lived in Cambridge
(iii)   Whitehead lived in Cambridge

such a proposal is quite unsuitable for

(iv)   Russell and Whitehead wrote *Principia Mathematica.*

We have here yet another problem raised by sentences involving plural noun phrases that admit of collective readings.

26. The results of some psycholinguistic experiments suggest that an "order-of-mention" strategy is applied fairly blindly in the earlier stages of language acquisition by children confronted with utterances containing the words 'before' and 'after'. In particular, children appear to grasp '*A* before *B*' and 'After *A, B*' before they grasp 'Before *B, A*' and '*B* after *A*'. See Clark (1971) and Johnson (1975).

27. Even if it is possible to treat the temporal and causal implications that attach to utterances in which 'and' is conjoining sentences in terms of conversational implicature, Carston (1988) points out that it is not at all clear how to extend the proposal to sentences like

(i)   Tell me a secret and I'll tell you one
(ii)   Shout at me again and I'll quit

in which 'and' seems to have the force of 'if . . . then'.

Carston proposes a way of holding onto the idea that 'and' is unambiguous while at the same time allowing for a difference between the proposition expressed by '*p* and *q*' and '*p* & *q*' on the grounds that linguistic meaning underdetermines the proposition expressed. Carston's approach may well inherit the positive characteristics of Grice's approach without inheriting many of its problems.

28. According to (e.g.) Gazdar (1979), an utterance of a sentence of the form 'some *F*s are *G*s' gives rise to a generalized conversational implicature to the effect that the speaker knows that some *F*s are not *G*s. But as Soames (1981, pp. 533–37) points out, it is more plausible to suppose that the generalized implicature is really that the speaker does not know whether all *F*s are *G*s, an additional particularized implicature to the effect that the speaker knows (or believes) that some *F*s are not *G*s, arising if the speaker can be presumed to know whether or not all *F*s are *G*s. In order

to avoid getting immersed in the details of this type of example, I have deliberately refrained from saying that the speaker conversationally implicates that some of the deaths were not accidental, or that the speaker believes (or knows) that some of the deaths were not accidental, opting instead for talk of the speaker implicating that he or she is willing to entertain the possibility that some Fs are not Gs.

29. Furthermore, as Martin Davies has pointed out to me, parity of reasoning would require that if S knew of a, b, c, d, and e that they were all of the Fs in existence, S could not use 'all Fs' as a quantifier. The real force of this point will emerge once we turn to referential uses of other quantifiers.

30. The existence of certain object-dependent beliefs on the part of the speaker is sometimes taken to suffice for a "referential" or "specific" use of an *indefinite* description in the literature on this topic (see, e.g., Fodor and Sag (1982)). In my opinion, this leads to considerable confusion. For discussion, see Ludlow and Neale (forthcoming).

31. Although there are counterexamples to (A2), I shall ignore them in what follows. The type of patching that is required would take us too far astray, and after all, I am only trying to provide the referentialist with a workable account of referential usage that can be utilized in conjunction with (A1), I am not trying to present a watertight conceptual analysis. The conjunction of (A1) and (A2) provides the referentialist with *a far more plausible position* than does the conjunction of (A1) with any alternative characterization of referential usage I have seen. (As Kripke (1977) and Searle (1979) observe, Donnellan's (1966) positive characterizations of referential and attributive usage lead to a classification that is neither exclusive nor exhaustive and problematic borderline cases can easily be constructed (on this point, see also Davies, 1981). No doubt the sorts of considerations that Kripke and Searle adduce could also be used to undermine (A2), but it still seems to me to provide the referentialist with the most reasonable position available.)

32. In conversation, it has more than once been suggested that the distinction between referential$_D$ and referential$_N$ uses is pedantic since the claim made by the referentialist is just the broad claim that descriptions used referentially function as referring expressions. But the distinction can only seem pedantic to those who presuppose a neo-Russellian conception of an object-dependent proposition. To someone who is as sensitive as Evans to the important differences between names and demonstratives, the distinction between referential$_D$ and referential$_N$ uses of descriptions will be vital if a semantically distinct referential interpretation turns out to be necessary. I do not want to presuppose any particular account of object-dependence; my reasons for adhering to the distinction concern satisfaction of the Justification Requirement.

33. Such an ambiguity is argued for by Chastain (1975), Wilson (1978), Donnellan (1978), Fodor and Sag (1982), Barwise and Perry (1983), and Stich (1986). For problems with this view, see King (1988) and Ludlow and Neale (forthcoming). As Kripke (1977) points out, many of the

considerations that favor a unitary Russellian account of definite descriptions carry over *mutatis mutandis* to indefinite descriptions.

34. This point is made by Sainsbury (1979), Davies (1981), and Blackburn (1984). The example I have used is based on an example due to Davies.

35. To the extent that such schemata seem to be adequate for many cases involving referential uses of descriptions, and to the extent that purely descriptive grounds for an assertion that the F is G are the exception rather than the rule, we might view such schemata as having the status of interpretive heuristics. More or less this suggestion is made by Klein (1980), though he does not distinguish between referential$_N$ and referential$_D$ uses.

36. This view has been contested by Recanati (1989) on the grounds that one can endorse (A1) and (A2) without being committed to an ambiguity in the definite article. I am baffled by this claim. Recanati explicitly assumes something akin to a three-way Gricean distinction between (*a*) the linguistic meaning of a sentence ϕ, (*b*) the proposition expressed by a particular utterance u of ϕ by a speaker S, and (*c*) the proposition(s) S meant by u. By analogy with the semantics of indexical and demonstrative referring expressions, Recanati suggests that a difference in the proposition expressed by distinct utterances of 'the F is G' does not correspond to distinct linguistic meanings of this sentence (or two linguistic meanings of the description 'the F' or two linguistic meanings of the definite article 'the').

   To fix ideas, let's return to the semantics of demonstratives. If I point to Recanati and say

   (i)   That man is French

I express a true object-dependent proposition about Recanati. If I point to David Lewis and utter (i) I express a false object-dependent proposition about Lewis. Of course, we do not have to say that (i) is ambiguous. It has a unique linguistic meaning; but because it contains an indexical component sensitive to a contextual coordinate, it may be used on different occasions to express different object-dependent propositions. In cases in which the proposition expressed exhausts the proposition(s) meant, we get the following picture (F1):

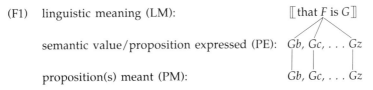

(F1)   linguistic meaning (LM): $[\![$ that F is G $]\!]$

       semantic value/proposition expressed (PE): $Gb, Gc, \ldots Gz$

       proposition(s) meant (PM): $Gb, Gc, \ldots Gz$

where each chain represents a distinct utterance of 'that F is G'.

   I have assumed until now that the referential use of a description 'the F' may be captured in one of two ways, which might be pictured as follows:

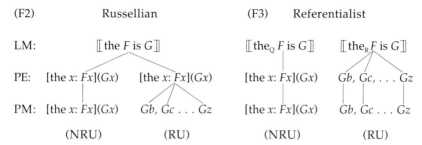

(F2)   Russellian   (F3)   Referentialist

LM: ⟦ the F is G ⟧   ⟦ the$_Q$ F is G ⟧   ⟦ the$_R$ F is G ⟧

PE: [the x: Fx](Gx)   [the x: Fx](Gx)   [the x: Fx](Gx) Gb, Gc, . . . Gz

PM: [the x: Fx](Gx) Gb, Gc . . . Gz [the x: Fx](Gx) Gb, Gc . . . Gz

          (NRU)   (RU)   (NRU)   (RU)

where 'NRU' and 'RU' signify nonreferential and referential usage, respectively. For the Russellian 'the F is G' has one linguistic meaning, represented as ⟦ the F is G ⟧; for the referentialist it has two linguistic meanings, represented as ⟦ the$_Q$ F is G ⟧ and ⟦ the$_R$ F is G ⟧.

Underlying the picture of the referentialist's position given in (F3) is the following argument: (*i*) if a particular utterance u of 'the F is G' expresses the object-independent proposition that whoever or whatever is uniquely F is also G, and a distinct utterance u^* of 'the F is G' expresses the object-dependent proposition that b is G, then the sentence 'the F is G' is semantically ambiguous, i.e., the sentence has two (or more) linguistic meanings (in the sense of 3.3); (*ii*) if the sentence 'the F is G' is ambiguous and the predicate 'is G' is unambiguous, then the definite description 'the F' is ambiguous, i.e., the description has two (or more) linguistic meanings; (*iii*) if the description 'the F' is ambiguous and the predicate 'F' is unambiguous, then the definite article 'the' is ambiguous, i.e., the article has two (or more) linguistic meanings.

It appears to be Recanati's view that descriptions can be treated on this model of indexicals and demonstratives, i.e., on the model of (F1) rather than (F3). That is, the sentence 'the F is G' does *not* have two linguistic meanings; rather, it is "indexical" and expresses either an object-dependent or an object-independent proposition according as the description is used referentially or nonreferentially. Recanati is, then, advocating the following picture:

(F4)   LM: ⟦ the F is G ⟧

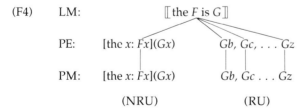

        PE: [the x: Fx](Gx) Gb, Gc, . . . Gz

        PM: [the x: Fx](Gx) Gb, Gc . . . Gz

              (NRU)   (RU)

I find this proposal puzzling. The word 'I' is unambiguous because it always refers to the speaker; a simple sentence of the form 'I am G' is unambiguous because it always expresses an *object-dependent* proposition about the speaker. The demonstrative expression 'that F' is unambiguous because it always refers to the object of the speaker's demonstration and a simple sentence of the form 'that F is G' is unambiguous because it always expresses an *object-dependent* proposition about the object of the speaker's demonstration. On Recanati's proposal, not only may different utterances of 'the *F* is *G*' express different *object-dependent* propositions, but other utterances of this same sentence may express the *object-independent* proposition that whatever is uniquely *F* is *G*. It all depends on whether the description is used referentially or nonreferentially.

It seems to me highly artificial to say that 'the *F* is *G*', 'the *F*' and 'the' are "unambiguous" on this proposal. On some occasions of use 'the *F*' *refers* (or is supposed to *refer*) to some contextually determined individual and the proposition expressed by 'the *F* is *G*' is object-dependent, whereas on other occasions of use 'the *F*' does *not* refer (and is not even intended to refer), and the proposition expressed is a complex quantificational affair. Since two utterly distinct *types* of proposition may be expressed, I fail to see how a theory with such flexibility can fail to be a theory that is postulating a semantical ambiguity. Despite Recanati's remarks to the contrary, it seems to me that his claim that 'the *F*' is unambiguous within his theory is close to being on a par with the claim that the noun 'bank' is unambiguous: on some occasions it is used for ground alongside a river and on others it is used for a type of financial institution.

Of course, even if Recanati is right that one can endorse (A1) and (A2) without postulating a genuine lexical ambiguity, a unitary Russellian theory of descriptions is still simpler than a theory that allows the proposition expressed to be either object-independent or object-dependent depending upon the context of utterance. Furthermore, the putative coherence of such a theory would not demonstrate that (A1) is true and (A3) is false. (There are also problems internal to Recanati's own positive proposal that I shall not address here.)

37. The general observation that one may succeed in conveying something about an individual by using a description that the individual does not satisfy is due to Hampshire (1959), p. 203. (See also Geach, 1962, and Linsky, 1963, 1966.) Indeed, Hampshire's brief discussion of descriptions (pp. 201–4) appears to anticipate quite a lot of subsequent discussion that appeals to misdescription and the distinction between the proposition expressed and the proposition(s) meant.

38. See (e.g.) Kripke (1977), Sainsbury (1979), Searle (1979), Davies (1981), Evans (1982), and Blackburn (1984). As pointed out by Kripke and Searle, we find a similar tension in cases where a proper name is misapplied. To borrow Kripke's example, suppose two people *A* and *B* see Smith in the distance but mistake him for Jones. *A* says "Jones is up early." *B* replies "Yes, he's hard at work too." Devitt (1981) points out some further troubling features of this sort of example that suggest that the distinction between the proposition expressed and the proposition(s) meant will not clear up all of its complexities.

39. Responses to the Argument from Misdescription in the same vein are also presented by Wiggins (1975), and in rather more detail by Kripke (1977), Sainsbury (1979), Searle (1979), and Davies (1981). For remarks that anticipate the Gricean response to the Argument from Misdescription, see Hampshire (1959), pp. 201–4, and Geach (1962), p. 8.

40. Up to now, I have considered only cases in which the speaker is genuinely mistaken about who or what satisfies the description that is being

employed. But as Donnellan (1966) points out, one might perfectly well use a description 'the F' referentially without being sure that the individual one has in mind is the F; indeed, as Hampshire (1959), Donnellan (1966), Grice (1981), and others have pointed out, conceivably one might use the description 'the F' while being quite sure that it does *not* apply to the individual one has in mind, or to any individual at all. The possibility of such cases does not force us to alter the general picture that has emerged so far, though it certainly adds interesting complications in providing an exact specification of when a description is being used referentially.

If the hearer is intended to reason as before, then such cases are no different from the ones we have been considering, except that [the x: $Fx](x = b)$, and very likely [the x: $Fx](Gx)$, will no longer furnish the speaker's grounds for his or her utterance. On the other hand, the speaker may be well aware that the hearer does not believe that b is the F, yet still think it possible to communicate a singular proposition to the effect that b is G by uttering 'the F is G'. (For example, Donnellan considers a case in which both speaker and hearer are aware that the description 'the king' does not strictly apply to the individual being referred to because that individual is a usurper; but they continue to use this description because they are fearful of reprisals. Another example: it may become the practice of the members of a certain group of individuals to use the description 'the F' when they wish to say something about a certain individual. Of course, at a certain point one might well be inclined to treat this description as a name on a par with 'The Holy Roman Empire' or 'The Evening Star'.) A variety of interesting cases can be constructed by tinkering with speakers' and hearers' beliefs about the satisfiers of descriptions and with beliefs about each others' beliefs, but the complexities involved do not seem to provide any insurmountable problems for the Russellian. Indeed, As Kripke (1977, p. 24, note 22) points out, if anything, the fact that many of these cases—for instance, Donnellan's king/usurper case—look a lot like cases involving irony or "inverted commas" seems to actually *weaken* the case for a semantical ambiguity. After all, we want a pragmatic account of irony, not an account that appeals to distinct literal and ironical meanings of expressions. (Once again, these considerations seem to carry over *mutatis mutandis* to other quantifiers, especially indefinite descriptions. On this matter, see Ludlow and Neale (forthcoming).)

41. Wettstein (1982) suggests that Salmon's argument turns on the mistaken assumption that a sentence relativized to a context of utterance C can be evaluated for truth or falsity at a possible world w, when in fact truth or falsity are properly predicated of the proposition expressed. But if Salmon is assuming a standard possible worlds semantics, it is unclear to me what technical or philosophical error Wettstein claims to have discovered in Salmon's discussion.

42. There seems to be no generally agreed upon label. Such phrases are known variously as *incomplete, improper, imperfect,* or *indefinite* definite descriptions.

43. According to Devitt (1981), incomplete descriptions ". . . are ones that are unsuitable for attributive use because only someone with crazy beliefs would use them: it is obvious that they do not denote" (p. 521). Peacocke's example is a clear counterexample to Devitt's claim, as are the examples from Donnellan (1968) and Evans (1982) quoted below.

44. This point is made by Quine (1940), Sellars (1954), Sainsbury (1979), Davies (1981), and Blackburn (1984).

45. Following Barwise and Cooper (1981), let's say that a quantifier $[Dx: Fx]$ is persistent just in case the following is a valid inference:

$$[Dx: Fx]\,(Gx)$$
$$\underline{[\text{every } x: Fx]\,(Hx)}$$
$$[Dx: Hx]\,(Gx)$$

for arbitrary G and H. Strictly speaking, the particular problem concerning incompleteness that I am addressing surfaces only with nonpersistent quantifiers, though a derivative problem surfaces for persistent quantifiers. A precise generalization does not seem to be possible here because of complex issues to do with predication, but very roughly we can say the following. For nonpersistent quantifiers the problem is that $[Dx: Fx](Gx)$ might be false while $[Dx: Fx \,\&\, Hx](Gx)$ is true; for persistent quantifiers the problem is that $[Dx: Fx](Gx)$ might be true while $[Dx: Fx \,\&\, Hx](Gx)$ is false.

46. There seems to be an even more general issue here. As (e.g.) Sellars (1954) and Sperber and Wilson (1986) have stressed, in many cases the linguistic meaning of a sentence—or sentence fragment—radically underdetermines the proposition it is used to express on a given occasion. We have already considered the sort of contextual supplementation that is required where an utterance contains overtly indexical or demonstrative components; but context-sensitivity does not end there. Suppose I ask S how old he is and he replies, "Twenty-five." We want to say that S has expressed the proposition that he is twenty-five years old. Or take the sentence 'This cup is mine'. Here there is no obvious ellipsis, but depending upon the context of utterance I might use this sentence to express the proposition that (e.g.) this cup is owned by me, or that it is being drunk from by me, or that it is being used by me, or that it has been assigned to me.

47. One could, of course, maintain that incompleteness is of no consequence once one takes into account the distinction between the proposition expressed and the proposition(s) meant. The idea here would be that my utterance of 'everybody was sick' expresses the manifestly false proposition that everybody was sick, but in the particular conversational setting it is very clear that I am attempting to *convey* the proposition that everybody who came to the dinner party I had last night was sick (standard forms of Gricean reasoning explaining the leap from the proposition expressed to the proposition meant). I know of no knock-down argument against this approach to incompleteness, but in view of the fact that

context-dependence is such a ubiquitous feature of the use of natural language, it seems likely that the explicit and implicit methods yield predictions more in accordance with our intuitive ascriptions of truth and falsity.

48. When all is said and done, the explicit and implicit methods might turn out to be notational variants of one another. For remarks that suggest otherwise, see Davies (1981) and Soames (1986).

49. For similar suggestions, see also Quine (1940), Vendler (1967), Lewis (1973), Cresswell (1973), and Grice (1981).

50. As noted at the outset, the problem of incompleteness affects plural as well as singular descriptions. In what follows, I shall restrict attention to singular descriptions, though nearly everything I shall have to say ought to carry over *mutatis mutandis* to plurals.

51. Even Kripke (1977) and Evans (1982), both of whom are very sympathetic to a unitary Russellian interpretation of descriptions, suggest that incompleteness may be just enough of a problem for the Russellian to warrant the postulation of a referential interpretation.

52. This has been noted by, e.g., Sellars (1954), Grice (1970, 1981), Evans (1982), Salmon (1982), and Soames (1986). After the bulk of the present chapter was completed, Nathan Salmon drew my attention to a recent paper by Blackburn (1988) in which the same point is made in the context of a discussion of Wettstein's argument.

53. To be more precise, saying that a Russellian description '[the x: Rbx]' may contain a referential component 'b' is very different from saying that the description is referential (in the intended sense) *as long as R is not the identity relation.* A phrase of the form '[the x: $x = b$]' is technically a Russellian definite description; but the claim that referential uses of descriptions do not require distinctive non-Russellian interpretations would indeed be hollow if the Russellian position could be maintained only by employing the identity relation to concoct descriptions of this form (e.g., '[the x: $x =$ that]'). There is nothing in the present work to suggest that descriptions of this form are required to account for referential usage. I am here indebted to Martin Davies.

54. The coordinates of a simple context $<s, a, <d_1,\ldots, d_n>, t, p>$ will not systematically supply a correct completion. Consider the incomplete description 'the President'. Suppose we are in the middle of a conversation right now somewhere in the U.S.A. and I say to you

(i)   The President is very ill.

The fact that the utterance takes place in the U.S.A. does not guarantee that the description 'the President' is elliptical for 'the U.S. President'. For suppose our entire conversation has been about the health of French politicians and I was in fact "talking about" the French President.

It may, at this stage, be tempting to add further coordinates to the formal notion of a context to cover such things as the *topic of discourse* and so on (see, e.g., Lewis, 1975). Husserl (1913, p. 85) suggests that "When a contemporary German speaks of 'the Emperor', he means the present German Emperor." A literal reading of this remark suggests that one's nationality is the relevant coordinate! In 3.4, I argued that we should not expect to be able to provide a formal specification of those features of context that play a role in the calculation of (e.g.) conversational implicatures. (This is not to say, of course, that one cannot attempt to provide a specification of the sorts of principles hearers bring to bear on the interpretation process.) For essentially the same reasons I, think it quite unlikely that an expansion of the formal notion of a context will be of much help in pinning down those factors that, on a given occasion of utterance, may play a role in the full specification of the content of an incomplete description. The important point to note here is that there is absolutely no requirement that a semantical theory be able to provide an account of which contextual features will be drawn upon in order to complete an incomplete description in any given scenario. It is enough if a semantical theory provide the general mechanisms with the aid of which actual complete contents can be specified.

55. In addition to the referential use of descriptions, it is possible to isolate several others.

Appositive Use. Searle (1979), and Barwise and Perry (1983) observe that descriptions may be used *appositively*, as in

(i)   John Smith, the man who threw strawberry ice cream at the Pope, was today sentenced to 50 years hard labor.

This example does not seem to present any sort of additional problem for Russell that will not have to be faced in any event by a semantical theory of apposition. One approach to (i) that might be explored is an analysis in terms of the conjunction of (ii) and (iii):

(ii)   John Smith was today sentenced to 50 years hard labor
(iii)   John Smith was the man who threw strawberry ice cream at the Pope.

Another approach that might be explored is to treat the subject of (i) as a complex definite description [the x: x = John Smith & x threw ice cream at the Pope]. Of course, these suggestions need to be investigated in detail before we can feel comfortable with either of them. Unlike the former proposal, the latter seems to carry over naturally to an example like

(iv)   The sculptor John Smith died today.

Predicative Use. No new problems are presented by an example like

(v)   John Smith is the man who threw strawberry ice cream at the Pope.

Indefinite Use. Tom Wasow has noted examples such as

    (vi)   Look it up in the dictionary!
    (vii)   Let's go to the beach.

These examples are (perhaps) best seen as idiomatic.

Chapter 4

Scope, Substitutivity, and Opacity

4.1 Introductory Remarks

In this chapter, I want to address several related questions concerning substitutivity, ambiguities of scope involving definite descriptions, and the intelligibility of quantified modal logic. Some of the most philosophically interesting scope permutations in natural language involve descriptions that interact with nonextensional operators such as modal expressions and propositional attitude frames. However, W. V. Quine has presented arguments designed to show that quantification into the contexts created by such operators is unintelligible; if these arguments are sound, a unitary Russellian analysis of definite descriptions seems to face some serious problems.

In 4.2, I make some preliminary remarks about the way definite descriptions interact with other operators, drawing upon ideas from Russell and Kripke. In 4.3, I examine the notion of a nonextensional operator and emphasize an important and frequently neglected point made by Russell concerning substitutivity and descriptions. In 4.4, I examine and reject Quine's arguments against quantifying into modal contexts. Expanding upon points made by Smullyan, I argue that the Principle of Substitutivity does not break down in modal contexts—or other intensional contexts—and that a formal derivation of the sort of paradoxical conclusion Quine requires cannot be constructed unless one stipulates in an entirely *ad hoc* fashion that definite descriptions cannot be treated in accordance with Russell's theory and cannot be treated as regular referring expressions. In 4.5, I turn to Quine's worries about quantification into attitude contexts and conclude, tentatively, that there is no obvious way to discredit Quine's claim when it comes to hyperintensional contexts. In 4.6, I turn briefly to descriptions of events. In the light of the discussion in 4.4, it is plausible to suppose that there are inherent ambiguities in sentences containing descriptions of events and modal operators, and that this type of ambiguity may be playing an important role in certain disagreements about the nature and identity of events.

4.2 Descriptions and Scope: Preliminaries

In 2.5, the Theory of Descriptions was disengaged from the formalism of *Principia Mathematica* and relocated within a more general theory of natural language quantification, a theory in which the determiners 'some', 'all', 'no', 'most', 'the', and so on, are treated as members of a unified syntactical and semantical category. Some notation for representing the quantificational structure of English sentences was also introduced, a notation that allowed us to capture the scope ambiguities that may be present in sentences containing two or more quantifiers. For example, very often a sentence that contains two quantifiers will be ambiguous. On the face of it, sentence (1) is ambiguous between (1_1) and (1_2):

(1)   Every man danced with a woman who was wearing Ray-Bans.

(1_1)   [every x: man x]
        ([a y: woman y & y was wearing Ray-Bans] (x danced with y))

(1_2)   [a y: woman y & y was wearing Ray-Bans]
        ([every x: man x] (x danced with y)).

As Whitehead and Russell observe in *Principia Mathematica*, in the simplest cases scope interactions between definite descriptions and many other quantifiers are truth-conditionally inert. For example, although (2) is *formally* ambiguous between (2_1) and (2_2), the two readings are logically equivalent:

(2)   The woman who was wearing Ray-Bans danced with a sailor

(2_1)   [the y: woman y & y was wearing Ray-Bans]
        ([a y: sailor y] (x danced with y))

(2_2)   [a y: sailor y] ([the y: woman y & y was wearing Ray-Bans]
        (x danced with y)).

Similarly with (3), which is formally ambiguous in the same way:

(3)   Every man danced with the woman who was wearing
        Ray-Bans

(3_1)   [the y: woman y & y was wearing Ray-Bans]
        ([every x: man x] (x danced with y))

(3_2)   [every x: man x] ([the y: woman y & y was wearing Ray-Bans]
        (x danced with y)).

Examples like these might tempt one to think that descriptions are always interpreted as if they took wide interpretive scope, and to see this as explicable on the assumption that descriptions are really more like referring expressions than genuine quantifiers. This would be a serious mistake. First, interactions between descriptions and monotone decreasing quantifiers show up truth-conditionally.[1] Recall that, on Russell's account, descriptions interact with negation. The two readings Russell found for (4),

(4)   The king of France is not bald

can be represented as (4_1) and (4_2), according as the description takes wide or narrow scope:

(4_1) [the x: present king of France x] $\neg$ (x is bald)

(4_2) $\neg$ [the x: present king of France x] (x is bald).[2]

The important point, for Russell, is that (4_2) can be true even if there is no present king of France. Now consider the following sentences, which contain monotone decreasing quantifiers:

(5)   Nobody has kissed the present king of France

(6)   Few Frenchmen have seen the present king of France

(7)   Fewer than fifty people have met the present king of France.

It is at least arguable that these sentences, like (4), also admit of readings that can be true even if there is no present king of France. And, presumably, the Russellian will capture these readings by giving the definite descriptions narrow scope.[3]

Second, as we saw in 2.4 and 2.6, definite descriptions may contain pronouns that function as variables bound by higher quantifiers; consequently there are sentences in which definite descriptions must be allowed to take narrow scope:

(8)   The mother of *each girl* waved to *her*
        [each y: girl y] ([the x: x mother-of y] (x waved to y))

(9)   The woman *every Englishman* loves is *his* mother
        [every x: Englishman x] ([the y: woman y & x loves y]
        ([the z: z mother of x] ($y = z$)))

(10)   *Every man* respects the woman *he* marries
        [every x: man x] ([the y: woman y & x marries y] (x respects y))

(11)   The man who bought *each donkey* vaccinated *it*

[each y: donkey y]

([the x: x man x & x bought y] (x vaccinated y)).[4]

Third, as Kripke (1972) has stressed, interpreting a description referentially is not at all the same thing as interpreting it as a wide-scope Russellian description. Following Russell (1905, p. 52) we can capture the so-called *de re–de dicto* distinction, as it shows up in sentences containing descriptions and nonextensional operators, as a product of scope permutation.[5] Consider the following sentences containing descriptions and psychological verbs:

(12)   Mary believes that the man who lives upstairs is a spy

(13)   Mary wants Bill to marry the richest debutante in Dubuque.[6]

Both of these sentences can be represented in either of the following canonical formats,

[the x: Fx] O (Gx)

O [the x: Fx] (Gx)

where O is a dummy unary sentential operator. For example, (12) is ambiguous between the following:

(12_1)   Mary believes that ([the x: man x & lives upstairs x] (spy x))

(12_2)   [the x: man x & lives upstairs x] (Mary believes that (spy x)).

Following Smullyan (1948), the same strategy can be used to account for the *de re–de dicto* distinction as it arises in sentences containing descriptions and modal operators, such as (14) and (15):

(14)   The first person in space might have been Alan Shepard

(15)   The number of planets is necessarily greater than 7.

For example, on the Russellian account (14) is ambiguous between the following:

(14_1)   possibly [the x: first-person-into-space x] (x = Alan Shepard)

(14_2)   [the x: first-person-into-space x] possibly (x = Alan Shepard).

(14_1) says that there is some counterfactual state of affairs in which Alan Shepard was the first person into space, something that is surely true. By contrast, (14_2) says that the person who was in fact the first person, viz. Yuri Gagarin, is such that there is some counterfactual state of affairs in which he is Alan Shepard, something that is surely false.

Sentences like (16) and (17), which contain descriptions and *temporal* operators can (perhaps) be handled in a similar fashion:

(16) The president will spend the week after the election in D.C.

(17) The mayor of Boston used to wear a wig.

It has seemed attractive to some philosophers to explicate the *de re* readings of sentences such as (12)–(17) in terms of referential interpretations of the definite descriptions they contain. For example, Rundle (1965) makes this suggestion for descriptions in modal contexts; and Stalnaker (1972) Partee (1972), and Cole (1978) suggest that a referential interpretation of descriptions can be used to characterize the *de re* readings of descriptions in nonextensional contexts more generally. However, as Cartwright (1968) and Kripke (1971, 1977) have pointed out, it is not possible to provide a fully general account of the *de re–de dicto* distinction in this way. A speaker may make a *de re* use of a sentence like

(18) The number of planets, whatever it is, is necessarily odd

without using the definite description 'the number of planets' referentially (in the sense of (A2) from 3.5). The following passage from Kripke makes the point very clearly:

> Suppose I have no idea how many planets there are, but (for some reason) astronomical theory dictates that that number must be odd. If I say, "The number of planets (whatever it may be) is odd," my description is used attributively. If I am an essentialist, I will also say, "The number of planets (whatever it may be) is necessarily odd," on the grounds that all odd numbers are necessarily odd; and my use is just as attributive as the first case (1977, p. 9).

The point, quite simply, is that the proposition expressed by an utterance of (18) is not *object-dependent*, even if the description is understood *de re*. The Russellian account is quite consistent with this fact. The proposition expressed is descriptive; the *de re* reading is obtained by giving the description wide scope over the modal operator:

(19) [the x: x numbers the planets] $\Box$ (x is odd).

And as Kripke goes on to point out, we find exactly the same situation with definite descriptions in attitude contexts. Suppose Mary has an object-dependent belief concerning the man who lives upstairs, that he is a spy. I may correctly report this state of affairs by saying

(12) Mary believes that the man who lives upstairs is a spy

with the definite description 'the man who lives upstairs' understood *de re*. But this does not mean that I have used the description referentially. I may have no relevant object-dependent thought about the man in question and no intention of communicating such a thought. Russell captures this *de re* reading by giving the definite description wide scope over 'believes that':

(12$_2$) [the x: man x & lives upstairs x] (Mary believes that (spy x)).

As Kripke (1977) and Higginbotham (1987) point out, the situation is the same with indefinite descriptions. Consider the following:

(20) Ralph thinks that an employee in his firm has been selling industrial secrets

(21) Each teacher overheard the rumor that a student of mine cheated

(22) A man from Chicago might have patented the zipper

(23) Next year a man from Texas will be President.

There are certainly readings of these sentences on which the indefinite descriptions are interpreted as existentially quantified phrases with wide scope. But contrary to what is assumed by (e.g.) Fodor and Sag (1982), it would be quite incorrect to account for these readings in terms of referential interpretations of the indefinite descriptions they contain.[7]

Furthermore, Kripke points out that no binary semantical distinction can *replace* Russell's notion of scope. A sentence like

(24) Watson doubts that Holmes believes that Smith's murderer is insane

is *three* ways ambiguous according as the description is given wide, intermediate, or narrow scope:

(24$_1$) [the x: x murdered Smith]
         (Watson doubts that (Holmes believes that (x is insane)))

(24$_2$) Watson doubts that ([the x: x murdered Smith])
         (Holmes believes that (x is insane)))

(24$_3$) Watson doubts that (Holmes believes that
         ([the x: x murdered Smith] (x is insane))).

The reading given by (20$_2$) is neither *de re* nor fully *de dicto*.

Again, the situation is the same with indefinite descriptions. As Kripke observes, the following example is three ways ambiguous according as 'a high American official' is given wide, intermediate, or narrow scope:

> (25) Hoover charged that the Berrigans plotted to kidnap a high American official.

(Similar examples can be constructed using (e.g.) iterated modalities.)

These facts demonstrate quite conclusively that descriptions understood *de re* cannot, in general, be identified with descriptions understood referentially, and that a semantic ambiguity between Russellian and referential interpretations of descriptions cannot *replace* either the *de re–de dicto* distinction or the wide scope-narrow scope distinction as it shows up in nonextensional contexts. So even if one could provide good arguments for the existence of referential interpretations of the definite and indefinite descriptions in some of the examples we have been considering, *the wide scope readings would still be needed.*[8]

It is still arguable, however, that there are serious problems for the Russellian, problems involving the status of quantification into clauses lying within the scope of nonextensional operators. And it has been claimed by at least one philosopher that such "unbridled" quantification leads to one or another kind of logical disaster. This claim will be examined in 4.4 and 4.5. But before any of this, we need to look in detail at the notion of substitutivity.

4.3 Substitutivity

The principle of *the indiscernibility of identicals* (or *Leibniz' Law*, as many people like to call it) says that if A and B are identical, then anything that is true of one is true of the other:

> (1) $(\forall x)(\forall y)(x = y \supset (Fx \supset Fy))$.

I shall take (1) to express a self-evident truth.

It is customary to see the truth of (1) as justifying an important rule of inference, particularly in systems of extensional logic. The rule in question is often called *the Principle of Substitutivity*, or *PS* for short.[9] Abstracting from the details of any particular deductive system, we might state the rule as follows: If (*i*) '*a* = *b*' is a true identity statement, (*ii*) α is a true sentence containing at least one occurrence of *a*, and (*iii*) β is the result of replacing at least one occurrence of *a* in α by an occurrence of *b*, then (*iv*) β is also true. (In the interests of brevity, I shall follow the common practice of talking about "the truth value of a sentence α." In keeping with the discussion in 3.3, this should be construed as shorthand for "the truth value of the proposition expressed by an utterance u of α." Similarly, where I talk of the "the truth conditions of α." No confusion should result from these abbreviatory conventions.)

To fix ideas, let's consider an elementary example. On the basis of the truth of (2), the Principle of Substitutivity sanctions a direct move from the truth of (3) to the truth of (4):

(2)   Cicero = Tully

(3)   It is not the case that (Cicero limped)

(4)   It is not the case that (Tully limped).[10]

Within the sort of system for predicate logic presented by Mates (1966) or Lemmon (1966), a deduction of (4) from (2) and (3) might be set out as follows (assumptions are in {braces}, line numbers are in [square brackets]):

{1}	[1]	$c = t$	P
{2}	[2]	$\neg(Lc)$	P
{1, 2}	[3]	$\neg(Lt)$	1, 2, PS.

Some of the most vexed questions in philosophical logic concern the extent to which PS can be retained as a valid rule of inference if the language under consideration is augmented with various nonextensional operators, such as the modal operators 'necessarily' and 'possibly', and propositional attitude frames like 'Tom thinks that', 'Mary doubts that', and 'I believe that'. In much of the literature on this important topic, there seems to be considerable terminological confusion. With a view to focussing on certain logical properties of linguistic constructions, the contexts created by sentential operators are said to be variously *transparent, opaque, oblique, extensional, nonextensional, intensional,* and *hyperintensional.* Some authors use (e.g.) 'nonextensional' and 'intensional' interchangeably; others do not. Some use 'opaque' and 'intensional' interchangeably; others do not. In order to forestall possible confusion, I propose to begin the present discussion by laying down some ground rules for my own use of 'extensional', and 'intensional' (the definitions I shall use are, I believe, grounded in actual philosophical usage, but they should still be viewed as somewhat stipulative).

First, let's stipulate the following: (*i*) the extension of a referring expression (singular term) 'b' is its referent; (*ii*) the extension of a predicate '— is G' is the class of things that are G; (*iii*) the extension of a sentence is its truth value.[11] An *extensional operator* operates on the extension of its operand. Consider a phrase '$O(\alpha)$' composed of an operator O and an operand α. O is an extensional operator if and only if the extension of '$O(\alpha)$' depends only upon the extension of α. For present purposes, I propose to restrict attention to a particular class of sentential operators. Let's say that an operator O is a *unary sentential* operator if and only if O combines with a single sentence α to form a well-formed expression '$O(\alpha)$'. And let's say that an operator O is a *sentence-forming* operator just in case it combines with its operand to form a *sentence* '$O(\alpha)$'. On this account, the negation sign '$\neg$', is a *unary, sentential, sentence-forming* operator: it combines with a single sentence to form another sentence. (By contrast, the conjunction sign '&' is a *binary*, sentential, sentence-forming operator, and Russell's *iota* operator '(ιx)' is a unary, sentential, *term-forming* operator.)

A unary, sentential, sentence-forming operator O is *extensional* if and only if any sentence β with the same truth value as α can be substituted for α in '$O(\alpha)$' to produce a sentence '$O(\beta)$' with the same truth value as '$O(\alpha)$'. As we might put it, for an extensional, unary, sentential, sentence-forming operator O, the truth value of '$O(\alpha)$' *depends only upon the truth value of* α. On this account, the truth-functional negation operator '$\neg$' is an extensional, unary, sentential, sentence-forming operator. If the following sentences are both true,

(5) $9 > 7$

(6)   Cicero limped

then their respective negations are both false:

(5_1) $\neg (9 > 7)$

(6_1) $\neg$ (Cicero limped).

(Similarly, we can say that an operator O is an extensional, *binary*, sentential, sentence-forming operator if and only if the truth value of '$O(\alpha, \beta)$' depends only upon the truth values of α and β. On this account, the truth-functional connectives '&', '$\supset$', '$\equiv$' and '$\vee$' are all extensional, binary, sentential, sentence-forming operators. Indeed, the class of extensional, sentential, sentence-forming operators is just the class of truth-functional operators.)

In contrast to the negation operator, the modal operator '$\square$' (or 'necessarily') is *non*extensional. (5) and (6) above are both true; but embedding them under '$\square$' produces one true sentence and one false sentence:

(5_2) $\square (9 > 7)$

(6_2) $\square$ (Cicero limped).

Among those sentential operators that are nonextensional, we can distinguish between *intensional* and *hyperintensional* operators (the label 'hyperintensional' is borrowed from Cresswell (1975)). Let's say that a unary, sentential, sentence-forming operator O is intensional just in case the truth value of '$O(\alpha)$' depends not just upon α's truth value but upon α's *truth conditions*. That is, O is intensional if and only if any sentence β with the same truth conditions as α can be substituted for α in '$O(\alpha)$' to produce a sentence '$O(\beta)$' with the same truth value (and truth conditions) as '$O(\alpha)$'.

One of the claims that I shall defend in 4.4 is that the modal operators '$\square$' and '$\diamond$' are intensional in this sense. Sentences (7) and (8) have the same truth conditions:

(7)   Cicero was a human being

(8)   Tully was a human being.

If '$\square$' is intensional, then (7_1) and (8_1) are either both true or both false:

(7_1) $\square$ (Cicero was a human being)

(8_1) $\square$ (Tully was a human being).

To the extent that it is possible to treat certain temporal modifiers as unary, sentential, sentence-forming operators, they are intensional operators. (9) and (10) have the same truth conditions:

(9)   Cicero hailed the news of Caesar's murder

(10)   Tully hailed the news of Caesar's murder.

If we treat 'in 44 B.C.' as a sentential, sentence-forming operator, from (9) and (10) we can produce (9_1) and (10_1), which have the same truth value (true):

(9_1) In 44 B.C. (Cicero hailed the news of Caesar's murder)

(10_1) In 44 B.C. (Tully hailed the news of Caesar's murder).

Let's say that a unary, sentential, sentence-forming operator O is *hyperintensional* if and only if it is neither extensional nor intensional. For a hyperintensional operator O, the truth value of '$O\alpha$' depends upon more than either the truth value or the truth conditions of α. To the extent that it is possible to treat propositional attitude frames like 'Bill thinks that', 'I doubt that', and 'Mary believes that' as unary, sentential, sentence-forming operators, they are hyperintensional. (In a fully worked out and genuinely compositional semantics that respects syntactical structure, propositional attitude frames will not be treated as primitive operators, but it will do no harm to think of them as sentential operators for the very limited semantical claims I shall be making about attitude constructions in this essay.) Although (9) and (10) have the same truth conditions, if we embed these sentences under, say, 'Tom believes that', we get sentences that may differ in truth value:

(9₂) Tom thinks that (Cicero hailed the news of Caesar's murder)

(10₂) Tom thinks that (Tully hailed the news of Caesar's murder).

We can now stipulate the following: (*i*) A word, phrase, or sentence ζ occurs in a *hyperintensional context* if and only if ζ is within the scope of a hyperintensional operator. (*ii*) ζ occurs in an *intensional context* if and only if ζ is within the scope of an intensional operator and not within the scope of any hyperintensional operator. (*iii*) ζ occurs in an *extensional context* if and only if ζ is not within the scope of any intensional or hyperintensional operator.

There are several important things to notice about these definitions. First, the presence of an intensional (or hyperintensional) operator O in a sentence α does not mean that every element in α occurs in an intensional (or hyperintensional) context. Consider the following sentence:

(11) Mary thinks that the number of planets is necessarily odd.

(11) appears to be ambiguous according as the definite description takes narrow, intermediate, or wide scope:

(11₁) Mary thinks that
       ($\Box$ ([the x: x numbers the planets] (x is odd)))

(11₂) Mary thinks that
       ([the x: x numbers the planets] ($\Box$ (x is odd)))

(11₃) [the x: x numbers the planets]
       (Mary thinks that ($\Box$ (x is odd)).[12]

Notice that we cannot talk about whether the quantifier 'the number of planets' in (11) appears in an extensional, intensional, or hyperintensional context. By the definitions given above, such talk makes sense only relative to particular scope assignments. Read as (11₁) or (11₂), 'the number of planets' occurs in a hyperintensional context (n.b. it does not occur in an intensional context when the sentence is read as (11₁)). Read as (11₃) it occurs in an extensional context (because it is not within the scope of any intensional or hyperintensional operator). To make this more concrete, let's assume that there are (at least) three homophonic sentences of English with the superficial syntactical structure we see in (11). Let's assume further that a full characterization of the syntactical structure of a sentence involves a specification of its surface syntax and a specification of its *logical form* understood as a further level of syntactical representation that is essentially a projection of surface syntax under scope assignment. I should stress that as far as the present chapter is concerned, nothing of consequence turns on these assumptions; they can be viewed as expository conveniences (the real motivation for positing this additional level of syntactical structure will emerge in 5.6).

The second thing to notice about the definitions is that no appeal was made to the Principle of Substitutivity (PS) in characterizing the notions of *extensional operator* and *extensional context*. It is clear that PS *does hold* in extensional contexts, but this is not explicitly part of the definition.

The third thing to notice is that PS holds in *intensional* contexts. If '*a*' and '*b*' are referring expressions that both refer to x, and if '*G*' is a simple monadic predicate, then '*Ga*' and '*Gb*' have the same truth conditions: they are both true if and only if x is G. Suppose O is an intensional operator. By definition, the truth value (and truth conditions) of '*O*(*Ga*)' depends only upon the truth conditions of '*Ga*'; and the truth value (and truth conditions) of '*O*(*Gb*)' depends only upon the truth conditions of '*Gb*'. But '*Ga*' and '*Gb*' have the same truth conditions (they are both true if and only if x is G). Hence '*O*(*Ga*)' is true if and only if '*O*(*Gb*)' is true. There is no controversy, then, over whether PS is a valid rule of inference in intensional contexts. The controversial question concerns which operators are intensional and which are hyperintensional. (In 4.4, we shall see that modal operators are intensional and that PS is therefore a valid rule of inference in modal contexts, contrary to claims made by Quine.)

Before looking in detail at substitutivity in nonextensional contexts, it will pay to spend some time on an important (and frequently overlooked) point about substitutivity and definite descriptions in extensional contexts. For historical and expository reasons, I propose to work with a standard formulation of predicate logic with identity.

To the system presented early on in *Principia Mathematica,* in *14 Russell adds nonprimitive terms of the form '$(\iota x)(Fx)$' to stand for descriptive phrases of the form 'the F'. Now it is vitally important to keep in mind that, on Russell's account, a "term" of the form

'$(\iota x)(Fx)$' is not an authentic singular term at all, it is an *abbreviatory device*, defined "contextually" as follows (for exposition, see 2.3):

    ＊14.01 $[(\iota x)(Fx)]G(\iota x)(Fx) =_{df} (\exists x)((\forall y)(Fy \equiv y = x) \& Gx)$.

So a statement of the form '$b = (\iota x)(Fx)$', which may *look like* an identity statement, is really just an abbreviation for a statement of the form

$$(\exists x)((\forall y)(Fy \equiv y = x) \& b = x).$$

This formula contains a genuine identity statement '$b = x$', but it is not *itself* such a statement.

One consequence of Russell's theory, then, is the following:[13]

(D4) Since a sentence of the form '$(\iota x)(Fx) = b$' is an *abbreviation* for a sentence of the form '$(\exists x)((\forall y)(Fy \equiv y=x) \& x=b)$', PS does not sanction a direct move from 'Gb' to '$G(\iota x)(Fx)$' (or vice versa) on the basis of the truth of '$(\iota x)(Fx) = b$'.[14]

Since there appears to be widespread confusion on this matter, I want to spell this out in some detail.

To fix ideas, let's contrast two very simple examples. On the basis of the truth of (12), the Principle of Substitutivity sanctions a direct move from the truth of (13) to the truth of (14):

(12) Cicero = Tully

(13) Cicero limped

(14) Tully limped.

The deduction might be set out as follows:

{1}	[1]	$c = t$	P
{2}	[2]	Lc	P
{1, 2}	[3]	Lt	1, 2, PS

Now consider the superficially similar argument from (15) and (16) to (17):

(15) Scott = the author of *Waverley*

(16) Scott limped

(17) The author of *Waverley* limped.

On a Russellian account of definite descriptions, this argument is of quite a different form from the previous one. To begin with, (15) is not a genuine identity statement: on one side of the identity sign we have 'the author of *Waverley*', which is not a referring expression (singular term). Consequently, the following derivation is illegitimate (where 'Wx' stands for 'x authored *Waverley*'):

{1}	[1]	$s = (\iota x)(Wx)$	P
{2}	[2]	Ls	P
{1, 2}	[3]	$L(\iota x)(Wx)$	1, 2, PS.

The derivation is illegitimate because PS does *not* license a direct from line [2] to line [3] on the basis of the truth of the entry on line [1]. Of course, if the entries on lines [1] and [2] are both true, then so is the entry on line [3]; but that is quite another matter. To say that the Principle of Substitutivity does not sanction a direct move from line [2] to line [3] on the basis of the truth of the entry on line [1] is *not* to say that one cannot *derive* the entry on line [3] from the entries on lines [1] and [2] using normal rules of inference (including, of course, PS). Indeed, it is a straightforward exercise to provide such a derivation if we explicitly introduce Russell's contextual definition for definite descriptions:

{1}	[1]	$s = (\iota x)(Wx)$	P
{2}	[2]	Ls	P
{1}	[3]	$(\exists x)((\forall y)(Wy \equiv y = x) \ \& \ s = x)$	1, *14.01
{4}	[4]	$(\forall y)(Wy \equiv y = b) \ \& \ s = b$	P
{4}	[5]	$s = b$	4, &-elim
{2, 4}	[6]	Lb	2, 5, PS
{4}	[7]	$(\forall y)(Wy \equiv y = b)$	4, &-elim
{2, 4}	[8]	$(\forall y)(Wy \equiv y = b) \ \& \ Lb$	6, 7, &-intro
{2, 4}	[9]	$(\exists x)((\forall y)(Wy \equiv y = x) \ \& \ Lx)$	8, EG
{1, 2}	[10]	$(\exists x)((\forall y)(Wy \equiv y = x) \ \& \ Lx)$	3, 4, 9, EI
{1, 2}	[11]	$L(\iota x)(Wx)$	10, *14.01.

It would certainly be a nuisance if one had to proceed in this way *every* time one wanted to set out a proof involving a definite description. In *Principia Mathematica*, Russell cuts down his workload by demonstrating that although a description '$(\iota x)(Fx)$' is not an authentic singular term, if we keep nonextensional operators out of the picture, then as long as there is exactly one F, for many purposes '$(\iota x)(Fx)$' can be treated *as if* it were an authentic singular term. The following theorem to this effect is proved (on p. 179):

*14.15 $\{(\iota x)(Fx) = b\} \supset \{G(\iota x)(Fx) \equiv Gb\}$.

As Russell puts it, ∗14.15 guarantees that one can "verbally substitute" a referring expression that refers to b for a definite description that denotes b (or vice versa). But it is still a mistake to think that when one performs a "verbal substitution" of this sort, one is making a direct application of PS. ∗14.15 is *not* PS; it is *a derived rule of inference* for a standard first-order language free of nonextensional operators. Adding ∗14.15 to our deductive system, the following derivation is now available:

{1}	[1]	$s = (\imath x)(Wx)$	P
{2}	[2]	Ls	P
{1, 2}	[3]	$L(\imath x)(Wx)$	1, 2, ∗14.15.

And so is the following:

{1}	[1]	$s = (\imath x)(Wx)$	P
{2}	[2]	$\neg(Ls)$	P
{1, 2}	[3]	$\neg(L(\imath x)(Wx))$	1, 2, ∗14.15.

It is surely only *because* ∗14.15 holds that Russell introduces descriptive terms into his formal language: they drastically simplify both his formulae and his proofs. And it is, perhaps, the truth of ∗14.15 that lures many philosophers and linguists into thinking of descriptions as referring expressions. For example, it is a striking feature of Quine's work that (*a*) he explicitly endorses contextual definition ∗14.01 (see Quine 1940, 1950), and (*b*) he very often treats a sentence in which a description flanks one side of the identity sign as if it were a genuine identity statement. (One disastrous consequence of this tension will be investigated in the next section.)

4.4 Descriptions and Modality

In various writings over the years, Quine has attacked the foundations of modal logic, particularly *quantified* modal logic. According to Quine, quantification into the contexts created by 'necessary' and 'possibly' is unintelligible. To be precise, Quine has argued that a variable occurring within the scope of a modal operator O may not be bound by a quantifier that has wider scope than O. If Quine is right about this, one interesting consequence for a Russellian account of definite descriptions is that such phrases may not be understood as taking wide scope over modal operators. In 4.2, it was assumed that the following sentences were ambiguous according as the descriptions take wide or narrow scope:

(1)   The number of planets is necessarily odd

(2)   The first person into space might have been Alan Shepard.

For example, (1) was taken to be ambiguous between (1_1) and (1_2):

(1_1) $(\exists x)((\forall y)(Py \equiv y = x) \ \& \ \Box \ (x \text{ is odd}))$

(1_2) $\Box \ (\exists x)((\forall y)(Py \equiv y = x) \ \& \ (x \text{ is odd})).$

where P stands for 'numbers the planets'.[15] But if quantification into modal contexts is unintelligible, we must apparently give up trying to make sense of (1_1) because the existential quantifier binds a variable within the scope of the modal operator.

Over the course of this section, I shall attempt to show that Quine's argument against quantifying into modal contexts is a failure. It is based on misunderstandings about the Principle of Substitutivity and definite descriptions. (In my opinion, the relevant objections were made very clearly by Smullyan (1948) but technical, conceptual, and scholarly errors by commentators (including Quine) seem to have prevented many people from fully appreciating Smullyan's points.)

Quine's argument against quantifying into modal contexts can be broken down conveniently into two stages. The first stage consists in demonstrating that modal contexts are "referentially opaque." The second consists in showing that quantification into opaque contexts is unintelligible. (There is a unfortunate tendency in the literature to use 'intensional' and 'opaque' interchangeably. One of the views I will be defending in this section is that modal contexts are intensional (in the sense of 4.3) but not opaque.)

Since 'Cicero' and 'Tully' are proper names of the same person, they are coreferring singular terms; thus (3) expresses a genuine identity:

(3)   Cicero = Tully.

Now consider (4):

(4)   Cicero limped.

If we substitute 'Tully' for 'Cicero' in (4), the truth value of the resulting sentence $(4')$ is the same as that of the original:

(4_1) Tully limped.

In Quine's terminology, the grammatical position that is the locus of the substitution in $(4)/(4_1)$ is "purely referential." (The idea behind this terminology seems to be that the contribution made by the position's occupant to determining the truth value of '( ) limped' is exhausted by the occupant's referent. Whatever other semantical features the occupant may have, only its referent is relevant to the truth value of the host sentence.)

As Frege observed, in sentences embedded under certain psychological verbs, there are positions that are *not* purely referential in this sense. Consider (5):

(5)   Bill thinks that Cicero limped.

Suppose (5) and (3) are both true. The Principle of Substitutivity apparently licenses a move from (5) to (5_1), *salva veritate*:

(5_1) Bill thinks that Tully limped.

But it is commonly held that (5) can be true even if (5_1) is false.[16] Linguistic contexts such as those created by 'Bill thinks that', 'I believe that', 'Mary hopes that', and so on, in which there are positions that are *not* purely referential (i.e., linguistic contexts in which the Principle of Substitutivity appears to break down) Quine calls *referentially opaque*.

Let us agree with Quine that attitude contexts are opaque in this sense. The question I want to address is whether *modal* contexts are also opaque. Quine argues that they are; and since he also argues that quantification into opaque contexts is incoherent, he concludes that attempts to make sense of quantification into modal contexts must be abandoned.

In my opinion, it is beyond doubt that Quine's argument for the referential opacity of modal contexts is flawed. And, consequently, even if it is true that quantification into opaque contexts is unintelligible, this is completely irrelevant as far as modal contexts are concerned.

Quine argues as follows. Since the truths of arithmetic are presumably necessary, (6) expresses a true claim:

(6)   □ (9 > 7).

(7) is also true:

(7)   9 = the number of planets.

And so, says Quine, if the occurrence of '9' in (6) occurs in a transparent (i.e., nonopaque) context, we should be able to substitute for it 'the number of planets', *salva veritate*:

(8)   □ (the number of planets > 7).

But (8) is patently false, says Quine. It is surely not a necessary truth that there are more than seven planets: there might well have been, say, six. Therefore, says Quine, the contexts created by 'necessarily' are referentially opaque.[17]

The fallacy in this argument was exposed by Smullyan (1947, 1948). However, a series of misunderstandings has managed to keep the argument alive for more than forty years, and it will take some time to demonstrate in a thoroughly satisfactory way that the argument is intrinsically incapable of making its point. Let me begin by just stating several points that I will go on to defend.

(A) If Quine treats definite descriptions in accordance with Russell's theory, his argument is based on an illegitimate application of PS. PS does *not* license a direct move from (6) to (8) on the basis of the truth of (7).

(B) To say that PS does not sanction a direct move from (6) to (8) on the basis of the truth of (7) is *not to say* that one cannot provide a *derivation* of (8) from (6) and (7) using standard rules of logical inference (including PS). The interesting question, then, is whether (8) is derivable from (6) and (7) if descriptions are treated in accordance with Russell's theory.

(C) The substitution of a definite description is an essential component of Quine's argument. Parallel examples that involve only genuine singular terms do not create even the illusion of a problem.

(D) If Quine decides not to use Russell's Theory of Descriptions and consistently treats 'the number of planets' as a referring expression, then the "paradox" disappears.

Let us now go through these points one at a time.

(A) In view of the discussion in 4.3, there is very little that needs to be added to the remarks already made. The main point is due to Church (1942), who points out that in Russell's system (presented in *Principia Mathematica*) and in Quine's system (presented in *Mathematical Logic*),

> . . . the translation into symbolic notation of the phrase 'the number of planets' would render it either as a description or as a class abstract, and in either case it would be construed contextually; any formal deduction must refer to the unabbreviated forms of the sentences in question, and the unabbreviated form of [(7)] is found actually to contain no name of the number 9 (p. 101).

The point here is that *if* Quine treats definite descriptions in accordance with Russell's theory—as he does in (e.g.) Quine (1940, 1950, 1960)[18]—then his argument is based on an illegitimate application of the Principle of Substitutivity. On a Russellian parsing, (7) is not a genuine identity statement—on one side of the identity sign there is a definite description—hence PS does not sanction a direct move from (6) to (8) on the basis of the truth of (7).

(B) Pursuing the line that 'the number of planets' is a Russellian description—alternatives will be considered under (D) below—the relevant question, then, is whether (8) is derivable from (6) and (7) using standard rules of inference (including PS). As Smullyan (1948) observes, on a Russellian analysis (8) is ambiguous according as the definite description has wide or narrow scope with respect to the modal operator:

(8_1) $(\exists x)((\forall y)(Py \equiv y = x)$ & $\Box\ (x > 7))$

(8_2) $\Box\ (\exists x)((\forall y)(Py \equiv y = x)$ & $(x > 7))$

where 'P' stands for 'numbers the planets'. (8_1) says: concerning the number x such that x in fact uniquely numbers the planets, x is necessarily greater than 7; this is surely true. (8_2), on the other hand, says that it is necessary that whatever number x uniquely numbers the planets, is greater than 7; this is surely false since there might have been, say, six planets.

On the assumption that Quine is presupposing a Russellian account of 'the number of planets', presumably it is (8_2) that provides the analysis of (8) he has in mind. (If Quine thinks that (8) is *false*, presumably he also thinks it is *intelligible*; so he can't opt for (8_1) because the intelligibility of (8_1) presupposes the intelligibility of quantification into modal contexts, which is precisely what Quine seeks to discredit. Similarly, in attempting to refute Quine, the defender of quantified modal logic cannot make any sort of direct appeal to (8_1)—as, say, a *true* reading of (8)—without begging the question against Quine. This is a matter about which there has been much confusion. For discussion, see below.)

The pertinent question, then, is whether (8_2)—the false but uncontroversial reading of (8)—is derivable from (6) and (7) using standard rules of inference (including PS). If (8_2) could be derived, this would show that at least one of the rules of inference employed in the derivation was unreliable in modal contexts.

(Of course, there will be no guarantee that *PS* breaks down; so, if we were being very strict about this, we ought to say that the putative existence of such a derivation would not demonstrate that modal contexts are *opaque* in Quine's sense. Of course, the existence of such a derivation would demonstrate *some* sort of problem, and to that extent surely Quine would be vindicated. Let's say that a context is *murky* if any of the standard rules of inference breaks down in that context. On this account, all opaque contexts are murky, since an opaque context is a context in which one particular rule, PS, breaks down. The interesting question, then, is whether all murky contexts are opaque. In order to give Quine the room to make his case, I shall assume that they are.)

As Smullyan (1948) first pointed out, only the controversial reading (8_1) is derivable from (6) and (7). A derivation of (8_1) might proceed as follows:

{1}	[1]	$9 = (\imath x)(Px)$	P
{2}	[2]	$\Box\,(9 > 7)$	P
{1}	[3]	$(\exists x)((\forall y)(Py \equiv y = x)\ \&\ x = 9)$	1, *14.01
{4}	[4]	$(\forall y)(Py \equiv y = b)\ \&\ b = 9$	P
{4}	[5]	$b = 9$	4, &-elim
{2, 4}	[6]	$\Box\,(b > 7)$	2, 5, PS
{4}	[7]	$(\forall y)(Py \equiv y = b)$	4, &-elim
{2, 4}	[8]	$(\forall y)(Py \equiv y = b)\ \&\ \Box\,(b > 7)$	6, 7, &-intro
{2, 4}	[9]	$(\exists x)((\forall y)(Py \equiv y = x)\ \&\ \Box\,(x > 7))$	8, EG
{1, 2}	[10]	$(\exists x)((\forall y)(Py \equiv y = x)\ \&\ \Box\,(x > 7))$	3, 4, 9, EI.

Since (8_1) *is* derivable from (6) and (7), but (8_2) is not, Smullyan quite rightly concludes that if Quine treats definite descriptions in accordance with Russell's theory, he has not demonstrated that modal contexts are opaque.

In his discussion of modal contexts, Quine does not explicitly reject Russell's Theory of Descriptions—indeed he *endorses* it elsewhere—but he does object to Smullyan's appeal to the theory. In a footnote to "Reference and Modality," he chastises Smullyan for letting a change in the scope of a nonempty description affect truth value. On *Russell's* account, says Quine,

[c]hange in the scope of a description was indifferent to the truth value of any statement, however, unless the description failed to name [sic]. This indifference was important to the fulfillment, by Russell's theory, of its purpose as an analysis or surrogate of the practical idiom of singular description. On the other hand, Smullyan allows difference of scope to affect truth value even where the description concerned succeeds in naming [sic] (p. 154, note 9).

In *Principia Mathematica*, Russell does say that when there is a unique ϕ we may "enlarge or diminish the scope of $(\imath x)(\phi x)$ as much as we please without altering the truth value of any proposition in which it occurs" (p. 70) and that "the scope of $(\imath x)(\phi x)$ does not matter to the truth value of any proposition in which $(\imath x)(\phi x)$ occurs" (p. 184). But it is quite clear (see pp. 70–74 and pp. 184–6) that he is talking about descriptions occurring in *extensional* contexts only (Smullyan empha- sizes this on p. 33 of his paper.) Indeed, one only has to turn to "On Denoting" to see that Quine is misrepresenting Russell. Concerning the nonextensional 'George IV wished to know whether so-and-so', where 'so-and-so' contains a definite description, Russell says,

> We may either eliminate this denoting phrase from the subordinate proposition 'so-and-so', or from the whole proposition in which 'so-and-so' is a mere constituent. Different propositions result according to which we do . . . [W]hen we say, 'George IV wished to know whether Scott was the au- thor of *Waverley*', we normally mean that 'George IV wished to know whether one and only one man wrote *Waverley* and Scott was that man'; but we *may* also mean: 'One and only one man wrote *Waverley*, and George IV wished to know whether Scott was that man'. In the latter, 'the author of *Waverley*' has a *primary* occurrence; in the former a *secondary*. The latter might be expressed by 'George wished to know, concerning the man who in fact wrote *Waverley*, whether he was Scott'. This would be true, for example, if George IV had seen Scott at a distance, and had asked 'Is that Scott?' (p. 52).

On Russell's account, then, (9) is ambiguous between (9₁) and (9₂):

(9)   George IV wished to know whether Scott was the author of *Waverley*

(9₁)   George IV wished to know whether
       $(\exists x)((\forall y)(y$ authored *Waverley* $\equiv y = x)$ & $x =$ Scott)

(9₂) $(\exists x)((\forall y)(y$ authored *Waverley* $\equiv y = x)$ &
       (George IV wished to know whether $(x =$ Scott)).

Even if 'the author of *Waverley*' describes exactly one individual, (9₁) can be true while (9₂) is false (or vice versa). Thus Quine is plainly mistaken when he claims that Smullyan is departing from Russell by allowing the scope of a properly-denoting description to affect truth value.[19] (It is true that Russell did not consider descriptions in *modal* contexts; but one would be hard-pressed to make any sort of case for the view that Russell would have been dismayed by the fact that the Theory of Descriptions predicts ambiguities of scope where descriptions interact with modal operators, ambiguities analogous to the ones it predicts when descriptions interact with attitude verbs.)

Quine's second objection to Smullyan is just as wide of the mark as the first:

> Still what answer is there to Smullyan? Notice to begin with that if we are to bring out Russell's distinction of scopes we must make two contrasting applications of Russell's contextual definition of description. But when the description is in a non-substitutive position, one of the two contrasting ap-

plications of the contextual definition is going to require quantifying into a non-substitutive position. So the appeal to scopes of descriptions does not justify such quantification, it just begs the question (1969, p. 338).

Here, Quine has simply misunderstood the main point of Smullyan's paper. We can agree with Quine that the intelligibility of (8_1) presupposes the intelligibility of quantifying into modal contexts. We can also point out that in a derivation of (8_1) from (6) and (7) it will have to be presupposed that modal contexts are not opaque (see the move from line [5] to line [6] in the derivation given above). But *as a response to Smullyan* this is all quite irrelevant. Smullyan does *not* attempt to refute Quine's argument against quantifying into modal contexts by exposing a scope ambiguity in (8) and then judiciously choosing the reading that does not conflict with the truth of (6) and (7). The ambiguity in (8), if it exists, is irrelevant to Smullyan's main point. What Smullyan demonstrates is that if 'the number of planets' is treated as a Russellian description, then *Quine's lemma that modal contexts are opaque* does not go through. And this he does (*a*) by pointing out, correctly, that the Principle of Substitutivity does not sanction a direct move from (6) to (8) on the basis of the truth of (7), and (*b*) by pointing out that no reading of (8) that does justice to Quine's intuitions of falsity can be derived from (6) and (7) using standard rules of inference. The existence or nonexistence of *another* reading of (8) is irrelevant to *this* point.[20] Of course, Smullyan thinks that (8_1) is intelligible, but this fact plays no direct role in his refutation of Quine because his main point is *not* that there is a true reading of (8), a reading that can be obtained by giving the description wider scope than the modal operator.[21,22]

We must conclude, along with Smullyan, that if 'the number of planets' is treated as a Russellian description, Quine does not succeed in demonstrating that modal contexts are opaque. And if modal contexts are not opaque, the second stage of Quine's argument—that quantification into opaque contexts is unintelligible—is irrelevant as far as *modal* contexts are concerned.

(C) The unlicensed substitution of a definite description turns out to be an *essential* component of Quine's argument. Analogous examples involving the substitution of referring expressions for other referring expressions create no problems whatsoever. For example, if (10) is true,

(10)   Cicero = Tully

PS licenses a direct move from (11) to (12), and there is not the slightest semblance of paradox here:

(11)   □ (Cicero was a human being)

(12)   □ (Tully was a human being).

But how can we be sure that we have not just picked one example for which we do not get a paradoxical result? Generalizing from this example, we get the following schema:

(R4) If '*a*' and '*b*' are genuine referring expressions and if '*a* = *b*' is true, then the Principle of Substitutivity licenses a direct move from '□ (*Fa*)' to '□ (*Fb*)', *salva veritate*.

As Quine observes, to subscribe to the validity of (R4) is to subscribe to the view that if an individual has a particular property necessarily, then it has that property however it (that individual) is singled out. Dubbing this view "Aristotelian essentialism," Quine proceeds to declare that (R4) is untenable.

But the notion of "essentialism" inherent in (R4) is extraordinarily weak and not obviously objectionable in itself. It is *not* the view that every object has an essence that distinguishes it from all other objects in all other circumstances; it is merely the view that *if* an object has any of its properties necessarily, it has them no matter what expression is used to pick out that object.[23] We may understand perfectly well what an essential property of an object would be; the controversial question is whether any nontrivial properties *are* essential, and (R4) is silent on this matter. As long as one is prepared to accept this weak form of "essentialism" there is no barrier to accepting (R4). And if (R4) is true, modal contexts are transparent quite generally: substituting one referring expression for another with the same referent does not affect truth value.

(D) It is clear, then, that modal contexts are unproblematic if definite descriptions are treated in accordance with Russell's theory. Consequently, if Quine is still determined to find a way of demonstrating that modal contexts are opaque (or at least murky), he will have to present an alternative to Russell's account of definite descriptions. Of course, to the extent that one is happy with an independently motivated Russellian account of descriptions, it would be rather pointless and perverse to construct an alternative designed solely to create trouble for modal contexts; so for expository purposes let's assume, for a moment, that the Quinean has some independent motivation for constructing an alternative to Russell's quantificational account.

The construction of an alternative theory presents Quine with three challenges. (*i*) The alternative analysis must deliver a reading of (7) that is true. (*ii*) It must deliver a reading of (8) that is false. (*iii*) The false reading of (8) must be derivable from (6) and the true reading of (7).

There appear to be only two serious options: (*a*) treat definite descriptions as referring expressions; (*b*) treat them as quasi-referring expressions that do *not* satisfy (R3), i.e., treat them as "nonrigid referring expressions."

(*a*) Suppose Quine treats definite descriptions as rigid referring expressions, in the spirit of the received treatments of names and demonstratives.[24] In particular, suppose he treats 'the number of planets' as a name of nine. Quine still cannot make his case. If 'the number of planets' as it occurs in (7) is interpreted as a referring expression (as referring to 9), then the reading of (8) in which the occurrence of the same description is also interpreted as a referring expression (again referring to 9) *does* follow from (6) and (7). But this reading of (8) is just as true as (6).[25]

(*b*) Suppose Quine treats descriptions as "nonrigid referring expressions." It looks as though Quine can then get his desired result on the assumption that PS, EG, and so on are valid rules of inference that may be used on sentences containing nonrigid singular terms. This is I believe, the heart of the matter. To the extent that there is a successful construal of Quine's argument for the referential opacity of modal contexts, such a construal will have to presuppose that definite descriptions are nonrigid referring expressions.

But there is no evidence that descriptions are nonrigid referring expressions; indeed, there is no good evidence for the existence of nonrigid referring expressions in natural language at all. The class of noun phrases appears to split very cleanly into two subclasses, the class of rigid referring expressions and the class of quantifiers. And we have seen plenty of good reasons for thinking that definite descriptions belong with the quantifiers and not with the referring expressions. Moreover, as we shall see in Chapters 5 and 6, there are good reasons for thinking that every pronoun occupying a noun phrase position is either a rigid referring expression or a quantifier. In short, there does not seem to be any good reason to suppose that we must complicate our semantical theory by positing a third category of noun phrases. So not only must Quine motivate such a category, he must also demonstrate that an analysis of descriptions as nonrigid referring expressions *has to be used* in analysing 'the number of planets' in (7) and (8). And to do that, he needs an argument against the Russellian analysis that does not beg the question—he cannot argue against Russell's theory by just pointing out that on Russell's account modal contexts are transparent. In the absence of the relevant arguments, we are perfectly justified in continuing the independently motivated and highly rewarding practice of treating definite descriptions as quantified expressions in accordance with Russell's theory.

To conclude, then, modal contexts are not opaque, they are just intensional. The real moral that emerges from the discussion is that the logical behavior of noun phrases in sentences that contain modal intensional operators provides yet another reason for treating descriptions as quantifiers rather than as referring expressions.

4.5 Descriptions and Attitudes

Propositional attitude ascriptions pose some very general semantical problems that I shall not attempt to address here. In this section, all I want to do is demonstrate that scope permutations involving descriptions and attitude frames do not give rise to any problems over and above those that must be faced in any case.

Consider the following three sentences:

(1)   Mary believes that the man who lives upstairs is a spy

(2)   Mary hopes that the manager is good-natured

(3)   Mary wants Bill to marry the richest debutante in Dubuque.

These sentences exhibit a *de re–de dicto* ambiguity that the Russellian would like to explain in terms of scope permutation. In particular, the *de re* readings are to be captured by giving the descriptions wider scope than the psychological verbs:

(1₁)   [the x: man who lives upstairs x] (Mary believes that (spy x))

(2₁)   [the x: manager x] (Mary hopes that (good-natured x))

(3₁)   [the x: richest debutante in Dubuque x]
(Mary wants (Bill to marry x)).

The question that confronts us now is whether these readings are genuinely intelligible. According to Quine (1956), quantification into attitude contexts is a "dubious business" (because such contexts are opaque) but at the same time it appears to be indispensible.

Why exactly, is Quine worried about quantification into attitude contexts? (4) is a genuine identity statement:

(4)   Cicero = Tully.

Consequently, the Principle of Substitutivity would appear to license a direct move from (5) to (6), *salva veritate*:

(5)   Bill thinks that Cicero denounced Catiline

(6)   Bill thinks that Tully denounced Catiline.

But it is commonly held that (5) can be true while (6) is false (or vice versa). In which case the position marked by '( )' in (7) is not purely referential:

(7)   Bill thinks that ( ) denounced Catiline.

In short, the contexts created by 'Bill thinks that' (and other attitude frames) are opaque, and this, Quine claims, leads to trouble with quantification.

Consider (8), which on Russell's account is ambiguous between (8_1) and (8_2):

(8)   Bill believes that someone denounced Catiline

(8_1) $(\exists x)$(Bill believes that x denounced Catiline)

(8_2) Bill believes that $(\exists x)(x$ denounced Catiline).

Quine has no worries about (8_2). But (8_1) he finds problematic: Who is this person x, Quine asks, such that Bill believes x denounced Catiline? By (4) Cicero, hence Tully? But to suppose this would be to conflict with the falsity of (5). Quantification into attitude contexts simply makes no sense. If a singular term position within a sentence is not purely referential, then that position may not be occupied by a variable bound by an initially placed quantifier.

There seem to be three premises in this argument: (*i*) attitude contexts are opaque (i.e., singular term positions in attitude contexts are not "purely referential"); (*ii*) no occurrence of a singular term in an opaque context is purely referential; and (*iii*) a bindable occurrence of a variable must be purely referential.[26]

Before we examine these premises, I want to make a brief point about the referential use of definite descriptions. Even if Quine's argument is successful, it lends no support to the view that definite descriptions are ambiguous between Russellian and referential interpretations. The following line of reasoning (which I have encountered several times in discussion) simply will not do: "*Any plausible semantical theory must be able to account for the* de re *readings of sentences (1)–(3)*:

(1)   Mary believes that the man who lives upstairs is a spy

(2)   Mary hopes that the manager is good-natured

(3)   Mary wants Bill to marry the richest debutante in Dubuque.

But if Quine is right that we cannot coherently quantify across verbs of propositional attitude, the Russellian is precluded from capturing the de re readings of such sentences by giving the descriptions wide scope. Therefore a unitary Russellian analysis of definite descriptions fails. Therefore we are forced to capture the relevant de re *readings by treating the definite descriptions as referring expressions rather than quantifiers."*

There is a serious mistake in this chain of reasoning. If quantification into an opaque context really is incoherent, the referentialist's account of the *de re* readings of (1)-(3) fails for the same reasons as the Russellian account. Since a singular term position in an opaque context is not purely referential, the position in which the referentialist would place an allegedly referential description—the position in which the Russellian would place a variable—is not purely referential. And by premise (*ii*) it therefore follows that neither the referentialist's description nor the Russellian's variable is purely referential. (Additionally, by premise (*iii*) the Russellian's variable is not bindable.) Consequently, if Quine's argument goes through, a definite description understood *de re* in an opaque context cannot be interpreted as a device of pure reference.

The referentialist might now attempt to devise some sort of composite theory according to which an allegedly referential description is not *purely* referential. On such an account, it might be suggested that the descriptive content of a referential description as well as its referent gets into a specification of truth conditions. But this gets the referentialist nowhere because there are cases in which *de re* readings are not correctly captured by treating the relevant descriptions referentially at all. Take (1) above. I may utter this sentence and say something true even though I have no idea who the man who lives upstairs is and no intention to communicate to you an object-dependent proposition about that man. And as Kripke (1977) has emphasized, although the sentence will receive its *de re* reading in such a situation, a referential interpretation, in the sense of (A2), of 'the man who lives upstairs' would be quite incorrect. *A fortiori*, the composite interpretation will also get things wrong. *Whether or not* Quine's argument goes through, a *general* account of the *de re* readings of sentences containing descriptions and attitude verbs cannot be provided by simply treating the descriptions as referring expressions, even impure referring expressions.

Let's now return to Quine's argument. Unlike the argument against quantifying into modal contexts, the argument against quantifying into attitude contexts cannot be defused by paying attention to the distinction between referring expressions and descriptions. There really *do* seem to be attitude ascriptions that do not license the substitution of coreferential expressions. However, as several philosophers have pointed out, it is by no means clear what follows from this. Suppose that '$a = b$' and 'Mary believes that $F(a)$' are both true, and 'Mary believes that $F(b)$' is false. What does this really show? As (e.g.) Kaplan (1986) observes, it shows that at least one of the occurrences of 'a' and 'b' is not purely referential. It does *not* show that *no* referring expression may have a purely referential occurrence in the embedded singular term position in 'Mary believes that $F(\ )$'. In particular, it does not show that an occurrence of a bindable variable in that position is not purely referential. So until premise (*ii*) of Quine's argument is established, we do not have to worry about quantification into attitude contexts. Whatever special problems attitude contexts pose for a semantical theory, we can rest content with the thought that the Russellian account of the *de re* readings of sentences like (1)-(3) seems to be intact.

4.6 Descriptions of Events

So far I have considered only descriptions of persons and material objects. However, following Davidson (1967) and Higginbotham (1983), it is plausible to suppose that phrases like 'the flood', 'the shortcircuit', 'the sinking of the *Titanic*', 'Nixon's resignation', 'Nixon's resigning', 'Mary's departure', 'Mary's departing' and so on, are definite descriptions of *events*. At this juncture, I should like to make one or two programmatic remarks about such phrases as they occur in modal contexts and about quantification over events more generally. There are several reasons for this. First, I want briefly to illustrate the applicability of Russell's theory to many event descriptions.[27] Second, it is at least arguable that an adequate semantics for expressions that purport to refer to, or quantify over, events might provide an alternative approach to the problem of incomplete quantifiers (3.7). Third, I want to sketch a difficulty that may arise if one does not pay careful attention to the logical forms of sentences containing event descriptions and modal operators. Talk of events is widespread in metaphysics, the philosophy of mind, and the philosophy of action; consequently it seems to me vitally important to be clear about the semantics of sentences containing expressions that purport to denote events, especially when these sentences contain modal operators. I expect such considerations to be of considerable importance to a future project, the aims of which I shall not delineate here. For the present, I shall restrict myself to a few brief and highly schematic remarks.

Davidson has argued that without an ontology of events—construed as unrepeatable particulars—much of our philosophical and daily discourse is unintelligible. Philosophical discussion of causation, for example, makes sense only if we assume that causes and effects are events and that causation is a relation that holds between events. Philosophical theses such as metaphysical determinism and the identity theory of mind are, according to Davidson, best understood as theses about events: Determinism is the thesis that every event is causally determined by antecedent events, and the identity theory is the thesis that every mental event is identical with some physical event. Moreover, Davidson argues that reference to events is built into natural language and that once we see this we can capture the logical structure of certain sentence types, in particular, *action* sentences.

Consider the following:

(1)   Mary left
(2)   Mary left hastily
(3)   Mary left on a bicycle
(4)   Mary left hastily on a bicycle.

Clearly (1) is entailed by each of (2)-(4). And (2) and (3) are both entailed by (4). Davidson suggests that we capture these logical relationships by quantifying over events. An ordinary action verb like 'leave' is said to contain an additional argument place for an event (construed as a particular) and the sentences above are then treated as existential quantifications over events. For instance, (1) is true if and only if there is an event that was a leaving of Mary; and so its logical form can be represented as

(1_1) $(\exists e)(\text{left}(\text{Mary}, e))$

where e ranges over events. If the adverb 'hastily' is then treated as an "adjective of events" the logical form of (2) can be rendered as

(2_1) $(\exists e)(\text{left}(\text{Mary}, e) \ \& \ \text{hasty}(e))$

and the entailment relationship thereby captured as a matter of first-order logic. (The fact that (4) entails (2) and (3) is to be captured in the same way.)

The semantic proposal of Davidson's I want to focus on here is the very natural one that noun phrases like 'Mary's departure', 'Mary's departing', 'the sinking of the Titanic', 'the short circuit that caused the fire', and so on, are *definite descriptions of events*. Consider the following sentences:

(5)   Mary's departure has upset Bill

(6)   Tom thinks that Mary's departure has upset Bill.

It is clear that 'Mary's departure' is not a referring expression that names an event. The reasoning here is straightforwardly Russellian and is exactly the same as that given in the discussion of referring expressions and description in 2.2. As long as 'Mary', 'Bill', and 'Tom' are referring expressions, utterances of (5) and (6) will expresses perfectly determinate propositions with perfectly determinate truth conditions *even if Mary has not departed*. Moreover, an utterance of (6) may express a *true* proposition even if Mary has not departed. That is, the absence of a denotation for 'Mary's departure' does not prevent utterances of (5) and (6) from expressing determinate propositions.

Following Chomsky (1970), let's call 'departure' a *derived nominal* and 'departing' a *gerundive nominal*. In early versions of transformational grammar, both types of nominal were derived by transformational rule from the underlying verb 'depart'. However, as Chomsky points out, there are some important syntactical and semantical differences between these types of phrases that ought to steer the syntactician away from a transformational analysis of derived nominals.[28] Derived nominals have all the key properties of genuine *common nouns*. They may combine with determiners to form full noun phrases, they admit prenominal adjectives, they pluralize, they can function as the direct objects of certain verbs, and they resist tense, aspect, adverbial-type modification, and negation.[29] Consequently, I propose to represent 'Mary's departure' in the same fashion as 'Mary's cat' or 'Mary's mother', viz., as a simple description:

(7)   [the e: e departure-of-Mary].

There are also semantic differences between derived and gerundive nominals. Whereas there is a regular and systematic relationship between verbs and gerundive forms, the relationship between verbs and corresponding derived nominals is irregular and idiosyncratic. There are verbs that have no corresponding derived nominal and derived nominals that do not really correspond to any verb. More importantly for our concerns, the semantic relationship between verbs and derived nominals is not at all systematic. From 'do' we get 'deed', from 'marry' we get 'marriage', from 'ignore' we get 'ignorance', and so on.

In view of the syntactical and semantical differences between gerundive and derived nominals, I propose to represent 'Mary's departing' rather differently from 'Mary's departure'. If we hold onto the idea that a noun phrase containing a gerundive nominal is derived from an underlying sentence, we can treat 'Mary's departing' as coming from 'Mary departs', which on Davidson's account has the following logical form:

(8) $(\exists e)(\text{depart}(\text{Mary}, e))$.

A simple operation then converts the underlying sentence into the definite description (9):

(9)   [the e: depart(Mary, e)].

By treating derived nominals as primitive nouns and gerundive nominals as derived from verbs we can continue to make use of our logical notation without positing any regular semantical connection between derived and gerundive nominals.

I want now to make a few brief remarks about event descriptions in modal contexts.

' I take it that, as a matter of historical fact, the following sentence is true:

(10)   Richard Nixon = the 37th U.S. President.

But remember, this is not a simple identity statement. On Russell's account, the logical form (10) is given by (11):

(11)   [the x: 37th President x] (x = Richard Nixon)

In the light of Smullyan's observations about descriptions in modal contexts, we can have no time for the following argument: (*i*) there are possible worlds in which Richard Nixon was not the 37th President; (*ii*) if $a = b$, then necessarily $a = b$; therefore (*iii*) sentence (10) is false.

The mistake here is obvious. Premise (*i*) is ambiguous between (12$_1$) and (12$_2$):

(12$_1$) $\Diamond$ [the x: 37th President x] (x = Richard Nixon)

(12$_2$)   [the x: 37th President x] $\Diamond$ (x = Richard Nixon).

Read as (12$_1$), premise (*i*) is very likely true; read as (12$_2$) it begs the question. And from (12$_1$) and premise (*ii*)—the necessity of identity—one cannot derive the negation of (11).

Now let's look at a similar example involving descriptions of events. In light of the fact that Richard Nixon was the 37th President, the gerundive nominals 'Nixon's resigning' and 'the 37th President's resigning' are satisfied by (describe/denote) the same event. That is, (13) expresses a truth:

(13)   Nixon's resigning = the 37th President's resigning.

(As Davidson frequently reminds us, we may describe the same individual event in different ways.) But again, this is not a simple identity statement; on the account we are considering, the logical form (13) is given by (13_1):

(13_1) [the e: resign(Nixon, e)]

([the f: [the x: 37th President x] (resign(x, f))] ($e \neq f$))).

Consider the following argument: (*i*) there are possible worlds in which the 37th President's resigning was not Richard Nixon's resigning (because there are possible worlds in which Richard Nixon was not the 37th President); (*ii*) if $a = b$, then necessarily $a = b$; therefore (*iii*) sentence (13) is false.

It seems to me that this argument is fallacious in the same way as the last one. Premise (*i*) is ambiguous between (14_1) and (14_2):

(14_1) $\Diamond$ ([the e: resign(Nixon, e)]

([The f: [the x: 37th President x] (resign(x, f))] ($e \neq f$)))

(14_2) [the e: resign(Nixon, e)]

([the f: [the x: 37th President x] (resign(x, f))] ($\Diamond$ ($e \neq f$))).[30]

Read as (14_1), premise (*i*) is true; read as (14_2) it begs the question. And from (14_1) and premise (*ii*)—the necessity of identity—one cannot derive the negation of (13_1).

I suspect that this particular type of ambiguity is responsible for a number of problems surrounding discussion of events. I do not want to dwell on this matter right now, but one or two brief remarks seem to be in order. Davidson (1968) and others have suggested that for events e and f, $e = f$ if and only if e and f have the same causes and effects. Other philosophers have professed adherence to something like the following: for events e and f, $e = f$ if and only if e and f occur within the same spatio-temporal regions. I don't wish to discuss the various merits of such proposals here; rather I want to look briefly at a certain type of argument against such proposals that is often appealed to by philosophers who are unsympathetic to one or other of them. Brand (1977, 1985), for instance, argues that neither causal indiscernibility nor spatio-temporal coincidence enough to nail down an event identity because distinct events may occur within the very same regions. Consider the following example. Jones raises his arm at noon and thereby signals the chairman. On both the causal indiscernibility and the spatio-temporal coincidence accounts, there may be nothing to prohibit Jones' raising his arm at noon and Jones' signaling the chairman at noon from being one and the same event (indeed, Davidson explicitly allows for such a possibility). So (15), the logical form of which can be given by (15₁), might well be true:

(15)   Jones's raising his arm at t = Jones signaling the chairman at t

(15₁)   [the f: raise(Jones, Jones's arm, f)]
([the e: signal(Jones, the chairman, e)]($e = f$).[31]

Brand feels that (15) is false:

> Since signaling by raising one's arm is a matter of convention, there are, to use the common idiom, possible worlds in which Jones raised his arm but did not signal and there are possible worlds in which he signaled without raising his arm. Hence [(25)] is false. There are, rather, two events that occurred in a single spatio-temporal region (1977, p. 334).

(On Brand's own account, only events that *necessarily* occur in the same region are to be identified. More precisely, if e and f range over events, r ranges over spatio-temporal regions, and W stands for 'occurs within', then

$$e = f \quad \text{iff} \quad \Box \, (\forall r)(Wer \equiv Wfr).[32]$$

According to Brand, this yields the right result when applied to the example at hand. Even if Jones signaled the chairman by raising his arm, and even if Jones's raising his arm and Jones's signaling the chairman occur in the same spatio-temporal region, it does not follow that his raising his arm and his signaling the Chairman are one and the same event.)

It seems to me that the modal consideration Brand brings into play against Davidson trades on the scope confusion outlined above. When Brand says that there are "possible worlds in which Jones raised his arm but did not signal and there are possible worlds in which he signaled without raising his arm," does he mean (16₁) or (16₂)?

(16₁)   ◇ ([the e: signal(Jones, the chairman, e)]
([the f: raise(Jones, Jones's arm, f)] ($e \neq f$))

(16₂)   [the e: signal(Jones, the chairman, e)]
([the f: raise(Jones, Jones's arm, f)] (◇ ($e \neq f$))).

Read as (16₁), this premise is quite likely true; read as (16₂) it simply begs the question. And from (16₁) together with the necessity of identity one cannot derive the negation of (15). I.e., it does not follow from that Jones's raising his arm and Jones' signaling the chairman—the events that took place in the actual world—are not to be identified. Perhaps they are *not* the same event; but this cannot be demonstrated in the way Brand envisages.

It is my belief that the type of scope consideration we have been looking at in this section needs to be taken very seriously if we are to get to the bottom of a certain type of dispute concerning accidental and essential properties of events, the relationship between the mental and the physical, and the alleged incompatibility of free will and determinism; but these are topics for another occasion.[33]

4.7 Concluding Remarks

In this chapter we have seen that the interpretation of definite descriptions in nonextensional contexts, such as those created by modal operators and verbs of propositional attitude, provides no support either for the view that descriptions are ambiguous between quantificational and referential interpretations.

Quine was wrong when he claimed that modal contexts are opaque; they are merely intensional, and the Principle of Substitutivity is a perfectly valid rule of inference in intensional contexts. To this extent, no problems arise in interpreting quantified modal logic once we distinguish clearly between referring expressions and quantified expressions such as definite descriptions. Consequently, we can make perfectly good sense of the *de re* readings of sentences containing descriptions and modal operators by giving the descriptions wide scope (the referential account of such readings fails in certain cases because a description may be given wide scope without being used referentially).[34]

Concerning attitude contexts, we have seen that Quine's argument cannot be defused by observing the distinction between referring expressions and quantifiers. The Russellian seeks to capture the relevant *de re* reading of sentences containing attitude verbs and descriptions by allowing descriptions to bind variables within attitude contexts. The viability of this seems to depend on whether or not Quine's argument from opacity to incoherence is sound.[35]

Notes

1.   Following Barwise and Cooper (1981), a quantifier $[Dx: Fx]$ is monotone decreasing just in case the following is a valid inference:

$[Dx: Fx] (Gx)$
$\underline{[\text{every } x: Hx] (Gx)}$
$[Dx: Fx] (Hx).$

2. It is not universally held that (4) is genuinely ambiguous. See, e.g., Kempson (1975). For a brief discussion, see the final note to this chapter.

3. If monotone decreasing quantifiers are treated as simple quantifiers, then the definite descriptions take narrow scope with respect to those quantifiers; if such quantifiers are decomposed, then the definite descriptions simply lie within the scope of the negation operators that result from decomposition.

4. Sentences (8)–(11) are counterexamples to Hornstein's (1984) claim that definite descriptions belong to a special class of quantifiers that insist on wide scope. According to Hornstein, there are several properties that distinguish quantifiers of the form 'a certain F', 'any F', and 'the F' ("Type I" quantifiers) from those of the form (e.g.) 'every F', and 'an F' ("Type II" quantifiers). Type I quantifiers are said to have "the same logical syntax as names" in that they do not form "operator-variable structures" and are "interpreted as if they had widest possible scope" (p. 44). Type II quantifiers, by contrast, form operator-variable structures and enter into scope interactions in the usual ways.

   Of concern to us here are Hornstein's views about the scope possibilities for definite descriptions. I have followed Russell in assuming that descriptions may enter into scope relations with other operators. But according to Hornstein, definite descriptions are Type I quantifiers and hence take widest possible scope. Since much of the discussion in the present chapter is predicated on the assumption that descriptions give rise to scope ambiguities in the presence of other operators, it is important to see straight away that descriptions are *not* Type I quantifiers. (For reasons that will become clear in Chapter 6, I doubt that there are *any* Type I quantifiers; but that is not something I want to assume or argue for right now.)

   Consider the following sentences:

   (i)   Every boy loves a girl
   (ii)   A girl loves every boy
   (iii) Every boy loves a certain girl
   (iv)   A certain girl loves every boy.

   According to Hornstein, although sentences (i) and (ii) are ambiguous, sentences (iii) and (iv) are not; the Type I quantifier 'a certain girl' must be understood as having wider scope than 'every man'. (I should mention that virtually everyone I have questioned disagrees with Hornstein's judgments that (iii) and (iv) are not ambiguous in the same way as (i) and (ii). Indeed, I notice that Lemmon (1966, p. 100) uses (iii)—which he attributes to Peter Geach—as his first example of a sentence that exhibits a scope ambiguity arising from the presence of two quantifiers. It seems to me that the real difference between 'an F' and 'a certain F' is not that the latter must take widest possible scope but rather that an occurrence of 'certain' after 'a' serves to conventionally implicate that the speaker has object-dependent grounds for his or her utterance or that someone to whom an attitude is ascribed in the utterance stands in some cognitive relation to an object-dependent proposition. For the sake of argument, however, let us grant to Hornstein that 'a certain F' must take wide scope and that consequently (iii) and (iv) are unambiguous. (For further discussion of Hornstein's analysis of 'a certain', see Hintikka (1986) and Hornstein (1988).)

According to Hornstein, a sentence like (v) is *un*ambiguous and so provides support for his view that definite descriptions are Type I quantifiers:

(v)   Every man danced with the woman wearing Ray-Bans.

As noted in the main text, (v) is indeed *truth-conditionally* unambiguous. That is, it doesn't matter to the truth conditions of (v) whether 'every man' or 'the woman wearing Ray-Bans' is given wider scope, because (vi) and (vii) are logically equivalent:

(vi)   [every x: man x] ([a y: woman y & y was wearing Ray-Bans] (x danced with y))

(vii)   [a y: woman y & y was wearing Ray-Bans] ([every x: man x] (x danced with y)).

But this fact by itself does not mean that (v) is not *formally* ambiguous (especially not for Hornstein, who claims (*a*) that truth conditions have no place in a semantical theory, and (*b*) that "scope is a syntactic notion describing formal relations among elements in a string" (p. 50).) Indeed, when thinking about the scope possibilities for definite descriptions it is important not to be taken in by the fact that relative scope assignment is truth-conditionally inert in a simple example like (v). In the sorts of Geach/Mates examples that initiated this note, the choice of scope is crucial:

(viii) The mother of *each girl* waved to *her*
        [each y: girl y] ([the x: x mother-of y] (x waved to y))

(ix)   The woman *every Englishman* loves is *his* mother
        [every x: Englishman x] ([the y: woman y & x loves y] ([the z: z mother of x] ($y = z$)))

(x)   *Every man* respects the woman *he* marries
        [every x: man x] ([the y: woman y & x marries y] (x respects y))

(xi)   The man who bought *each donkey* vaccinated *it*
        [each y: donkey y]([the x: x man x & x bought y] (x vaccinated y)).

On the anaphoric readings intended, the definite descriptions clearly take narrow scope. The upshot of this is that some occurrences of descriptions clearly *are* interpreted as taking narrow scope; *so by one of Hornstein's own criteria*, definite descriptions are not Type I quantifiers. (When we turn to nonextensional contexts, we shall see that there are many other cases in which descriptions take narrow scope.)

One might be tempted to respond on Hornstein's behalf by pointing out that what he actually *says* is that Type I quantifiers take "widest possible scope" not "maximally wide scope". With this phrasing in mind, one might then suggest that Hornstein's idea is that Type I quantifiers take maximally wide scope *whenever they can*, but may be forced to take narrower scope in certain linguistic environments. But a principled account would then be needed of when and why, exactly, a Type I quantifier would be allowed to take less than maximally wide scope, an account that (a) managed to respect the Type I-Type II distinction (in particular, the allegedly crucial difference in their scope properties), and (b) could be reconciled with the claim that Type I quantifiers have "the same logical syntax as names" and hence do not form "operator-variable structures." Hornstein's discussion of (ix) suggests that he is aware of part of the problem. In order to get 'every Englishman' (which is embedded in a restrictive relative clause) to bind the anaphoric pronoun 'his', he appeals to "reconstruction," a mechanism that allows one to interpret 'every Englishman' *as if* it took wide scope. But this is an empty appeal. As Soames (1987) points out, Hornstein cannot appeal to a mechanism that allows one to "interpret" the Type II quantifiers "as if" they took wide scope over the Type I quantifiers in (viii)–(x) because he rejects the standard semantical notion of scope needed to make sense of this idea in favor of a purely *syntactical* notion. At this point Hornstein could either (a) reject the alleged syntactical notion of scope in favor of the standard semantical notion, or (b) retain the alleged syntactical notion and treat descriptions as quantifiers that (α) form operator-variable structures and (β) are permitted to take narrow scope. In either case, descriptions would no longer be treated as quantifiers that insisted on widest interpretive scope.

One possible source of Hornstein's problems is a confusion about Russell's formal theory. According to Hornstein, on Russell's account "definite descriptions were adjoined to predicates to yield terms" (p. 157, note 3). This is incorrect. On Russell's account, neither a definite description $(\imath x)(Fx)$ nor the definite description operator $(\imath x)$ combines with a predicate to form a term. Rather, a definite description $(\imath x)(Fx)$ combines with a one-place predicate G to form a *formula* $G(\imath x)(Fx)$. And the definite description *operator* $(\imath x)$ combines with a *formula* to form a term. (For discussion, see 2.3.) And it is the latter fact that makes it possible for a description to contain a variable that can be bound by a quantifier taking wider scope.

Hornstein also claims that certain facts about pronominal anaphora support his view that definite descriptions are Type I quantifiers. The relevant facts are examined in notes to Chapters 5 and 6. For further problems with Hornstein's views about descriptions, see note 8 to the present chapter.

5. A unary sentential operator O is extensional just in case the truth-value of '$O\alpha$' depends only upon the truth-value of the embedded sentence α (see 4.3 for extended discussion of extensional and nonextensional operators). Thus the negation sign '$\neg$' is an extensional operator, whereas the modal operators 'necessarily' and 'possibly' are not. In the literature there is an unfortunate tendency to characterize the notion of an extensional operator in terms of substitutivity. Some of the disastrous consequences of this move are examined in 4.3 and 4.4.

6. I have deliberately not used a sentence like

    (i)   Bill wants to marry the richest debutante in Dubuque

so as to avoid the philosophical problem of *de se* attitude reports, and the syntactical problem of how best to handle what linguists once called "equi noun phrase deletion." In early versions of transformational grammar, in the "underlying" syntactical structure for (i), a second occurrence of 'Bill' occupied the subject position of the embedded sentence, ('Bill to marry the richest debutante in Dubuque') and was then deleted by a transformational rule in the derivation of the sentence's "surface structure" representation. More recent theories from the same camp posit the existence of a phonetically empty noun phrase that is "controlled by" 'Bill'. Particular syntactical details aside, there is surely consensus among linguists and philosophers alike that the "understood subject" of 'marry' in (i) is 'Bill'; however, it will probably not do to say that (i) is equivalent to

(ii)   Bill wants Bill to marry the richest debutante in Dubuque

where the two occurrences of 'Bill' refer to the same individual, as there appear to be circumstances in which (ii) is true and (i) false. For discussion, see Castañeda (1967), Perry (1977), and Lewis (1979).

If the two readings of (i) are to be attributed to a scope ambiguity, then it would seem that what follows 'wants' will have to be sentential in character. Of course, a certain amount of (rather less innocuous) violence to syntax is required if this idea is to be extended to a sentence like

(iii)   Bill wants a new car.

Indeed, it seems to be held by many philosophers and linguists that there is no principled way of treating verbs like 'look for', 'seek', 'fear', 'want', and so on as taking sentential complements, and consequently, no principled way of providing two readings of (iii) and related sentences in terms of scope permutation. I am not aware of any knock-down argument against a scope-based analysis but the generality of the alleged problem is worth noting. As Church, Montague, and others have observed, the same problem—if it is a problem—arises with sentences such as the following:

(iv)   Henry is looking for a unicorn
(v)   Mary is hunting centaurs
(vi)   The Greeks worshipped many gods
(vii)   Mary advertized for three elves
(viii)   Ponce de Leon searched for the Fountain of Youth.

In none of these examples does there appear to be any relevant operator with respect to which the quantifiers in question can take narrow scope. Since the problem would appear to be a quite general one about the interpretation of quantifiers in such contexts—and not just about the interpretation of definite descriptions in such contexts—we should have no sympathy with the limited claim (voiced by (e.g.) Zalta 1988) that the truth of a sentence like (viii), or the truth of variants of (iv)-(vii) involving definite descriptions, forces us to abandon Russell's quantificational analysis. A theory of descriptions aims to explicate the logic of descriptions, not the logic of seeking, hunting, worshipping, and advertizing. As Smiley (1981, p. 330) remarks, ". . . descriptions occur everywhere, but a logic of descriptions is not a logic of everything."

7. Kripke's point effectively undermines *all* of Fodor and Sag's arguments for a referential interpretation of indefinite descriptions. Fodor and Sag's general strategy is (*a*) to uncover readings of sentences in which indefinite descriptions appear to take widest possible scope, and then (*b*) argue that plausible syntactical constraints on quantifier scope in natural language—so-called "island constraints"—are violated if the indefinite descriptions in question are given the required scope assignments. Their "solution" is to treat the offending indefinite descriptions as referring expressions. But, of course, this type of argument is powerless: indefinite and definite descriptions can take wide scope without being used referentially, and in such cases referential interpretations are quite wrong. So even if one could demonstrate conclusively (in some other way) that indefinite descriptions have referential interpretations, the referentialist would *still* have to appeal to Russell's notion of scope in order to capture the readings on which the indefinite descriptions in (20)-(23) take maximally wide scope. For detailed discussion of Fodor and Sag's arguments, see Ludlow and Neale (forthcoming).

8. In the light of the publication of Kripke's (1977) therapeutic remarks on scope, the tendency to confuse referential and wide scope readings appears to have abated (though see Fodor and Sag (1982), Hornstein (1984), and Stich (1986).)

    It should be pointed out that Hornstein's accounts of both definite and indefinite descriptions are undermined by the behavior of descriptions in nonextensional contexts. (This has been stressed by Soames (1987), but in the context of the present discussion some of Soames' main points need to be amplified.) First, since Hornstein claims that *definite* descriptions are Type I quantifiers (see note 4), his account predicts (falsely) that only *wide* scope readings are available for the definite descriptions in sentences such as the following:

    (i)   Mary believes that the man who lives upstairs is a spy
    (ii)   John thinks he has proved that the largest prime number lies somewhere between 10^{27} and 10^{31}
    (iii) Mary wants Bill to marry the richest debutante in Dubuque
    (iv)   Watson doubts that Holmes believes that Smith's murderer is insane
    (v)   The first man in space might have been American
    (vi)   The number of planets is necessarily odd
    (vii) Next year the President will be a democrat
    (viii) The Lord Mayor of London used to wear a wig.

    Second, since Hornstein claims (*a*) that *indefinite* descriptions are Type II quantifiers (see note 4), and (*b*) that Type II quantifiers cannot take wide scope over certain sentence-embedding operators, then to the extent that it is possible to get clear predictions from his account, it predicts (falsely) that only *narrow* scope readings are available for the indefinite descriptions in the following sentences:

(ix)   Ralph thinks that an employee in his firm has been selling industrial secrets

(x)   Each teacher overheard the rumor that a student of mine cheated

(xi)   Hoover charged that the Berrigans plotted to kidnap a high American official

(xii)   A man from Chicago might have patented the zipper

(xiii) Next year a man from Texas will be President.

Hornstein attempts to rescue his accounts of definite and indefinite descriptions by appealing to largely unspecified nonlinguistic considerations. With respect to definite descriptions, Hornstein claims (falsely) that the ambiguities in (i)–(viii) turn on whether or not the descriptions succeed in denoting. Something that does the work of the (linguistically prohibited) narrow scope reading is allowed to materialize at a level of semantic representation external to "the language faculty." With indefinite descriptions, the situation is apparently reversed: something that does the work of the (linguistically prohibited) *wide* scope reading is generated by obscure nonlinguistic factors. It is quite unclear to me how such plasticity is compatible with a firm and genuine distinction between Type I and Type II quantifiers. On this matter, see also note 4 and Soames (1987).

9. My reasons for not equating the Principle of the Indiscernibility of Identicals and the Principle of Substitutivity are, for the most part, those given by Cartwright (1971). The former is a self-evident truth about objects; the latter is a claim about language and (arguably) does *not* hold in full generality. For example, it is widely held that the propositions expressed by 'John believes that Cicero denounced Catiline' and 'John believes that Tully denounced Catiline' can differ in truth-value. And this is quite compatible with the fact that if Tully = Cicero then there is no property that Cicero has and Tully lacks. For further discussion, see below and 4.5.

10. Of course, those of a neo-Fregean persuasion may want to argue that (3) and (4) express different *propositions*, but that is not what we are interested in right now.

11. Cf. Carnap (1947), ch. 1.

12. The relative scopes of 'Mary thinks that' and 'necessarily' appear to be dictated by surface syntax. That is, in (11) the modal operator cannot take wider scope than the attitude frame. By contrast, in (11′) the attitude frame cannot take wider scope than the modal operator (except (perhaps) with a very contrived stress contour):

    (11′)   Necessarily, Mary thinks that the number of planets is odd.

13. See in particular Russell (1905), p. 47 and pp. 51–52, and *Principia Mathematica* *14. (Of course, the Russellian will have to allow that *if* we are forced to postulate the existence of semantically referential descriptions (in addition to quantificational descriptions), then a statement of the form (e.g.) 'b = the F' is a genuine identity statement when, but only when, 'the F' is a referential description.)

14. Nor does it sanction a direct move from '$G(\iota x)(Fx)$' to '$G(\iota x)(H'x)$' on the basis of the truth of '$(\iota x)(Fx) = (\iota x)(Hx)$', since this last sentence is also an abbreviation. (D4) should be understood in this broader sense.

15. In the restricted quantifier notation of 2.5, (1) is ambiguous between (1_i) and (1_{ii}):

    (1_i)   [the x: Px] $\square$ (x is odd)

    (1_{ii}) $\square$ [the x: Px] (x is odd).

    (As I mentioned in 4.3, for historical and expository purposes I shall continue to use a standard first-order notation in this section.)

16. For discussion of 'can' in this type of locution, see Kripke (1979).

17. It is worth noting that parallel arguments can be constructed with the aim of demonstrating that, say, temporal operators create opaque contexts. Consider the following example, adapted from Sharvy (1969):

    (6_1)   In 1962 George Bush did not appear on TV
    (7_1)   George Bush = the U. S. President
    (8_1)   In 1962 the U. S. President did not appear on TV.

    (8_1) seems to be derivable from (6_1) and (7_1) in the same way as (8) is derivable from (6) and (7). And there is clearly a reading of (8_1) that can be false while (6_1) and (7_1) are both true. Consequently, one might suggest that temporal contexts are also referentially opaque. It will become clear that this argument suffers from the same defects as Quine's argument.

18. Actually Quine goes further. Not only does he treat definite descriptions in accordance with Russell's theory, he also treats proper names as disguised definite descriptions. He apparently fails to see that this severely constrains his use of the Principle of Substitutivity.

19. The ellipsed material in the passage quoted from Russell makes the same point with another example of some independent interest:

    I have heard of a touchy owner of a yacht to whom a guest, on first seeing it, remarked, 'I thought your yacht was larger than it is'; and the owner replied, 'No, my yacht is not larger than it is'. What the guest meant was, 'The size that I thought your yacht was is greater than the size your yacht is'; the meaning attributed to him is, 'I thought the size of your yacht was greater than the size of your yacht'.

    Russell's idea here seems to be that we can use the Theory of Descriptions to characterize the logical form of sentences containing comparatives, and that sentences containing comparatives and verbs of propositional attitude may therefore exhibit scope ambiguities. We find the same situation with comparatives in modal contexts:

    (i)   Henry could be a lot thinner than he is.
    (ii)   Henry could earn more money than he does.

20. Interestingly, Smullyan does not really come out and explicitly accuse Quine of an illicit application of the Principle of Substitutivity. Fully

cognizant of the fact that if definite descriptions are defined contextually PS does not sanction a direct move from (6) to (8) on the basis of the truth of (7), Smullyan seems to assume—rather charitably in my opinion—that Quine also sees this. So rather than chastize Quine for an illicit application of PS, Smullyan is content to point out that the false reading of (8)—given by (8_2)—cannot be derived from (6) and (7) using standard rules of logical inference. This is, indeed, enough to show that Quine's argument fails if descriptions are treated in accordance with Russell's theory.

21. Linsky (1977, 1983) appears to make the same mistake as Quine in his interpretation of Smullyan's paper:

> Smullyan totally by-passes the problem of making sense of construc-tions such as (8_1). Has Quine not shown that the attempt to bind a variable in a referentially opaque context by a quantifier outside the context produces nonsense? According to Quine, (8_1) is nonsense, so it cannot represent a possible sense of (8). Thus Smullyan's argument from ambiguity is destroyed. Friends of Smullyan's view-point will be quick to answer that Quine's *argument* for the unintelli-gibility of constructions such as (8_1) rests on the fallacy of ambiguity exposed by Smullyan. Quine's argument against quantifying into modal contexts assumes the unintelligibility of such constructions as (8_1), so it begs the question. Smullyan's argument against Quine as-sumes the intelligibility of these quantifications, but no attempt is made to explain them. Thus Quine and Smullyan can each find the other begging the question at issue (1977, p. 127; see also 1983, pp. 112–13).

The intelligibility of (8_1) is irrelevant to Smullyan's argument against Quine; and to the extent that Linsky is agreeing with Quine that "Smullyan's argument assumes the intelligibility of these quantifications" he is simply in error. Even if (8) were unambiguously read as (8_2), Smullyan's main point would still hold. There is no sense in which Smullyan is begging the question.

22. Føllesdal (1961) also claims to find problems with Smullyan's proposal. According to Føllesdal, the following example, due to Wilson (1959), shows that Smullyan has not provided a fully general rebuttal of Quine's argument. Let '$(\iota x)(Wx)$' stand for the author of *Waverley*, and '$(\iota x)(Mx)$' stand for 'the author of *Marmion*'. According to Føllesdal, on Smullyan's account, it is now possible to derive a false conclusion (iii) from two true premises (i) and (ii):

(i) $(\iota x)(Wx) = (\iota x)(Mx)$

(ii) $\square\{[(\iota x)(Wx)]G(\iota x Wx) \equiv [(\iota x)(Wx)]G(\iota x Wx)\}$

(iii) $\square\{[(\iota x)(Wx)]G(\iota x Wx) \equiv [(\iota x)(Mx)]G(\iota x Mx)\}.$

But on Smullyan's account (iii) is *not* derivable from (i) and (ii), even with the indicated scopes. Using $(\iota u)(Mu)$ in place of $(\iota x)(Mx)$ so as to avoid obvious confusion, on his Russellian analysis of descriptions Smullyan must unpack (i)-(iii) as follows:

(i$_1$) $(\exists x)((\forall y)(Wy \equiv y=x)$ & $(\exists u)((\forall v)(Mv \equiv v=u)$ & $x=u))$

(ii$_1$) $\square\,\{(\exists x)((\forall y)(Wy \equiv y=x)$ & $Gx) \equiv (\exists x)((\forall y)(Wy \equiv y=x)$ & $Gx)\}$

(iii$_1$) $\square\,\{(\exists x)((\forall y)(Wy \equiv y=x)$ & $Gx) \equiv (\exists u)((\forall v)(Mv \equiv v=u)$ & $Gu)\}.$

And (iii$_1$) simply does *not* follow from (i$_1$) and (ii$_1$).

Føllesdal's mistake is to assume that Smullyan's proposal reduces to the following two propositions: (*a*) a sentence containing a description and a modal operator is ambiguous, and (*b*) once one has established the scope of a description, one can substitute for it a codenoting description having the same scope. Smullyan certainly holds (a), but he does *not* subscribe to (*b*). Indeed, he *could not* because, by virtue of being a Russellian about descriptions, he subscribes to (D4). And it is because Smullyan subscribes to (D4) that he subscribes to (*a*). (Since writing the bulk of this note, it has come to my attention that Reeves (1973) makes substantially the same point against Føllesdal.)

Føllesdal's own solution to the alleged problem of quantifying into modal contexts is predicated on the mistaken assumption that Smullyan's response is inadequate because of examples like Wilson's (Føllesdal present similar examples of his own, and makes the same mistake in his discussion of the examples). That is, Føllesdal (1961, 1965, 1969, 1986) argues that the way out of trouble is to count as real singular terms only those noun phrases that are rigid designators. On this account, rigid descriptions can be treated as singular terms as far as (e.g.) PS and EG are concerned. But this is all superfluous. Once it is seen that descriptions are quantifiers and not singular terms, all of the desired results follow without Føllesdal's constraint because Referring expressions and variables are rigid designators. Descriptions take care of themselves.

23. For discussion, see Føllesdal (1986).

24. See 2.2 and 3.3 for the reasons why names and demonstratives must be treated as rigid designators (the arguments, of course, are due to Kripke, for names, and to Kaplan, for demonstratives).

25. In its main respects, this point is due to Rundle (1965). After drawing a distinction between referential and Russellian interpretations of descriptions in extensional contexts, Rundle suggests that Quine's troubles arise from neglecting this ambiguity. As Rundle correctly observes, if the description in (7) is Russellian, then the Principle of Substitutivity does not sanction a direct move from (6) to (8) on the basis of the truth of (7) because (7) is not a genuine identity statement (here, Rundle is agreeing whole-heartedly with Russell and Smullyan, though curiously he does not mention Smullyan's paper). However, if the description in (7) is interpreted as a referring expression (as referring to 9)—as Rundle's theory allows—then the reading of (8) in which the same description is also interpreted as a referring expression (again referring to 9) *does* follow from (6) and (7). But this reading is true.

Unlike Smullyan, then, Rundle sees the ambiguity in (8) as lexical rather than scope-related (it concerns the *semantics* of the description itself). And herein lies the problem with Rundle's account: unlike

Smullyan's account of *de re* modal statements, Rundle's is not sufficiently general because of the possibility of nonreferential *de re* uses of descriptions noted by Cartwright and Kripke (see 4.2).

26. I am grateful to Scott Soames for suggesting this way of setting out the second stage of Quine's argument.

27. One reason for a degree of caution here is that it is at least arguable that in many contexts nominal phrases appear to denote general events or types of events (rather than particular events). Consider the following:

    (i)   My leaving always upsets Mary
    (ii) Bill's singing usually startles the cat.

    With the support of a theory of 'always', 'usually', and other adverbs of quantification—see Lewis (1975)—perhaps the Theory of Descriptions can be suitably extended to take into account sentences like these, but I shall not attempt such manoeuvres here.

    A further complication emerges from Thomason's (1986) observation that in certain contexts gerundive nominals are more appropriately regarded as denoting propositional objects.

28. The presence of 'derived' in 'derived nominal' is misleading: it is derived nominals that Chomsky claims are *not* derived from underlying sentences by syntactical transformation.

29. Using 'DN' and 'GN' as shorthand for 'derived nominal' and 'gerundive nominal', and 'DNP' and 'GNP' for the full phrases containing DNs and GNs (e.g., 'Mary's departure' and 'Mary's departing'), the relevant data are the following:

    (i) The head of a DNP can be replaced by an overt determiner; the head of a GNP cannot:

    > The/each/no departure upset James
    > *The/each/no departing upset James.

    (ii) DNs allow adjectival modification, GNs do not:

    > Mary's subsequent departure upset James
    > *Mary's subsequent departing upset James.

    (iii) DNs pluralize, GNs do not:

    > Mary's departures always upset James
    > * Mary's departings always upset James.

    (As Richard Larson has pointed out to me, gerundive nominals of an idiomatic nature *do* seem to pluralize. E.g., 'Mary's comings and goings'.)

    (iv) DNPs can appear as complements to verbs of perception, GNPs cannot (this is was pointed out by Gee (1977) and is not one of Chomsky's original data):

    > James saw Mary's departure
    > * James saw Mary's departing.

    (v) GNPs may have aspect, DNPs may not:

    > * Mary's having departure has upset James

Mary's having departed has upset James.

(vi) GNs allow adverbial-type modification, DNs do not:

* Mary's departure like that upset James
Mary's departing like that upset James.

(vii) GNP's allow negation, DNP's do not:

* Mary's not departure has upset James
Mary's not departing has upset James.

30. There is, of course, an additional reading of (10), obtained by giving the modal operator intermediate scope. For present concerns this reading can be ignored. (There may even be other readings because of the embedded quantifier 'the 37th President'.)

31. For ease of exposition, I have not unpacked the definite descriptions 'Jones' arm' and 'the chairman', and I have suppressed the temporal parameter.

32. There may well be substantial difficulties involved in making sense of (B), but I shall let these pass. For discussion, see Tye (1979) and Horgan (1980).

33. Taylor (1985, pp. 92–93) also stresses the importance of scope distinctions in discussions of events. As he points out, the claim that Caesar's death might have taken place later than it did can be understood in at least two ways because of the possibility of scope permutations. The following is probably true:

(i)   [the e: die(Caesar, e)] ($\Diamond$ ([the f: die(Caesar, f)] ($e < f$))).

where '<' is understood as 'temporally precedes'. But it does not follow from the truth of (i) that the temporal location of an event is not one of its "essential" properties.

34. A rather different approach to the ambiguities found in sentences containing descriptions and nonextensional operators is suggested by Smiley (1981). Smiley's idea is that an incomplete description like 'the President' is elliptical for 'the President at (time) t' in a sentence such as 'the President was a democrat', and elliptical for 'the President at (world) w' in a sentence containing a modal operator. Perhaps it is possible to mimic scope in this way (or by appealing to parametric objects) but it is quite unclear to me what the payoff is, especially when genuinely opaque contexts are taken into account. (I suspect that much of the residual aversion to the notion of quantifier scope comes from thinking about this semantical notion far too syntactically.)

35. At this juncture, a few brief remarks on negation are in order. Notoriously, negation brings up a variety of complex semantical issues, many of which are not at all well understood. Some of the most perplexing issues concern the interaction of negation with quantifiers. Nothing I can say here will do justice to the intricacies involved; however, I think it is possible to get reasonably clear about several issues that are of some relevance to a quantificational analysis of descriptions.

Recall that by allowing scope permutations involving descriptions and negation, Russell was able to capture the fact that

(i)   The King of France is not bald

might be used to say something true even if there is no king of France. On his account, (i) is ambiguous between (ii) and (iii):

(i₁)   [the x: King of France x] ¬ (x is bald)
(i₂)   ¬ [the x: King of France x] (x is bald).

If the description has wide scope, as in (i₁), then the sentence entails the existence of a unique King of France. By contrast, if the description has narrow scope, as in (i₂), then there is no such entailment; on this reading, the truth of an utterance of (i) is perfectly consistent with there being no king of France.

One question here is whether or not the scope permutation posited for (i) captures a genuine semantical ambiguity. (The existence of an ambiguity appears to be doubted by (e.g.) Kempson (1975).) If an ambiguity is to be posited, two interesting observations need to be explained at some point. First, as Grice (1981, p. 189) points out, ". . . without waiting for disambiguation, people understand an utterance of [(i)] as implying (in some fashion) the unique existence of a king of France." Second, as (e.g.) Hornstein (1984) points out, sentences containing negation and various other quantifiers do not seem to exhibit precisely the same range of scope permutations as those containing descriptions and negation.

Let's take the latter observation first. Unfortunately, when it comes to the scope permutations involving negation and quantifiers, judgments as to the availability of possible readings are not very robust; however, there is, I think, just about enough of a consensus for the very limited aims I have here. Consider a pair of sentences like (ii) and (iii):

(ii)   John didn't talk to the king of France
(iii)   John didn't talk to every woman who turned up.

On Russell's account, (ii) is ambiguous; and on the assumption that negation may interact with the quantifier 'every woman who turned up', (iii) ought to be ambiguous in the same way, i.e., it ought to be ambiguous between (iii₁) and (iii₂):

(iii₁)   [every x: woman x & x turned up] ¬ (John talked to x)
(iii₂)   ¬ [every x: woman x & x turned up] (John talked to x).

But (iii₁) does not seem to be a legitimate reading of (iii). Hornstein (1984) takes this as evidence for the view that there is no scope interaction involving negation quantifiers and that the alleged ambiguity in (ii) is not the product of a genuine scope permutation. Notice that it is the reading on which the quantifier has *narrower* scope than the negation that is available. But now contrast (iii) with (iv):

(iv)   John didn't talk to some women who turned up

In (iv) it is the reading on which the quantifier has *wider* scope than the negation that is preferred. And, as (e.g.) Kaplan (1986) points out, a sentence like (v) seems to be straightforwardly ambiguous:

(v)   Everyone is not hungry.

It seems clear, then, that there is no hard and fast generalization to the effect that quantifiers must take wide (or narrow) scope with respect to negation.

Concerning the other observation, in support of Russell, Grice (1981) suggests that it is explicable on the assumption that when (i) is read as (i_2) the utterance will typically carry a conversational implicature to the effect that there is a unique king of France. (An alternative to Grice's strategy would be to argue that (i_1) is the "unmarked" or "default" reading of (i) and special contextual circumstances are required before reading (i_2) comes to mind.) Kempson (1975) appears to disagree with Russell by suggesting that (i) is unambiguously represented as (i_2), presumably in deference to the fact that (i_1) entails (i_2). It is not clear to me that this approach has any advantages over the Russellian-Gricean account.

Chapter 5

Pronouns and Anaphora

5.1 Introductory Remarks

A comprehensive semantical theory must account for the ways in which pronouns function. A variety of questions need to be answered: Should pronouns be assimilated to the class of referring expressions or the class of quantifiers, or are matters more complicated? Are there important semantical differences between, say, *demonstrative* and *anaphoric* occurrences of pronouns? What syntactical constraints are imposed on the semantics of the latter?

In the context of the present essay, the most pressing questions concern pronouns anaphoric on definite descriptions and other quantifiers. It is not infrequently claimed that facts about pronominal anaphora undermine Russellian analyses of definite and indefinite descriptions. In my opinion, many such claims have been somewhat rashly made, and over the course of this chapter and the next, I shall do my best to show that none of them stands up to serious scrutiny.

By way of examining anaphoric objections to Russell, I want to map out a general theory of the semantics of pronouns. The theory is straightforward, but in view of certain superficial complexities that are going to arise, it will be useful to outline the central theses prior to the main discussion. In previous chapters, I have suggested several times that there is no good reason to posit more than two classes of noun phrases, the class of (rigid) referring expressions and the class of (restricted) quantifiers. As far as I have been able to ascertain, the semantical behavior of pronouns does not require any deviation from this picture. Every pronoun is either a referring expression or a quantifier. Very roughly, we can say the following: (*i*) nonanaphoric pronouns are referring expressions; (*ii*) pronouns anaphoric on referring expressions are themselves referring expressions; (*iii*) pronouns anaphoric on quantifiers are either bound variables or quantifiers depending on the syntactical relationship between antecedent and anaphor. This is more or less the picture I shall explore in this chapter.

In 5.2, I look at those pronouns that are interpreted as referring expressions. In 5.3, I turn to pronouns that function like the bound variables of quantification theory. Following Evans (1977), a sharp semantical and syntactical distinction is made between bound and unbound anaphora. In 5.4, the main challenge to Russell is presented. In 5.5, I argue for the view that unbound pronouns that are anaphoric on quantifiers go proxy for definite descriptions, drawing upon the work of Evans and upon various modifications suggested in subsequent literature. In 5.6, the notion of variable-binding that has been operative throughout this essay is made more precise with the help of some ideas from contemporary grammatical theory. Solutions to some longstanding anaphoric puzzles are then presented. In 5.7, I return to the challenge to Russell.

5.2 Referential Pronouns

As Evans (1977, 1980) observes, a typical taxonomy of the way pronouns function will include their use as genuine referring expressions and their use as something akin to the bound variables of quantification theory. Let us look at these in turn.

The clearest sorts of examples involving referential pronouns are those in which a pronoun is used as a device of *demonstrative* reference to an object (or objects) in view, as in a particular utterance *u* of (1) accompanied by some sort of demonstration or gesture:

(1)   *He* looks tired.

A pronoun used in this way will fall under a theory of demonstrative referring expressions of the sort sketched in 3.3.

Notice that neither a demonstration nor immediate perceptual contact is required for a pronoun to receive a referential interpretation; a pronoun may be used as a device of quasi-demonstrative reference to an object (or objects) made salient in some other way. For instance, Pope Jean-Paul may render himself salient by fainting in the middle of a sermon, and I might then say to you,

(2)   He must be exhausted from all that traveling.

No demonstration was necessary in this case. Suppose we are at a cocktail party and a very loud, boring man has been dominating the conversation with talk about his wealth. As soon as he leaves, I say,

(3)   I'm glad *he*'s gone.

Here the referent of 'he' is not in the immediate perceptual environment at the time of utterance. (As in Chapter 4, talk of "the referent of an expression ζ" is to be understood as shorthand for talk of "the referent of a particular utterance u of ζ.")

In (1)-(3), the occurrences of 'he' seem to be functioning as genuine referring expressions. They certainly satisfy (R1):

(R1) If 'b' is a referring expression, then for a (monadic) predicate '— is G', it is necessary to identify the referent of 'b' in order to understand the proposition expressed by an utterance of 'b is G'.

If the occurrence of 'he' in an utterance u of, say, (1) has no referent, then there is nothing identification of which would constitute identifying its referent, and hence nothing that would constitute *understanding* the proposition expressed. And if nothing constitutes understanding the proposition expressed, it makes no sense to say that a proposition *was* expressed. Thus (R2) also appears to be satisfied:

(R2) If 'b' has no referent, then for a (monadic) predicate '— is G', no proposition is expressed by an utterance of 'b is G'.

In short, the proposition expressed by an utterance u of (1) is *object-dependent*. Thus (R3) is also satisfied:

(R3) If 'b' is a genuine referring expression that refers to x, then 'b' is a rigid designator; i.e., x enters into a specification of the truth conditions of (the proposition expressed by) an utterance u of 'b is G' with respect to actual and counterfactual situations.[1]

Let us now turn to *anaphoric* pronouns. Roughly, we can say that an expression α is *anaphoric* on an expression β if and only if (*i*) the semantical value (in the sense of 3.3) of α is determined, at least in part, by the semantical value of β, and (*ii*) β is not a constituent of α. Where α *is* anaphoric on β, let's say that β is the *antecedent* of α.

The occurrences of 'he' in (4) and (5) surely admit of anaphoric interpretations:

(4)   *That man* is a crook; *he* tried to bribe the judge

(5)   *Jones* is a crook; *he* tried to bribe the judge.

And when they are interpreted anaphorically—*italics* will be used throughout to indicate anaphoric connections—these pronouns are surely referential. In short, a pronoun that has as its antecedent a referring expression refers to the same thing as its antecedent.

There are several ways of implementing this proposal. First, it might be suggested that such pronouns are what Geach (1962) calls "pronouns of laziness," in the sense that they go proxy for repeated occurrences of their antecedents. Second, it might be suggested that while they are not actually devices of laziness, they still "inherit" their referents from the phrases upon which they are anaphoric ('that man' and 'Jones'). Third, it might be suggested that the use of a referring expression like 'that man' or 'Jones' raises its referent to some sort of perceptual or conversational salience. In the case of the demonstrative 'that man', the individual will often be (or have been) in the shared perceptual environment and in any case will be an easy target for a demonstrative use of 'he'. In the case of the name 'Jones', although Jones need not be in the shared perceptual environment, he will still have been raised to *conversational* salience and is therefore an easy target for a quasi-demonstrative use of 'he'.

On each of these accounts, the occurrences of 'he' in (4) and (5) are *referential*; and the proposition expressed in each case by 'He tried to bribe the judge' is object-dependent. But it is important to see that on each proposal the locus of explanation is rather different. According to the first proposal, the pronoun literally goes proxy for another occurrence of its antecedent. According to the second proposal, there is rule-governed anaphora, the pronoun, *inheriting* its reference from its antecedent. On the third proposal, the utterance of the clause containing the antecedent has raised some individual (the referent of the antecedent) to perceptual and/or conversational salience, and a referential pronoun may now be used to refer to that individual. Of course, in the cases we have considered there is not a lot to choose between these proposals, but more sophisticated examples may lead one to favor one over the others or to construct some sort of hybrid account. Since I shall be concerned primarily with pronouns anaphoric on quantified noun phrases, it is not terribly important to come down firmly in favor of any one of these approaches here.[2] I shall simply make the fairly neutral assumption that a pronoun that has a referring expression as its antecedent refers to the same thing as its antecedent, remaining silent on the nature of the mechanism by which this effect is achieved.[3]

5.3 Pronouns and Bound Variables

Not all pronouns can be treated as straightforward referring expressions. To begin with, there are pronouns that seem to function like the bound variables of quantification theory, what we can call *bound pronouns* or *bound anaphors*. Below are some English sentences containing pronouns anaphoric on quantifiers, along with their respective logical forms:

(1) *Some boy* thinks *he* is immortal
     [some x: boy x] (x thinks (immortal x))

(2) *Every boy* loves *his* mother
     [every x: boy x] ([the y: y mother-of x] (x loves y))

(3) *No boy* liked the girl who kissed *him*
     [no x: boy x] ([the y: girl y & y kissed x] (x liked y)).[4]

The champions of the bound interpretation of such pronouns are Geach (1962) and Quine (1960). The proposal seems to me both natural and recommended on independent syntactical grounds (see below).[5]

On the assumption that definite descriptions are quantifiers, the pronouns in the following variants of (1)-(3) can also be treated as bound variables:

(4) *The boy* thinks *he* is immortal
     [the x: boy x] (x thinks (immortal x))

(5) *The boy* loves *his* mother
     [the x: boy x] ([the y: y mother-of x] (x loves y))

(6) *The boy* liked the girl who kissed *him*
     [the x: boy x] ([the y: girl y & y kissed x] (x liked y)).

It might be thought that we can provide bound analyses of the pronouns in examples like the following, since they are also anaphoric on quantifiers:

(7) *The man in the gabardine suit* is a spy. *He* tried to bribe me.

(8) John bought *some donkeys* and Harry vaccinated *them*.[6]

On such an account, the two-sentence sequence in (7) comes out as (7$_1$):

(7$_1$) [the x: man ... x] (spy x & x tried to bribe me).

This certainly gets the right truth conditions for (7) *as a whole*; but it does so by allowing the scope of the quantifier in the first sentence to vault across a sentence boundary. Suppose the hearer replies to (7) with "I was at college with him; I always suspected he would end up doing that sort of work." We will now have to say that the initial quantifier, 'the man in the gabardine suit', binds a variable in a sentence uttered by *someone else*. And if the discourse contains further anaphoric pronouns, the scope of the description will have to be extended again. This seems to conflict with our intuitions that each utterance of a complete indicative sentence in a discourse typically expresses some proposition or other (relative to the context of utterance) and hence ought to be evaluable for truth or falsity.

I suspect that one cannot turn this sort of intuitive consideration into a knock-down argument against cross-sentential binding. But that does not matter; as soon as we turn to example (8) we find powerful semantical and syntactical considerations that thoroughly discredit the idea. If the pronoun 'them' in (8) is treated as a variable bound by 'some donkeys', the sentence comes out as (8_1):

(8)   John bought *some donkeys* and Harry vaccinated *them*.

(8_1) [some x: donkeys x] (John bought x & Harry vaccinated x).

But as Evans (1977, 1980) observes, this is wrong on several related counts. Let me amplify and expand upon Evans' more important points. Note that (8_1) will be true as long as Harry vaccinated *some* of John's donkeys; but on its most natural reading, the truth of (8) requires Harry to vaccinate *all* of them. (For example, if John bought ten donkeys and Harry vaccinated only three of them, (8_1) is true but (8) is not.) The bound proposal simply delivers the wrong truth conditions. As a corollary, it runs into another problem that it will be fruitful to explore. A conjunction is true if and only if both of its conjuncts are true, so the truth of (8) implies the truth of (9):

(9)   John bought some donkeys.

The bound analysis does in fact make the right prediction in this case because (9_1), which represents (9), is a consequence of (8_1):

(9_1) [some x: donkeys x] (John bought x).

But this is due solely to the choice of example. The bound analysis misfires with examples like the following:

(10)   John bought *exactly two donkeys* and Harry vaccinated *them*

(11)   *Few politicians* came to the party, but *they* had a good time

(12)   *Just one man* drank rum, and *he* was ill.

Take (12); if this is true, then so is (13):

(13)   Just one man drank rum.

But the bound analysis goes astray here. If the scope of the quantifier phrase 'just one man' is extended to the second conjunct so as to capture the pronoun 'he', (12) will come out as (12₁), making it equivalent to (14):

(12₁) [just one x: man x] (x drank rum & x was ill)

(14)   Just one man drank rum and was ill.

But the truth of (12₁)/(14) is quite compatible with the falsity of (13₁), which represents the logical form of (13):

(13₁) [just one x: man x] (x drank rum).

Thus the bound analysis of (12), as given by (12₁), will not do. In particular, (12₁) can be true if two (or more) men drank rum, but (12) cannot.

Exactly parallel considerations preclude bound analyses of the pronouns in (10) and (11). Indeed, whenever the quantified antecedent is not *monotone increasing* the bound analysis will slip up in this way.[7] With quantifiers of the form 'no Fs' the problem is especially acute. The bound analysis predicts that the incoherent (15) is equivalent to (16):

(15)   John bought *no donkeys* and Harry vaccinated *them*

(16)   John bought no donkeys that Harry vaccinated.

Of course, if cross-sentential binding is prohibited, none of these problems arises.[8] The upshot of all this is that among pronouns anaphoric on quantifiers we need to distinguish between those that function as bound variables and those that do not.[9]

There turns out to be a simple and precise syntactical characterization of when an anaphoric pronoun functions as a bound variable.[10] First, a very rough characterization: If P is a pronoun P that is anaphoric on a quantifier Q, then P is bound by Q only if P is located inside the smallest clause containing Q. We can make this precise with the aid of some elementary configurational notions from contemporary grammatical theory. Moreover, we can (I think) get at the relevant notions without getting fully submerged in the details of this or that version of any particular grammar. For the sake of simplicity, let's assume that the following very elementary set of phrase structure rules provides an adequate syntactical characterization of a certain finite fragment of English:

1.   S → NP VP

2.   NP → NAME   NAME = {Bill, Tom}

3.   NP → DET N   DET = {every, the, a, some, no}

N = {spy, man, boy}

4.   NP → PRON   PRON = {he, him, himself}

5.   VP → IV   IV = {snores, procrastinates}

6.   VP → TV NP   TV = {likes, respects}.

(Gloss: S, NP, and VP are the *phrasal* categories of sentence, noun phrase, and verb phrase; NAME, DET, N, PRON, IV, and TV are the *lexical* categories of proper name, determiner, common noun, pronoun, intransitive verb, and transitive verb.[11])

Using this simple grammar, we can represent the syntactical structure of (17) using a "tree" diagram:

(17)   The boy likes himself

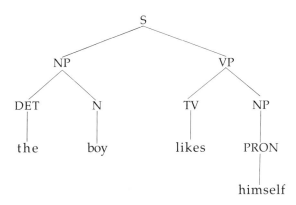

Alternatively, we can use the labeled bracketing given in (17₁):

(17₁)   [$_S$ [$_{NP}$ [$_{DET}$ the] [$_N$ boy]] [$_{VP}$ [$_{TV}$ likes] [$_{NP}$ [$_{PRON}$ himself]]]].

If we now add to our grammar a lexical category SV of sentential verb (i.e., verb taking a sentential complement) and the following phrase structure rule, we can generate some propositional attitude constructions:

7.   VP → SV S   SV = {thinks, believes, hopes}.

For example, we can represent the syntactical structure of (18):

(18)   The boy thinks Bill likes him

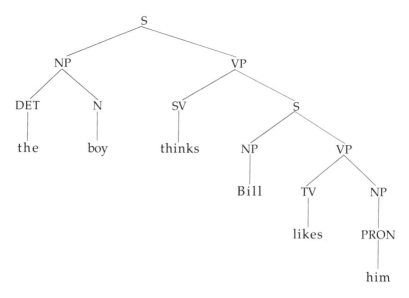

Or, again, with a labeled bracketing:

(18₁) [s [NP [DET the] [N boy]]
       [VP [SV thinks] [S [NP [NAME Bill]] [VP [TV likes] [NP [PRON
       him]]]]]].

(Notice that the grammar now recursively generates an infinite number of sentences because VP is introduced under S in rule 1 and S is
reintroduced under VP in rule 7.)

Both (17) and (18) contain pronouns that may be interpreted as
variables bound by the quantifier 'the boy'. The first notion we need
in order to syntactically characterize the binding relation in these
examples is that of *dominance*, which concerns the hierarchical
organization of constituents. A node (point) x in a tree *dominates* its
constituents, that is, every node beneath it that can be traced back to
it. For instance, in (18) the VP 'likes him' dominates the verb 'likes'
as well as the NP 'him'. And the NP 'the boy' dominates 'the' and
'boy'.

The central notion we need in order to characterize bound anaphora
is Reinhart's notion of *c-command*:

(P1) A phrase α c-commands a phrase β if and only if the first
      branching node dominating α also dominates β (and neither α
      nor β dominates the other).[12]

By this definition, in (18) the subject NP 'the boy' c-commands the
VP and all of its constituents; in particular it c-commands the pronoun

'him'. Similarly, in (17), 'the boy' c-commands the reflexive pronoun 'himself'.

We are now in a position to state the syntactical constraint on bound anaphora that Evans (1977) uncovers:

> (P2) A pronoun P that is anaphoric on a quantifier Q is interpreted as a variable bound by Q if and only if Q c-commands P.[13]

On this account, since the pronoun 'him' in (18) is c-commanded by 'the boy', if the former is understood as anaphoric on the latter—it may also be understood *demonstratively*, of course—it is interpreted as a bound variable. And in (17), since the reflexive pronoun 'himself' is c-commanded by 'the boy', it is also interpreted as a bound variable. (Indeed, it has to be interpreted as a bound variable because a reflexive pronoun must have a c-commanding antecedent in the same clause, and in (17) 'the boy' is the only NP satisfying this criterion.[14])

We can now add a few binary connectives to our fragment of English:

8.   S → S CONN S   CONN = {and, or, if, only if, but}.

If we now form a sentence S_0 from two sentences S_1 and S_2 together with a binary sentential connective, notice that no proper constituent of S_1 will c-command anything in S_2; hence no pronoun in S_2 can be interpreted as bound by a quantifier in S_1. (P2) therefore tells us that the pronouns in (7), (8), (10), (11), and (12) are not bound variables: they are not c-commanded by (and hence not within the scope of) their antecedents. If (P2) is a genuine constraint on bound anaphora— and the data suggest it is—then we must reject cross-sentential binding.

Let's take stock. We need to distinguish between bound and unbound anaphora involving quantified antecedents. A pronoun P that is anaphoric on a quantifier Q is a bound variable only if Q c-commands P. If Q does not c-command P, then an analysis of P as a bound variable will not, in general, deliver the correct truth conditions. This failure comes through very clearly with examples such as (8), (10), (11), and (12), where the quantified antecedents are of the form 'some Fs', 'exactly two Fs', 'few Fs', and 'just one F'. Where the antecedent is of the form 'the F' as in (7),

(7)   *The man in the gabardine suit* is a spy; *he* tried to bribe me

a bound variable analysis would, in fact, deliver the right truth conditions. But this is a theoretically uninteresting by-product of the semantics of the quantificational determiner 'the' (and the simple nature of the example). We must look for a more satisfactory account of the anaphoric pronoun in (7), an account that also covers the anaphoric pronouns in (8), (10), (11), (12), and similar examples. One of the things I have been trying to demonstrate in this essay is that definite descriptions are regular quantifiers, that the determiners 'every', 'some', 'exactly two', 'few', 'just one', 'the', 'all', 'many', 'most' 'a', etc., belong to a unified syntactical and semantical category. Consequently, it would be most inappropriate to ascribe to definite descriptions the dexterity to bind pronouns they do not c-command, when this property cannot be ascribed to the other quantifiers.[15] A satisfactory semantical theory should provide a systematic treatment of quantifiers and a systematic treatment of pronouns that are anaphoric on them. At this juncture, we have a preliminary account of bound anaphora, which will be sharpened in 5.6. A preliminary account of unbound anaphora will be presented in 5.5, but first we need to look at the nature of the problem unbound anaphora is supposed to create for the Russellian.

5.4 Anaphora and Referential Usage

A number of philosophers have claimed that the possibility of cross-sentential anaphora undermines unitary Russellian accounts of definite and indefinite descriptions.[16] Consider the following examples involving anaphora on definite descriptions:

(1)   *The man in the gabardine suit* is a spy. *He* tried to bribe me

(2)   *The inventor of the wheel* was a genius. I suspect *s/he* ate fish on a daily basis.

We saw in the last section that it is not feasible to treat the pronouns in such examples as bound variables. Consequently, it is natural to explore the possibility that they are straightforwardly referential. Indeed, it has been claimed by some philosophers that the pronouns in such examples must be referential and that this is explicable only if their antecedents are also referential. That is, it has been claimed that the anaphoric pronouns in these pairs inherit their referents from their antecedents, and that this requires their antecedents to be referring expressions rather than quantifiers. Let's call the sentence containing the antecedent description the *antecedent sentence*, and the sentence containing the anaphoric pronoun the *anaphor sentence*.[17] Focusing on a particular utterance *u* of (1), we can set out one central argument behind the above claim as follows:[18]

(pr1)   The occurrence of 'he' in the anaphor sentence is anaphoric on the occurrence of 'the man in the gabardine suit' in the antecedent sentence.

(pr2)   If an occurrence of a pronoun P is anaphoric on an occurrence of another noun phrase Q, then P is either a bound variable or a genuine referring expression.

(pr3)   The occurrence of the pronoun 'he' in the anaphor sentence is not a bound variable.

(c1)   Therefore, the occurrence of 'he' in the anaphor sentence is a referring expression.

(pr4)   If an occurrence of a pronoun P is (*i*) a referring expression, and (*ii*) anaphoric on an occurrence of another noun phrase Q, then P inherits its reference from Q.

(c2)   Therefore, the occurrence of 'he' in the anaphor sentence inherits its reference from the occurrence of 'the man in the gabardine suit' in the antecedent sentence.

(pr5)   If an occurrence of a noun phrase P inherits its reference from an occurrence of another noun phrase Q, then Q must be a referring expression.

(c3)   Therefore, 'the man in the gabardine suit' in the antecedent sentence is a referring expression.

We can call this argument a version of the "Argument from Anaphora" for a semantically referential interpretation of definite descriptions.[19]

It was pointed out in Chapter 3 that if an argument for a referential interpretation of a description carries over to quantifiers quite generally, then the argument is weakened to that extent, since it is implausible to suppose that *all* quantifiers are ambiguous between quantificational and referential interpretations. The Argument from Anaphora actually starts off weak, then, as it is usually intended to apply equally to definite and indefinite descriptions and in fact also carries over to other quantifiers.[20] For example, the same type of argument might be used to argue for referential interpretations of the indefinite descriptions in (3) and (4):

(3)   *A cat* is on the lawn. *He* looks like a stray to me

(4)   *An insurance agent* is coming to see me today. I'm sure *s/he* just wants to sell me a policy.

And since we established in 5.3 that the pronouns in (5)-(7) below are not bound variables, parallel arguments ought to demonstrate the existence of referential interpretations of 'just one man', 'few professors', and 'several donkeys':

(5)   *Just one man* drank rum. *He* was ill afterwards

(6)   *Few professors* came to the party but *they* had a good time

(7)   John bought *several donkeys*. Harry vaccinated *them*.

All this suggests that there is something seriously wrong with the Argument from Anaphora. In fact, most of the premises have been challenged in the literature, either explicitly or implicitly. For example, Kripke (1977) and Lewis (1979) are challenging either (pr1) or (pr4) when they suggest that a (putatively) anaphoric pronoun may refer to an individual *raised to salience* by the utterance of the antecedent sentence. Evans (1977), Parsons (1978), and Cooper (1979), on the other hand, are challenging either (pr2) or (pr4) when they provide analyses of unbound anaphoric pronouns in terms of Russellian descriptions recoverable from antecedent sentences. (In the light of the discussion in 5.3, I take it that (pr3) is uncontroversial.)

Whatever the merits of the suggestion made by Kripke and Lewis, it is clear that the descriptive approach pioneered by Evans has better prospects for providing the basis of a unified theory of unbound anaphora.[21] Section 5.5 will address the descriptive approach in detail; for the remainder of this section I want to look briefly at the limitations of the alternative suggestion.

The basic idea behind the suggestion made by Kripke and Lewis is that a speaker can use a pronoun to refer to an object raised to salience by an utterance of a sentence containing the pronoun's (putative) antecedent. Consider an utterance u of (1) in which S uses 'the man in the gabardine suit' referentially:

(1)   *The man in the gabardine suit* is a spy. *He* tried to bribe me.

Although the proposition expressed by the antecedent sentence is descriptive, the proposition *meant* is object-dependent (recall from 3.5 that when S makes a referential use of a definite description in an utterance u of 'The F is G', there is some object b such that S *means* by u that b is G). And since a particular individual b has been raised to perceptual salience, S may use a subsequent referential pronoun to refer to b; that is, S may use the subsequent sentence 'He tried to bribe me' to express an object-dependent proposition about b.

The following passage from Lewis (1979) makes the point very clearly for an example such as (3),

(3)   *A cat* is on the lawn; *he* looks like a stray to me

which involves an indefinite description:

> I may say 'A cat is on the lawn' under circumstances in which it is apparent to all parties to the conversation that there is some one particular cat that is responsible for the truth of what I say, and for my saying it. Perhaps I am looking out of the window, and you rightly presume that I said what I did because I saw a cat; and further (since I spoke in the singular) that I saw only one. What I said was an existential quantification; hence, strictly speaking, it involves no reference to any particular cat. Nevertheless it raises the salience of the cat that made me say it. . . . Thus although indefinite descriptions—that is, idioms of existential quantification—are not themselves referring expressions, they may raise the salience of particular individuals in such a way as to pave the way for referring expressions that follow (p. 243).

On this account, the "anaphoric" pronouns in (1) and (3) are referring expressions while their "antecedents" are quantifiers.

The limitations of this approach to unbound anaphora can be illustrated by considering examples in which antecedent descriptions are used nonreferentially. Consider (2) and (4) again:

(2) *The inventor of the wheel* was a genius. I suspect *s/he* ate fish on a daily basis

(4) *An insurance agent* is coming to see me today. I'm sure *s/he* just wants to sell me a policy.

Suppose I use the description 'the inventor the wheel' nonreferentially in an utterance *u* of (2). I have no idea who invented the wheel and no intention to communicate an object-dependent proposition about any particular person; but I suspect that whoever it was that invented the wheel ate a lot of fish. In this case, there is no temptation to say that the pronoun in the anaphor sentence in (2) is a referring expression. No identifiable individual has been raised to salience. Similarly for an utterance of (4) involving a nonreferential use of the indefinite description 'an insurance agent'. For now we can just note that although the salience-based suggestion seems to work for some cases—specifically, those in which the "antecedent" description is used referentially as in (1) and (3)—it cannot be the whole story.[22]

The discussion of examples (2) and (4) shows that premise (pr2) of the Argument from Anaphora is not in general true. We have just constructed cases in which anaphoric pronouns are neither bound variables nor straightforward referring expressions. So it looks as though any complete theory of unbound anaphora will have to treat at least some pronouns in a rather different way. But how? The first clue comes from the following observation: to endorse (pr2) is to reject the possibility that some anaphoric pronouns are "pronouns of laziness" of one form or another. Suppose the pronouns in (1)-(4) are treated as going proxy for repeated occurrences of their antecedents. This would, in fact, give us the right truth conditions for (1) and (2), where the antecedents are definite descriptions, but not for (3) and (4), where the antecedents are indefinite descriptions:

(1_1) The man in the gabardine suit is a spy. The man in the gabardine suit tried to bribe me

(2_1) The inventor of the wheel was a genius. I suspect the inventor of the wheel ate fish on a daily basis

(3_1) A cat is on the lawn. A cat looks like a stray to me

(4_1) An insurance agent is coming to see me today. I'm sure an insurance agent just wants to sell me a policy.

However, as is well known, if the pronouns in (3) and (4) are treated as going proxy for the *definite* descriptions 'the cat on the lawn' and 'the insurance agent who is coming to see me today', respectively, things look a lot better. The importance of this fact, emphasized by Evans (1977) and others, will be explored in 5.5.

Let's take stock. We saw in 5.3 that the anaphoric pronouns in (1)-(4) are not bound variables. Consequently, we need to supplement a theory of bound anaphora with a theory of unbound anaphora. A treatment of unbound anaphors as referring expressions appears to succeed only with examples in which the antecedent quantifier is used referentially as in the scenarios we constructed for utterances of (1) and (3). It does not work in cases where the antecedents are used nonreferentially, such as those we created for utterances of (2) and (4). By contrast, a simple pronoun-of-laziness treatment appears to succeed with examples like (1) and (2), where the antecedents are definite descriptions, but not with examples like (3) and (4), where the antecedents are indefinite descriptions. Moreover, as Evans (1977) has emphasized, *both* approaches appear to fail with examples like (5)-(7), where the antecedents are other quantifiers:

(5)   *Just one man* drank rum. *He* was ill afterwards

(6)   *Few professors* came to the party but *they* had a good time

(7)   John bought *several donkeys*. Harry vaccinated *them*.

In short, we do not yet have any sort of general account of unbound anaphora. What is needed is comprehensive theory that applies to all pronouns that are anaphoric on, but not c-commanded by, quantified antecedents. It is the task of the next section to map out a plausible theory.

5.5 Descriptive Anaphora

Recall from 2.6 that a definite description, whether singular or plural, is just a type of (restricted) universal quantifier, one with existential import. Where 'F' is singular, '[the x: Fx] (Gx)' is true if and only if all Fs are Gs and there is *exactly one F*; where 'F' is plural, '[the x: Fx] (Gx)' is true if and only if all Fs are Gs and there is *more than one F*. To borrow Vendler's (1967) wording, the use of the definite article typically signals the speaker's intention to exhaust the range of a particular predicate. (As we saw in 3.7, the precise content of the predicate may depend upon various contextual factors, for instance when the description is incomplete or otherwise improper.) If just one thing is taken to fall under the predicate, a singular description should be used; if more than one, a plural description. As shorthand for this, let's say that the definite article is used to *signal   maximality*, which in the case of a singular description is the same thing as *signalling* uniqueness. More generally, let's say that

(P3)   A quantifier '[Dx: Fx]' is *maximal* if and only if '[Dx: Fx](Gx)' entails '[every x: Fx](Gx)', for arbitrary G.[23]

On this account, quantifiers of the form 'the F', 'the Fs' 'each F', 'each of the Fs', 'every F', 'all Fs' are maximal.

Recall from 5.3 that the pronoun in (1) is not functioning as a bound variable:

(1)   John bought *some donkeys* and Harry vaccinated *them*.

A plausible paraphrase of (1) is (2):

(2)   John bought some donkeys and Harry vaccinated *the donkeys John bought*.

This suggests to Evans (1977) that the unbound pronoun 'them' in (1) should be interpreted *via* the plural description 'the donkeys John bought', as what he calls an *E-type* pronoun.[24] We might, therefore, represent the logical form of (1) as (1₁):

(1₁)   [some x: donkeys x] (John bought x) &

[the y: donkeys y & John bought y] (Harry vaccinated y).[25]

It is instructive to compare (1_1) with Geach's bound variable analysis of (1) as (1_2):

(1_2) [some x: donkey x] (John bought x & Harry vaccinated x).

The problem with (1_2), recall, is that it is true if Harry vaccinated just *some* of John's donkeys. But intuitively, the truth of our target sentence (1) requires him to vaccinate *all* of them. This, of course, is exactly what an analysis of the plural pronoun 'them' as a plural definite description captures.

As noted at the end of the last section, we find the same sort of paraphrase relation where the antecedent is a singular indefinite description. A plausible paraphrase of (3) is (4):

(3)   John bought *a donkey* and Harry vaccinated *it*

(4)   John bought *a donkey* and Harry vaccinated *the donkey John bought.*

We might therefore represent the logical form of (3) as (3_1):

(3_1) [an x: donkey x] (John bought x) &

[the y: donkey y & John bought y] (Harry vaccinated y).[26]

As Evans points out, it is tempting to think that we have here the beginnings of a quite general account of the semantical content of unbound pronouns anaphoric on quantifiers. First, the presence of a connective like 'and', 'but', 'yet', 'or', 'if...then', etc., is inessential. For example, no substantial change results if we switch from (3) to the two-sentence sequence (5):

(5)   John bought *a donkey*. Harry vaccinated *it*.

Second, the descriptive analysis is not specific to those (unbound) pronouns that have indefinite descriptions as their antecedents. It appears to be applicable to pronouns anaphoric on quantified antecedents far more generally. For instance, the second sentence in (6) is plausibly equivalent to (6_1):

(6)   *Just one man at my party* drank rum. *He* was ill afterward

(6_1) *The man who drank rum at my party* was ill afterward.

Similarly for the following pairs:

(7)   *A few policemen* came; *they* seemed to enjoy themselves

(7_1) *The policemen who came* seemed to enjoy themselves

(8)   John owns *many donkeys*; Harry vaccinates *them*

(8$_1$)   Harry vaccinates *the donkeys John owns*

(9)   John found *several minor mistakes* in his proof, but he managed to correct *them* without too much difficulty

(9$_1$)   He managed to correct *the mistakes he found in the proof* without too much difficulty

(10)   Either there's *no bathroom* in this house or *it*'s in a strange place

(10$_1$)   *The bathroom (there is) in this house* is in a strange place

(11)   *The inventor of bifocals* was a genius; *he* ate a lot of fish

(11$_1$)   *The inventor of bifocals* ate a lot of fish

(12)   *The women who came to the party* were irritated by Bill; *they* complained, in particular, about his chauvinism

(12$_1$)   *The women who came to the party* complained, in particular, about Bill's chauvinism.[27]

Let us now adopt the following definition:

(P4)   The *antecedent clause* for a pronoun P that is anaphoric on a quantifier Q occuring in a sentence ϕ is the smallest well-formed subformula of ϕ that contains Q as a constituent.[28]

(Although the intent of (P4) is clear, in due course we will need to forge some connections between logical representations and surface syntax if it is to have application once we get away from all but the simplest cases, for example when we get to sentences involving relative clauses. But this can wait until 5.6.)

We might now put forward the following generalization:

(P5)   If x is a pronoun that is anaphoric on, but not c-commanded by, a quantifier '$[Dx: Fx]$' that occurs in an antecedent clause '$[Dx: Fx](Gx)$', then x is interpreted as the most "impoverished" definite description directly recoverable from the antecedent clause that denotes everything that is both F and G.[29]

More usefully for present purposes, (P5) can be spelled out as the conjunction of (P5$_a$) and (P5$_b$):

(P5$_a$)   If x is a pronoun that is anaphoric on, but not c-commanded by a nonmaximal quantifier '$[Dx: Fx]$' that occurs in an antecedent clause '$[Dx: Fx](Gx)$', then x is interpreted as '$[$the $x: Fx$ & $Gx]$'

(P5$_b$) If x is a pronoun that is anaphoric on, but not c-commanded by a maximal quantifier '$[Dx: Fx]$' that occurs in an antecedent clause '$[Dx: Fx](Gx)$', then x is interpreted as '$[$the $x: Fx]$'.[30]

Let's run through an example. Consider (1) again:

(1)   John bought *some donkeys* and Harry vaccinated *them*.

The logical form of the antecedent sentence can be given by

(1$_3$)   [some x: donkeys x] (John bought x).

By (P4) this is also the antecedent clause for 'some donkeys' in (1). Since 'some Fs' is nonmaximal, the force of (P5) is captured by (P5$_a$). If (P5$_a$) is applied to 'they' the anaphor sentence comes out as:

(1$_4$)   [the x: donkeys x & John bought x] (Harry vaccinated x).

Now consider (11) again:

(11)   The *inventor of bifocals* was a genius; *he* ate a lot of fish.

Since 'the F' is maximal, the force of (P5) is captured by (P5$_b$). If this is applied to 'he' the net result is that the pronoun goes proxy for a repeated occurrence of its antecedent, giving it the illusion of being a pronoun of laziness (in Geach's (1962) strict sense).

Now if this treatment of unbound anaphors succeeds, it is obvious that the Argument from Anaphora presented in 5.4 is defeated again. One of the premises, (pr2), in that argument is that if a pronoun P is anaphoric on another noun phrase Q, then P is either a bound variable or a referring expression. But if unbound anaphors go proxy for definite descriptions and definite descriptions are quantifiers, (pr2) is false. Both antecedent and anaphor can be treated in accordance with Russell's theory. When it comes to descriptive pronouns that are anaphoric on definite descriptions, we are not going to encounter any *new* problems in specifying descriptive content: the pronoun (typically) has the same content as its antecedent.[31] If the antecedent description is elliptical or otherwise incomplete, so is the anaphor, and in exactly the same way.

This point naturally leads one to question the precise status of (P5). Should it be understood as a linguistic rule, a processing heuristic, or a mere generalization? Or some combination of these? The analogous rule in Evans' theory is treated by him as a genuine linguistic rule: on Evans account E-type anaphora is just as rule-governed as bound anaphora. However, he concedes that "We should allow the reference of an E-type pronoun to be fixed not only by predicative material explicitly in the antecedent clause, but also by material which the speaker supplies on demand" (1977, p. 130). In one respect this is as expected. It is impossible to provide the correct truth conditions for sentences containing quantifiers without allowing context to play a role in specifying their full content, if only because of indexicality and incompleteness (see Chapter 3).

Consideration of further data might lead the semanticist in either of two general directions. At one extreme, one might consider working up (P5) into a full-blown syntactical transformation (that is, one might opt for the view that the description for which a descriptive pronoun goes proxy is actually present at some level of linguistic representation). At the other extreme, the semanticist might think of (P5) as a pretty reliable descriptive generalization: when we interpret utterances we operate under broadly Gricean constraints and bring to bear a lot of background assumptions and contextual information, including information derived from preceding utterances (and perhaps fragments of the utterance being processed), and we use this in filling out those aspects of the utterance that are underspecified by linguistic form, including the assignment of referents to those pronouns that are referential and the assignment of descriptive content to some of those that are not.) Or one might opt for any one of a number of intermediate positions. My own inclination is to see (P5) as a very reliable descriptive generalization, and perhaps also as a processing heuristic, though as we shall see, a rather impressive array of facts can be accounted for on the assumption that (P5) is a genuine linguistic rule that operates on syntactical representations in which scope assignments have been made. For the sake of precision, let us proceed as if (P5) were a linguistic rule and be ready to back down where necessary.

It is plausible to suppose that the bound/referential/descriptive trichotomy provides a near-exhaustive classification of pronominal content.[32] Taking the class of bound pronouns to be delimited syntactically by (P2), a distinction between referential and descriptive pronouns makes good explanatory sense if we take seriously the distinction between object-dependent and object-independent thoughts and have an interest in opening up the possibility of the distinction being extended to sentences with pronouns as subjects. For as we have seen, we use pronouns where we might use genuine referring expressions, and we also use them where we might otherwise use descriptions.

Let's now look in detail at the semantics of descriptive pronouns. As I mentioned earlier, Evans (1977) explicitly rejects the view that E-type pronouns *go proxy for* descriptions in favor of the view that they *have their referents fixed* by description in Kripke's (1972) sense. Consequently, *E-type* pronouns are, for Evans, a hybrid category: they are not genuine referring expressions—they are not subject to (R1) and (R2)—but they *are* supposed to be rigid designators, i.e., subject to (R3). According to Evans, they function just like names whose references are fixed by description.[33] As Evans puts it, an E-type pronoun refers to "those objects which verify (or that object which verifies) the sentence containing the antecedent quantifier" (1977, p. 111).

Evans' main reason for rejecting the proxy view in favor of the reference-fixing view is that he thinks descriptive pronouns do not give rise to the sorts of scope ambiguities that overt descriptions delight in when they interact with sentential operators (4.2). According to Evans, if we take a sentence S containing a descriptive pronoun P and replace P with the favored description, the resulting sentence S' may exhibit a scope ambiguity that is not exhibited by S. First let's look at descriptive pronouns in attitude contexts. On the proxy theory, (13) will come out as (14):

(13) *A man* murdered Smith, but John does not believe that *he* murdered Smith

(14) A man murdered Smith, but John does not believe that the man who murdered Smith murdered Smith.

Thus it delivers two readings for the anaphor sentence—the so-called *de re* and *de dicto* readings (see 4.2 and 4.5)—according as the description delivered by (P5$_a$) is given wide or narrow scope:

(15$_1$) [the x: man x & x murdered Smith]

(John does not believe that (x murdered Smith))

(15$_2$) John does not believe that

([the x: man x & x murdered Smith] (x murdered Smith)).

Evans points out that it is natural to interpret (13) as attributing to John "merely a non-contradictory belief of the murderer that he is not the murderer" (1977, p. 133). (This is the reading delivered by his own formal theory.) On the proxy theory, this attribution is captured by (15$_1$), the *de re* reading of the second conjunct.

It is (15$_2$), the *de dicto* reading of the second conjunct, that Evans finds troubling. As he points out, (15$_2$) attributes to John the self-contradictory belief that the man who murdered Smith did not murder Smith, a highly unlikely reading. The fact that this unlikely *de dicto* reading emerges on the proxy theory suggests to Evans that the correct analysis of descriptive pronouns is that they are rigid designators that have their referents fixed by description, an analysis that prevents them from being interpreted as if they took narrow scope.

There are several points here. First, as Soames (1989) points out, although Evans claims that E-type pronouns rigid designators whose references are fixed by description, we must really take him to be making the ("weaker") claim that they are equivalent to wide scope descriptions—which is the way they are treated in his semantical formalism.[34] The reason for this is that being rigid and being equivalent to a description that insists upon wide scope do not amount to the same thing. And as Soames points out, typically E-type pronouns are not rigid, because at different circumstances of evaluation the clauses containing their antecedents will be verified by different objects; in which case the pronoun will refer to different objects (or a different object) at different circumstances. Consider (1):

(1)   John bought *some donkeys* and Harry vaccinated *them.*

If 'them' were rigid, it would refer to the donkeys John actually bought—let's say, Eeyore and Dinah—and so the proposition expressed by (i) would be true at any circumstance of evaluation in which Harry vaccinated Eeyore and Dinah so long as John bought some donkeys there, though not necessarily Eeyore and Dinah. We must conclude, then, that descriptive pronouns are not typically rigid designators.

Second, it's not clear that (13) poses a problem for the proxy view at all. Notice that the *de dicto* reading of the second clause of (14) is also highly unlikely. Consequently, the proxy theorist might well argue that the *de dicto* reading of the second clause in (13) is technically available but so unlikely that it cannot be taken seriously. All the example really shows, the proxy theorist can say, is that the preferred reading is the same in both (13) and (14).

Third, as Davies (1981) and others have pointed out, there are examples of the same general form as (13) in which the *de dicto* reading of the anaphor sentence is clearly available, if not preferred:[35]

(16)   *A man* murdered Smith. The police have reason to think *he* injured himself in the process

(17)   Hob thinks that *a witch* killed Trigger. He also suspects that *she* blighted Mathilda.

Similarly where the antecedent is a definite description:

(18)   *The inventor of the wheel* was a genius. I suspect *s/he* ate a lot of fish

(19) I suspect that *the man who murdered Smith* was from out of town. In fact, I suspect *he* was a foreigner.

The most plausible readings of the anaphor clauses in (18) and (19) are the ones that ascribe to me *de dicto* suspicions, the descriptions delivered by (P5) taking narrow scope.[36]

Fourth, Kripke's (1977) point that Russell's notion of the scope of a description cannot be replaced with a binary semantical ambiguity (4.2) carries over to descriptive pronouns.[37] For example, the proxy view seems to handle examples such as the following in which the descriptive pronoun can take intermediate scope:

(20) *A man* murdered Smith. John thinks Bill knows where *he* is staying.

To the extent that it makes available different scope readings of anaphor sentences, the proxy theory must, I believe, be viewed as superior to Evans' own theory, at least for descriptive pronouns in contexts of propositional attitude.[38] To avoid confusion, henceforth let us borrow the terminology of Sommers (1982) and call pronouns that literally go proxy for definite descriptions *D-type* (rather than E-type) pronouns.[39]

What of unbound anaphors in temporal and modal contexts? Are they E-type or D-type? According to Evans, (21) presents a problem for the D-type theory:

(21) Boston has a Mayor. He used to be a Democrat.

The *de re* reading of the anaphor sentence in (21) is certainly preferred and perhaps even more so than the *de re* reading of the anaphor sentence in (22), which Evans takes to be the prolix version of (21):

(22) Boston has a Mayor. The Mayor of Boston used to be a
      Democrat.

But it is not at all clear that this example tells against the D-type theory. First, the *de dicto* reading *does* seem to be available, it's just not preferred. Second, application of (P5) to 'he' in (21) does not yield 'the Mayor of Boston', it yields 'the Mayor Boston has', and if this description is substituted for 'he' in (21) the resulting pair of sentences seems to pattern with the pair in (21) rather than the pair in (22). Furthermore, it is possible to construct similar examples in which the purported *de dicto* reading is just as likely as the *de re* reading. Consider:

(23) Next year a man from Texas will be President and he'll certainly help the oil business

(24) Right now the Mayor of Boston is a Republican, but next year he'll be a Democrat.[40]

Take (25); if the pronoun 'he' is analyzed in accordance with (P5), the second conjunct can be interpreted as either (25_1) or (25_2):

(25_1) next-year ([the x: Mayor of Boston x] (Democrat x))

(25_2) [the x: Mayor of Boston x] (next-year (Democrat x))

the descriptive pronoun taking either wide or narrow scope with respect to the temporal operator.[41] This suggests very strongly that the pronoun in (24) is D-type.[42]

Descriptive pronouns also interact with modal operators. Consider the following sort of sentence from Karttunen (1976):

(26) Mrs Jones wants Mary to marry *a rich man*; *he* must be a banker.[43]

The *de dicto–de dicto* reading of this pair of sentences is perfectly natural. On this reading the logical form of the antecedent sentence is given by:

(27) Mrs Jones wants ([an x: man x & rich x] (Mary marry x)).

By (P4) the logical form of the antecedent clause is just

(28) [an x: man x & rich x] (Mary marry x).

If we now apply (P5) to 'he' in the anaphor sentence, that sentence as a whole comes out as either (29_1) or (29_2)

(29_1) [The x: man x & rich x & Mary marry x] O (banker x))

(29_2) O [The x: man x & rich x & Mary marry x] (banker x))

where O is whatever modal operator is introduced by 'must'. And it is clear that it is (29_2) that is required where the antecedent sentence is read *de dicto*.

The possibility of descriptive pronouns taking narrow scope appears to throw some light on Karttunen's observation that if the antecedent sentence in (26) is given its *de dicto* reading, the modal auxiliary has to be there for the anaphora to work. Compare (26) with (30):

(30) Mrs Jones wants Mary to marry *a rich man*; *he* is a banker.

If the antecedent sentence in (30) is read *de re*, there is no problem construing the pronoun in the anaphor clause as anaphoric on 'a rich man'. But the anaphoric relation seems to be illicit if the antecedent sentence is read *de dicto*. Unpacking the pronoun 'he' in the anaphor clause as a definite description yields only one reading for that clause because there is no modal expression with which the description may interact. And on this reading the description will give rise to an implication of existence that will be infelicitous if the antecedent clause is read *de dicto*.

We find more or less the same situation with certain conditionals. Consider the following type of contrast discussed by Roberts (1988):

(31_1) If I had the money, I'd hire *a gardener*.
I'd pay *him* $10 an hour

(31_2) ? If I had the money, I'd hire *a gardener*.
I pay *him* $10 an hour.

In (31_1) the descriptive pronoun can take wide or narrow scope with respect to the contracted modal auxiliary 'would', and the reading in which the pronoun has narrow scope makes perfectly good sense. In (31_2), on the other hand, the pronoun is not within the scope of such a device.[44] Evans' E-type theory simply provides no means of accounting for the anaphoric relations exemplified in (26) and (31). Indeed, in view of the fact that we need to interpret some unbound anaphoric pronouns as taking wide scope with respect to certain sentential operators and that we need to interpret other occurrences as taking narrow scope, it is not at all clear how a theory of the semantics of anaphoric pronouns can do justice to the full range of anaphoric relations if it does not treat some pronouns quantificationally.[45] I shall henceforth assume that all descriptive pronouns are D-type, i.e., that there are no E-type pronouns in natural language.

By taking into account both syntax and semantics we have seen that a distinction between bound and unbound anaphoric pronouns seems to be called for. We have further seen that unbound pronouns anaphoric on quantifiers can be treated as D-type pronouns, i.e., as going proxy for definite descriptions. There is no reason to impose any sort of structural constraint on the type of description a D-type pronoun stands in for:

The description may be *relational* (2.2) as in

(32) *Smith's murderer* is insane. *He* should be jailed for life.

The description may be *indexical* (3.3) as in

(33) *My parrot* has escaped. I suppose *it* was unhappy.

The description may be *elliptical* (3.6) as in

(34) *The mayor* is a crook. *He* should be impeached.

The description may be *relativized* (2.6) as in (35) and (36):

(35) *The father of each girl* cheered her. Then *he* waved to her
(36) *Each girl's father* cheered her. Then *he* waved to her.

The description may be interpreted *distributively* or *collectively*. Many plural noun phrases may be interpreted collectively when combined with the right sorts of predicates (see Chapter 2, note 55). This includes plural descriptions. Consider the following:

(37) The men washed their hands
(38) The men carried the piano down the stairs.

Whereas (37) is naturally interpreted distributively—i.e., as saying that *each* of the men washed his hands—(38) is naturally interpreted collectively—i.e., as saying that the men carried the piano down the stairs *together*, not that *each* of them did so. D-type pronouns also admit of both types of reading:

(39) *The men* washed their hands. Then *they* went home
(40) *The men* carried the piano down the stairs. Then *they* loaded it onto a truck.

In (39) 'they' will naturally receive its distributive reading, whereas in (40) it will naturally receive its collective reading.

There is no pressure to preserve distributive and collective continuity:

(41) *The men* carried the piano down the stairs. Then *they* washed their hands and went home.[46]

In this section, I have attempted to spell out the view that unbound pronouns that are anaphoric on quantifiers are interpreted as definite descriptions. In some sense, that's all there is to the theory I am inclined to endorse. The cases we have considered have mostly involved rote applications of (P5), and it is clear that we can do quite a lot without appealing to very much in the way of contextual considerations. But so far we have said nothing about sentences containing two or more pronouns anaphoric on quantifiers or sentences in which the antecedent quantifier is buried in a relative clause or in the antecedent of a conditional. As we shall see, (P5) seems to work very well in these constructions too—although there are certain examples that might steer the theorist towards the view that the precise content of any particular descriptive pronoun is really determined by contextual considerations, not least of which is the immediate linguistic environment. Before we look at more complex cases, however, we need to say a little more about the notion of variable-binding and its relation to syntactical structure.

5.6 Variable-binding and Logical Form

For expository purposes, up to this point I have made the simplifying assumption that we can adequately characterize the syntactical structure of a sentence in terms of its surface structure. One consequence of this is that (P2) has been implicitly understood as a constraint on surface syntax:

(P2) A pronoun P that is anaphoric on a quantifier Q is interpreted as a variable bound by Q if and only if Q c-commands P.

However, for reasons that will emerge in a moment, it seems clear that (P2) must ultimately be viewed as a constraint operating at a level of syntactical representation at which scope relations are made explicit. Here we can draw upon some interesting ideas concerning the representation of quantifier scope within a broadly Chomskyan theory of syntax.[47] Again, for the limited syntactical aspirations of this essay we can ignore many of the technical intricacies; it is just the general idea that we need.

In Chomsky's theory, a distinction is made between *S-Structure* and *LF* ("Logical Form").[48] For present purposes, we can think of an S-Structure representation as a representation of *surface* syntactical structure. An LF representation is a further syntactical representation derived from an S-Structure representation by a formal operation. In effect, LF is the syntactical level at which scope assignments are made explicit and, derivatively, the syntactical level relevant to semantical interpretation.[49] Consider (1), the logical form of which we have been representing as (2):

(1) The girl snores

(2) [the x: girl x] (x snores).

On the assumption that definite descriptions are quantified NPs, something very similar to (2) will be the LF representation for (1). This LF representation is derived from the S-Structure representation by a syntactical scoping rule QR ("Quantifier Raising") that adjoins the quantifier to the S node dominating the subject NP and the VP. In effect, QR maps the S-Structure in (3) into the LF in (4):

(3)   [$_S$ [$_{NP}$ the girl] [$_{VP}$ snores]]

(4)   [$_S$ [$_{NP}$ the girl]$_x$ [$_S$ [$_{NP}$ t]$_x$ [$_{VP}$ snores]]

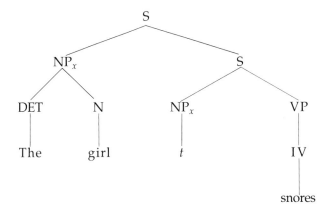

There are several points here. First, QR creates an S node dominating the original S node. Second, at LF the quantifier that has been "raised" is an immediate constituent of the new S node and a "sister" to the original S node. (As the linguists put it, the quantifier is "Chomsky-adjoined to S.") Third, the scope of the raised quantifier is everything it c-commands at LF, i.e., everything under the S node to which it has been Chomsky-adjoined. Fourth, the quantifier leaves behind a "trace" t that functions as a bound variable. Thus (4) is interpreted as (5):

(4)   [$_S$ [$_{NP}$ the girl]$_x$ [$_S$ [$_{NP}$ t]$_x$ [$_{VP}$ snores]]

(5)   [the x: girl x] (x snores).

In a sentence like

(6)   Every girl danced with a boy

the reading obtained depends upon which quantifier QR applies to first. Consequently, (6) is predicted to be ambiguous because it has two distinct LFs:

(6$_1$)   [$_S$ [every girl]$_x$ [$_S$ [a boy]$_y$ [$_S$ [t]$_x$ danced with [t]$_y$]]]

(6$_2$)   [$_S$ [a boy]$_y$ [$_S$ [every girl]$_x$ [$_S$ [t]$_x$ danced with [t]$_y$]]].[50]

Now consider the anaphoric relations in the following examples:

(7)   The father of *each girl* waved to *her*

(8)   The woman *every Englishman* respects is *his* mother

(9)   An F.B.I. agent in *each C.I.A. division* is keeping tabs on *it*.

As noted in 4.2, the interesting feature of these examples is that, from the point of view of surface syntax, the quantifier upon which the pronoun is anaphoric is embedded in another quantifier, despite being interpreted as taking wide scope (on the more natural reading):

(7$_1$)   [each y: girl y] ([the x: x father-of y] (x waved to y)

(8$_1$)   [every y: Englishman y] ([the x: woman x & y respects x]
         ([The z: z mother of y] ($x = z$)

(9$_1$)   [each y: C.I.A. division y] ([an x: F.B.I. agent x & x in y]
         (x is keeping tabs on y)).

Let's focus on (7). Notice that the pronoun 'her' has been treated as a bound variable in (7$_1$). Now if (P2) holds at S-Structure this is illicit because 'her' is not c-commanded by its antecedent at that level of representation. But if (P2) is construed as a constraint on LF representations, things seem to fall neatly into place.[51] Applying QR first to the subject quantifier in the S-Structure (7$_2$) we get (7$_3$):

(7$_2$)   [$_S$ [$_{NP}$ the father of [$_{NP}$ *each girl*]] [$_{VP}$ waved to *her*]]

(7$_3$)   [$_S$ [$_{NP}$ the father of [$_{NP}$ *each girl*]]$_x$ [$_S$ [$_{NP}$ t]$_x$ [$_{VP}$ waved to *her*]]].

Applying QR next to 'each girl' we get (7$_4$):

(7$_4$)   [$_S$ [$_{NP}$ each girl]$_y$ [$_S$ [$_{NP}$ the father of [$_{NP}$ t]$_y$]$_x$
         [$_S$ [$_{NP}$ t]$_x$ [$_{VP}$ waved to her$_y$]]]].

At LF, then, 'each girl' c-commands 'her'; and since it is the reading on which 'her' is understood as anaphoric on 'each girl' that we are interested in, the pronoun can be legitimately treated as a bound variable.

Such examples suggest very strongly that (P2) ought to be understood as a constraint operating at LF rather than S-Structure, and this is what I shall henceforth assume. For ease of exposition, however, I shall continue to use the logical notation introduced in Chapter 2 rather than official LF representations, but the formulae might as well be thought of as LF representations (or as transparently related to LF representations).[52]

In the logical notation introduced in 2.5, both determiners and quantifiers function as variable-binding operators. A determiner Dx binds every free occurrence of x in the formula ϕ with which it combines to form a unary quantifier $[Dx: \phi]$. And a unary quantifier $[Dx: \phi]$ binds every free occurrence of x in the formula ψ with which it combines to form a formula $[Dx: \phi](\psi)$. From the point of view of LF representations of sentences of English, traces resulting from QR and pronouns c-commanded by quantified antecedents function as variables bound by quantifiers. By contrast, it has been implicit in the discussion that the relative pronouns 'who', 'whom', and 'which' (as they occur in restrictive relative clauses) are variables bound by determiners. For example, in the notation of 2.5 (10) comes out as (10_1), and (11) comes out as (11_1):

(10) The man who loves Mary is happy

(10_1) [the x: man x & x loves Mary] (x is happy)

(11) The man whom Mary loves is happy

(11_1) [the x: man x & Mary loves x] (x is happy).

On the natural assumption that English determiners combine with complex nouns like 'man who loves Mary' and 'man whom Mary loves', in the S-Structure representations of (10) and (11) the relative pronouns 'who' and 'whom' are c-commanded by the determiner 'the'. And in the LF representations of these sentences, the pronouns are still c-commanded by 'the' since neither is transplanted to a position outside the description's c-command domain. Consequently, if relative pronouns are treated as bound variables at LF, we can specify a more general constraint on the operator-variable relationship:

(P6) A variable v is bound by an operator Ov if and only if Ov c-commands v at LF.[53]

Furthermore, if a pronoun cannot be treated as a bound variable unless it is c-commanded by its antecedent at LF, we can use semantical facts in support of syntactical hypotheses. Consider the semantical difference between restrictive and nonrestrictive relative clauses, exemplified by (12) and (13):

(12) John bought some donkeys which were vaccinated by Harry

(13) John bought some donkeys, which were vaccinated by Harry.

In accordance with the previous discussion, in (12) the relative pronoun 'which' is part of the noun phrase 'some donkeys which were vaccinated by Harry'. Moreover, since it is c-commanded by the determiner 'some', by (P6) it is interpreted as a bound variable. On this account, (12) comes out as

(12$_1$) [some x: donkeys x & x were vaccinated by Harry]

   (John bought x).

This seems to get the correct truth conditions; like (12), the truth of (12$_1$) is perfectly consistent with John buying *some* donkeys that Harry did *not* vaccinate.

But notice that a bound analysis of 'which' in (13) would deliver the wrong truth conditions; (13) cannot be true unless Harry vaccinated *all* of the donkeys John bought. Indeed, as Evans (1977) observes, the arguments against treating 'them' as bound in

   (14)   John bought *some donkeys* and Harry vaccinated *them*

can be converted into arguments against treating 'which' as bound in (13). This suggests very strongly that, unlike the relative pronoun 'which' in the restrictive relative clause in (12), the relative pronoun 'which' in the nonrestrictive relative clause in (13) is not c-commanded by (is not within the scope of) 'some'. And this comports with our syntactical intuitions: in (13), the nonrestrictive relative clause 'which Harry vaccinated' surely modifies the entire quantifier 'some donkeys'. And on the assumption that the relative pronoun in (13) is not c-commanded by 'some', by (P5) it goes proxy for 'the donkeys John bought', which gets things exactly right. On this account (13) comes out equivalent to the conjunction of 'John bought some donkeys' and 'Harry vaccinated the donkeys John bought', i.e., it comes out as equivalent to (14).[54]

We can now address an anaphoric objection to the Theory of Descriptions due to Heim (1982, pp. 227–29). Consider

   (15)   Every boy who likes *his mother* visits *her* at Christmas.

The interesting thing about this example is that the antecedent is embedded in a restrictive relative clause. According to Heim, since 'her' is not within the scope of 'his mother', a treatment of the antecedent as a Russellian description denies one the possibility of accounting for the anaphoric relation in question. However, on the present proposal, since the pronoun is not c-commanded by its antecedent, by (P5) it goes proxy for a description and the sentence as a whole comes out as

   (15$_1$) [every x: boy x & [the y: y mother of x] (x likes y)]

   ([the y: y mother of x] (x visits y at Christmas)

just as required.[55]

We are now in a position to look at the anaphoric relationships in Bach-Peters sentences like the following:

(16)   The pilot who shot at *it* hit *the MiG that chased <u>him</u>*

(17)   The boy who was fooling *her* kissed *the girl who loved <u>him</u>*.

These examples involve what has come to be called—rather misleadingly as far as the Russellian is concerned—*crossing coreference*, or what I shall henceforth call just *crossing*. The characteristic feature of sentences involving crossing is that one noun phrase NP_1 contains a pronoun that is anaphoric on another noun phrase NP_2, while NP_2 contains a pronoun anaphoric on NP_1.[56] Since there is a lot going on these examples, it will pay to construct them a piece at a time. Consider sentence (18), which is somewhat simpler than (16):

(18)   The pilot who shot at *it* hit *the oncoming MiG*.

Technically, this sentence is ambiguous because it contains two definite descriptions. If 'the oncoming MiG' has wider scope, then (on the assumption that quantified noun phrases undergo QR) the pronoun 'it' can be treated as a bound variable because it is c-commanded by its antecedent at LF:

(18_1)   [the y: oncoming-MiG y]

([the x: pilot x & x shot-at y] (x hit y)).

By contrast, if the subject description 'the pilot who shot at it' takes wider scope, the pronoun 'it' will not be c-commanded by its antecedent at LF and hence cannot be treated as a bound variable:

[the x: pilot x & x shot-at *it*]

([the y: oncoming-MiG y] (x hit y)).

By (P5) the pronoun is therefore a D-type pronoun that goes proxy for the definite description 'the oncoming MiG', and the logical form of the sentence is given by

(18_2)   [the x: pilot x & [the y: oncoming-MiG y] (x shot-at y)]

([the y: oncoming-MiG y] (x hit y))

which is equivalent to (18_1). The two readings of (18) do not differ truth-conditionally.

Now consider the following sentence:

(19)   *The pilot* shot at the MiG that chased *him*.

This sentence is ambiguous in the same way as (18). If 'the pilot' is given wider scope, the sentence comes out as

(19$_1$) [the x: pilot x] ([the y: MiG y & y chased x] (x hit y))

with the pronoun 'him' bound. By contrast, if 'the MiG that chased him' is given wider scope, the pronoun 'him' is unbound. By (P5) the it therefore goes proxy for 'the pilot' and the logical form of the sentence is given by

(19$_2$) [the y: MiG y & [the x: pilot x] (y chased x)]
[the x: pilot x] (x hit y))

which is logically equivalent to (19$_1$).

Now let's return to the Bach-Peters sentence (16):

(16) The pilot who shot at *it* hit *the MiG that chased him*.

There are two interesting features of this example. First, whatever the choice of relative scope, only one of the two pronouns can be bound, the other is D-type. Second, the two readings are not equivalent. If 'the pilot who shot at it' is given wider scope, 'him' is bound and 'it' is D-type:

(16$_1$) [the x: pilot x & [the y: MiG y & y chased x] (x shot-at y)]
([the y: MiG y & y chased x] (x hit y)).

If 'the MiG that chased him' is given wider scope, 'it' is bound and 'he' is D-type:

(16$_2$) [the y: MiG y & [the x: pilot x & x shot-at y] (y chased x)]
([the x: pilot x & x shot-at y] (x hit y)).[57]

The fact that (16$_1$) and (16$_2$) capture the two nonequivalent readings of (16) uncovered by Karttunen (1971) suggests very strongly that the theory under consideration is on the right track and that (P6) and (P2) hold at LF rather than S-Structure.[58]

5.7 Anaphora and Referential Usage Revisited

Before looking at some residual problems concerning referential uses of descriptions and pronominal anaphora, let's summarize the position we have reached. In Chapter 3, I defined what I called a *basic case* of a referential use of a definite description 'the F' as it occurs in a particular utterance u of 'the F is G' made by a sincere speaker S. In the basic case four conditions obtain:

(a)   There is an object b such that S knows that b is uniquely F;
(b)   It is b that S wishes to communicate something about;
(c)   'The F' occurs in an extensional context;
(d)   There are no pronouns anaphoric on this occurrence of 'the F'.

According to the referentialist, if these four conditions are satisfied, the proposition expressed by u is true if and only if b is G. In the basic case, then, the proposition expressed by u will be true on the referential interpretation if and only if it is true on the Russellian interpretation. This is what makes it so hard for the referentialist to provide an argument against Russell using a basic case. To succeed, the referentialist must provide an argument that demonstrates beyond any doubt that one must entertain an object-dependent proposition about b in order to understand the utterance.

Over the course of the last three chapters, we have looked at several quite distinct arguments for a referential interpretation of descriptions that have involved departing from the basic case in one way or another. The Argument from Misdescription (3.6) involved tinkering with conditions (a) and (b) in order to produce cases in which the Russellian and referential analyses delivered propositions with different truth values. The referentialist then urged that our ordinary intuitions favored the referential interpretation. Once the Theory of Descriptions was located within a broadly Gricean theory of communication, this argument was seen to collapse. The Argument from Incompleteness (3.7) involved relaxing condition (a) to allow consideration of cases involving "incomplete" descriptions like 'the table', which seem to resist the Russellian analysis on account of not being uniquely-denoting. Supplemented with an independently motivated theory of context-dependence, the Theory of Descriptions emerged intact. And in Chapter 4 we saw that the introduction of nonextensional operators did not advance the case for a referential interpretation.

If the theory of anaphora advanced in this chapter is on the right track, the Argument from Anaphora presented in 5.4 fails too. The referentialist urges that the pronouns in (1) and (2) are referential:

(1)   *The man in the gabardine suit* is a spy. *He* tried to bribe me.
(2)   *The inventor of the wheel* was a genius. I suspect *s/he* ate fish on a daily basis.

And on the basis of this, the referentialist goes on to claim that the descriptions functioning as their antecedents are also referential. According to the theorist of D-type anaphora, the occurrences of 'he' in (1) and (2) are interpreted as Russellian descriptions, not as referring expressions. It is clear, then, that the referentialist needs to find fault with the D-type analysis if the Argument from Anaphora is to be revived.

Consider an utterance of (1) where 'the man in the gabardine suit' is used *referentially*. For instance, you and I are at a party together and a man in a gabardine suit walks in. I am pretty sure you have seen him, and I utter (1). The referentialist might argue that in this scenario, since it is perfectly clear just who the speaker intends to communicate information about, it is really stretching things to provide a D-type analysis of the anaphoric pronoun in the second clause.

But the Russellian can respond to this objection in various ways. First, the Russellian might argue that the objection is based on a confusion between the proposition *expressed* and the proposition(s) *meant* (in the sense of 3.4). Just as we must distinguish between the (descriptive) proposition expressed, and the (object-dependent) proposition meant by the utterance of the antecedent sentence 'The man in the gabardine suit is a spy', so we must distinguish between the (descriptive) proposition expressed and the (object-dependent) proposition meant by the utterance of the anaphor sentence 'He tried to bribe me'. And of course if the referentialist now appeals to the Arguments from Misdescription, Incompleteness, or Opacity in an attempt to demonstrate that the pronoun is referential rather than descriptive, the Russellian will disarm each argument in exactly the same way as for overt descriptions. The upshot of all this is that if the Russellian opts for an independently motivated D-type analysis of unbound anaphoric pronouns, then the Argument from Anaphora is powerless by itself; any force it has depends upon the prior success of one of the other arguments (applied to unbound pronouns).[59]

Second, suppose (*a*) the referentialist manages to construct a case in which a description is used referentially, and (*b*) a referential interpretation of a subsequent anaphoric pronoun seems intuitively more plausible than a descriptive interpretation. This would still not pose a serious threat to the Russellian: it is still open to appeal to the suggestion made by Kripke (1977) and Lewis (1979), and discussed briefly in 5.4, that an unbound anaphoric pronoun may refer to an individual raised to salience by the utterance of the sentence containing its antecedent. Indeed, one interesting idea is that referential and D-type accounts of unbound anaphora are complementary rather than competing.[60] Something very much like this suggestion seems to lie behind Kripke's (1977, p. 21) discussion of the following dialogues involving misdescription and referential uses of the definite description 'her husband':

Dialogue I   A: Her husband is kind to her.
               B: No, he isn't. The man you are referring to isn't
                  her husband.

Dialogue II   A: Her husband is kind to her.
               B: He is kind to her, but he isn't her husband.

In dialogue I, the occurrence of 'he' is naturally interpreted as going proxy for 'her husband'. But in dialogue II, the pronoun is naturally interpreted as referring to the person misdescribed.[61] In the terminology of the present discussion, the idea here is that unbound pronouns that are anaphoric on definite descriptions used referentially can receive *either* D-type or referential interpretations.[62] (If a description is used nonreferentially then a subsequent anaphoric pronoun must receive a D-type interpretation.)

The interesting thing about this idea is that it encompasses no *syntactical* criterion with which to distinguish between referential and D-type anaphors. Purely linguistic factors tell us only whether or not a pronoun can be construed as a bound variable. If a pronoun is not c-commanded by its antecedent, it is not bound by it, and all that a linguistic theory dictates is that it will therefore receive either a referential or a D-type interpretation. (A *semantical* theory need say no more at this point; but a pragmatic theory will have to concern itself with the types of speech situations in which D-type or referential interpretations are more appropriate.)

Up to now, the content of D-type anaphors has been established by rote application of (P5). There are, however, cases in which more flexibility seems to be required. As noted in 5.4, one obvious type of case is where the description delivered by (P5) is incomplete, as in (3) and (4),

(3)   Right now *the Mayor* is a republican but next year *he*'ll be a democrat

(4)   *A man* came into the office today. *He* tried to sell me an encyclopedia.[63]

What we have here, of course, are instances of the more general problem of incomplete descriptions (3.7), and it is reasonable to suppose that solutions to the more general problem will carry over to these examples. Where the speaker uses 'the Mayor' or 'a man' referentially in utterances of (3) and (4), the Russellian might bypass any potential problem by treating the anaphoric pronouns referentially in accordance with the discussion above. But suppose the speakers are using the descriptions nonreferentially yet have particular individuals in mind (the grounds for their utterances are furnished by object-dependent beliefs). Here, D-type rather than referential analyses of the anaphoric pronouns seem to be called for, and it is clear that the content of each pronoun will have to be filled out in one way or another so as to be uniquely-denoting. Of course, this does not tell against either a unitary Russellian analysis of descriptions or a descriptive approach to unbound anaphora. At most it shows that the content of a D-type anaphor is not always determined by a mechanical application of (P5). And this should occasion no surprise: as we saw in 3.7, even the descriptive content of an *overt* description is not always fixed by purely linguistic factors.

A rather more interesting type of case is exemplified by the following dialogue, based on examples from Strawson (1952) and Donnellan (1978):

(5)   A: The psychologist we met at Macys yesterday just phoned.
       B: He's not a psychologist, he's a psychiatrist.

Let's make the natural assumption that the definite description 'the psychologist we met at Macys yesterday' is being used referentially, i.e., that A is attempting to communicate an object-dependent thought about some particular individual by using this particular description. Now if the anaphoric pronoun in B's utterance goes proxy for the description 'the psychologist we met at Macys yesterday', the clause 'He's not a psychologist' will come out as:

(6)   The psychologist we met at Macys yesterday is not a
       psychologist

which is false in every state of affairs. Let's call this the problem of *pronominal contradiction*.

Those who believe in a semantical ambiguity in definite descriptions might be tempted, at this juncture, to seize on this sort of example in support of their cause.[64] That is, they might argue as follows: If the definite description in A's utterance is interpreted as a referring expression (that need not refer to the unique entity satisfying its descriptive condition), and if the anaphoric pronoun inherits its reference from its antecedent, the problem of pronominal contradiction is solved. Therefore, we should treat the description referentially.

There are several things the Russellian can say in response to this. First, it should be repeated that it is not only the referentialist who may treat the anaphoric pronoun referentially. The Russellian is at liberty to endorse the split D-type/referential thesis and take the anaphoric pronoun 'he' to refer to the individual raised to salience by the utterance of the sentence containing its antecedent, the description 'the psychologist we met at Macys yesterday'.

Second, as Strawson (1952) observes, the phenomenon of pronominal contradiction is not peculiar to definite descriptions. Consider the following exchange:

(7)   *A*: A man from the IRS insulted me today.
       B: He wasn't from the IRS, he was from the INS.

A naïve application of (P5) to *B*'s remark gives us

(8)   The man from the IRS who insulted me today wasn't from the IRS, he was from the INS

which comes out false in every state of affairs. And consider (9):

(9)   *A*: Three people who ate at *Luigi's* last Monday died from food poisoning.
       B: No one ate at *Luigi's* last Monday; it's closed on Mondays. They must have eaten there on Tuesday.

This suggests that we are once again dealing with a phenomenon having to do with the use of quantifiers quite generally, rather than something specific to the use of definite descriptions.

Third, notice that even if a referential interpretation of the anaphoric pronoun in (5) provides a solution to the problem of pronominal contradiction in this particular case, a *general* solution to the problem cannot be constructed along these lines. We find pronominal contradiction even when the quantifier is not used referentially. In example (7) for instance, *A* would probably be making a nonreferential use of the indefinite description 'a man from the IRS'. Moreover, as Davies (1981) points out, it is not even necessary that the grounds for the speaker's utterance are furnished by an object-dependent belief:

Suppose that *A* has a reputation for making predictions about criminal activity, by employing certain mathematical functions and a telephone directory, and that *A* says

A tall blond man murdered Smith at 4 p.m.

Speaker *B*, who also claims powers of prediction and doubts *A*'s accuracy in matters of detail, might reply

He was tall but he wasn't blond

and *B*'s remark would intuitively be correct provided that a tall, non-blond man uniquely murdered Smith at 4 p.m.

An interpretation of the indefinite description 'a tall blond man' as a genuine referring expression in Davies' example is incorrect. There may be no such man, and in any case (R1) and (R2) would both be violated. Similarly for the anaphoric pronoun 'he' in B's utterance. And as Davies goes on to point out, we find the same situation with definite descriptions. Suppose Smith and Jones have been found dead and that it is common knowledge between A and B that each believes a single person murdered both men, but neither has an inkling who it was. Suppose that A now hears that Brown has been found dead, while B hears that Smith actually died of a heart attack. The following exchange takes place:

(10) A: Smith's murderer has been at it again.
 B: He didn't murder Smith. Smith died of a heart attack.

By Donnellan's own criterion, we have here an *attributive* use of 'Smith's murderer', and of course a referential interpretation of this description is out of the question. (All three men may have died of natural causes, and in any case (R1) and (R2) would be violated.) Thus, whatever problems these examples of pronominal contradiction pose for a theory of anaphora, one thing is quite clear: they provide no support for the view that there are semantically distinct referential interpretations of definite and indefinite descriptions.

But cases of pronominal contradiction are still interesting, and it would be nice to be able to throw some light on what is going on in them. Davies suggests that the pronouns in such examples—which he calls "nonliteral" uses—might be treated as having an *ironical* character that can be captured by marking off their descriptive content (or part of it) with scare quotes. For instance, B's utterance in (5) of might be interpreted as (11):

(11) The "psychologist" we met at Macys yesterday is not a psychologist.

The logical form of (11) might be given by (12):

(12) [the x: we met x at Macys yesterday & x was just classed as a psychologist] ($\neg$(psychologist x) & psychiatrist x).

Certainly B might have uttered (11) and conveyed the same point.[65]

We can draw two conclusions from the discussion in this section. First, pronominal anaphora on definite descriptions used referentially does not force us to posit a semantically distinct referential interpretation of such phrases. Second, although (P5) delivers the right descriptive content of D-type anaphors in a wide variety of cases, there are cases in which contextual factors have an important bearing on content specification.[66]

5.8 Concluding Remarks

In this chapter we have seen that the existence of cross-sentential anaphora poses no threat to the approach to quantified noun phrases set out in Chapter 2. In particular, we have seen that anaphora poses no threat to Russell's quantificational analysis of definite descriptions. Indeed, we have seen that some apparently troublesome antecedent–anaphor relations between descriptions and pronouns can be handled rather well within a theory of anaphora that itself makes crucial use of the Theory of Descriptions.

The theories of bound and unbound anaphora that we have examined have much to recommend them. Not only do they mutually dovetail, they also comport with many received ideas in contemporary grammatical theory and provide us with the correct truth conditions for all sorts of sentences involving anaphora on quantified noun phrases. However, there are several matters concerning number agreement and anaphora on *in*definite descriptions that I have not yet addressed. These are not really pertinent to the defence of Russell's account of definite descriptions *per se*; but in the interests of seeing just how far we can go with the D-type approach to unbound anaphora, the next chapter is devoted to such matters.

Notes

1. For discussion of this feature of demonstrative referring expressions, see 3.3.

2. Apart from saying that genuine referring expressions satisfy (R1), (R2), and (R3), in this essay I have deliberately avoided committing myself to particular theories of the interpretation of proper names and demonstratives; in particular I have avoided any sort of commitment to either the neo-Russellian or neo-Fregean conceptions of an object-dependent proposition (2.2). However, as Scott Soames has pointed out to me, choices made here will constrain the options available for dealing with the sort of anaphora discussed above. For example, if a referring expression contributes just an object to the proposition expressed (the neo-Russellian view), then there is nothing to choose between (*i*) the view that a pronoun anaphoric on a referring expression goes proxy for another occurrence of its antecedent, and (*ii*) the view that it inherits its reference from its antecedent. On the other hand, if a referring expression contributes an object-dependent sense to the proposition expressed (the neo-Fregean view), then whether or not these mechanisms are equivalent

will depend upon whether or not the inheritance view is interpreted in such a way that the pronoun inherits the *sense* of its antecedent. As Soames (1988) notes, the difference becomes especially clear if the anaphoric pronoun is within the scope of a psychological verb, as in (i):

    (i)   Mary met *John* yesterday. She thought *he* was very attractive.

3.   For discussion, see Lasnik (1976) and Evans (1980). Several complications and alternative suggestions should be mentioned here. First, the "neutral" assumption seems to be wrong in certain interesting cases. Consider the following example from Nunberg (1977):

    (i)   *Yeats* did not enjoy hearing *himself* read in an English accent.

We can make sense of this example on the assumption that 'himself' is a pronoun of laziness that leads its own semantical life. (Perhaps this should be the model for pronouns anaphoric on referring expressions quite generally.) Second, there is the problem of *de se* attitude reports like (ii) and (iii):

    (ii)   *Yeats* thought *he* was a truly great poet
    (iii)   Yeats wanted to die in Ireland.

(See Chapter 4, note 6.) Third, Salmon (1986) and Soames (1987) have argued that reflexive pronouns anaphoric on referring expressions should be treated not as expressions that refer to the same things as their antecedents but as devices that combine with n-place predicates to form $n - 1$-place predicates. For example, the two-place predicate 'admires' combines with the reflexive pronoun 'himself' to form the one-place predicate '$[\lambda y](\text{admire } y, y)$'. On this account, (iv) comes out as (v):

    (iv)   Yeats admires himself
    (v) $[\lambda y](\text{admire } y, y)$Yeats.

The initial motivation for this view comes from thinking about reflexives in contexts of propositional attitudes. However, as pointed out by Soames (1989), the fact that many of the same problems arise for the interpretation of nonreflexive pronouns in the same contexts might well lead one to widen the domain of application of such an approach.

4.   Examples (2) and (3) are counterexamples to Hornstein's (1984) claim that definite descriptions must take wide scope. (See Chapter 4, notes 4 and 8.) It is unclear what Hornstein's theory predicts for examples like (5) and (6) below.

5.   Of course, to say that some pronouns are interpreted as variables rather than straightforward referring expressions is not to say anything very radical. First, as Kaplan (1977) has emphasized, the variable under an assignment is in some sense the paradigm rigid referring expression. Second, as Evans (1977, 1980) has emphasized, the ability to understand pronouns anaphoric on quantifiers is surely intimately connected to the ability to understand pronouns anaphoric on referring expressions. It is no coincidence that for any sentence containing a pronoun bound by a quantifier we can construct another well-formed sentence by replacing

the quantifier phrase with a referring expression (of the same syntactical number and semantical gender). For example, from (i) we can form (ii):

(i)   *Every bishop* thinks *he* is immortal
(ii)   *John* thinks *he* is immortal.

6. See, especially, Geach (1962, 1964, 1969).

7. A quantifier [*Dx*: *Fx*] is *monotone increasing* just in case the following is a valid inference:

$$[Dx: Fx](Gx)$$
$$\underline{[\text{every } x: Gx](Hx)}$$
$$[Dx: Fx](Hx)$$

for arbitrary *G* and *H*. Examples: 'every *F*', 'some *F*', 'most *Fs*'. For discussion of monotonicity and related properties, see Barwise and Cooper (1981) and van Benthem (1983).

8. The possibility of collective readings for anaphoric pronouns poses a further problem for cross-sentential binding. Consider (i):

(i)   *Three men* got off their bikes and then *they* pushed the VW up the hill.

The more likely reading of the second conjunct of (i) is the one on which the three men who got off their bikes pushed the VW up the hill *together* (though the reading on which each of them pushed the VW up the hill individually is still available). However, this collective reading cannot be obtained by treating the pronoun as bound by 'three men'—at least not in the manner familiar from first-order logic—because 'three men' is still interpreted distributively in the first conjunct.

9. Alternatively, one could devise some sort of alternative to the standard account of bound anaphora. On this score, see (e.g.) Kamp (1981), Heim (1982), Wilson (1984), and Barwise (1987). One of the main points I want to make in this chapter and the next is that there is no good reason to reject the standard account.

10. Indeed, as Higginbotham (1980) points out, there is ultimately a simple and precise syntactical characterization of Russell's notion of the *scope* of a quantifier; see 5.6. To say that there is a syntactical characterization of quantifier scope is not, of course, to deny that scope is a semantical phenomenon.

11. In most contemporary work, linguists do not distinguish in this simplistic way between intransitive and transitive verbs; rather the distinction emerges from consideration of syntactical context.

12. In its crucial respects, (P1) is taken from Reinhart (1976, 1978). The basic idea behind c-command can also be found in Klima (1964), Wasow (1972), and Culicover (1976). In the linguistics literature a variety of competing refinements of Reinhart's definition have emerged. For the very limited syntactical aspirations of this essay, we will not go too far astray if we work with (P1).

13. Strictly speaking, Evans formulates (P2) with an 'only if'; but as we shall see, the stronger formulation seems to hold. It might be thought that sentences like the following are counterexamples to the stronger formulation:

(i)   Most philosophers think they are smart
(ii)   Many junior professors think they are underpaid.

In both of these sentences the anaphoric pronoun is c-commanded by the quantifier in subject position. Although there are readings of these sentences on which the pronouns are interpreted as variables bound by the quantifiers, as Sommers (1982) observes, each appears to have another reading. For example, (ii) might be interpreted as meaning that many junior professors feel that *junior professors* are underpaid. It seems to me that the existence of this reading does not threaten the stronger formulation of (P2). On the reading in question, 'they' is not anaphoric on 'many junior professors', it is anaphoric on 'junior professors' (which does not c-command it) and functions as what Geach (1962) calls a "pronoun of laziness."

The fact that (P2) explicitly tells us when a pronoun may be interpreted as a bound variable, and does so using *syntactical* notions, clashes head on with the following remarks from Hintikka and Kulas:

> We consider it a serious mistake to try to assimilate the semantical modus operandi of anaphoric pronouns to that of bound variables of quantification theory. This assimilation should appear to an unbiased observer extremely unlikely a priori because of the absence of explicit syntactical ties between quantifier phrases and the "variables" allegedly bound to them, and because of the absence of scope indicators in natural language (1985, p. 94).

In 5.6, we will see examples that suggest very strongly that (P2) holds at a level of syntactical representation removed from surface structure. However, as we shall also see, this modification entails no concession to Hintikka and Kulas. Indeed, as Higginbotham (1980) points out, with a few minor assumptions a definition of scope in terms of c-command is interdefinable with Russell's notion.

It might be wondered whether (P2) should also stipulate that a quantifier *precede* a pronoun that it binds. Reinhart (1978) argues that mention of linear precedence is superfluous in English and actually wrong for *left-branching* languages like Malagasy.

Evans (1977) thinks there may be two minor problems for an analysis of bound anaphora in terms of c-command. First, it is held by some philosophers that the determiners 'a certain' and 'any' may be used to form quantifiers that just seem to insist on wide scope in certain environments. (For reasons that will emerge in Chapter 6, this is undoubtedly a mistake.) Second, Evans thinks that one can sometimes "hear" certain occurrences of the standard quantifiers as taking wide scope when, from the point of view of (P2) they cannot, as in (i) for example:

(i)   If a friend of mine sees us, he will be angry.

(As we shall see in Chapter 6, there are reasons to think that this problem is also illusory.) It should be noted that, contrary to what is claimed by Fodor and Sag (1982), even if 'a friend of mine' took wide scope in (i), this would not provide any sort of evidence for a semantically distinct referential treatment of indefinite descriptions. As Kripke (1977) has emphasized, to give a definite or indefinite description wide scope is not at all the same thing as interpreting it referentially. For discussion, see 4.2 and Ludlow and Neale (forthcoming).

14. Thus in (i), 'the man' is the only possible antecedent of 'himself',

    (i)   John thought the man liked himself

and in (ii), there is no possible antecedent:

    (ii)   John thought the woman liked himself.

In a sentence like (iii)

    (iii)   *John*'s mother thought *he* had killed *himself*

the name 'John' does not c-command the reflexive pronoun 'himself'. All this shows is that the pronoun 'he' functions as the c-commanding antecedent of 'himself'. ('John' is the antecedent of 'he'.)

15. Hornstein (1984) claims that quantifiers of the from 'any *F*', 'a certain *F*' and 'the *F*' are members of a class of so-called Type I quantifiers that can (in effect) bind pronouns they do not c-command. I shall be arguing that the facts surrounding anaphora on such quantifiers do not require us to view them as Type I quantifiers. Indeed, in the light of the discussions in Soames (1986), and notes 4 and 8 to Chapter 4 of this essay, it is clear that there are no Type I quantifiers in Hornstein's sense.

16. See (e.g.) Strawson (1952), Chastain (1975), Donnellan (1978), Wilson (1978), Kamp (1981), Heim (1982), Stich (1986), and Barwise (1987). Hornstein (1984) claims that the existence of the anaphoric relations in (1) and (2) below supports his view that definite descriptions are so-called Type I quantifiers. The fact that the anaphoric relations in (3) and (4) below are just as acceptable (even though indefinite descriptions are Type II quantifiers) ought to make one immediately suspicious of this claim.

17. This terminology is borrowed from Sommers (1982).

18. None of the philosophers mentioned in note 16 lays out the argument in this sort of detail; I have extrapolated from informal statements. A rather more schematic reconstruction is presented in Ludlow and Neale (forthcoming) in the context of a discussion of anaphora on indefinite descriptions.

19. An interesting variant of the problem allegedly raised by (1)–(4) concerns the anaphoric links that may exist in sentences containing restrictive relative clauses. For example, it has been argued that the Russellian cannot account for the anaphoric relationships in sentences like the following:

    (i)   Every boy who likes *his mother* visits *her* at Christmas
    (ii)   *The pilot who shot at it* hit <u>the MiG that chased *him*</u>
    (iii)   Every man who bought *a donkey* vaccinated *it*.

Sentences (i) and (ii) are addressed in 5.6; sentence (iii) is addressed in Chapter 6.

20. I am indebted to Martin Davies for stressing this point.

21. To say that the descriptive approach has better prospects for providing the basis of a unified theory of unbound anaphora is not to say that Kripke and Lewis are in error. Both philosophers suggest only that *some* pronouns anaphoric on descriptions may refer to individuals raised to salience by the utterances of the sentences containing their (putative) antecedents. The possibility of reconciling their suggestions with the account of descriptive anaphora proposed in 5.5 is examined in 5.7.

22. Modifying an example due to Geach (1962, p. 117), Evans (1977*b*, p. 160) notes the following asymmetry (where '?' indicates an infelicity of some sort):

    (i)   John owns a donkey. Mary beats it
    (ii)   ? John is a donkey-owner. Mary beats it.

Heim (1982, p. 24) argues that this sort of asymmetry undermines the suggestion made by Kripke and Lewis. She suggests that since 'John owns a donkey' and 'John is a donkey-owner' are equivalent, an utterance of either sentence would render John's donkey salient, and that since the two occurrences of 'it' are not equally felicitous, salience cannot be the operative notion. One possible reply to this would be to say that the infelicity in (ii) is syntactical rather than semantical, i.e., that (ii) is perfectly comprehensible because John's donkey has been raised to salience, but is still odd because anaphoric pronouns—even referential ones—take noun phrases as their syntactical antecedents. The only noun phrases in the first sentence in (ii) are 'John' and 'a donkey-owner', and the context dictates that neither of these is a suitable antecedent. Similarly for (iii) and (iv), which Heim (pp. 21, and 119) attributes to Barbara Partee:

    (iii)   I dropped ten marbles and found them all except for one. It's probably under the sofa.

    (iv)   ? I dropped ten marbles and found only nine of them. It's probably under the sofa.

Notice, however, that it does seem to be possible to construct scenarios in which examples of this ilk seem to work. Suppose I have ten pet mice, one of whom is called 'Hector'. Hector is always getting out of the cage in which I keep all ten mice, and whenever he does so he goes and hides under the sofa. I open up the cage and begin counting mice: "One, two, three, . . ." When I reach 'nine' I turn to you and with a knowing look I say,

    (v)   I put all ten mice in the cage an hour ago, and there are only nine here now.

Knowing Hector's habits, you might then reply,

    (vi)   I bet he's under the sofa again.

The idea would be that (vi) is at most *syntactically* infelicitous.

But do we still want to call this *anaphora*? How different is this case from the following examples (due to Paul Grice):

(vii)   I spent last summer in Persia; *they* are very dissatisfied with the present regime

(viii) His leg was cancerous; he contracted *it* in Africa.

Grice suggests that the "anaphora" in these cases may be less a matter of grammar than conversational reasonableness (3.4) given the salience of the purported denotations of the pronouns.

23. A word of caution is in order here. One often hears it said that 'a plural definite description 'the F' is maximal in the sense that it refers to a "maximal collection" of Fs (or perhaps to some pragmatically determined maximal collection of Fs). I claim no such thing; indeed, I think such talk is ultimately very misleading, even for collective readings.

24. See also Parsons (1978), Cooper (1979), Davies (1981), and Sommers (1982).

25. Although (1_1) might be palatable to Parsons (1978) and Cooper (1979), strictly speaking, Evans would *not* claim that (1_1) provides the logical form of (1). On his final account, E-type pronouns do not *go proxy* for descriptions but rather have their *references fixed* by them, in Kripke's (1972) sense. Although Evans explicitly considers and rejects the proxy view, we shall see later that it is superior to his own account. (The idea that unbound anaphoric pronouns might go proxy for definite descriptions goes back at least to Quine (1960) at pp. 102–3 and p. 113.)

26. In keeping with the English sentences they represent, I have used 'donkeys' in (1_1) and 'donkey' in (3_1). With respect to definite descriptions the difference is important. The truth conditions of '[The x: Fx] (Gx)' are sensitive to whether F is singular or plural (see above). With respect to indefinite descriptions, the distinction between singular and plural may, or may not be important (see 6.3).

If (3_1) is an accurate rendering of (3), then the pronoun 'it' in (3) carries an implication of uniqueness. Heim (1982), Sommers (1982), and Wilson (1984) have taken issue with Evans on the grounds that such an implication is not generally present when an unbound pronoun is anaphoric on a singular indefinite description—indeed they are both sceptical about maximality quite generally. (Heim (1982) contains a lucid discussion of the problems Evans faces.) Although an account of incomplete descriptions (such as the one sketched in 3.7) will help in many cases, there are still some problematic cases left over. I shall defer discussion of such cases until Chapter 6.

27. Examples (6)–(9) are variants of examples used by Evans (1977, 1980); example (10) is due to Barbara Partee, cited in Roberts (1988). Notice that none of (6)–(13) involves anaphora on quantifiers of the form 'every F', 'each F', 'all Fs', or 'any Fs'. Such examples are addressed in 6.3.

Evans observes that the range of cases in which an E-type pronoun may be anaphoric on a quantifier of the form 'no F(s)' is severely limited: (10) is fine, and so is (i), but (ii) and (iii) are not:

(i)   *No professors* were allowed into the party. *They* were stopped at
       the door by bouncers
(ii)   ? John bought *no donkeys* and Harry vaccinated *them*
(iii) ? Every man who bought *no donkeys* vaccinated *them*.

For discussion, see 6.3.

28. I am here indebted to David Lewis.

29. (P5) has its origins in the generalizations offered by Evans (1977, p. 111)
    and by Davies (1981, p. 171), neither of which I find entirely satisfactory.
    The most important differences are the following: (*i*) Evans treats descrip-
    tive anaphors as having their references fixed by description rather than
    as going proxy for descriptions. For reasons given by Davies (1981) and
    by Soames (1989), and recapitulated later in this section, this view must
    be rejected (along with the "weaker" view that descriptive pronouns are
    equivalent to wide scope descriptions); thus (P5) is stated in such a way
    that it does not preclude scope interactions between descriptive
    pronouns and other operators. (*ii*) Evans and Davies both treat deter-
    miners as *binary* quantifiers (in the sense of 2.5). Furthermore, on the
    basis of so-called "donkey" anaphora, Evans argues that quantified noun
    phrases in natural language *cannot* be unary restricted quantifiers; for
    reasons given in 6.3, I think Evans is quite mistaken on this point so I
    have continued to use the unary-restricted notation in stating (P5). (*iii*)
    Evans treats unbound pronouns that are anaphoric on definite descrip-
    tions as "pronouns of laziness" rather than as E-type pronouns; (P5) is
    stated in such a way that it is appropriate in cases where the relevant pro-
    nouns are anaphoric on singular and plural definite descriptions, as in
    (11) and (12); if Davies' generalization were applied to these cases it
    would yield incorrect results (although the problems only show up clearly
    in more complex cases involving nonextensional operators). In cases
    where the antecedent is not maximal, (P5) is, I believe, equivalent to
    Davies' generalization, *modulo* my use of restricted quantifiers. I am here
    indebted to Peter Ludlow and Scott Soames for valuable discussion.

30. At this point, I should say a few words about unbound anaphora on
    certain maximal quantifiers and a few words about unbound pronouns
    that precede their antecedents (the matters are connected). Consider the
    following:

    (i)   Although *he* was furious about the decision, *Simon* decided not to
           quit
    (ii)   Although *he* was furious about the decision, *the filing clerk* de-
           cided not to quit
    (iii) ? Although *he* was furious about the decision, *every filing clerk* de-
           cided not to quit.

The fact that the proper name 'Simon' and the definite description 'the
filing clerk' may serve as "antecedents" for preceding occurrences of
'he', whereas the quantifier 'every filing clerk' may not, is sometimes
treated as evidence for a referential (or otherwise non-Russellian) interpretation of descriptions. The thought behind this claim seems to be that

only a referential expression may serve as the antecedent of a pronoun to its left.

This view does not stand up to serious scrutiny. To begin with, notice that (iv) is fine, even if the definite description is used *non*referentially:

(iv)   Although *he* left no clues, the police have a hunch that *the man who murdered Smith* was a professional.

Furthermore, the contrast between (ii) and (iii) is not a reliable means of diagnosing an alleged distinction between the behavior of descriptions and other quantifiers. There are two points to note here. First, there appears to be a more general problem with unbound anaphora on 'every'-phrases, a problem that surfaces even when we are not dealing with backwards anaphora:

(v)   ? Although *every filing* clerk was furious about the decision, *he* decided not to quit.

As we shall see in 6.3, the right conclusion to draw from this is *not* that unbound anaphora on 'every'-phrases is prohibited; there are more subtle semantical and pragmatic factors at work. Second, if we replace the occurrences of 'every filing clerk' in (iii) and (v) by other quantifiers, we do not find any problems:

(iii$_1$)   *a.*   Although *he* was furious about the decision, *a filing clerk I talked to* decided not to quit

    b.   Although *they* were furious about the decision, *most/several/the/some/many filing clerks* decided not to quit

(v$_1$)   *a.*   Although *a filing clerk I talked to* was furious about the decision, *he* decided not to quit

    b.   Although *most/several/some/the/many filing clerks* were furious about the decision, they decided not to quit.

Hornstein (1984) claims that the anaphoric relations between quantifiers and pronouns to their left supports his view that definite descriptions are so-called Type I quantifiers (see Chapter 4, note 4). According to Hornstein, a Type I quantifier but not a type II quantifier, "can bind a pronoun to its left" (p. 47). Hornstein gives us examples similar to the following:

(vi)   That *he* might be insulted didn't bother *a certain man*
(vii)   That *he* might be insulted didn't bother *any man*
(viii)   ? That *he* might be insulted didn't bother *every man*.

But as Soames (1987) points out, there are plenty of counterexamples to Hornstein's claim:

(ix)   That *he* might be insulted didn't bother *one man I know*
(x)   That *he* might be insulted didn't bother *a man from Idaho*
(xi)   That *they* might be insulted didn't bother *most candidates* at all
(xii)   That *they* might be insulted didn't bother *several candidates*.

Hornstein seems to have focused on a quirk of 'every' rather than anything intrinsic to his Type II quantifiers. Consequently, the fact that (xiii) patterns with (vi) and (vii) and not with (viii) provides no evidence for the view that definite descriptions are Type I quantifiers:

(xiii) That *he* might be insulted didn't bother *the man in the corner*.

In short, the phenomenon of backwards anaphora lends no support to those who would posit a non-Russellian interpretation of definite descriptions.

For further remarks on backwards anaphora, see 5.6. For more detailed discussion of unbound pronouns anaphoric on maximal quantifiers, see 6.3.

31. The caveat is needed because of examples involving contradiction discussed in 5.7.

32. One reason the classification is not exhaustive is the existence of "pronouns of laziness." Consider the occurrences of 'one' in sentences like (i) and (ii):

(i)   John owns a donkey and Harry owns one too
(ii)   John bought a brown donkey yesterday and a grey one today.

In (i), 'one' appears to be functioning as a genuine pronoun of laziness (in Geach's original sense) by virtue of going proxy for a noun phrase that is formally identical to some other noun phrase in the vicinity. (See Geach (1962), pp. 124–25.) In (ii), on the other hand, 'one' seems to be going proxy for 'donkey'.

The occurrences of 'them' in the following sentences also admit of lazy readings:

(iii)   John shot some deer even though they were protected by law
(iv)   John shot some deer even though they are protected by law
(v)   People who buy books tend to read them
(vi)   People who buy flowers tend to grow them.

In (iii), 'them' may be anaphoric either on 'some deer' or on 'deer'. If the former, it is interpreted descriptively as, e.g., 'the deer he shot'. If the latter, it is interpreted lazily as 'deer'. In (iv), the lazy reading is clearly preferred. In (v), both readings are equally plausible, and in (vi) the lazy reading is preferred for obvious pragmatic reasons.

As pointed out earlier, we find a similar situation in sentences like (vii) and (viii):

(vii)   Most philosophers think they are smart
(viii) Many junior professors think they are underpaid.

33. See Evans (1979, 1982). I must admit I am not particularly sympathetic to this hybrid category of noun phrase, which comprises just E-type pronouns and descriptive names. For reasons I give in the text, I think E-type pronouns actually go proxy for descriptions and should therefore be assimilated to the quantifiers. The issues surrounding descriptive names are rather more complex.

34. At one place Evans (1977, p. 132, note 67) does actually *say* that "E-type pronouns are like descriptions which insist upon widest scope."

35. See also Sommers (1982), Richards (1984) and Wilson (1984). Example (16) is adapted from Davies (1981); example (17) is adapted from Geach (1967).

36. Examples like (17) and (19) highlight an interesting discourse phenomenon. Since both the antecedent clause and the anaphor clause contain nonextensional operators, both clauses admit of *de re* and *de dicto* readings. Yet it seems to be the case that the anaphor clause must be read in the same way as the antecedent clause, mixed *de re–de dicto* readings being infelicitous. In these particular cases, what we can call "intensional continuity" seems to be preserved, though doubtless examples can be constructed in which it need not be.

37. This point has been emphasized to me by James Higginbotham and Peter Ludlow.

38. Notice that the pronoun of laziness 'one' may also enter into scope interactions with other operators:

    (ii)   Mary is marrying an artist. Fred wants to marry one too.

    (iii)   Mary wants to marry an artist. Fred wants to marry one too.

39. This is not *exactly* the way Sommers uses 'D-type', but it is near enough for present purposes. It is a weakness of the present essay that it does not take into account Sommers' own rich and interesting proposals concerning the interpretation of pronouns and other noun phrases.

40. Example (24) is adapted from Sharvy (1969).

41. For present purposes I am not going to choose between alternative ways of representing tenses and temporal modifiers in natural language; I shall just appeal to the fact that many of the devices we use to express temporal relations do indeed give rise to the sorts of ambiguities that we can, in very many cases, represent as scope ambiguities.

    Again, we find examples in which pronouns may take intermediate scope:

    (i)   *The mayor* is a democrat. John thinks that next year *he*'ll be a republican.

42. Since it is something equivalent to the reading on which the descriptive pronoun has *narrow* scope that lies beyond Evans' grasp, it will not do to reply on his behalf that the ambiguity in (24) is due to the fact that the definite description 'the Mayor of Boston' is ambiguous between Russellian and referential interpretations. Besides, (*a*) as noted in 4.2, wide scope and referential readings of descriptions are not the same thing, (*b*) no binary distinction can capture intermediate readings in more complex cases, and (*c*) for more or less the same reasons as those given in 3.4, Evans (1977a, 1979, 1982) favors a unitary Russellian analysis of definite descriptions as quantifiers.

    Evans (1977) suggests that he would follow Geach (1962) and Sharvy (1969) in treating the pronoun in (24) as a pronoun of laziness rather than as an E-type pronoun. Since Evans treats descriptions as quantifiers this would indeed allow him to capture the ambiguity in (24), though not in (23) of course. Even so, on such an account—which seems to be motivated only by Evans' desire to provide a solution to the Bach-Peters paradox, a paradox that disappears if one provides a D-type analysis (see 5.6)—we are left with no account of why unbound pronouns anaphoric on quantifiers are pronouns of laziness when the quantifier in question is a definite description and an E-type pronoun otherwise. A D-type analysis would have (*a*) saved Evans from making this *ad hoc* stipulation, and (*b*) allowed him to capture narrow scope readings of descriptive pronouns where the antecedent is a quantifier other than a definite description.

43. Karttunen actually uses 'Mary wants to marry a rich man' as his antecedent sentence. I have changed this so as to avoid distracting issues concerning equi-NP deletion and *de se* attitude reports.

44. This point is made in Neale and Ludlow (1987). Example (31_2) exemplifies what Roberts (1988) calls "modal subordination." In the text I do not mean to be claiming that a descriptive analysis of the anaphoric relation in a conditional like (31_1) takes away all its intrigue. Such sentences raise quite general problems that I shall not even attempt to address in this chapter. (Anaphora in conditionals is discussed briefly in Chapter 6, however.) For present concerns we can at least say that it is a fact about the nature of rational discourse that the elements of a sequence of utterances containing modal operators are often taken to be linked to the same range of possibilities. For instance, in (31_1) the force of the modal 'would' in the anaphor sentence is presumably inherited in some fashion from the occurrence in the antecedent sentence. Thus we might paraphrase the force of the pair as "In any world in which I have the money, I hire a gardener. *In those same worlds*, I pay the gardener I hire $10 an hour." This suggests that it may be possible to view modal continuity as a species of D-type anaphora. I am here indebted to discussion with Leora Weitzman.

45. This is one area in which the original theories of anaphora presented by Kamp (1981) and Heim (1982) appear to fall short. For an attempt to account for the relevant data within a broadly Kamp/Heim framework, see Roberts (1988).

46. As I mentioned earlier, I am not going to say anything here about the semantics of collective readings; suffice to say that an account that works for plural descriptions should carry over naturally to D-type pronouns that are anaphoric on plural descriptions and other plural quantifiers.

47. See (e.g.) Chomsky (1986), chap. 2.

48. For the purposes of this essay we can ignore *D-Structure*, which is the "first" syntactical level in the sense that it is a projection of lexical properties in accordance with a general constraint on well-formedness known as X' ("X-bar") theory. X' theory virtually obviates the need for explicit phrase structure rules. For a clear and relatively nontechnical discussion, see Chomsky (1986).

49. See (e.g.) Higginbotham (1980, 1983), Higginbotham and May (1981, 1981*a*), Ludlow (1985), and May (1985). May (1985), chap. 2 contains a lucid account of the role of LF.

50. If the identity of a sentence is determined by a D-Structure representation, an S-Structure representation, and an LF representation, then it is more accurate to say that two distinct sentences have the superficial form of (6) rather than saying that (6) is *ambiguous*.

51. This observation is due, essentially, to May (1977, 1985).

52. In earlier work (Neale, 1988), I challenged Higginbotham's (1983) use of LF as a tool with which to capture a variety of facts concerning the semantics of "naked-infinitive" perceptual reports, originally treated by Barwise (1981). It now seems to me that the problems I raised—most of which concerned the precise relationship between LF representations and surface syntax—can, in fact, be disposed of without abandoning the spirit of Higginbotham's theory.

53. I have simplified matters here. It is common to think of relative pronouns as devices of predicate abstraction rather than as variables. (See, e.g., Quine (1960), Montague (1973), and Evans (1977).) On such an account, (10) and (11) are interpreted as (10_2) and (11_2), respectively:

    (10)   The man who loves Mary is happy

    (10_2) [the x: man x & $[\lambda z](z$ loves Mary$)x$] (x is happy)

    (11)   The man whom Mary loves is happy

    (11_2) [the x: man x & $[\lambda z]$(Mary loves $z)x$] (x is happy).

By lambda-elimination (10_2) and (11_2) are equivalent to (10_1) and (11_1) respectively

    (10_1) [the x: man x & x loves Mary] (x is happy)

    (11_1) [the x: man x & Mary loves x] (x is happy)

Spelling out the semantical structure of (10) and (11) as (10_2) and (11_2) seems to mesh nicely with Chomsky's view that at S-Structure a relative pronoun is an operator that binds a variable occupying its D-Structure position. (See (e.g.) Chomsky, 1986, chap. 2.) I am here indebted to Richard Larson for discussion.

54. I shall not attempt to work out the syntactical details of this semantics for nonrestrictive relative clauses. I shall be concerned only with restrictive relative clauses in the remainder of this essay.

55. Heim also argues that the anaphoric relation in the structurally isomorphic sentence (i) undermines Russell's quantificational analysis of *in*definite descriptions (see chapter 6):

    (i)   Every man who bought a donkey vaccinated it.

56. This type of sentence was used by Emmon Bach and Stanley Peters in the late 1960's to undermine the (then popular) view that pronouns are derived transformationally from full NPs (see Bach 1970). The fact that each antecedent contains a pronoun anaphoric on the other apparently presented the transformationalist with an infinite regress.

57. The well-formedness of (16_1) and (16_2) falsifies Hintikka and Kulas's (1985) claim that Bach-Peters' sentences cannot be translated into

Russell's *iota*-notation. The particular example Hintikka and Kulas claim is untranslatable is (i):

(i)   The boy who was fooling *her* kissed *the girl who loved him*.

If the subject description is given wider scope, (i) comes out as (ii), which is equivalent to (iii) in Russell's notation:

(ii)   [the x: Bx & [the y: Gy & Lyx] (Fxy)] ([the y: Gy & Lyx] (Kxy))

(iii) $[(\iota x)(Bx\ \&\ Fx(\iota y)(Gy\ \&\ Lyx)]K(\iota x)(Bx\ \&\ Fx(\iota y)(Gy\ \&\ Lyx))$
         $(\iota y)(Gy\ \&\ Lyx)$.

Mutatis mutandis for the reading of (i) on which the object description is given wider scope.

There is apparently a third reading of (16), the truth of which requires that *each* pilot who shot at the unique MiG that was chasing him hit that MiG. If this is a genuine reading, it may well be tied to the quasi-universal readings of simpler sentences such as 'The man who drinks hemlock will die.'

58.   (*a*) One interesting crossing puzzle concerns the following contrast discussed by Jacobson (1977) and Higginbotham (1983):

(i)   *The man who married her loved his wife*
(ii)   *Her husband loved his wife*.

Sentence i seems to be fine with 'his' anaphoric on 'the man who married her', and 'her' anaphoric on 'his wife'; indeed in relevant respects it does not differ markedly from the sentences we have been considering. But for some reason (ii) cannot be interpreted with 'her' anaphoric on 'his wife', and 'his' anaphoric on 'her husband'. Suppose 'his wife' and 'her husband' are cashed out as the descriptions '[The x: x wife-of *him*]' and '[The y: y husband-of *her*]'. On the model of the treatment of (24) given in the text, if the subject description is given wider scope, (i) will come out as

(iii)   [the x: man x & [the y: y wife-of x] (x married y)]
         ([the y: y wife-of x] (x loves y)).

It is not clear to me why (ii) is unacceptable. If it is treated on the model of (i) we get

(iv)   [the x: [the y: y wife-of x] (x husband-of y)]
         ([the y: y wife-of x] (x loves y)).

But (ii) cannot be understood this way. If, for some reason, *both* anaphoric pronouns have to be treated as bound variables, (ii) would come out as

(v)   [the x: x husband-of y] ([the y: y wife-of x] (x loves y))

which contains a free variable y in the first description. (With the scope of the descriptions reversed, the same problem would arise for x. Whichever description gets wider scope will be able to bind the anaphoric pronoun inside the other, but then we are left with the problem of interpreting the remaining anaphoric pronoun.) This would "explain" why (ii) does not work; but then an explanation of why both pronouns are supposed to be bound would be required. (I am here indebted to James Higginbotham.)

(b) I have not said much about *reflexive* pronouns like 'himself', 'herself', 'themselves', etc., but it is plausible to suppose that they do not require any sort of radical departure from the theory examined in the text. There are two types of case to take into consideration, those in which the antecedent is a quantifier and those in which it is a referring expression, as in (i) and (ii), respectively:

(vi)   Every bishop washes himself
(vii)   John washes himself.

One simple approach would be to treat the occurrence of 'himself' in (vi) as a variable bound by 'every bishop' and the occurrence in (vii) as referential, i.e., as referring to whoever 'John' refers to. This would give us (viii) and (ix):

(viii)   [every x: bishop x] (x washes x)
(ix)   John washes John.

But perhaps this is not the best approach. Recall that we have treated noun phrases like 'Smith's murderer' and 'his mother', as definite descriptions that we can represent as '[the x: x murdered Smith]' and '[the x: x mother of him]', where the occurrence of 'him' in the latter is either bound, referential, or descriptive, depending upon the usual considerations. Now if one were to treat 'himself' as a description of the form '[the y: y = him]', (vi) and (vii) would come out as (x) and (xi):

(x)   [every x: bishop x] ([the y: y = x] (x washes y))
(xi)   [the y: y = John] (John washes y).

One possible advantage of treating reflexives in this way emerges if we look at the phenomenon linguists call *VP-deletion*. Consider (xii):

(xii)   John saw Bill and Eric did too.

It is plausible to suppose that the content of the second conjunct in (xii) is given by 'Eric saw Bill (too)'. Now consider a case involving a definite description:

(xiii)   John phoned his mother and Bill did too.

The second conjunct of (xiii) is ambiguous. One might be asserting that Bill phoned his (Bill's) mother, or that Bill phoned John's mother. We can represent these possibilities as (xiv) and (xv):

(xiv)   [the x: x mother-of Bill] (Bill phoned x)
(xv)   [the x: x mother-of John] (Bill phoned x).

One way of capturing these facts is to see the content of the second conjunct as established by copying over material from the first conjunct. For example, (xiv) might be derived by copying over '[the x: x mother-of *him*]' with 'him' uninterpreted, and hence free to pick up its referent from 'Bill'. By contrast, (xv) might be derived by copying over '[the x: x mother-of *him*]' with 'him' already assigned John as its referent. (This is just a first thought; attempting to spell out the details of such a proposal may well uncover a variety of technical problems.) Maria Bittner has pointed out to me that one merit of handling VP-deletion in this way is that (xvi) and (xii) are predicted to be unambiguous, which seems right:

(xvi)   John phoned his mother and so did Mary

(xvii) John and Mary sent their mother flowers and so did Bill.

However, consider (xviii), which Stanley Peters pointed out to me:

(xviii) John defended himself most skillfully and so did his lawyer.

This sentence seems to be ambiguous in the same way as (xiii), and this can be accounted for on the assumption that the reflexive pronoun 'himself' is a description of the form '[the x: $x = him$]', as was suggested for examples (vi) and (vii).

Richard Larson has pointed out to me that bound variables also seem to be copied over uninterpreted, as in the following pair of sentences

(xix)   Most philosophers think they are smart. Most linguists do too

on the reading given in (xx):

(xx)   [most x: philosophers x] (x think (smart x)) &
        [most x: linguists x] (x think (smart x)).

The fact that a variable/pronoun that is the product of some sort of copying or construction process may end up being bound by a different operator from the one binding the variable/pronoun on its original occurrence seems to open up the way to an account of what is going on in Karttunen's (1969) *paycheck* sentence:

(xxi)   The man who gave *his paycheck* to his wife was wiser than the man who gave *it* to his mistress.

The interesting thing about this sentence is that even though 'it' is anaphoric on 'his paycheck', it is clear that (on the more natural interpretation of the sentence) they are not interpreted as denoting the same object. (Cf, 'The man who gave *his wife* a bouquet was wiser than the man who gave *her* chocolates', in which it is quite natural to interpret 'his wife' and 'her' as denoting the same individual.) In accordance with previous discussion, we can analyze 'his paycheck' and 'his wife' as the definite descriptions that we can represent as '[The y: y paycheck-of *him*]' and '[The z: z wife-of *him*]', respectively. But what of the occurrence of 'him' inside each of these descriptions? Notice that the descriptions are themselves constituents of the restrictive relative clause 'who gave his paycheck to his wife', which is itself a constituent of another definite description 'the man who gave his paycheck to his wife', which we can represent as

(xxii) [the x: man x & [the y: y paycheck-of *him*]
        ([the z: z wife-of *him*] (x gave y to z))].

The reading of (xxi) that we are interested in is the one in which the man in question gave his own paycheck to his own wife. Since both 'occurrences of 'him' are within the scope of (i.e., c-commanded by) 'the x', on this reading they are bound variables. By (P5) the pronoun 'it' in (xxi) goes proxy for another occurrence of the description 'his paycheck', which is itself a constituent of the description 'the man who gave it (his paycheck) to his mistress', which we can represent as:

(xxiii) [the a: man a & [the y: y paycheck-of him]
([the b: b wife-of him] (a gave y to b))].

Since this occurrence of 'him' is within the scope of 'the a', it is, on the reading we are interested in, a bound variable. The entire sentence therefore comes out as

(xxiv) [the x: man x & [the y: y paycheck-of x]
([the z: z wife-of x] (x gave y to z))]
([the a: man a & [the y: y paycheck-of a]
([the b: b mistress-of a] (a gave y to b))] (x was wiser than a)).

Compare (xxi) with

(xxv) The man who gave *his wife* a bouquet was wiser than the man who gave *her* chocolates

where the variable inside the description for which 'her' goes proxy is naturally interpreted as bound by the subject description 'the man who gave his wife a bouquet.' In this note I am indebted to Richard Larson for discussion.

59. I am here indebted to Martin Davies for discussion.

60. See also Sommers (1982). For pronouns anaphoric on indefinite descriptions, this suggestion is made in Neale and Ludlow (1987) and is examined in more detail in Ludlow and Neale (forthcoming).

61. Kripke also points out that the referentialist may be hard-pressed to provide a coherent account of dialogue I. For further discussion, see Devitt (1981), p. 522.

62. Informants seem to agree that if no special stress is placed on 'he', dialogue II is less natural than dialogue I.

63. Example (4) is from Donnellan (1978).

64. See, e.g., Chastain (1975), Donnellan (1978), and Wilson (1978).

65. For a similar suggestion, see Sommers (1982). As Peter Ludlow has observed, ironic uses of *overt* definite descriptions are not uncommon. But as Nathan Salmon has pointed to me, there is still a strong feeling that an ironic use of a description has a certain rhetorical effect that the pronoun lacks, an asymmetry that the proxy view seems to leave unexplained.

66. The following examples (due to Richard Holton) involving monotone decreasing quantifiers, raise some related issues (similar examples can be found in Sommers (1982)):

(i)   *Few Hondurans* voted. *They* were intimidated by the secret police

(ii)   *No Hondurans* voted. *They* were intimidated by the secret police.

A naive application of (P5) to 'they' in, say, (i) would yield

(iii)   The *Hondurans* who voted were intimidated by the secret police which is not the most natural reading of (i). There is clearly a more natural reading on which it is *Hondurans* more generally that were intimidated by the secret police. One possible way of obtaining this reading would be to see 'they' as anaphoric on *Hondurans* (or 'the *Hondurans*', on the assumption that 'few *Hondurans*' is elliptical for 'few of the *Hondurans*') in accordance with earlier discussion. Now consider (iv):

(iv)   No philosophers were allowed into the party. They were turned back at the door by a huge bouncer

Here the pronoun seems to go proxy for something like 'the philosophers who tried to get into the party'. Thus (iv) seems to provide good evidence for the view that context must play a role in determining the content of at least some D-type pronouns.

Another type of case in which we may want to allow more than the immediate linguistic environment to affect descriptive content involves what Geach (1967) calls *intentional identity*. Consider (v):

(v)   Hob thinks *a witch* blighted Daisy, and Nob thinks *she* killed Trigger.

If 'she' as it occurs in the second conjunct of (v) is treated as a D-type pronoun, there will be two readings for that clause as a whole:

(vi$_1$)   [the x: witch x & Hob thinks (x blighted Daisy)]
(Nob thinks (x killed Trigger))

(vi$_2$)   Nob thinks ([the x: witch x & Hob thinks (x blighted Daisy)]
(x killed Trigger)).

(vi$_1$) captures the *de re* reading in which there is some particular witch such that Hob thinks she blighted Daisy and Nob thinks she killed Trigger. Unlike (vi$_1$), (vi$_2$) can be true even if there are no such things as witches. Suppose Hob thinks there are witches and has been led to believe that a witch blighted Daisy. He tells Nob about this. Nob also believes in witches and is led to believe that a witch killed Trigger; in fact he thinks that *one* witch is responsible for both acts. (vi$_2$) seems to capture this state of affairs. (Just as the Theory of Descriptions gave Russell the power to deal with nondenoting descriptions, it gives *us* the power to deal with nondenoting *pronouns*.)

Now a complication. Suppose the inhabitants of a certain village have come to believe (erroneously) in the existence of a witch. Geach suggests that someone reporting on events in the village could be justified in asserting (v) because he had heard Hob say "The witch has blighted Daisy" and heard Nob say "The witch has killed Trigger," even if Hob had not said or thought anything about Trigger nor Nob about Daisy. This may well be right; but as Geach points out, in such a case (vi$_2$) is not an adequate rendering of (v), because (v) is true and (vi$_2$) is false. (On the assumption that there are no witches, (vi$_1$) is, of course, out of the question.) If Geach's intuitions are sound—many informants find (v) unacceptable in the envisioned scenario—the pronoun 'she' in (v) will have to come out as something like 'the local witch', or 'the witch we have been hearing about'.

Chapter 6

Further Notes on Descriptive Anaphora

6.1 Introductory Remarks

In this chapter, I want to refine the theory of D-type anaphora and apply it to some residual semantical puzzles. In 6.2, I provide the background for later discussion by laying out the problems that Geach's notorious "donkey" sentences pose for a unitary Russellian analysis of singular indefinite descriptions and for theories of bound and descriptive anaphora. In 6.3, I turn to the relationship between syntactical and semantical number as it applies to quantifiers, and to the matter of number agreement between antecedents and anaphors. This leads to plausible solutions to the central problems involving donkey anaphora. In 6.4, I conclude my discussion of anaphora with some remarks about residual matters that cannot be dealt with at length within the confines of the present essay.

6.2 Donkey Anaphora: The Problem

By making some important modifications to the accounts of bound and unbound anaphora presented by Evans (1977), we have managed to construct a powerful theory that provides a plausible semantics for a variety of sentences containing pronouns anaphoric on quantifiers. However, as it stands the subtheory of unbound (D-type) anaphora faces some of the same problems as Evans' original account.

Consider the following so-called "donkey" sentences:

(1)   Every man who bought *a donkey* vaccinated *it*

(2)   If John buys *a donkey* he vaccinates *it*.

Heim (1982), Richards (1984), and Wilson (1984) have argued that descriptive approaches to unbound anaphora are undermined by the anaphoric relations between 'a donkey' and 'it' in both (1) and (2). And Kamp (1981) and Heim (1982) have argued that the anaphoric relations in (1) and (2) actually preclude the provision of a unitary

Russellian (i.e., existential) treatment of indefinite descriptions.[1] Furthermore, Evans (1977, 1982) himself has argued that the anaphoric relation in (1) cannot be captured by a theory that treats the subject expression 'every man who bought a donkey', as a unary restricted quantifier.

By the time we reach the end of 6.3, we shall see that sentences like (1) and (2) do not force us to abandon the conceptions of quantification and anaphora that have been put to use in the last five chapters. That is, one can pursue the general approach to pronominal anaphora taken in the last chapter without abandoning either Russell's semantics for indefinite descriptions or a general treatment of quantified noun phrases as unary restricted quantifiers.

In order to characterize the initial problem for the Russellian, it will be convenient to revert to the notation of the predicate calculus. On Russell's account, since indefinite descriptions are existentially quantified phrases, the logical form of (3) might be rendered as (3_1):

(3)   Every man who bought a donkey was happy

(3_1) $(\forall x)((\text{man } x \ \& \ (\exists y)(\text{donkey } y \ \& \ x \text{ bought } y)) \supset x \text{ was happy}).$[2]

Since $(\exists x\phi) \supset \psi$ and $(\forall x)(\phi \supset \psi)$ are logically equivalent (where ψ contains no free occurrences of x), notice that (3_1) is logically equivalent to (3_2):

(3_2) $(\forall x)(\forall y)((\text{man } x \ \& \ \text{donkey } y \ \& \ x \text{ bought } y) \supset x \text{ was happy}).$

Now consider (1):

(1)   Every man who bought *a donkey* vaccinated *it*.

Following Geach (1962), it is pretty generally agreed that (1) is true just in case every man who bought at least one donkey vaccinated *every* donkey he bought.[3] We might therefore render (1) as (1_2):

(1_2) $(\forall x)(\forall y)((\text{man } x \ \& \ \text{donkey } y \ \& \ x \text{ bought } y) \supset x \text{ vaccinated } y).$

Now despite the equivalence noted above, there is no first-order formula that is to (1_2) as (3_1) is to (3_2). The "closest" we get is

(1_1) $(\forall x)((\text{man } x \ \& \ (\exists y)(\text{donkey } y \ \& \ x \text{ bought } y)) \supset x \text{ vaccinated } y)$

in which the final occurrence of y lies outside the scope of the existential quantifier that ought to be binding it.[4] It would seem, then, that we cannot represent (1) with a formula that reflects an existential treatment of 'a donkey' (on the intended reading). Consequently, a uniform Russellian analysis of indefinite descriptions would seem to be thwarted.[5]

In my opinion, this is all a bit hasty. Russell's semantics for indefinite descriptions works so very well elsewhere that we should think very hard before abandoning it. Not only does it work for indefinites as subjects and direct or indirect objects in simple sentences, it also works for indefinites in restrictive relative clauses, as in (3). But for some reason, when there is *anaphora* on an indefinite contained in such a clause, as in (1), we must apparently resign ourselves to a treatment of the indefinite as a device of *universal* quantification.[6,7]

Anaphora across conditionals gives rise to virtually the same problem. Consider (4):

(4) If John buys a donkey he is happy.

If we follow the common practice of taking a conditional to be composed of two sentences and a binary sentential connective, and then take the pronoun 'he' in the consequent of (4) to refer to John (see 5.2), we might assign to the sentence as a whole the following logical form:[8]

(4_1)   ($\exists x$)(donkey x & John buys x) $\supset$ John is happy.

By the familiar equivalence again, (4_1) is equivalent to (4_2):

(4_2)   ($\forall x$)((donkey x & John buys x) $\supset$ John is happy).

Notice that the scope of the existential quantifier in the antecedent of (4_1) does not extend to the consequent; in a word, its scope is *clausal*. It should come as no surprise, then, that if the consequent contains a pronoun that is anaphoric on the indefinite description in the antecedent, that pronoun will not be captured by the existential quantifier. Take (2):

(2) If John buys *a donkey* he vaccinates *it*.

If the indefinite description is treated existentially and if 'it' is treated as a variable, (2) will come out as

(2_1)   ($\exists x$)(donkey x & John buys x) $\supset$ John vaccinates x

in which the final occurrence of x lies outside the scope of the existential quantifier that ought to be binding it.[9]

It is not difficult to find a sentence of first-order logic that will get us the right truth conditions:

(2_2)   ($\forall x$)((donkey x & John buys x) $\supset$ John vaccinates x).

Again, apparently the indefinite description must be seen as introducing wide-scope universal quantification.

But there is a *prima facie* absurdity in the claim that indefinite descriptions in certain subordinate structures—restrictive relative clauses and the antecedents of conditionals—have universal rather than existential import. As (3) and (4) make clear, it is just false that *every* indefinite description occurring in such a position requires a universal interpretation. The problem seems to arise only when there is *anaphora* of the sort exemplified in (1) and (2).

From the point of view of simply capturing the truth conditions of (1) and (2) (and some related sentences), it will, perhaps, suffice to treat indefinite descriptions as introducing universal quantification when (and only when) they are constituents of certain subordinate structures. But the intrinsic weakness of such a proposal is plain to see. Insofar as we are seriously engaged in the construction of a semantical theory for a learnable language, we must aim for more than this limited brand of truth-conditional adequacy. We want a a *systematic* deliverance of truth conditions, a theory that projects the truth conditions of sentences on the basis of the "meanings" of their parts and their syntactical structures. And on this score, treating indefinite descriptions in (and only in) certain subordinate structures as devices of wide-scope universal quantification is, at best, a tottering first step. Such a treatment gives us no *explanation* of the apparent "universalization" in (1) and (2).

There are good grounds for thinking that the universalization of the indefinite descriptions in (1) and (2) is a logical illusion. I want to explore the idea that it is, in fact, the anaphoric pronoun, not the indefinite description, that has a universal character. The existence of sentences like the following suggests that this might be a good way to proceed:

(5)   Every man who bought *two or more donkeys* vaccinated *them*

(6)   If John buys *several donkeys* he vaccinates *them*.

Here again there is universalization. Take (5); this is true just in case every man who bought two or more donkeys vaccinated *every* donkey he bought.[10] But we cannot capture this fact by treating 'two or more donkeys' as a wide-scope quantifier—universal or otherwise—that binds 'them'. If the quantifier were universal, (5) would be equivalent to (1), which it is not.[11] And if the quantifier were 'two or more', (5) would mean that there are two or more donkeys such that every man who bought them vaccinated them, which it does not. All this suggests very strongly that if we are to understand what is going on in (1), (2), (5), and (6), we need to think about the semantics of the anaphoric pronouns, not the semantics of their antecedents.

What light can we shed on the problem of donkey anaphora using the theory of restricted quantification outlined in Chapter 2 and the theory of D-type anaphora developed in Chapter 5?

Recall from 5.6 that we can think of relative pronouns that introduce restrictive relative clauses as bound variables. On such an account, the relative pronoun 'who' in our target sentence (1) functions as a variable bound by 'every', so the subject noun phrase 'every man who bought a donkey' has the following logical structure:

(1_4)   [every x: man x & [a y: donkey y] (x bought y)].

Now what of the pronoun 'it' in the verb phrase? Since its antecedent, 'a donkey', does not c-command it, by (P2) the pronoun is not a bound anaphor. By (P5), it is therefore a D-type pronoun that goes proxy for a definite description recoverable from the antecedent clause. By (P4), the antecedent clause for the indefinite description 'a donkey' is

(1_5)   [a y: donkey y] (x bought y)

which contains a free occurrence of x. Applying (P5) to the anaphoric pronoun 'it' we get

(1_6)   [the y: donkey y & x bought y]

which represents the English description 'the donkey he bought'.[12] Thus, (1) as a whole will be interpreted as either (1_7) or (1_8), according as the subject quantifier or the descriptive pronoun is given wider scope:

(1_7)   [every x: man x & [a y: donkey y] (x bought y)]
          ([the y: donkey y & x bought y] (x vaccinated y))

(1_8)   [the y: donkey y & x bought y]
          ([every x: man x & [a y: donkey y] (x bought y)]
          (x vaccinated y)).

(1_8) is no good because it contains a free occurrence of x. But (1_7) is formally impeccable. It represents the English sentence

(1_3)   Every man who bought a donkey vaccinated the donkey he bought on the reading on which the pronoun 'he' is interpreted as a variable bound by 'every man who bought a donkey' (the pronoun is c-commanded by the quantifier as (P2) requires).

There is no formal trick here. We have respected (P2) and (P6), used (P4) to determine the anaphor clause, and applied (P5) in a rote fashion, opting for the reading upon which the descriptive pronoun takes narrow scope.

As it stands, there is an obvious worry about the truth conditions of (1_3). But before examining this worry, let me pause to stress a formal point: the intelligibility of (1_7) refutes Evans's claim that the anaphoric connection between 'a donkey' and 'it' in (1) precludes a treatment of the subject noun phrase 'every man who bought a donkey' as a "logical unit," i.e., as a unary restricted quantifier.[13] In 2.5, it was pointed out that one can treat the English determiners 'some', 'a', 'every', 'most', 'the', etc., *either* as unary (restricted) quantifier-formers or as binary quantifiers (i.e., as devices that combine with pairs of predicates (or open sentences) to form sentences). I claimed that the resulting systems were equivalent in expressive power and that, from a semantical point of view, neither was superior to the other. I chose the unary system on purely aesthetic grounds: it treats quantified noun phrases as syntactical and semantical units, its formulae tend to be easier to parse, and it makes it easier to state (P5). Evans claims that sentence (1) brings out a crucial formal difference between the two systems. In particular, he claims that the anaphoric relation in (1) cannot be captured if the subject phrase 'every man who bought a donkey' is treated as a unary (restricted) quantifier, but it can be captured if 'every' is treated as a binary quantifier. The theory under consideration—a theory that (*a*) treats quantified noun phrases in English as restricted quantifiers, and (*b*) treats unbound pronouns that are anaphoric on quantifiers as definite descriptions—has delivered a perfectly intelligible reading of (1), viz., (1_7). Furthermore, (1_7) is *equivalent* to the reading that Evans claims his theory delivers for (1). So either *both* theories provide a correct account of the truth conditions of (1), or *neither* does: they stand or fall together.[14]

In my opinion, they fall (but not in a way that imperils the view that 'every man who bought a donkey' is a logical unit). It is not a consequence of (1) that every man who bought a donkey bought *exactly one* donkey; but this *is* a consequence of (1_7) because of the implication of uniqueness built into singular Russellian descriptions. Consequently, the D-type analysis given by (1_7) and the standard Geachian analysis given by (1_2)

(1_2) $(\forall x)(\forall y)((\text{man } x \ \& \ \text{donkey } y \ \& \ x \text{ bought } y) \supset x \text{ vaccinated } y)$

yield divergent truth conditions for (1). In particular, if there is a man who bought two (or more) donkeys and who vaccinated both (or all) of them, (1_7) will be false whereas (1_2) can still be true. I think it must be conceded that this a genuine failing on the part of the D-type analysis as it stands.[15]

A variation of the same problem arises with a D-type analysis of the pronoun in (2):

(2)   If John buys *a donkey* he vaccinates *it*.

Again, assuming that an indicative conditional like (2) is composed of two sentences and a binary sentential connective, the pronoun 'it' in (2) is a D-type rather than a bound anaphor because it is not c-commanded by its antecedent. A routine application of (P5) delivers

(2_3) [an x: donkey x] (John buys x) $\supset$
[the x: donkey x & John buys x](John vaccinates x)

which, unlike (2), cannot be true if John buys more then one donkey.

We appear to face a dilemma. The standard Geachian analyses of (1) and (2) provide plausible truth conditions at the expense of an unsatisfactory treatment of indefinite descriptions. The D-type analysis, on the other hand, respects the standard semantics of indefinite descriptions at the expense of unacceptable truth conditions for (1) and (2). In the next section, I shall look at a natural way of repairing the D-type analysis that does not compromise its general appeal.[16]

6.3 Numberless Pronouns

At this stage, the Russellian might consider rejecting the standard Geachian truth conditions for

(1)   Every man who bought *a donkey* vaccinated *it*.

Geachian truth conditions for (1) have, in fact, been rejected by Cooper (1979) and (more tentatively) Parsons (1978), who suggest that sentences like (2) and (3) support the view that there *is* an implication of (relative) uniqueness in constructions like (1):

(2)   Every man who has a daughter thinks she is the most beautiful girl in the world

(3)   Every man who has a son wills him all his money.

On Geach's account, the truth of (2) entails that every man who has more than one daughter has contradictory beliefs (each such man believing that each of his daughters is the most beautiful girl in the world).[17] But according to Cooper, this should not follow from the truth of (2). Intuitions are certainly not very clear here, but it is worthy of note that even if Geachian truth conditions for (2) are incorrect, it is far from clear that an analysis of the anaphoric pronoun as a singular description will succeed, for on that view, (2) will be false if any man has more than one daughter.

Let's return to (1). Can the distinction (made in 3.4) between propositions expressed (PE) and propositions meant (PM) be used to explain why (1) is normally understood in the way it is, i.e., as having Geachian truth conditions? One idea here would be that although an utterance of (1) would normally *convey* that every man who bought a donkey vaccinated every donkey he bought, this is not the proposition literally expressed. In keeping with Grice's derivability requirement, if such a position is to have any merit, an explanation of the mismatch between PE and PM must be provided. One might suggest something like the following. When a speaker S uses a sentence of the form 'An F is G', typically some object-dependent belief or other furnishes the grounds for S's utterance (3.3, 3.4). However, if one is using an indefinite description that is within the scope of, say, a universal quantifier, it is very likely that the grounds for S's utterance are not furnished by a set of object-dependent beliefs but by an object-independent one. Indeed, it is not difficult to construct scenarios in which an utterance of (1) is grounded only by an object-independent belief. On the assumption that S is being truthful, informative, and relevant (3.3), and on the assumption that the particular utterance of (1) is not grounded by a set of object-dependent beliefs, it is plausible to suppose that S would not wish to be committed to the view that every man who bought a donkey bought exactly one donkey. S is then faced with a problem when wishing to use a pronoun anaphoric on 'a donkey'. What S wants to say is 'Every man who bought a donkey (i.e., at least one donkey), vaccinated the donkey or donkeys he bought'. But S is lazy, or at least is attempting to observe Grice's maxim enjoining brevity, and so utters (1). The utterance is literally false, but in the circumstances S manages to get across the desired message.

I don't know if this is a viable story or not. Would it be a conversational implicature of an utterance of (1) that every man who bought a donkey vaccinated every donkey he bought? If so, then it ought to cancelable. Perhaps (4) would be an example involving explicit cancellation:

(4)   Every man who bought a donkey vaccinated it, but every man who bought more than one donkey was so excited that he forgot to vaccinate any of his.

Unfortunately, intuitions are not very clear on whether or not this is contradictory. Similarly with (5):

(5)   Every man who has a daughter thinks she is the most beautiful girl in the world.

Perhaps an utterance of this sentence would involve an implicit cancellation of the implicature because of the fact that there can only be one *most* beautiful girl in the world. Again, intuitions are hazy. (Indeed, one might be just as well off with the view that Geachian truth conditions are right, an utterance of (5), although strictly false, giving rise to an implicature concerning uniqueness.)[18]

A more interesting (and, I think, more fruitful) account of what is going on in donkey sentences emerges if one pays careful attention to the *cardinality implications* associated with certain quantifiers and to the matter of *number agreement* between antecedents and anaphors. Number agreement between bound pronouns and their antecedents is generally a *syntactical* matter.[19] In particular, the syntactical number on a bound pronoun agrees with that of its antecedent. For example, if we use 'all boys', we must use 'they', 'them', 'their', or 'themselves'; if we use 'every boy' or 'each boy', we must use 'he', 'him', 'his', or 'himself':

(6)   All boys respect their mothers
(7)   Every boy respects his mother
(8)   Each boy respects his mother.

There may well be shades of difference in "meaning" between (6), (7), and (8), differences in the circumstances in which each is appropriate, but they are truth-conditionally equivalent. In an introductory logic course, each might be rendered as

(9) $(\forall x)(Bx \supset Rx(\imath y)(Myx))$

which makes it clear that whether the pronoun is singular or plural is of no truth-conditional significance. Of course this is a quite general fact about bound anaphora. The variables of quantification theory are unmarked for number (and gender), so if a bound pronoun is to be treated as the natural language counterpart of the logician's bound variable, its overt number is truth-conditionally inert.

With D-type anaphora matters are more complicated. In the examples we have looked at so far, anaphoric pronouns have agreed in syntactical number with their antecedents. And there has been an implicit assumption that the syntactical number of a D-type pronoun determines its *semantical* number. Consequently, unbound pronouns anaphoric on 'the *F*', 'just one *F*', 'some *F*', and 'an *F*', have come out as singular definite descriptions, whereas those anaphoric on 'the *Fs*', 'most *Fs*', 'several *Fs*', 'some *Fs*', 'many *Fs*', and 'a few *Fs*', have come out as plural descriptions.

But what happens to unbound pronouns that are anaphoric on *universally quantified* noun phrases? Evans notes that there seems to be a problem with unbound anaphora on 'every'-phrases:

(10)   *Every congressman* came to the party and *he* had a marvelous time.

This seems to be unacceptable on the anaphoric reading intended. Evans offers an explanation in terms of a *semantical number clash* between antecedent and anaphor: (*i*) the pronoun is unbound (since its antecedent does not c-command it), therefore (*ii*) since it is singular, it is interpreted via the singular definite description 'the congressman who came to the party'; yet (*iii*) the antecedent sentence asserts the existence of a plurality of congressmen who came to the party.[20]

There are problems with this explanation. First, it is not clear that the antecedent sentence in (10) is false if there is only one congressman. We know there are more, and this fact may be well affect the way we react to (10). Contrast (10) with (11):

(11)   *Every frisbee major* got a job this year. *He* is very happy about it.

Of course, someone who uttered (11) would normally be aiming for some sort of rhetorical effect, but it is clear that the anaphora still works. A partial explanation of the joke-like quality of (11) surely lies in the fact that if the speaker knows that exactly one person satisfies the descriptive condition expressed by 'frisbee major', typically he or she will use a definite description like 'the frisbee major' or 'our frisbee major', rather than 'every frisbee major'. It's not that 'every frisbee major' carries with it an implication of plurality, rather it's that it does *not* carry with it an implication of singularity. (As we shall soon see, the difference is important.)

The second problem with Evans' explanation is that it fails to explain the oddity of (12):

(12)   *Every congressman* came to the party. *They* had a marvelous time.

Perhaps (12) is an *improvement* over (10), but it still seems a little strained. The reason, I suspect, is that in moving from (10) to (12) we have traded an alleged clash in semantical number for a very real clash in *syntactical* number.

We are faced here with some quite general questions about number agreement and about cardinality implications present in maximal quantifiers. Recall that D-type anaphora is not always acceptable when the antecedent is of the form 'no *F*' or 'no *Fs*':

(13) John bought *no donkeys*. Harry vaccinated *them*

(14) Every man who bought *no donkeys* vaccinated *them*.

However, in my opinion it would be a mistake to construct a semantical theory that prevented unbound pronouns from being anaphoric on quantifiers of the form 'no *F*(s)'. First, an example like the following would be ruled out:

(15) Either there's· *no bathroom* in this house or *it*'s in a funny place.

Second, the following sentences are just as bad as (13) and (14), but we don't want to prohibit unbound anaphora on indefinite descriptions:

(16) John didn't buy *a donkey* and Harry vaccinated *it*

(17) Every man who didn't buy *a donkey* vaccinated *it*.[21]

The syntactical and semantical rules of the language should not conspire to block examples like (13), (14), (16), and (17); they are perfectly well-formed. The problem is simply that, in the normal course of things, it would *make no practical sense* to use these sentences. The theory of D-type anaphora explains this. Consider (13); the anaphoric pronoun will come out as 'the donkeys John bought', so the sentence as a whole will be straightforwardly contradictory. Similarly for the other examples.

Related considerations apply where the antecedent is a universally quantified noun phrase. In the light of the alleged anaphoric difficulties in (10) and (11) and in examples like the following:

(18) Every man who bought *every donkey* vaccinated *it*

(19) Every man who bought *every donkey* vaccinated *them*

some people have argued that an adequate semantical theory must prevent pronouns from being interpreted as anaphoric on 'every' phrases that do not c-command them.[22] In my opinion, this is a mistake. Consider (19); since this sentence could be true only in a situation in which just one man bought any donkeys, it would certainly be much more natural to use (20):

(20)   The man who bought *every donkey* vaccinated *them*.[23]

And notice that this sentence falsifies the view that pronouns anaphoric on 'every' phrases must be bound (i.e., c-commanded) by them. So do the following:

(11)   *Every frisbee major* got a job this year. *He* is very happy about it

(21)   Everyone who managed to listen to *every prophet* was asked to rank *them*

(22)   If John manages to acquire *every Rembrandt* he will build a museum in which to house *them*.

Let's now turn to the matter of semantical number. Even if it is true that phrases of the form 'every *F*' and 'each *F*' have existential import—which is itself open to debate—it is untrue that these quantifiers are always genuinely plural, and untrue that *singular* unbound pronouns can never be anaphoric on them. Consider the following sentences:

(23)   *Every Swiss male over the age of twenty-one* owns a gun. *He* is required to do so by law

(24)   *Each candidate* will be debriefed by Mrs Hendrix. *He* will given some advice on how to tackle the press.

But as Evans notes, on the face of it, singular descriptive pronouns seem to carry implications of singularity and plural descriptive pronouns seem to carry implications of plurality. The upshot of all this is that in cases where we do not wish to prejudice the issue, we feel uneasy using *either*. Unbound anaphora on phrases of the form 'every *F*' and 'each *F*' is *awkward* however you look at it. To preserve syntactical agreement, a singular pronoun is required; but from a pragmatic standpoint, a plural pronoun will seem more appropriate unless there is doubt (or feigned doubt) as to whether there is more than one *F*. If I am certain that are several candidates for the new job, I might use (25):

(25)   Mrs Hendrix introduced herself to *every candidate for the new job*. Later she had a reception for *them* over at her house.

But if I know that there is only one candidate, a certain John Jones, I will be inclined to use (26):

(26)   Mrs Hendrix introduced herself to *the candidate for the new job*. Later she had a reception for *him* over at her house.

For rhetorical effect, however, in certain imaginable situations I might say

(27)   Mrs Hendrix introduced herself to *every candidate for the new job*. Later she had a reception for *him* over at her house.

But what about cases in which we don't want to commit ourselves one way or the other? One interesting idea is that in many such cases unbound anaphoric pronouns go proxy for definite descriptions that are, from a semantical perspective, *numberless*. The following sentences are surely equivalent:

(28)   Every new recruit is armed

(29)   All new recruits are armed.[24]

Now suppose we want to continue with a sentence containing an anaphoric pronoun. Preserving syntactical agreement we get the following:

(28_1)   *Every new recruit* is armed. *He* is ready for combat at a moment's notice

(29_1)   *All new recruits* are armed. *They* are ready for combat at a moment's notice.

Since the pronouns in these pairs are not bound by their antecedents, D-type analyses are called for. But this seems to present a problem. The antecedent sentences in (28_1) and (29_1) are truth-conditionally equivalent. But if the subsequent anaphoric pronouns are cashed out as singular and plural definite descriptions respectively, the two *anaphor* sentences will not be equivalent. By (P5), the pronoun in (28_1) will come out as 'the new recruit', and the one in (29_1) will come out as 'the new recruits'. And on the analyses of singular and plural descriptions provided earlier, neither of these is right: (28_1) will now be false if there is *more than one* new recruit, and (29_1) will be false if there is *exactly one* new recruit. The anaphoric pronouns will have added *cardinality implications* not supplied by their antecedents. From the point of view of truth conditions, 'every new recruit' and 'all new recruits' are neither singular nor plural, which is why (28) and (29) are equivalent.

Following up on a remark made by G. E. Moore, in 2.6 I suggested that phrases like 'whoever wrote *Waverley*', and 'whoever shot John F. Kennedy' might profitably be viewed as definite descriptions that are semantically numberless. Using '[whe $x: Fx$]' to represent a numberless description, the following truth clause was suggested:

(∗8) '[whe $x: Fx$] (Gx)'   is true iff $|F - G| = 0$ and $|F| \geq 1$.

With a view to honoring the truth-conditional number-neutrality of their antecedents, we might think of D-type pronouns that are anaphoric on quantifier phrases of the form 'every F', 'all Fs', and 'each F' as semantically numberless.[25]

If we take seriously the view that anaphoric pronouns should not add cardinality implications not already supplied by their antecedents, we should expect to find numberless occurrences elsewhere. On Russell's account, a sentence of the grammatical form 'An F is G' has the same logical form as a sentence of the form 'Some Fs are Gs'. In the notation of 2.5, '[an $x: Fx$](Gx)' and '[some $x: Fx$](Gx)' are logically equivalent; both are true if and only if there is at least one F that is G.[26] On a *completely* Russellian account of indefinite descriptions, then, since there can be no difference between the truth-conditional contributions of 'a donkey' and 'some donkeys', the same must be true of the complex noun phrases (*i*) 'every man who bought a donkey' and (*ii*) 'every man who bought some donkeys' (with minimal assumptions concerning compositionality). So in our target sentence (1), we should be able to substitute (*ii*) for (*i*) *salva veritate*. But notice that we cannot substitute *salva congruitate*: we must replace 'it' with 'them' in order to maintain syntactical agreement between anaphor and antecedent:

(1)   Every man who bought *a donkey* vaccinated *it*

(33) Every man who bought *some donkeys* vaccinated *them*.

Now if we interpret singular and plural descriptive pronouns as singular and plural descriptions respectively, not only do we get—as we have already seen—unacceptable truth conditions for (1), we get *different* truth conditions for (33). If 'them' is interpreted as 'the donkeys he bought', (33) will be false if every man who bought a donkey bought just one donkey.[27] To the (complete) Russellian, this divergence might suggest that we pursue the suggestion, made in passing by Parsons (1978, p. 20) and by Davies (1981, p. 175), that descriptive pronouns anaphoric on indefinite descriptions are, or at least can be, interpreted as numberless descriptions.[28] After all, independent evidence for the existence of such pronouns has already been provided. On such an account, the logical forms of (1) and (33) will be (34) and (35), respectively:

(34) [every x: man x & [a y: donkey y] (x bought y)]
      [whe z: donkey z & x bought z] (x vaccinated z)

(35) [every x: man x & [some y: donkeys y] (x bought y)]
      [whe z: donkey z & x bought z] (x vaccinated z).

On Russell's assumption that '[a y: Fy](Gy)' and '[some y: Fy](Gy)' are equivalent, (34) and (35) are also equivalent. Moreover, (34) gives us the right truth conditions for (1), viz., those given by Geach in

(36) $(\forall x)(\forall y)$((man x & donkey y & x bought y) $\supset$ x vaccinated y).

So it *does* seem to be possible to provide an analysis of (1) that (*a*) delivers the correct (Geachian) truth conditions, and (*b*) honors a Russellian treatment of singular indefinite descriptions. The universalization of the indefinite description 'a donkey' in (1) is a logical illusion: It is the *pronoun* that has universal force, by virtue of standing in for a definite description.

Now let's turn to some possible objections to this proposal.

First, it might be objected that (1) and (33) have different truth conditions, that even if (34) captures the force of (1), (35) misrepresents the force of (33), the truth of which does not depend on how things are with any man who bought only *one* donkey. But this is not really an objection to the proposed treatment of the *pronoun* in (33), nor to Russell's treatment of singular indefinites; it is an objection to Russell's treatment of *plural* indefinites. The objector is contesting Russell's claim that 'An F is G' and 'Some Fs are Gs' are equivalent. In short, the objector is urging the following split:

(∗3_1) 'Some Fs are Gs' is true iff $|F \cap G| > 1$

(∗4)   'An F is G'   is true iff $|F \cap G| \geq 1$.

($|F|$ is the cardinality of F, the set of all things that are F; see 2.5.) I am inclined to agree. But analyzing plural indefinites in this way does *not* create a problem for the pronominal theory under consideration. If (∗3_1) is adopted, the relevant difference in truth conditions between (1) and (33) will follow as a consequence of distinct treatments of the *antecedents* 'a donkey' and 'some donkeys' (rather than distinct treatments of the anaphors 'it' and 'them').

Second, it might be suggested that the numberless proposal cannot be correct because some pronouns anaphoric on singular indefinite descriptions are semantically *singular*. After all, in 5.5 we looked at some examples in which analyses of such pronouns as singular descriptions seemed to be appropriate.

There are several things one might say in response to this. First, one might maintain that, as a matter of fact, some D-type pronouns anaphoric on singular indefinites are singular while others are numberless. This would not, of course, be to abandon the spirit of the theory of D-type anaphora; it would simply be to bestow upon it a welcome degree of flexibility. The line of reasoning here would be as follows. When a speaker S uses a sentence of the form 'An F is G', very often some object-dependent belief or other furnishes the grounds for S's utterance, and a subsequent pronoun anaphoric on the indefinite will, in all probability, be interpreted as semantically singular. But if the indefinite description is within the scope of, say, a universal quantifier, very likely S has object-independent grounds for the assertion. In which case S is less likely to want to be committed to any implication of (relative) uniqueness. Consequently, if we are not to complicate the language by adding a new numberless pronoun, we must allow for the possibility of a numberless interpretation of 'it' in cases where the antecedent does not *force* a singular interpretation, i.e., where the antecedent is genuinely numberless.

And it is clear that singular indefinites themselves *are* genuinely numberless. Compare (*4) and (*3_1) with (*6) and (*7):

(*6) 'The F is G'   is true iff $|\mathbf{F} - \mathbf{G}| = 0$ and $|\mathbf{F}| = 1$

(*7) 'The Fs are Gs'   is true iff $|\mathbf{F} - \mathbf{G}| = 0$ and $|\mathbf{F}| > 1$.

'The F is G' and 'The Fs are Gs' can never be true together.[29] But singular *indefinite* descriptions are not *semantically* singular; they do not generate uniqueness implications. When we just wish to say that $|\mathbf{F} \cap \mathbf{G}| = 1$, we say 'Exactly one F is G' or 'Just one F is G'. The truth of 'An F is G' does not require that $|\mathbf{F} \cap \mathbf{G}| = 1$, it just requires that $|\mathbf{F} \cap \mathbf{G}| \geq 1$, and this is perfectly consistent with the truth of 'Some Fs are Gs', even on the non-Russellian analysis of plural indefinites given in (*3_1). In short, singular indefinites are not *semantically* singular.

Now according to the proposal under consideration, a pronoun anaphoric on a singular indefinite occurs in the singular so as to maintain syntactical agreement. At this stage the theorist may proceed in one of two directions. One option, of course, is to say that the pronoun *has to be interpreted as a numberless description* so as not to add any cardinality implication to the truth conditions not already supplied by its antecedent. The other option is to say that the pronoun *may be either singular or numberless* depending upon various contextual or linguistic factors. In view of the fact that informants have insecure and divergent intuitions when questioned about the truth conditions and/or grammaticality of many donkey sentences—see especially some of those listed below—I am inclined to think that the flexibility introduced by the latter option is called for. Compare the following:

(1)   Every man who bought *a donkey* vaccinated *it*

(2)   Every man who has *a daughter* thinks that *she* is the most beautiful girl in the world

(37)   Some man who bought *a donkey* vaccinated *it*

(38)   Some men who bought *a donkey* vaccinated *it*

(39)   Most men who bought *a donkey* vaccinated *it*.

As we have already seen, in (1) the numberless interpretation of the pronoun seems to be preferred. But as Parsons (1978) points out, in an example like (2)—which is of the same general form as (1)—it is arguable that a singular interpretation of the pronoun is preferred. A reasonable explanation is that immediate linguistic context, and lexical and background knowledge, conspire to defeat the numberless interpretation. (In the normal run of things, there cannot be *two* most beautiful girls in the world.)

In (37) and (38) there is no obvious reason to prefer either interpretation, but the singular interpretation is apparently preferred; perhaps it is the default interpretation.[30] In (39) the numberless interpretation is preferred—probably for the same sorts of reasons it is preferred in (1). The theory at hand will therefore represent (39) as

(40)   [most x: men x & [a y: donkey y] (x buys y)]
       ([whe z: donkey z & x buys z] (x vaccinates z)).[31]

Sentence (41) seems to provide very strong evidence for the existence of numberless D-type pronouns:

(41)   Every man who bought *a beer* bought five others along with *it*.

If the pronoun 'it' is interpreted as a singular description then the sentence will be automatically false.[32] But if it is interpreted as a numberless description, things come out exactly right. The sentence will be true just in case every man who bought at least one beer bought five other beers along with each of the beers he bought.[33] (Of course, there may be more general worries about the alleged maximality implications attributable to D-type pronouns anaphoric on indefinite descriptions, but such worries are nothing to do with donkey sentences *per se*. For discussion, see 5.7 and 6.4.)

Further evidence for semantically numberless pronouns comes from sentences like the following:

(42) Every man who bought *a donkey and a mule* vaccinated *them*

(43) Every man who bought *a donkey or a mule* vaccinated *it*

(44) Every man who bought *more than one donkey* vaccinated *it*

(45) Every man who bought *two or more donkeys* vaccinated *them*.

In (42) the pronoun appears to be going proxy for the conjunctive description 'the donkey(s) he bought and the mule(s) he bought', which is syntactically plural as well as semantically plural (given the semantics of conjunction), so 'them' is the correct choice. In (43) the pronoun appears to be going proxy for 'the donkey(s) he bought or the mule(s) he bought'. The semantics of disjunction requires that for (43) to be true every man who bought a donkey vaccinated it, every man who bought a mule vaccinated it, and every man who bought a mule and a donkey vaccinated them; hence the pronoun seems to demand a numberless interpretation. (This suggests, perhaps, that when a numberless interpretation is required and there is no syntactical reason to use a plural pronoun, it is the singular pronoun that is called upon.)

Many speakers find (44) and (45) truth-conditionally equivalent. But notice that in (44) the pronoun is syntactically singular so as to agree with 'more than one donkey', even though it cannot be interpreted as *semantically* singular for fear of contradiction.

It seems to be clear, then, that donkey anaphora of the sort exemplified in sentences of this general form—i.e., where the antecedent is a constituent of a restrictive relative clause—does not *by itself* undermine either a unitary Russellian analysis of indefinite descriptions or a D-type analysis of unbound anaphora. The maximality implication that (1) apparently gives rise to can be captured once it is seen that D-type pronouns anaphoric on numberless antecedents may, and in some cases *must*, receive numberless interpretations, and that agreement between anaphors and antecedent noun phrases is, by and large, a syntactical matter.

Virtually everything that has just been said carries over *mutatis mutandis* to conditional donkey sentences. Notoriously, conditionals give rise to all sorts of problems in philosophical logic, and it is with great trepidation that I bring them up at all. However, it is worth remarking that, under the present proposal, anaphoric relations in the simplest types of conditionals do not appear to raise any *new* or *additional* problems.[34] Indeed, the proposal seems to help with some old ones. Consider:

(46) If John buys *a donkey* he vaccinates *it*.

As noted in 6.2, it has been claimed in the literature that this type of conditional donkey sentence thwarts the existential analysis of indefinite descriptions. The truth conditions of (46) are apparently captured by (47), a fact that allegedly commits us to a wide-scope universal rather than a narrow-scope existential treatment of the indefinite description:

(47) [every x: donkey x] (John buys $x \supset$ John vaccinates x).

But we can now provide a coherent account of (46) that comports with the existential analysis of the indefinite. On the assumption that a conditional is composed of two sentences and a binary sentential connective, the pronoun 'it' in (46) is not a bound anaphor because it is not c-commanded by its antecedent. So on the numberless D-type proposal, (46) will come out as (49):

(49) [an x: donkey x] (John buys x) $\supset$
      [whe x: donkey x & John buys x] (John vaccinates x)

which does not seem to invite any objection over and above those standardly brought up against the material analysis of conditionals. It would seem, then, that we are not forced to treat indefinite descriptions in the antecedents of conditionals as universally quantified expressions that mysteriously take wide scope.

This is a good point at which to say something about quantifiers of the form 'any F'. According to (e.g.) Evans (1977) and Hornstein (1984), quantifiers of this form are special in that they appear to insist on wide scope in certain environments. In particular, it is sometimes argued that the scope of an occurrence of 'any F' in the antecedent of a conditional extends to the consequent. Consider the following example from Chrysippus:[35]

(50) If *any man* is born at the rising of the Dog Star, *he* will not die at sea.

By treating 'any man' as a universally quantified expression with wide scope over the entire conditional, and by treating 'he' as a variable bound by 'any', one can capture the force of (50) with (51):

(51) [every x: man x] (x is born at the rising of the Dog Star $\supset$
      x will not die at sea).

But this is thoroughly unilluminating; it forces us to attribute to 'any F' properties that the other quantifiers simply do not possess, viz., the capacity to take scope over an entire conditional when embedded in its antecedent.

Under the D-type proposal, we no longer need to treat 'any' as exceptional. On the assumption that (*a*) it receives its existential reading in (51) and (*b*) its scope is restricted to the antecedent of the conditional (i.e., everything it c-commands), the pronoun 'he' is a D-type anaphor and comes out as a numberless description, which gives us the following:

(52) [any x: man x] (x is born at the rising of the Dog Star) ⊃
      [whe x: man x & x is born at the rising of the Dog Star]
      (x will not die at sea).[36]

6.4 Maximality, Events, and Variable-binding

In this last major section on pronominal anaphora, I want to look at several related matters that cannot be examined in any great detail here. My purpose is simply to locate potential weaknesses in the theory of D-type anaphora and to highlight one or two areas in which the theory may interact with other semantical subtheories.

In the previous section, we saw that the provision of an adequate account of the relationship between indefinite descriptions and anaphoric pronouns in donkey sentences is not, by itself, incompatible with a unitary existential analysis of indefinite descriptions. However, as we saw in 5.7, in the literature a more general worry has been voiced about the interpretation of unbound pronouns anaphoric on indefinite descriptions, a worry about the uniformity of the implications of maximality that result from interpreting unbound anaphoric pronouns as (or via) definite descriptions. In the light of the discussion of incomplete quantifiers in 3.7, I suggested that quite general contextual considerations must play a role in spelling out the descriptive content of D-type pronouns in exactly the same way that such considerations play a role in spelling out the contents of overt definite descriptions and other quantifiers. Whatever mechanisms come into play in completing elliptical descriptions can be appealed to in spelling out (elliptical) D-type pronouns.

I have several times heard it suggested that appeals to context and to numberless descriptive pronouns can be eliminated by paying attention to the hidden quantifications over events that Davidson (1967) has uncovered in ordinary action sentences (see 4.6). It would be quite an undertaking to investigate how the anaphoric theory I have been using fares when theories of event quantification, temporal and aspectual modifiers, quantificational adverbs, and so on are brought into the picture in earnest, and I have no intention of beginning such an investigation here. For one thing, there does not seem to be much in the way of consensus about the semantics of such phrases, and much of the work would involve the construction of plausible theories with which the theories of bound and D-type anaphora could systematically interact. However, I do want to indicate in a brief and relatively informal manner why I think that numberless pronouns will still be needed even if Davidsonian event quantifiers are officially introduced into LF representations.

Let's start by considering an exchange between Geach and Evans over the following example:

(1)   Socrates kicked *a dog* and it bit *him*.

Geach has objected to any implication of uniqueness generated by a theory that analyzes 'it' in (1) as (or via) a Russellian description, on the grounds that it would be perfectly coherent to utter the conjunction of (1) and (2):

(2)   Socrates kicked *another dog* and *it* did not bite him.

The Russellian who is sympathetic to the discussion in 3.7 will, of course, reply that Geach's example just shows that the problem of incomplete descriptions emerges for D-type pronouns as well as for overt descriptions (and other quantifiers). As we might expect, the phenomenon of underspecified D-type pronouns is not restricted to cases involving anaphora on singular indefinite descriptions. Consider (3) and (4):

(3)   Harry bought *some books*. He put *them* in his office with some other books he bought

(4)   *Several politicians* entered the room. *They* went straight over and talked to several other politicians.

The moral, once again, is that we need, in certain cases, a degree of contextual flexibility in spelling out descriptive content.

While Evans seems to agree that contextual factors may play a role in fixing content, in response to Geach he floats one rather formal method of augmenting content using only linguistic material from the antecedent sentence:

> . . . the tense in the verb effectively introduces an initial existential quantifier *There was a time such that* . . . , and my claim is that the truth of the sentence requires that there be a time such that Socrates kicked only one dog *at that time*, not that Socrates kicked only one dog *ever* (1980, p. 223, note 7).

Unfortunately Evans does not expand upon this remark, and we shall be forced to project somewhat if we are to make much sense of it. When he says that the tense in the verb introduces "an initial existential quantifier," Evans appears to be claiming that the temporal quantifier takes wide scope over any overt quantifiers in the smallest sentence containing the verb that gives rise to it. Let's use '[∃t]' as shorthand for 'there is a time t such that'. On this account, the first conjunct in (1) will come out as (5):

(5)   [∃t] ([an x: dog x] (Socrates kicked x at t)).

Heim (1982) and Wilson (1984) understand Evans as claiming that the pronoun 'it' in the second conjunct of (1) is interpreted as 'the dog that Socrates kicked at t' with 't' bound by the '[∃t]' at the beginning of the first conjunct. Let's spell this out. Since 'bit' in the second conjunct of (1) is a tensed verb, presumably it also generates an existential quantification over times. The sentence as a whole will therefore come out as

(6)   [∃t] ([an x: dog x] (Socrates kicked x at t) &
       [∃t'] ([the x: dog x & Socrates kicked x at t]
       (x bit Socrates at t'))).

Three things about this proposal are worthy of note. First, it appears to be inconsistent with Evans' staunch opposition to cross-sentential binding (see 5.5), since it requires the scope of a temporal quantifier in one sentence to extend into *subsequent* sentences. (I am not unsympathetic to this as an objection in principle to Evans' proposal if this is what he intended.)

The second point concerns simultaneity. Consider (7):

(7)   Socrates kicked two dogs.

While there may well be a reading of (7) in which the alleged temporal quantifier has wide scope—that is, a reading in which Socrates kicked two dogs simultaneously (by, e.g., jumping up in the air and kicking one dog with each foot while in mid-air)—it cannot be denied that the reading in which 'two dogs' takes wider scope than the temporal quantifier is at least as natural. (The possibility of simultaneous kickings brings up another problem that I shall address in a moment.) Example (8) brings this home with a vengeance:

(8)   Every Greek philosopher constructed six moral theories.

Giving Evans' temporal quantifier widest possible scope in (8) produces the least plausible reading of this sentence. If we are to take Evans' existential temporal quantifiers seriously, and if we are to capture the more natural readings of (8), at the very least we shall have to allow temporal quantifiers to take narrow scope with respect to overt quantifiers.[37] Let's assume in the first instance, then, that all scope readings are available.

The third point also concerns simultaneity. Suppose Socrates kicks two dogs at the same time. In such a scenario (1) could still be true. But the second conjunct of (6)—the rendering of the second conjunct of (1)—must be false as there is no unique dog that Socrates kicked at t.[38] (Altering the relative scopes of the quantifiers in accordance with the previous discussion will not help.) What this suggests is that we replace talk of *times* with talk of *events*. Invoking Davidson's (independently motivated) proposal for representing event quantification once again, (1) will now come out as (9):

(9) $[\exists e]$ ([an x: dog x] (kick(Socrates, x, e) &

    $[\exists f]$ ([the x: dog x & (kick(Socrates, x, e)]

    (bite(x, Socrates, f)))

(where '$[\exists e]$' is shorthand for 'there is an event e such that'). This is both compatible with Geach's observation and immune to the simultaneity problem.

It has been suggested to me several times that that event quantification gives one the means to dispense with the idea that some D-type pronouns are numberless. Recall (from 6.3) that one of the main motivations for numberless D-type pronouns is unbound anaphora on indefinite descriptions as in (10):

(10)   Every man who bought *a donkey* vaccinated *it*.

The suggestion I have encountered aims to treat the pronoun 'it' in (10) as equivalent to a singular description that is relativized to events. Intuitively, the idea seems to be that (10) is true just in case every man for whom there is a donkey for which there is an event that consists in that man buying that donkey is such that there is some other event that consists in that same man vaccinating the donkey he bought in the previous event. Such an analysis is supposed to be immune to the original objection concerning uniqueness because now uniqueness is relativized to events.

Within the general framework I have attempted to spell out here, it is not clear that event-based relativization can really do what is asked of it. If we prohibit numberless D-type pronouns, the best analysis of (10) that can be provided using the theory embodied in

(P1)-(P6), supplemented with event quantification, seems to be the following:

(11) [every x: man x & [an y: donkey y] [$\exists e$] (buy(x, y, e)]

([the y: donkey x & [$\exists e$] (buy(x, y, e)] [$\exists f$] (vaccinate(x, y, f))).

But this still comes out false if there is some man b such that b bought two donkeys. In such a scenario there is no unique donkey c for which there is an event in which b buys c. At the very least, then, if the event-based approach to securing uniqueness is to succeed, some modifications to (P1)–(P6) are going to be necessary. But if we allow for numberless D-type pronouns, we can leave (P1)–(P6) alone.

Furthermore, Irene Heim has developed a particular type of counterexample that threatens to undermine the general idea behind the event-based proposal even if the formal details could be worked out satisfactorily.[39] Consider the following examples:

(12) If *a man* buys an apartment with <u>another man</u>, *he* shares the fee with with <u>him</u>

(13) Every man who buys an apartment with *another man* shares the fee with *him*.

Take (12). If the pronoun 'he' goes proxy for a singular description the nature of the problem is clear. There can be no unique man who buys an apartment with another man. For suppose b is such a man; then there is a distinct man c with whom b buys an apartment. But *buying an apartment with* is symmetric, therefore c is also a man who buys an apartment with another man, viz., b. As Heim points out, the reason that this type of example causes a problem for an event-based approach to maximality is that there is no event in which a unique man buys an apartment with another man.

The theory of D-type anaphora that allows for numberless pronouns appears to fare remarkably well with examples like (12) and (13)? In order to see this, let's look first at a simpler example. Consider (14):

(14) If *a man* buys <u>a donkey</u> *he* vaccinates <u>it</u>.

Since the antecedent in this conditional contains two indefinite descriptions, technically the antecedent sentence is ambiguous between (15_1) and (15_2):

(15_1) [an x: man x] ([a y: donkey y] (x buys y))

(15_2) [a y: donkey y] ([an x: man x] (x buys y)).

Let's begin with (15_1), the reading obtained by applying the rule of Quantifier Raising (see 5.6) first to 'a donkey' and then to 'a man'. By (P4), the antecedent clause for 'a man' is the whole of (15_1); so if we apply (P5) to 'he' we get (16)

(16) [whe x: man x & [a y: donkey y] (x buys y)].

On the assumption that (P4) holds at LF, the antecedent clause for 'a donkey' is just '[a y: donkey y] (x buys y)', which contains a free occurrence of x. If we now apply (P5) to 'it' we get

(17) [whe y: donkey y & x buys y]

which also contains a free occurrence of x. Thus the consequent of (14) is ambiguous between (18_1) and (18_2) according as (16) or (17) takes wider scope:

(18_1) [whe x: man x & [a y: donkey y] (x buys y)]
     ([whe y: donkey y & x buys y] (x vaccinates y))

(18_2) [whe y: donkey y & x buys y]
     ([whe x: man x & [a y: donkey y] (x buys y)] (x vaccinates y)).

(18_1) is fine because the description for which 'he' goes proxy binds a variable inside the description for which 'it' goes proxy; but (18_2) is of no use because the description for which 'it' goes proxy contains a free variable. In other words, if the antecedent of (14) is read as (15_1), the sentence as a whole is still technically ambiguous but only one of the resultant readings is fully interpretable.

The same is true if the antecedent of (14) is read as (15_2). The consequent will come out as either (19_1) or (19_2), but only (19_2) is fully interpretable:

(19_1) [whe x: man x & x buys y]
     ([whe y: donkey y & [an x: man x] (x buys y)] (x vaccinates y))

(19_2) [whe y: donkey y & [an x: man x] (x buys y)]
     ([whe x: man x & x buys y] (x vaccinates y)).

So (2) is actually four ways ambiguous. Two of the readings—(18_2) and (19_1)—are apparently useless because they contain free variables and the other two—(18_1) and (19_2)—are logically equivalent.[40]

Now let's return to (12) and (13):

(12) If *a man* buys an apartment with <u>another man,</u> *he* shares the
     fee with <u>him</u>

(13) Every man who buys an apartment with *another man* shares the fee with *him*.

In order that we do not get swamped with quantifiers, let's use '*P*' as shorthand for the two-place predicate 'buys an apartment with', and '*R*' as shorthand for the two-place predicate 'shares the fee with'. I shall focus on (12). The only interpretable reading of the antecedent sentence is given by (20):

(20) [an x: man x] ([a y: man y & $y \neq x$] (Pxy)).

By (P4) this also represents the antecedent clause for 'a man'. If we apply (P5) to the anaphoric pronoun 'he' (in the consequent), we get

(21) [whe x: man x & [a y: man y & $y \neq x$] (Pxy)].

By (P4) the antecedent clause for 'another man' is

(22) [a y: man y & $y \neq x$](Pxy).

If we apply (P5) to the anaphoric pronoun 'him', we get

(23) [whe y: man y & $y \neq x$ & Pxy].

Combining these descriptions with the matrix clause 'Rxy', the consequent of (12) comes out as either (24$_1$) or (24$_2$), according as (21) or (23) has wider scope:

(24$_1$) [whe x: man x & [a y: man y & $y \neq x$](Pxy)]
         ([whe y: man y & $y \neq x$ & Pxy](Rxy))

(24$_2$) [whe y: man y & $y \neq x$ & Pxy]
         ([whe x: man x & [a y: man y & $y \neq x$](Pxy)](Rxy)).

(24$_2$) is of no use because it contains a free occurrence of x. But (24$_1$) seems to be exactly right; it says that every man who buys an apartment with another man shares the fee with every other man with whom he buys an apartment. Sentences (12) and (13) would therefore seem to provide strong support for the view that D-type pronouns anaphoric on singular indefinite descriptions can be numberless and evidence against the view that the maximality of D-type pronouns can be secured by taking into account event quantifications.[41]

I want now to make a few brief remarks about sentences containing what Lewis (1975) calls *adverbs of quantification*. Here I think there may be good grounds for thinking that the theory of D-type anaphora interacts with theories that posit hidden quantifications over events (and states-of-affairs). (Lewis's theory may also help in the construction of a more refined account of conditionals.) Consider the following sentences:

(25)   If a man buys a donkey he always vaccinates it
(26)   Sometimes if a man buys a donkey he vaccinates it
(27)   Usually if a man buys a donkey he vaccinates it.

On the face of it, these sentences do not appear to pose any new problems. In each case, the D-type pronoun 'he' is interpreted as 'the man/men who buys a donkey', and the D-type pronoun 'it' is interpreted as 'the donkey(s) he buys', with the occurrence of 'he' in the latter description bound by the former description. However, it will be instructive to look in more detail at how we might explicate the semantical structure of sentences of this form.

On Lewis's account, adverbs of quantification (AQs) like 'always' 'sometimes', 'usually', 'often', 'seldom', 'never', and so on, function as binary quantifiers. Each combines with an if-clause 'if-ϕ' and a matrix clause 'ψ' to form a sentence '[AQ] (if-ϕ) (ψ)'. Equivalently, we can think of the adverb as a unary quantifier-former that combines with an if-clause 'if-ϕ' to form a unary restricted quantifier '[AQ: if-ϕ]', which combines with a matrix clause 'ψ' to form a sentence of the form '[AQ: if-ϕ] (ψ)'. With a view to uniformity with previous discussion, let's adopt the unary system.[42]

Roughly speaking, on Lewis's account an AQ indiscriminately binds all free variables inside 'if-ϕ' and 'ψ', and in this sense it is an *unselective* quantifier. For 'always', Lewis posits the following:

(L1)   '[always: if-ϕ] (ψ)' is true iff every assignment of values to free variables in 'ϕ' that satisfies 'ϕ' also satisfies 'ψ'.

Take (25). This will have the following logical structure:

(25$_1$)   [always: if- man x & donkey y & x buys y] (x vaccinates y).

That is, the indefinite descriptions 'a man' and 'a donkey', and the pronouns 'he' and 'it' introduce variables that the unselective quantifier 'always' captures. By (L1), sentence (25$_1$) is true just in case every assignment of values to x and y that satisfies the open sentence (28) also satisfies the open sentence (29):

(28)   man x & donkey y & x buys y
(29) x vaccinates y.

Naturally enough, rules analogous to (L1) can be constructed for other adverbs. For 'sometimes', the rule will be

(L2) '[sometimes: if-ϕ] (ψ)' is true iff some assignment of values to free variables in 'ϕ' that satisfies 'ϕ' also satisfies 'ψ'.

For 'usually', we want *most* assignments of values to free variables, for 'seldom' we want *few* assignments, for 'never', we want *none*, and so on.

As Lewis points out, when there is no overt adverb of quantification, as in

(30) If a man buys a donkey he vaccinates it

it as though there were an implicit 'always' present. That is, (30) seems to be true just in case (25) is true; so we can treat it as if it were also subject to (L1).[43] Consequently, Lewis's theory and the theory of D-type anaphora both predict that (14) is true just in case every man who buys a donkey vaccinates every donkey he buys.

My interest in Lewis's theory is not in what it says about pronouns or indefinite descriptions but in what it says about adverbs of quantification.[44] Although the theory of D-type anaphora does not treat the pronouns in examples like (25)–(27) as variables, there may well be *other* variables around that adverbs of quantification can bind, and these are of interest to both Lewis and the theorist of descriptive anaphora. Consider (31):

(31) Usually if a policeman sees a fight he stops it.

The rule for handling this sentence is the following:

(L3) '[usually: if-ϕ] (ψ)' is true iff most assignments of values to free variables in ϕ that satisfy ϕ also satisfy ψ.

Consequently, (31) will be true just in case most assignments of values to free variables in (32) that satisfy (32) also satisfy (33):

(32) policeman x & fight y & x sees y
(33) x stops y.

This seems right. But now consider (27):

(27) Usually if a man buys a donkey he vaccinates it.

Since it is possible to buy the same donkey twice on separate occasions (selling it in between), it seems that (L3) makes a false prediction if the only available variables in (27) are those introduced by 'a man', 'a donkey', 'he', and 'it'. Suppose Pedro buys Eeyore on twenty separate occasions but never once vaccinates the poor thing; and suppose two other men each buy one donkey once and that each vaccinates the donkey he buys. (L3) incorrectly predicts that (27) is true in such a scenario. A particular fight comes and then goes for good, but a particular donkey like Eeyore might turn up again and again.

Recognizing the possibility of examples like this, Lewis suggests that we may want to allow adverbs of quantification to bind event variables that are explicit in "underlying structure." Let me sketch one way of implementing this idea that may provide us with the means of accepting Lewis's general theory of AQs without accepting that indefinite descriptions and pronouns in conditionals introduce variables that AQs may (unselectively) bind.

Suppose, following Davidson again, that we construe simple action sentences as expressing existential quantifications over events. Suppose, in addition, that it is the sole semantical function of the word 'if' in an *if*-clause 'if-ϕ' to override the main existential event quantifier in ϕ. On this account, an *if*-clause will always contain an event variable that an AQ can get its hands on. If we now bring into play the theory of D-type anaphora, (27) will be true just in case most assignments of values to e that satisfy (34) also satisfy (35):

(34)   [an x: man x] ([a y: donkey y] (buys(x,y,e)))

(35)   [whe x: man x & [a y: donkey y] (buys(x,y,e))]
       ([whe y: donkey y & buys(x,y,e)] ([∃f] (vaccinates(x,y,f)))).

(Analyses of (25) and (26) could be provided in the same way.)

I don't know if it *is* possible to construct an adequate semantics for adverbs of quantification in which they bind only free event (or state-of-affair) variables.[45] But it does seem to me that, in the first instance, a semantical subtheory for adverbs of quantification ought to be constructed independently of a semantical subtheory for anaphoric pronouns: there are sentences that contain anaphoric pronouns and no AQs, and there are sentences that contain AQs and no anaphoric pronouns ('I usually go to bed before midnight'). The theories must, of course, interact in productive ways when it comes to sentences like (25)–(27), but that is to be expected in a modular semantics. What I have tried to do here is sketch, in a very rough-and-ready manner, one possible way in which Lewis's independently motivated approach to AQs might interact with an independently motivated theory of unbound anaphora.

It has been observed that Lewis's approach to AQs might well provide the basis of a more general account of conditionals.[46] Recall that Lewis suggests treating (30), which is just like (25)–(27) except that it contains no AQ, as if it contained an implicit 'always':

(30)   If a man buys a donkey he vaccinates it.

On this account, (30) is true just in case every assignment of values to *x* and *y* in (28) that satisfies (28) also satisfies (29):

(28)   man *x* & donkey *y* & *x* buys *y*

(29)   *x* vaccinates *y*.

On the modification we are entertaining, the idea would be that (30) is true just in case every assignment of values to *e* that satisfies (34) also satisfies (35). More generally, then, a theory might be constructed in which a conditional 'if-ϕ, ψ' is true if and only if *every* assignment of values to the main event (or state-of-affairs) variable in ϕ that satisfies ϕ also satisfies ψ: "*every* assignment" is, as it were, the default setting for a conditional that an overt AQ may override.[47,48]

This is all very sketchy of course. A lot more investigative work needs to be done on adverbs of quantification—and on the representation of event quantification more generally—before we can feel comfortable with this type of proposal. The following questions spring to mind immediately: How general is event quantification? Do AQs sometimes bind *time* variables? Can they bind state-of-affair variables in sentences that do not seem to involve quantification over events (or times)? If so, can the general idea be extended to a sentence like 'A quadratic equation usually has two different solutions'? How do AQs interact with nonextensional operators? Can the quantification introduced by AQs be adequately represented using the restricted quantifier machinery introduced in 2.5?[49] How might this type of proposal for AQs be integrated with the proposals for descriptions of events sketched in 4.7? And so on. Such questions need to be looked at before this type of proposal can be evaluated properly; but the place to address them is not here.

6.5 Concluding Remarks

In this chapter I have attempted to fine-tune the theory of D-type anaphora presented in Chapter 5. First, it was noted that the syntactical number on a bound pronoun plays no semantical role and that unbound pronouns anaphoric on 'every' and 'all' phrases must be semantically numberless despite agreeing syntactically with their antecedents. It was then argued that unbound pronouns anaphoric on singular indefinite descriptions can also be numberless because their antecedents are numberless. As a consequence, many of the problems raised by donkey anaphora seem to disappear. Second, it was suggested that the anaphoric theory might interact with an independently motivated theory that makes explicit quantification over events and an independently motivated theory of the semantics of adverbs of quantification, thereby enabling the theory of anaphora to come into contact with some rather more interesting cases.

Notes

1. Kamp (1981) goes on to claim that such anaphoric relations warrant a "radical departure from existing frameworks" and "a major revision of semantic theory" (p. 2). Barwise (1987) also seems to think that cross-sentential anaphora of the sort found in donkey sentences requires the construction of fundamentally new semantical machinery.

2. Russell's treatment of indefinite descriptions is presented in most detail in Russell (1919), pp. 167–72. For a detailed commentary, see Ludlow and Neale (forthcoming).

3. Geach focuses primarily on conditionals of the form 'If any man buys a donkey he vaccinates it' (pp. 126ff).

4. Notice that there is a second reading of (1) in which 'a donkey' is given wide scope; but this is not the reading we are interested in here. A wide scope reading comes through more clearly in sentences like (i) and (ii):

   (i)   Everyone who saw *a painting I bought* wanted to buy *it* from me
   (ii)   Some man who bought *a donkey* vaccinated *it*.

   In neither of these sentences does the indefinite description c-command the anaphoric pronoun at S-Structure. This seems to provide further support for the view that (P2) holds at LF rather than S-structure. (For discussion, see 5.6.)

5. This is the view of (e.g.) Kamp (1981) and Heim (1982), both of whom advocate a wholesale rejection of Russell's quantificational analyses of indefinite and definite descriptions, and of traditional attempts to account for the semantics of pronominal anaphora. (They both construct theories in which descriptions (definite and indefinite) and pronouns introduce variables that get bound by various types of operators. For discussion, see note 31.) In effect, I shall be arguing that donkey anaphora does not demonstrate the need for any sort of "radical departure from existing frameworks" or for any sort of "major revision of semantic theory" since the phenomenon can be incorporated perfectly well into current syntactical and semantical theories that make use of Russell's evident insights.

6. It is this apparent influence of the pronoun in the predicate on the semantics of the subject that leads Evans to claim that any theory in which determiners are treated as unary quantifier formers (rather than as binary quantifiers) must fail. However, as we shall see in 6.3, Evans is quite mistaken on this point.

7. Positing a full-blown ambiguity in the indefinite article will not help; there is simply no reading of (e.g.) 'A man from London came to see me last night', or 'I met a doctor in Spain', in which the indefinite has universal

force. The ambiguity theory is also susceptible to criticisms raised by Hintikka and Carlson (1978).

It should be clear that, contrary to what is claimed by Hornstein (1984), the phenomenon under investigation is not something that arises only when the indefinite description requires a so-called *generic* or *quasi generic* reading. This is the reason I have used sentence (1) rather than, say, 'Every man who buys a donkey vaccinates it', which apparently admits of a quasi-generic reading.

8. By using the material conditional in setting out this particular problem involving donkey anaphora, I do not mean to be committing myself to the view that this is the best way of thinking about 'if...then' constructions in English. (An alternative, and perhaps better, analysis of conditionals, based on an idea due to Lewis (1975), is entertained in passing in 6.4.) My purposes here are mainly expository.

9. Of course, if (P2) is a genuine constraint on bound anaphora, this is exactly as expected.

10. The fact that we find universalization in sentences containing quantified phrases other than indefinite descriptions is noted by Harman (1972). See also Higginbotham and May (1981*a*).

11. This problem generalizes, of course, to *all* sentences of the form 'Every man who bought *n or more donkeys* vaccinated *them*', for arbitrary *n*.

12. A theory entertained by Parsons (1978) also cashes out the pronoun in terms of such a description.

13. Evans (1977), pp. 136–39, and Evans (1982), pp. 58–59. The discussion in Evans (1977) concerns the sentence 'Most men who own a car wash it on Sunday', which differs in no relevant respects from (1).

14. A point of clarification is in order here. Geach (1962) claims that 'man who bought a donkey', as it occurs in (e.g.) 'every man who bought a donkey' is not a logical unit. Evans refutes this claim by constructing a viable semantical theory in which the phrase *is* a logical unit. But then Evans goes on to claim that 'every man who bought a donkey' as it occurs in (e.g.) 'every man who bought *a donkey* vaccinated *it*' is not a logical unit. And Evans' claim has been refuted in the same way as Geach's, i.e., by the construction of a viable semantical theory in which the phrase in question (viz., 'every man who bought a donkey') *is* treated as a logical unit.

Although Evans' claim is clearly false, there is no quick way to explain exactly where and why his *argument* breaks down; this is (mainly) because a charitable reconstruction of his argument turns crucially on certain technical details of Evans' own formal theories of quantification, anaphora, and relative clauses (see Neale (forthcoming)). For present purposes, the following informal remarks will suffice. The breakdown of Evans' argument is connected in important ways to (*a*) his belief that descriptive pronouns cannot take narrow scope, and (*b*) his preference for a "Fregean" interpretation of quantifiers. When certain constraints imposed by his own formal machinery are superimposed on these prior strictures, he is unable to countenance the idea that 'it' in (1) is equivalent to a description that takes *narrow* scope with respect to the quantifier 'every man who bought a donkey'. At most, Evans could hope to demonstrate that *if* one endorsed his view that descriptive pronouns have their references fixed by description, and *if* one endorsed his "Fregean" interpretation of the quantifiers, then in order to generate an interpretable reading of (1), one would have to treat 'every' as a binary quantifier instead of treating 'every man who bought a donkey' as a restricted quantifier. But we have already seen that there are cases in which descriptive pronouns take narrow scope. The upshot of all this is that rather than providing support for the view that quantified noun phrases cannot be treated as restricted quantifiers, sentence (1) provides further support for the view that descriptive pronouns are D-type rather than E-type anaphors.

15. This point is made by Heim (1982), who provides a comprehensive discussion of the most notable attempts to deal with donkey anaphora before presenting her own theory. The same objection to Evans's theory is made by Richards (1984) before he presents his theory. Perhaps, the same worry lies behind the failure of Kamp (1981) and Barwise (1987) to engage Evans's theory—Kamp makes only one fleeting reference to Evans's influential work and Barwise does not mention it at all.

16. In the light of the discussion of events in 4.6, it might be thought that making explicit the event quantification in (1) will clear the way for some sort of general solution to this sort of problem. But this appears not to be so; for discussion, see 6.4.

17. According to the theory of D-type anaphora, there are two distinct readings of (2) according as 'she' ('the daughter he has') is given wide or narrow scope with respect to the attitude verb 'thinks'. (A third reading, on which the pronoun has maximally wide scope is unavailable—or, at least, not fully interpretable—because the description for which it would go proxy contains a free variable.)

18. Along with others, I have, at times, felt that the absence of firm and consistent intuitions about the truth conditions of donkey sentences is a serious obstacle to the provision of *any* sort of theory that can achieve general appeal. However, I think there are enough *firmish* intuitions to make investigation worthwhile.

19. There are counterexamples such as 'Someone has left their copy of the *Phaedo* behind', when uttered in a deliberate attempt to avoid using the masculine pronoun. Tom Wasow has pointed out others, such as 'Pat bought a *Veg-o-matic* after seeing them advertized on TV'. Here the pronoun is surely not descriptive in the sense I have been describing. Perhaps this occurrence of 'them' functions as a plural pronoun of laziness standing in for '*Veg-o-matics*'.

20. Evans (1980), p. 220.

21. Of course, (16) is fine if 'a donkey' is given wide scope, but we are not concerned with that reading here.

22. See (e.g.) Hintikka and Carlson (1978), Kamp (1981), and Barwise (1987).

23. There are conceivable circumstances in which one might take utterances of (20) to be making stronger claims. Suppose that Mike bought every donkey on Monday, Tom bought them all from Mike on Tuesday, and Willy bought them all from Tom on Wednesday. The stronger reading I have in mind is the one that is true just in case Mike vaccinated every donkey, Tom vaccinated them, and Willy vaccinated them. (Notice the anaphora in this note.)

24. Similarly for 'Each new recruit is armed'. To say that these sentences are equivalent is not to say that 'every', 'all', and 'each' are "synonymous" in any strong sense. They may have rather different *appropriateness* conditions; since we are here concerned only with *truth* conditions, this can be ignored.

25. This idea is hinted at by Wilson (1984) pp. 44-45.

26. Russell enters the following caveat: ". . . rhetorically there is a difference, because in the one case there is a suggestion of singularity, and in the other case of plurality" (Russell (1919) p. 171). Grice's (1967) notion of *conventional* implicature might be of help in spelling out what Russell has in mind by "rhetorical effect" here. The idea would be that although 'An F is G' and 'Some Fs are Gs' do not differ truth-conditionally, the use of (say) the singular indefinite gives rise to a non-truth-conditional suggestion of singularity. It is, of course, open to challenge Russell on the truth-conditional equivalence of 'An F is G' and 'Some Fs are Gs'. Thus Strawson: ". . . 'some' in its most common employment as a separate word, carries an implication of plurality. . ." (1952, p. 177-78). On this matter, see below.

27. Similarly for the pair (i) and (ii)

    (i)   If John buys a donkey he vaccinates it
    (ii)   If John buys some donkeys he vaccinates them

    which will be discussed in due course.

28. I am grateful to James Higginbotham for directing my attention to the former reference and to Martin Davies for directing my attention to the latter. Richards (1984), p. 294, seems to be on the verge of making a similar suggestion.

    Nouns in English are marked for number, and typically there is a correlation between syntactical and semantical number. Note however, that even where there is a mismatch (e.g., 'trousers', 'scissors', etc.), an anaphoric pronoun must agree in *syntactical* number with its antecedent: 'This morning I bought some trousers. They are grey.' (Compare the equivalent French: 'Ce matin j'ai acheté un pantalon. Il est gris.')

29. If $|F - G| = 0$, then $|F| = |F \cap G|$. I have used $|F \cap G|$ rather than $|F|$ in these restatements of (✳6) and (✳7) only to bring out the relationship between definite and indefinite descriptions.

30. The reading on which 'a donkey' takes wide scope and binds 'it' is also available. As mentioned earlier, sentence (1) also seems to admit of a reading in which the indefinite description takes wide scope. The existence of such readings seems to provide support for the view that

there is a level of syntactical representation at which scope assignments are made and at which (P2) holds.

31. (40) captures the preferred truth conditions of (39), on the assumption that (⁎5) is an adequate truth clause for 'most Fs are Gs':

(⁎5) '[most x: Fx] (Gx)'   is true iff $|F \cap G| > |F - G|$.

(Some informants get additional readings of (39), viz., one that requires that most men who bought at least one donkey vaccinated *at least one* of the donkeys they (*qua* individuals) bought, or another that requires that most men who bought at least one donkey vaccinated *most* of the donkeys they (*qua* individuals) bought.)

This is a good point to bring out, in a brief and schematic way, the main differences between the theory of D-type anaphora and the theories of "discourse representation" (DR) proposed by Kamp (1981) and Heim (1982), both of whom reject Russell's analyses of definite and indefinite descriptions as well as descriptive approaches to unbound anaphora. (There are some differences between Kamp's theory and Heim's theory, but we can, I think, put these aside for present concerns.) Two ideas stand out: (*a*) definite and indefinite descriptions introduce variables rather than quantifiers; (*b*) a quantified sentence '[Dx: φ](ψ)' is true if and only if D assignments of values to free variables in φ that satisfy φ also satisfy ψ. (As Heim stresses, this second idea has its origins in Lewis's (1975) proposals concerning adverbs of quantification like 'always', 'usually', 'sometimes', and so on. The similarities show up especially in the analysis of conditional donkey sentences; for discussion see 6.4.) On this account, our target sentence (1) is true if and only if *every* assignment of values to x and y that satisfies (ii) also satisfies (iii):

(ii)   man x & donkey y & x bought y
(iii)   x vaccinates y.

Thus, the DR theory and the D-type theory (that allows number-neutral pronouns) deliver equivalent analyses of (1).

But the ways in which these two theories achieve this result are, of course, rather different: the theory of D-type anaphora locates the implication of maximality in (1) in the anaphoric pronoun, whereas DR theory locates it in the determiner 'every'. Example (39), brings out this difference very clearly. On the DR proposal, (39) is true if and only if *most* assignments of values to x and y that satisfy (ii) also satisfy (iii). And as Richards (1984, p. 281) points out, this is incorrect: suppose Alan bought ninety donkeys, and five other men bought exactly two donkeys each. DR theory predicts that (39) is true if Alan vaccinated fifty-one or more of the donkeys he bought and the other five men failed to vaccinate any of their donkeys.

The problem here is that in (39) 'most' is quantifying over donkey-buying men and not over pairs of donkey-buying men and donkeys, as DR theory requires. This suggests that the success DR theory has in capturing the implication of maximality in (1) is due to an artifact of first-order logic, and that it will need to be supplemented by some additional machinery if it is to handle the full range of examples.

While (39) seems to favor the D-type over the DR approach, it is arguable that (iv) provides evidence the other way (though this will ultimately depend upon one's final analyses of nonsingular descriptions and monotone decreasing quantifiers):

   (iv)   No man who bought *a donkey* vaccinated *it*.

On the DR proposal, (iv) is true just in case no man who bought a donkey vaccinated *any* of the donkeys he bought, which seems to me like the preferred reading. On the D-type proposal, if the pronoun goes proxy for the singular description 'the donkey he bought', we get a less desirable reading with an implication of relative uniqueness. If it goes proxy for a numberless description we get a reading equivalent to 'No man who bought a donkey vaccinated *each* of the donkeys he bought', which does not seem to be a genuine reading of (iv). As Irene Heim has pointed out to me, (iv) does not actually pose a problem for the view that the pronoun goes proxy for a numberless description—on its preferred reading, (iv) can be paraphrased as 'No man who bought a donkey vaccinated the donkey or donkeys he bought'—rather it poses a more general problem concerning the interpretation of nonsingular definite descriptions within the scope of monotone decreasing quantifiers. The following examples bear out Heim's point:

   (v)   *No man* vaccinated the donkeys *he* bought
   (vi)   *Few men* vaccinated the donkeys *they* bought.

Again, the descriptions are naturally interpreted as 'any of the donkeys he (they) bought' rather than 'each of the donkeys he (they) bought'.

The situation, then, seems to be as follows: (*a*) DR theory has problems with a sentence like (39), in which the indefinite description is within the scope of a non-first-order determiner such as 'most'; (*b*) If the D-type theory utilizes the standard distributive analysis of plural and numberless descriptions, then it will have a problem with a sentence like (iv), in which the indefinite description is within the scope of a monotone decreasing determiner like 'no'. Consequently, if we use a determiner like 'few', which is both monotone decreasing *and* non-first-order, we can construct a sentence that may be problematic for both approaches:

   (vii)   Few men who bought *a donkey* vaccinated *it*.

A further difference between the D-type and DR approaches is that the latter—along with the theories proposed by Hintikka and Carlson (1978) and Barwise (1987)—by its very nature explicitly prohibits cross-sentential anaphoric relations where the purported antecedent is a quantified noun phrase—according to DR theory, definite and indefinite descriptions are not quantified noun phrases. Thus DR theory cannot capture many of the legitimate anaphoric relations discussed in 5.5. In this note I am indebted to discussion with Irene Heim and David Lewis.

32. The problem for Evans raised by sentences of this type is pointed out by Heim (1982) and Le Pore and Garson (1983).

33. A numberless analysis of the pronoun 'it' in (41) does *not* mean that the sentence cannot be true unless every man who bought a beer bought *eleven* beers; *nor* does it mean that it cannot be true unless every man

who bought a beer bought an *infinite number* of beers. (In discussion, it has more than once been claimed that the numberless analysis makes one or other of these undesirable predictions.) As I mentioned earlier, I am confining my talk about plural and numberless descriptions to cases in which they receive *distributive* readings. This is reflected in the contextual definitions (✻II) and (✻III) and in the truth clauses (✻7) and (✻8). As noted in Chapter 2, many plural noun phrases may be interpreted *collectively* when combined with the right predicates; and, naturally enough, this includes plural descriptions and (as pointed out in 5.5) plural D-type pronouns. It is, of course, the simple distributive reading of the numberless D-type pronoun 'it' in (41) that we are interested in. Confused talk of men buying eleven (or an infinite number of) beers results from thinking that nonsingular descriptive pronouns have to be interpreted collectively even though nonsingular descriptions do not. I suspect that the origin of this confusion lies in popular but loose talk of plural E-type pronouns as referring to "sets," "classes," "maximal collections," and the like. (Evans himself says nothing that commits him to just collective readings of nonsingular E-type pronouns, and for good reason.)

34. Conditionals that contain adverbs of quantification bring up some interesting orthogonal issues that appear to have a bearing on the theory of D-type anaphora and on the analysis of conditionals more generally. For the purposes of the present section, I shall continue to work with the material conditional. In 6.4, however, I shall suggest that an idea due to Lewis (1975), and used in his analysis of adverbs of quantification, may provide the basis for a better treatment of conditionals that interacts in interesting ways with the theory of D-type anaphora.

35. The example is from Cicero, *De Fato*, pp. 311–12.

36. On Hornstein's (1984) account (which is summarized in note 4 to Chapter 4), 'any *F*' is a Type I quantifier that may bind a variable across a sentence boundary. The existence of the anaphoric relation in examples like (50) and (i)

(i)   If *any man* buys a donkey *he* is happy

is supposed to support this view. We have already seen that there is no good reason to suppose that any quantifiers have *all* of the properties that Hornstein ascribes to his Type I quantifiers. The D-type analysis of the pronouns in (50) and (i) really closes the book altogether: there is no reason to depart from the view that *all* quantified noun phrases are Type II quantifiers that create "operator-variable structures." The anaphora exemplified in (i) is no different from that exemplified in the following:

(ii)   If *a man* buys a donkey *he* is happy
(iii)   If *some man* buys a donkey *he* is happy
(iii)   If *just one man* wins the jackpot *he* will be very happy
(iv)   If *eight people* share the jackpot *they* will be very happy.

To sum up, Hornstein provides no evidence against the view that a pronoun *P* anaphoric on a quantifier *Q* is (i) a bound variable if and only if *Q* c-commands *P* (at LF).

37. Whether or not we can do everything of truly *semantical* import by always giving temporal quantifiers narrowest possible scope is something I shall not go into here.

38. The same point is made by Wilson (1984), p. 5, and (with respect to conditionals) by Heim (1982), p. 3.

39. See Heim (forthcoming) for discussion. Heim notes an indebtedness to Jan van Eijck and Hans Kamp in developing this type of counterexample to event- or situation-relativized uniqueness.

40. We find a parallel situation in the following example:

(i)   Every man who bought *a woman* <u>a diamond</u> gave *it* to *her* in private.

(This particular example is due to George Wilson.) Since the relative clause inside the subject noun phrase contains two indefinite descriptions the subject NP is ambiguous between (ii_1) and (ii_2):

(ii_1) [every x: man x & [a y: diamond y] ([a z: woman z] (x bought y for z))]

(ii_2) [every x: man x & [a z: woman z] ([a y: diamond y] (x bought y for z))].

Suppose the subject NP is interpreted as (ii_1). If we now apply (P5) to 'it' we get

(iii)   [whe y: diamond y & [a z: woman z] (x bought y for z)].

If we then apply (P5) to 'her' we get

(iv)   [whe z: z: woman z & x bought y for z].

If (iii) is given wider scope than (iv), the sentence as a whole comes out as

(v)   [every x: man x & [a y: diamond y] ([a z: woman z] (x bought y for z))]
([whe y: diamond y & [a z: woman z] (x bought y for z)]
([whe z: z: woman z & x bought y for z]
(x gave y to z in private)))

which gets us exactly the right result. (If (iv) is given wider scope than (iii) we are left with a free occurrence of y.)

If the subject NP is read as (ii_2), only the reading on which 'her' has wider scope than 'it' is fully interpretable:

(vi)   [every x: man x & [a y: diamond y] ([a z: woman z] (x bought y for z))]
([whe z: z: woman z & [a y: diamond y] (x bought y for z)]
([whe y: diamond y & x bought y for z]
(x gave y to z in private)))))

(v) and (vi) are equivalent; the only formal difference is that in (v) the description for which 'it' goes proxy binds a variable inside the description for which 'her' goes proxy, and in (vi) the description for which 'her' goes proxy binds a variable inside the description for which 'it' goes proxy.

In this note I am indebted to Scott Soames for extensive discussion.

41. This is a good point at which to spell out a problem that will arise for any account of D-type anaphora that is bent on construing (P5$_a$) and (P5$_b$) as *bona fide* linguistic rules.

In the light of the discussion in 5.5 and 5.7, for expository purposes I have been proceeding as if (P5$_a$) and (P5$_b$) were linguistic rules, but as I mentioned earlier, in view of the fact that there appear to be genuine counterexamples and in view of the fact that broadly Gricean considerations impose strong constraints on utterance interpretation, in my opinion (P5$_a$) and (P5$_b$) should really be thought of as descriptive generalizations, and perhaps also as processing heuristics. Consider (i):

(i)   *Every boy* danced with <u>a girl</u>. Afterward, *he* gave <u>her</u> flowers.

The antecedent sentence is ambiguous between (ii$_1$) and (ii$_2$), which are not equivalent:

(ii$_1$)   [every x: boy x] ([a y: girl y] (x danced with y))
(ii$_2$)   [a y: girl y] ([every x: boy x] (x danced with y)).

Take (ii$_1$). Applying (P5) to 'he' in the anaphor sentence we get

(iii)   [whe x: boy x].

Applying (P5) to 'her' we get

(iv)   [the y: girl y & x danced with y]

which contains a free occurrence of x. Putting this all together with 'x gave y flowers' the interpretable reading we get for the anaphor sentence is given by (v):

(v)   [whe x: boy x]
       ([the y: girl y & x danced with y] (x gave y flowers))

in which the occurrence of x inside the description for which 'her' goes proxy is captured by the description for which 'he' goes proxy, exactly as required.

But what of a case like the following?

(vi)   Every boy danced with *a girl*. *She* was a ballerina.

First, let's construe the antecedent sentence on the reading given by (ii$_2$). If we apply (P5) to 'she', the anaphor sentence will come out as

(vii)   [the y: girl y & [every x: boy x] (x danced with y)] (ballerina y).

We also appear to get a sensible reading of (vi) on which the indefinite description in the antecedent sentence takes narrow scope, i.e., as (ii$_1$) (this comes through more clearly with an example like 'Every car come with *a spare tire; it* is located on the left-hand side of the trunk', which is adapted from Sells (1985)). On the assumption that this reading is available, if we apply (P5) to 'she', the anaphor sentence will come out as

(viii)   [the y: girl y & x danced with y)] (ballerina y)

with a free occurrence of x. When we spelled out the anaphor sentence of (i), the counterpart to this occurrence of x was captured by the description for which 'he' went proxy; but in the anaphor sentence of (vi) there is no operator around to bind x.

What are we to make of this situation? It is clear that this type of example does not threaten the general idea that unbound anaphors go proxy for descriptions; we find exactly the same situation where an overt description is used instead of a pronoun:

(vi$_1$)   Every boy danced with *a girl. The girl* was a ballerina.

Indeed, (vi$_1$) is ambiguous in the same way as (vi). In the light of the discussion of in 3.7, 5.5, and 5.7, the natural move, of course, is remind ourselves (*a*) that (P5) is not genuine semantical rule but a generalization about D-type content (and possibly a processing heuristic), and (*b*) that nonpersistent quantifiers must often be completed by context anyway. In most speech situations, the anaphor sentence in both (vi) and (vi$_1$) will probably be interpreted as something like

(ix)   [every x: boy x]
        ([the y: girl y & x danced with y)] (ballerina y))

The point here is that the heuristic (P5) just does not deliver enough information by itself so additional contextual information must be brought into play if a sensible interpretation is to be provided.

Of course, if one were convinced that (P5) should be accorded the status of a rule of semantics, one could attempt to rework the theory in such a way that the offending variable in (viii) were assigned some descriptive content, or rework it in such a way that (P5) has access to more information than it has under the formulation I gave it in 5.5. On the first count, I suppose one might attempt to provide a D-type treatment of the offending variable on the grounds that it is not c-commanded by its antecedent. On the assumption that the occurrence of 'every boy' in the antecedent sentence is the antecedent of the variable, by (P5) the variable would then come out as

(x)   [whe x: boy x].

The antecedent sentence of (vi) would come out as

(xi)   [whe x: boy x]
        ([the y: girl y & x danced with y)] (ballerina y)).

On the second count, one might suggest modifying modify (P5) in such a way that the content of an anaphor sentence containing a D-type pronoun whose antecedent is contained in an antecedent sentence ϕ containing free variables $x_1,...,x_n$ must, under certain specifiable syntactical conditions, and in a systematic way, inherit all of the descriptive material contained in the quantifiers outside ϕ that bind $x_1,...,x_n$. (I suspect that in order to handle relative clause donkey sentences such a theory would have to distinguish two different types of binding relation, one that quantifiers bears to the variables they bind, and another that determiners bear to the variables they bind.) My own inclination is to steer well clear of either of these ideas.

42. Again, there is no gain in semantical power or technical coherence is obtained by choosing one system rather than the other. For discussion, see Neale (1989*a*).

43. This is one of the starting points of the DR theory developed by Heim (1982). Heim agrees on the following two counts: (i) indefinite descriptions and pronouns introduce variables that unselective quantifiers may bind; and (ii) sentence (30) involves implicit universal quantification. For discussion, see note 31.

44. Lewis's theory was not originally intended to form the basis of a general theory of the semantics of anaphoric pronouns, the semantics of indefinite descriptions, or the semantics of conditionals; it was intended to explicate the semantical structure of a certain class of conditional donkey sentences, those containing adverbs of quantification like 'always', 'sometimes', 'usually', etc. This is not to say that the theory cannot be generalized in certain directions with a view to producing more comprehensive theories of anaphora and indefinite descriptions. Indeed, as Heim (1982) makes clear, her DR theory is, in many respects, an attempt to do just that.

45. I have been making parenthetical reference to state-of-affair variables for the simple reason that for many simple sentences it is not plausible to suppose that there is quantification over *events* as such. Consider (i):

   (i)   If *a man* owns a donkey *he* is happy.

   If there is a hidden quantification here, it is surely a quantification over something more like states-of-affairs or situations.
   But even the introduction of state-of-affair variables may not do justice to an example like the following:

   (ii)   If *a number* is prime and greater than two then *it* is always odd.

   It is examples like this that suggest to Lewis that AQs are predominantly quantifiers over *cases*, where a case is just a tuple.

46. See (e.g.) Kratzer (1979).

47. On such a proposal there is still no way to dispense with numberless D-type pronouns by paying attention to event parameters. First, the event parameter does not help with relative clause donkey sentences. Second, Heim's devious examples of the form 'If a man buys an apartment with another man, he shares the fee with him' will remain to be reckoned with.

48. In 4.6, it was suggested that we follow Davidson in treating nominals like 'Mary's departure', 'Mary's departing', 'Nixon's resignation', and so on, as definite descriptions of events. On such an account, the anaphora exemplified in (i) can be treated in the same way as that in (ii):

   (i)   John saw *Mary's departure*. I saw *it* too
   (ii)   John saw *Mary's dog*. I saw *it* too.

   By (P5) the anaphoric pronoun in (i) comes out as 'Mary's departure' too. Now consider:

   (iii)   Mary kissed John. I saw it.

   Following a suggestion made by Wiggins (1985), it ought to be possible in a fully worked out theory to treat the pronoun 'it' in this example as a D-type anaphor that goes proxy for 'Mary's kissing John'. If we follow

Davidson in making explicit the implicit event quantification in (iii), the antecedent sentence comes out as

(iv)   ($\exists e$)(kiss(Mary, John, e)).

The idea would be that the pronoun 'it' can then be interpreted as the definite description '[the e: kiss(Mary, John, e)]'; I shall not attempt to work out the precise details of such a proposal here.

Paul Grice has suggested (in unpublished work) that it may be preferable to explicate the putative anaphoric relation in examples like (iv) in a rather different way. Discussing the example

(v)   The manager of the Minneapolis Moonrakers resigned last week, and Ann Landers made a joke about it in her column

Grice suggests that the utterance of the antecedent sentence raises the manager's resignation to salience and thereby makes that event available as the referent of 'it' in the anaphor sentence. However, Grice suggests that on this account the anaphoric relationship may not be a matter of pure grammar; that is, it might be better explained on the model of the "anaphoric" relations exemplified in (vi) and (vii):

(vi)   I spent last summer in Persia; *they* are very dissatisfied with the present regime
(vii)   His leg was cancerous; he contracted *it* in Africa.

(There are obvious points of contact between Grice's suggestion and the suggestion made by Kripke and Lewis that is discussed in 5.4.)

49. For example, we will be able to construct a semantics in which, say, (i) comes out as something like (ii)?

(i)   Usually if *a man* buys a donkey *he* smiles
(ii)   [most e: event e & [an x: man x] ([a y: donkey y] (buys(x,y,e)]
       ([whe: x: man x & [a y: donkey y] (buys(x,y,e)]
       ([some f: event f] (smile(x,f))).

If it is possible to proceed in this way, this ought to give us a handle on sentences like (iii) and (iv):

(iii)   I usually go to bed before midnight
(iv)   Sometimes Lisa forgets her name.

Appendix

Definitions and Principles

(A1) If a speaker S uses a definite description 'the F' referentially in an utterance u of 'the F is G', then 'the F' functions as a referring expression and the proposition expressed by u is *object-dependent* (rather than descriptive).

(A2) A speaker S uses a definite description 'the F' referentially in an utterance u of 'the F is G' iff there is some object b such that S means by u that b is the F and that b is G.

(A3) If a speaker S uses a definite description 'the F' referentially in an utterance u of 'the F is G', 'the F' still functions as a quantifier and the proposition expressed by u is the object-independent proposition given by '[the x: Fx](Gx)'.

(D1) If 'the F' is a definite description, then for a (monadic) predicate phrase '— is G', the proposition expressed by an utterance of 'the F is G' can be perfectly well understood by a person who does not know who or what is denoted by 'the F' (indeed, even if nothing satisfies 'the F', and even if that person knows that nothing satisfies 'the F').

(D2) If 'the F' is a definite description, then for a (monadic) predicate phrase '— is G', an utterance of 'the F is G' expresses a perfectly determinate proposition whether or not there is any individual that satisfies 'the F'. .

(D3) The individual x that actually satisfies a definite description 'the F' does not enter into a specification of the truth conditions of 'the F is G' in either actual or counterfactual situations.

(G1)   By uttering ϕ, S means that p only if for some audience H, S utters ϕ intending:

   (1) H to actively entertain the thought that p, and
   (2) H to recognize that S intends (1).

(P1)   A phrase α c-commands a phrase β if and only if the first branching node dominating α also dominates β (and neither α nor β dominates the other).

(P2)   A pronoun P that is anaphoric on a quantifier Q is interpreted as a variable bound by Q if and only if Q c-commands P.

(P3)   A quantifier '$[Dx: Fx]$' is *maximal* if and only if '$[Dx: Fx](Gx)$' entails '$[every\ x: Fx](Gx)$', for arbitrary G.

(P4)   The *antecedent clause* for a pronoun P that is anaphoric on a quantifier Q occuring in a sentence ϕ is the smallest well-formed subformula of ϕ that contains Q as a constituent.

(P5)   If x is a pronoun that is anaphoric on, but not c-commanded by, a quantifier '$[Dx: Fx]$' that occurs in an antecedent clause '$[Dx: Fx](Gx)$', then x is interpreted as the most "impoverished" definite description directly recoverable from the antecedent clause that denotes everything that is both F and G.

(P5$_a$)   If x is a pronoun that is anaphoric on, but not c-commanded by a nonmaximal quantifier '$[Dx: Fx]$' that occurs in an antecedent clause '$[Dx: Fx](Gx)$', then x is interpreted as '$[the\ x: Fx\ \&\ Gx]$'.

(P5$_b$)   If x is a pronoun that is anaphoric on, but not c-commanded by a maximal quantifier '$[Dx: Fx]$' that occurs in an antecedent clause '$[Dx: Fx](Gx)$', then x is interpreted as '$[the\ x: Fx]$'.

(P6)   A variable v is bound by an operator Ov if and only if Ov c-commands v at LF.

(Q1)   If ϕ is a well-formed formula with x free, and
   if D is one of 'some', 'no', 'every', 'all', 'a', 'the', 'most', etc.,
   then '$[Dx: \phi]$' is a well-formed quantifier phrase.

(Q2)   If ψ is a well-formed formula with x free, and
   if '$[Dx: \phi]$' is a well-formed quantifier phrase,
   then '$[Dx: \phi](\psi)$' is a well-formed formula.

(Q1')   If ϕ is a well-formed formula that contains at least one occur-
         rence of b, and if D is one of 'some', 'no', 'every', 'all', 'a',
         'the', 'most', etc., then '$[Dx: \phi(b/x)]$' is a well-formed
         quantifier phrase, where '$\phi(b/x)$' is the result of replacing at
         least one occurrence of b in ϕ by x.

(Q2')   If ψ is a well-formed formula that contains at least one occur-
         rence of b, and if '$[Dx: \phi]$' is a well-formed quantifier phrase,
         then '$[Dx: \phi](\psi(b/x))$' is a is a well-formed formula, where
         '$\psi(b/x)$' is the result of replacing at least one occurrence of b
         in ψ by x

(R1)   If 'b' is a genuine referring expression (singular term), then for
         a (monadic) predicate '— is G', it is necessary to identify the
         referent of 'b' in order to understand the proposition expressed
         by an utterance u of 'b is G'.

(R2)   If 'b' has no referent, then for a (monadic) predicate '— is G',
         no proposition is expressed by an utterance u of 'b is G'.

(R3)   If 'b' is a genuine referring expression that refers to x, then 'b'
         is a rigid designator; i.e., x enters into a specification of the
         truth conditions of (the proposition expressed by) an utterance
         u of 'b is G' with respect to actual and counterfactual
         situations.

Bibliography

Bach, E. (1970). Problominalization. *Linguistic Inquiry* 1, 121–122.

Bar-Hillel, Y. (1954). Indexical Expressions. *Mind* 63, 359–379.

Barwise, J. (1981). Scenes and Other Situations. *Journal of Philosophy* 77, 269–397.

Barwise J. (1987). Noun Phrases, Generalized Quantifiers, and Anaphora. In P. Gärdenfors (ed.), *Generalized Quantifiers*. Dordrecht: Reidel, 1–29

Barwise, J., and R. Cooper (1981). Generalized Quantifiers and Natural Language. *Linguistics and Philosophy* 4, 159–219.

Barwise, J., and J. Perry (1983). *Situations and Attitudes*. Cambridge, Mass.: MIT Press.

van Benthem, J. (1983). Determiners and Logic. *Linguistics and Philosophy* 6, 447–478.

Blackburn, S. (1984). *Spreading the Word: Groundings in the Philosophy of Language*. Oxford: Clarendon Press.

Blackburn, W. (1988). Wettstein on Definite Descriptions. *Philosophical Studies* 53, 263–278.

Boër, S., and W. Lycan (1976). *The Myth of Semantic Presupposition*. Bloomington, Ind.: Indiana University Linguistics Club.

Brand, M. (1977). Identity Conditions for Events. *American Philosophical Quarterly* 14, 329–337.

Brand, M. (1985). *Intending and Acting*. Cambridge, Mass.: MIT Press.

Carnap, R. (1947). *Meaning and Necessity*. Chicago: University of Chicago Press.

Carston, R. (1988). Implicature, Explicature, and Truth-theoretic Semantics. In R. Kempson (ed.) *Mental Representations*. Cambridge: Cambridge University Press, 155-181.

Cartwright, R. (1968). Some Remarks on Essentialism. *Noûs* 2, 229–246.

Castañeda, H. N. (1966). "He": A Study in the Logic of Self-Consciousness. *Ratio* 8, 130–157.

Castañeda, H. N. (1967). Indicators and Quasi-indicators. *American Philosophical Quarterly* 4, 85–100.

Castañeda, H. N. (1967). On the Philosophical Foundations of the Theory of Communication: Reference. In In P. A. French, T. E. Uehling, Jr., and H. K. Wettstein, *Contemporary Perspectives in the Philosophy of Language*. Minneapolis: University of Minnesota Press, 125–146.

Chastain, C. (1975). Reference and Context. In K. Gunderson (ed.), *Minnesota Studies in the Philosophy of Science, vol. VII: Language, Mind, and Knowledge*. Minneapolis: University of Minnesota Press, 194–269.

Chomsky, N. (1970). Remarks on Nominalization. In *Studies on Semantics in Generative Grammar*. The Hague: Mouton, 1972, 11–61.

Chomsky, N. (1975). Questions of Form and Interpretation. *Linguistic Analysis* 1, 75–109.

Chomsky, N. (1981). *Lectures on Government and Binding*. Dordrecht: Foris.

Chomsky, N. (1986). *Knowledge of Language*. New York: Praeger.

Church, A. (1942). Review of Quine's "Whitehead and the Rise of Modern Logic." *Journal of Symbolic Logic* 7, 100–101.

Church, A. (1943). Review of Quine's "Notes on Existence and Necessity." *Journal of Symbolic Logic* 8, 45–47.

Clark, E. (1971). On the Acquisition of the Meaning of "before" and "after." *Journal of Verbal Learning and Verbal Behavior* 10, 266–275.

Cole, P. (1978). On the Origins of Referential Opacity. In P. Cole (ed.), *Syntax and Semantics, vol 9: Pragmatics*. New York: Academic Press, 1-22.

Cooper, R. (1979). The Interpretation of Pronouns. In F. Heny and H. Schnelle (eds.), *Syntax and Semantics, vol. 10: Selections from the Third Gröningen Round Table*. New York: Academic Press, 61–92.

Cresswell, M. (1973). *Logics and Languages*. London: Methuen.

Cresswell, M. (1975). Identity and Intensional Objects. *Philosophia* 5, 47–68.

Culicover, P. (1976). A Constraint on Coreferentiality. *Foundations of Language* 14, 109–118.

Davidson, D. (1967). The Logical Form of Action Sentences. In N. Rescher (ed.), *The Logic of Decision and Action*. Pittsburgh: University of Pittsburgh Press, 81–95. (Reprinted in *Essays on Actions and Events*. Oxford: Clarendon Press, 1980, 105–148.)

Davidson, D. (1969). The Individuation of Events. In N. Rescher (ed.), *Essays in Honor of Carl Hempel*. Dordrecht: Reidel, 216–234. (Reprinted in *Essays on Actions and Events*. Oxford: Clarendon Press, 1980, 163–180.)

Davidson, D. (1986). A Nice Derangement of Epitaphs. In R. Grandy and R. Warner (eds.), *Philosophical Grounds of Rationality, Intentions, Categories, Ends*. Oxford: Clarendon Press, 157–174.

Davies, M. (1981). *Meaning, Quantification, Necessity*. London: Routledge and Kegan Paul.

Devitt, M. (1981). Donnellan's Distinction. In P. A. French, T. E. Uehling, Jr., and H. K. Wettstein (eds.), *Midwest Studies in Philosophy VI*. Minneapolis: University of Minnesota Press, 511–524.

Dominicy, M. (1984). *La Naissance de la Grammaire Moderne: Langage, Logique et Philosophie à Port Royal*. Bruxelles: Pierre Mardags Editeur.

Donnellan, K. (1966). Reference and Definite Descriptions. *Philosophical Review* 77, 281–304.

Donnellan, K. (1966a). Substitution and Reference. *Journal of Philosophy* 63, 685–688.

Donnellan, K. (1968). Putting Humpty Dumpty Back Together Again. *Philosophical Review* 77.

Donnellan, K. (1978). Speaker Reference, Descriptions, and Anaphora. In P. Cole (ed.), *Syntax and Semantics, vol. 9: Pragmatics*. New York: Academic Press, 47–68.

Donnellan, K. (1981). Presupposition and Intuitions. In P. Cole (ed.), *Radical Pragmatics*. New York: Academic Press, 129–142.

Dummett, M. (1973). *Frege: Philosophy of Language*. London: Duckworth.

Evans, G. (1973). The Causal Theory of Names. *Proceedings of the Aristotelian Society* 47, 187–208. (Reprinted in Evans (1985), 1–24.)

Evans, G. (1977). Pronouns, Quantifiers and Relative Clauses (I). *Canadian Journal of Philosophy* 7, 467–536. (Reprinted in Evans (1985), 76–152.)

Evans, G. (1977a). Pronouns, Quantifiers and Relative Clauses (II), *Canadian Journal of Philosophy* 7, 777-797. (Reprinted in Evans (1985), 153–175.)

Evans, G. (1979). Reference and Contingency. *The Monist* 62, 161–189. (Reprinted in Evans (1985), 178–213.)

Evans, G. (1980). Pronouns. *Linguistic Inquiry* 11, 337–362. (Reprinted in Evans (1985), 214–248.)

Evans, G. (1982). *The Varieties of Reference*. Oxford: Clarendon Press.

Evans, G. (1985). *The Collected Papers*. Oxford: Clarendon Press.

Fillmore, C. (1966). The Syntax of Preverbs. Manuscript, University of California, Berkeley.

Fodor, J. D., and I. Sag (1982). Referential and Quantificational Indefinites. *Linguistics and Philosophy* 5, 355–398.

Føllesdal, D. (1961). *Referential Opacity and Modal Logic*. Doctoral thesis, Harvard University.

Føllesdal, D. (1965). Quantification into Causal Contexts. In R. S. Cohen and M. W. Wartofsky (eds.), *Boston Studies in the Philosophy of Science. Volume II: In Honor of Philipp Frank*, Dordrecht: Reidel, 263–274. (Reprinted in Linsky (1971), 52–62.)

Føllesdal, D. (1969). Quine on Modality. In D. Davidson and J. Hintikka (eds.), *Words and Objections*. Dordrecht: Reidel, 175–185.

Føllesdal, D. (1986). Essentialism and Reference. In L. E. Hahn and P. A. Schilpp (eds.), *The Philosophy of W. V. Quine*. La Salle: Open Court, 97–113.

van Fraassen, B. (1966). Singular Terms, Truth-value Gaps, and Free Logic. *Journal of Philosophy* 63, 481–494.

van Fraassen, B. (1968). Presupposition, Implication, and Self-reference. *Journal of Philosophy* 65, 136–152.

van Fraassen, B. (1969). Presupposition, Supervaluation, and Free Logic. In K. Lambert (ed.), *The Logical way of Doing Things*. New Haven: Yale University Press, 67–91.

Frege, G. (1879). *Begriffsschrift*. English translation in J. van Heijenoort (ed.), *From Frege to Gödel*. Cambridge, Mass.: Harvard University Press, 1967.

Frege, G. (1893). Uber Sinn and Bedeutung. *Zeitschrift fur Philosophie und Philosophische Kritik*, 25–50. Translated as "On Sense and Reference," in P. T. Geach and M. Black (eds.), *Translations from the Philosophical Writings of Gottlob Frege*. Oxford: Blackwell, 1952, 56–78.

Gale, R. (1970). Strawson's Restricted Theory of Referring. *Philosophical Quarterly* 20, 162–165.

Gazdar, G. (1979). *Pragmatics: Presupposition, Implicature, and Logical Form*. New York: Academic Press.

Geach, P. (1962). *Reference and Generality*, Ithaca, NY: Cornell University Press.

Geach, P. (1964). Referring Expressions Again. In *Logic Matters*. Oxford: Blackwell, 1972, 97–102.

Geach, P. (1969). Quine's Syntactical Insights. In In D. Davidson and J. Hintikka (eds.), *Words and Objections*. Dordrecht: Reidel, 146–157. (Reprinted in *Logic Matters*. Oxford: Blackwell, 1972, 115–127.)

Geach, P. (1967). Intentional Identity. In *Logic Matters*. Oxford: Blackwell, 1972, 146–153.

Gee, J. (1977). Comments on the Paper by Akmajian. In P. Culicover, T. Wasow, and A. Akmajian (eds.), *Formal Syntax*. New York: Academic Press, 461–481.

Grice, H. P. (1957). Meaning. *Philosophical Review* 66, 377–388.

Grice, H. P. (1961). The Causal Theory of Perception. *Proceedings of the Aristotelian Society*, suppl. vol. 35, 121–52.

Grice, H. P. (1967). Logic and Conversation. (William James Lectures.) In *Studies in the Way of Words*. Cambridge, Mass.: Harvard University Press, 1989. (Lectures II and III published as Grice (1975) and Grice (1978).)

Grice, H. P. (1968). Utterer's Meaning, Sentence Meaning and Word Meaning. *Foundations of Language* 4, 225–242.

Grice, H. P. (1969). Vacuous Names. In D. Davidson and J. Hintikka (eds.), *Words and Objections*. Dordrecht: Reidel, 118–145.

Grice, H. P. (1969a). Utterer's Meaning and Intentions. *Philosophical Review* 78, 147–177.

Grice, H. P. (1970). Lectures on Logic and Reality. University of Illinois at Urbana. (Lecture IV published as Grice (1981).)

Grice, H. P. (1975). Logic and Conversation. In P. Cole and J. Morgan (eds.), *Syntax and Semantics, vol. 3: Speech Acts*. New York: Academic Press, 41–58.

Grice, H. P. (1978). Further Notes on Logic and Conversation. In P. Cole (ed.), *Syntax and Semantics, vol. 9: Pragmatics*, New York: Academic Press, 113–128.

Grice, H. P. (1981). Presupposition and Conversational Implicature. In P. Cole (ed.), *Radical Pragmatics*. New York: Academic Press, 1981, 183–198.

Hampshire, S. (1959). *Thought and Action*. New York: Viking Press.

Harman, G. (1972). Deep Structure as Logical Form. In D. Davidson and G. Harman (eds.), *Semantics of Natural Language*. Dordrecht: Reidel, 25–47.

Heim, I. (1982). *The Semantics of Definite and Indefinite Noun Phrases*. Doctoral thesis, University of Massachusetts, Amherst.

Heim, I. (forthcoming). E-Type Pronouns and Donkey Anaphora. To appear in *Linguistics and Philosophy*.

Higginbotham, J. (1980). Pronouns and Bound Variables. *Linguistic Inquiry* 11, 679–708.

Higginbotham, J. (1983). Logical Form, Binding, and Nominals. *Linguistic Inquiry* 14, 395–420.

Higginbotham, J. (1987). Indefinites and Predication. In E. J. Reuland and A. ter Meulen (eds.), *The Representation of (In)definiteness*. Cambridge, Mass.: MIT Press, 43–70.

Higginbotham, J., and R. May (1981). Questions, Quantifiers, and Crossing. *Linguistic Review* 1, 41–80.

Higginbotham, J., and R. May (1981a). Crossing, Markedness, Pragmatics. In A Belletti, L. Brandi, and L. Rizzi (eds.), *Theory of Markedness in Generative Grammar*. Pisa: Scuola Normale Superiore, 423–444.

Hintikka, J. (1967). Individuals, Possible Worlds, and Epistemic Logic. *Nous* 1, 33–62.

Hintikka, J. (1986). The Semantics of 'a certain'. *Linguistic Inquiry* 17, 331–336.

Hintikka, J., and L. Carlson (1978). Conditionals, Generic Quantifiers, and Other Applications of Subgames. In F. Guenthner and S. J. Schmidt (eds.), *Formal Semantics and Pragmatics for Natural Language*. Dordrecht: Reidel, 1–36.

Hintikka, J., and J. Kulas (1985). *Anaphora and Definite Descriptions*. Dordrecht: Reidel.

Horgan, T. (1980). Nonrigid Event Designators and the Modal Individuation of Events. *Philosophical Studies* 37, 341–351.

Hornsby, J. (1977). Singular Terms in Contexts of Propositional Attitude. *Mind* 86, 31–48.

Hornstein, N. (1984). *Logic as Grammar*. Cambridge, Mass.: MIT Press.

Huang, C.-T. J. (1982). Move *WH* in a Language Without *Wh*-movement. *Linguistic Review* 1, 369–416.

Husserl, E. (1913) *Logische Untersuchungen, Zweiter Band*. 2nd ed., Halle: Niemeyer. English tr. by J. N. Findlay, London: Routledge and Kegan Paul, 1970.

Jacobson, P. (1977). *The Syntax of Crossing Coreference Sentences*. Doctoral thesis, Massachusetts Institute of Technology.

Johnson, H. (1975). The Meaning of "before" and "after" for Preschool Children. *Journal of Experimental Child Psychology* 19, 88–99.

Kamp, H. (1981). A Theory of Truth and Semantic Interpretation. In J. Groenendijk et al. (eds.), *Formal Methods in the Study of Natural Language*. Amsterdam: Amsterdam Centre, 277–322. (Reprinted in J. Groenendijk et al. (eds.), *Truth, Interpretation, and Information*. Dordrecht: Foris, 1984, 1–43.)

Kaplan, D. (1972). What is Russell's Theory of Descriptions? In D. F. Pears (ed.), *Bertrand Russell: A Collection of Critical Essays*. Garden City, NY: Doubleday Anchor, 227–244.

Kaplan, D. (1975). How to Russell a Frege-Church. *Journal of Philosophy* 72, 716–729.

Kaplan, D. (1977). Demonstratives. In J. Almog, J. Perry, and H. Wettstein (eds.), *Themes from Kaplan*. New York: Oxford University Press, 1989, 481–563.

Kaplan, D. (1978). Dthat. In P. Cole (ed.), *Syntax and Semantics, vol. 9: Pragmatics*. New York: Academic Press, 221–243.

Kaplan, D. (1986). Opacity. In L. E. Hahn and P. A. Schilpp (ed.), *The Philosophy of W. V. Quine*. La Salle: Open Court, 229–289.

Karttunen, L. (1969). Pronouns and Variables. In *Papers from the Fifth Regional Meeting of the of the Chicago Linguistic Society*. Chicago: University of Chicago Press, 108–115.

Karttunen, L. (1971). Definite Descriptions and Crossing Coreference. *Foundations of Language* 7, 157–182.

Karttunen, L. (1976). Discourse Referents. In J. McCawley (ed.), *Syntax and Semantics, vol. 7: Notes from the Linguistic Underground*. New York: Academic Press, 363–385.

Kempson, R. (1975). *Presupposition and the Delimitation of Semantics*. Cambridge: Cambridge University Press.

King, J. (1988). Are Indefinite Descriptions Ambiguous? *Philosophical Studies* 53, 417-440.

Klein, E. (1980). Defensible Descriptions. In F. Heny (ed.), *Ambiguities in Intensional Contexts*. Dordrecht: Reidel, 1981, 83–102.

Klima, E. (1964). Negation in English. In J. Fodor and J. Katz (eds.), *The Structure of Language*. Englewood Cliffs, NJ: Prentice Hall, 246–323.

Kratzer, A. (1979). Conditional Necessity and Possibility . In R. Bäuerle, U. Egli, and A. von Stechow (eds.), *Semantics form a Different Point of View*. New York: Springer-Verlag, 117–147.

Kripke, S. A. (1963). Semantical Considerations on Modal Logic. *Acta Philosophica Fennica* 16, 83–94. (Reprinted in Linsky (1971), 63–72 with addendum on p. 172.)

Kripke, S. A. (1971). Identity and Necessity. In M. K. Munitz (ed.), *Identity and Individuation*. New York: New York University Press, 135–164. (Reprinted in S. P. Schwartz (ed.), *Naming, Necessity, and Natural Kinds*. Ithaca, New York: Cornell University Press, 66–101.)

Kripke, S. A. (1972). Naming and Necessity. In D. Davidson and G. Harman (eds.), *Semantics of Natural Language*. Dordrecht: Reidel, 253–355, and 763–769.

Kripke, S. A. (1977). Speaker Reference and Semantic Reference. In P. A. French, T. E. Uehling, Jr., and H. K. Wettstein, *Contemporary Perspectives in the Philosophy of Language*. Minneapolis: University of Minnesota Press, 6–27.

Kripke, S. A. (1979). A Puzzle about Belief. In A. Margalit (ed.), *Meaning and Use*. Dordrecht: Reidel, 239–283.

Kripke, S. A. (1980). Preface to "Naming and Necessity." In *Naming and Necessity*, Cambridge, Mass.: Harvard University Press.

Lasnik, H. (1976). Remarks on Coreference. *Linguistic Analysis* 2, 1–22.

Lemmon, E. J. (1965). *Beginning Logic*. London: Thomas Nelson and Sons.

Le Pore, E., and J. Garson (1983). Pronouns and Quantifier-Scope in English. *Journal of Philosophical Logic* 12, 327–358.

Lewis, D. (1972). General Semantics. In D. Davidson and G. Harman (eds.), *Semantics of Natural Language*. Dordrecht: Reidel, 169–218.

Lewis, D. (1973). *Counterfactuals*. Cambridge, Mass.: Harvard University Press.

Lewis, D. (1975). Adverbs of Quantification. In E. Keenan (ed.), *Formal Semantics of Natural Language*, Cambridge: Cambridge University Press, 3-15.

Lewis, D. (1979). Scorekeeping in a Language Game. *Journal of Philosophical Logic* 8, 339–359.

Link, G. (1983). The Logical Analysis of Plurals and Mass Terms: A Lattice-Theoretical Approach. In R. Bäuerle, C. Schwarze, and A. von Stechow (eds.), *Meaning, Use, and Interpretation*. Berlin: Walter de Gruyter. 302–323.

Link, G. (1987). Generalized Quantifiers and Plurals. In P. Gärdenfors (ed.), *Generalized Quantifiers*. Dordrecht: Reidel, 151–180.

Linsky, L. (1963). Reference and Referents. In C. E. Caton (ed.), *Philosophy and Ordinary Language*, Urbana: University of Illinois Press, 74–89.

Linsky, L. (1966). *Referring*. London; Routledge and Kegan Paul.

Linsky, L. (1971). *Reference and Modality*. Oxford: Oxford University Press.

Linsky, L. (1977). *Names and Descriptions*. Chicago: University of Chicago Press.

Linsky, L. (1983). *Oblique Contexts*. Chicago: University of Chicago Press.

Lønning, J. T. (1987). Collective Readings of Definite and Indefinite Noun Phrases. In P. Gärdenfors (ed.), *Generalized Quantifiers*. Dordrecht: Reidel, 203–255.

Ludlow, P. (1985). *The Syntax and Semantics of Referential Attitude Reports*. Doctoral thesis, Columbia University.

Ludlow, P. (1989). Implicit Comparison Classes. *Linguistics and Philosophy* 12, 519–533.

Ludlow, P., and S. Neale (forthcoming). Indefinite Descriptions: In Defence of Russell.

Lycan, B. (1984). *Logical Form in Natural Language*. Cambridge, Mass.: MIT Press.

Mackay, A. F. (1968). Mr. Donnellan and Humpty Dumpty on Referring. *Philosophical Review* 77, 197–202.

Marcus, R. (1947). The Identity of Individuals in a Strict Functional Calculus of First Order. *Journal of Symbolic Logic* 12, 12–15.

Marcus, R. (1962). Modalities and Intensional Languages. *Synthese* 27, 303–322. (Reprinted in I. M. Copi and J. A. Gould (eds.), *Contemporary Philosophical Logic*. New York: St. Martin's Press, 1978, 257–272.)

Mates, B. (1973). Descriptions and Reference. *Foundations of Language* 10, 409–418.

May, R. (1977). *The Grammar of Quantification*. Doctoral thesis, Massachusetts Institute of Technology.

May, R. (1985). *Logical Form: its Structure and Derivation*. Cambridge, Mass.: MIT Press.

McDowell, J. (1977). On the Sense and Reference of a Proper Name. *Mind* 86, 159–185

McDowell, J. (1982). Truth-value Gaps. *Logic, Methodology, and the Philosophy of Science Vol VI*, 299–313.

McDowell, J. (1986). Singular Thought and the Extent of Inner Space. In P. Pettit and J. McDowell (eds.), *Subject, Thought, and Context*. Oxford: Clarendon Press, 137–168.

McKinsey, M. (1986). Mental Anaphora. *Synthese* 66, 159–175.

Meinong, A. (1904). The Theory of Objects. In *Untersuchungen zür Gegenstandstheorie und Psychologie*. In G. Isemenger (ed.), *Logic and Philosophy*. New York: Appleton-Century-Crofts, 1968.

Mitchell, D. (1962). *An Introduction to Logic*. London: Hutchison.

Montague, R. (1968). Pragmatics. In R. Thomason (ed.), *Formal Philosophy: Selected Papers of Richard Montague*. New Haven: Yale University Press, 1974, 95–118.

Montague, R. (1970). English as a Formal Language. In R. Thomason (ed.), *Formal Philosophy: Selected Papers of Richard Montague*. New Haven: Yale University Press, 1974, 188–221.

Montague, R. (1973). The Proper Treatment of Quantification in Ordinary English. In R. Thomason (ed.), *Formal Philosophy: Selected Papers of Richard Montague*. New Haven: Yale University Press, 1974, 247–270.

Moore, G. E. (1944). Russell's "Theory of Descriptions." In P. A. Schilpp (ed.), *The Philosophy of Bertrand Russell*, New York: Tudor, 177–225.(reprinted in G. E. Moore, *Philosophical Papers*. London: George Allen and Unwin, 1959, 151–195.)

Mostowski, A. (1957). On a Generalization of Quantifiers. *Fund. Math.* 44, 12–36.

Neale, S. (1988). Events and "Logical Form." *Linguistics and Philosophy* 11, 303–321.

Neale, S. (1988a). Descriptive Pronouns and Donkey Anaphora. Paper presented to the American Philosophical Association, Pacific Division, Portland Oregon, April, 1988.) To appear in the *Journal of Philosophy*.

Neale S. (1989). "One" as an Anaphor. *Behavioral and Brain Sciences* 12, 2, 353–354.

Neale, S. (1989a). Unary Quantifiers and Binary Quantifier-formers. Paper presented to the Association for Symbolic Logic, Berlin, July 1989.

Neale, S., and P. Ludlow (1989). Russellian Indefinites, Russellian Anaphors. Abstract in *Journal of Symbolic Logic* 54, 666–7.

Nerlich, G. (1965). Presupposition and Entailment. *American Philosophical Quarterly* 2, 33–42.

Nunberg, G. (1977). The Pragmatics of Reference. Doctoral thesis, CUNY.

Parsons, T. (1978). Pronouns as Paraphrases. Manuscript, University of Massachusetts at Amherst.

Partee, B. (1972). Opacity, Coreference and Pronouns. In D. Davidson and G. Harman (eds.), *Semantics of Natural Language*. Dordrecht: Reidel, 415–441.

Peacocke, C. (1975). Proper Names, Reference, and Rigid Designation. In S. Blackburn (ed.), *Meaning, Reference, and Necessity*. Cambridge: Cambridge University Press, 109–132.

Peacocke, C. (1983). *Sense and Content*. Oxford: Clarendon Press.

Perry, J. (1977). Frege on Demonstratives. *Philosophical Review* 86, 474–497.

Perry, J. (1979). The Essential Indexical. *Noûs* 13, 13–21.

Prior, A. (1963). Is the Concept of Referential Opacity Really Necessary? *Acta Philosophica Fennica* 16, 189–198.

Quine, W. V. (1940). *Mathematical Logic*. Cambridge, Mass.: Harvard University Press, revised edition 1951.

Quine, W. V. (1941). Whitehead and the Rise of Modern Logic. In P. A. Schillp (ed.), *The Philosophy of Alfred North Whitehead*. Evanston, Illinois: Northwestern University Press, 127–163.

Quine, W. V. (1943). Notes on Existence and Necessity. *Journal of Philosophy* 40, 113–127.

Quine, W. V. (1947). On the Problem of Interpreting Modal Logic. *Journal of Symbolic Logic* 12, 43–48.

Quine, W. V. (1950). *Methods of Logic*. Cambridge Mass.: Harvard University Press, fourth edition 1982.

Quine, W. V. (1953). Reference and Modality. In *From a Logical Point of View*. Cambridge, Mass.: Harvard University Press, 139–57. (Reprinted in Linsky (1971), 17–34.)

Quine, W. V. (1953a). Three Grades of Modal Involvement. *Proceedings of the XIth International Congress of Philosophy* 14, 65–81. (Reprinted in in *The Ways of Paradox and Other Essays*, New York: Random House, 156–174.)

Quine, W. V. (1956). Quantifiers and Propositional Attitudes. *Journal of Philosophy* 53, 177–187. (Reprinted in Linsky (1971), 101–111.)

Quine, W. V. (1960). *Word and Object*. Cambridge, Mass.: MIT Press.

Quine, W. V. (1969) Replies. In D. Davidson and J. Hintikka (eds.), *Words and Objections*. Dordrecht: Reidel, 292–352.

Ramsey, F. (1931). *The Foundations of Mathematics and Other Logical Essays*. London: Routledge and Kegan Paul.

Rawls, J. (1971). *A Theory of Justice*. Cambridge, Mass.: Harvard University Press.

Recanati, F. (1981). On Kripke on Donnellan. In H. Parrett, M. Sbisa, and J. Verschueren (eds.), *Possibilities and Limitations of Pragmatics*. Amsterdam: John Benjamins, 595–630.

Recanati, F. (1986) Contextual Dependence and Definite Descriptions. *Proceedings of the Aristotelian Society* 87, 57–73.

Recanati, F. (1989). Referential/Attributive: A Contextualist Proposal. *Philosophical Studies* 56, 217–249

Reeves, A. (1973). In Defence of a Simple Solution. *Australasian Journal of Philosophy* 51, 17–38.

Reinhart, T. (1976). *The Syntactic Domain of Anaphora*. Doctoral thesis, Massachusetts Institute of Technology.

Reinhart, T. (1978). Syntactic Domains for Semantic Rules. In F. Guenthner and S. J. Schmidt (eds.), *Formal Semantics and Pragmatics for Natural Languages*. Dordrecht: Reidel, 107–130.

Rescher, N. (1962). Plurality Quantification. Abstract in *Journal of Symbolic Logic* 27, 373-374.

Richards, B. (1984). On Interpreting Pronouns. *Linguistics and Philosophy* 7, 287–324.

Roberts, C. (1988). Modal Subordination and Pronominal Anaphora in Discourse. Report No. CSLI–88–127, CSLI, Stanford University. To appear in *Linguistics and Philosophy*.

Rundle, B. (1965). Modality and Quantification. In R. J. Butler (ed.), *Analytical Philosophy, Second Series*. Oxford: Blackwell, 27–39.

Russell, B. (1903). *The Principles of Mathematics*. London: George Allen and Unwin.

Russell, B. (1904). Letter to Frege. Published in G. Frege, *Philosophical and Mathematical Correspondence*. Chicago: University of Chicago Press, 1980, 166-170.

Russell, B. (1905). On Denoting. *Mind* 14, 479–493. (Reprinted in R. C. Marsh (ed.), *Logic and Knowledge*. London: George Allen and Unwin, 1956, 41–56.)

Russell, B. (1911). Knowledge by Acquaintance and Knowledge by Description. In *Mysticism and Logic*. London: George Allen and Unwin, 1917, 152–167.

Russell, B. (1912). *The Problems of Philosophy*. Oxford: Oxford University Press.

Russell, B. (1918). The Philosophy of Logical Atomism. In R. C. Marsh (ed.), *Logic and Knowledge*. London: George Allen and Unwin, 1956, 177–281.

Russell, B. (1919). *Introduction to Mathematical Philosophy*. London: George Allen and Unwin.

Russell, B. (1944). Reply to Criticisms. In P. A. Schilpp (ed.), *The Philosophy of Bertrand Russell*. New York: Tudor.

Russell, B. (1948). *An Inquiry into Meaning and Truth*. Harmondsworth: Penguin.

Russell, B. (1959). Mr. Strawson on Referring. In *My Philosophical Development*. London: George Allen and Unwin, 238–245.

Sainsbury, R. M. (1979). *Russell*. London: Routledge and Kegan Paul.

Salmon, N. (1980). *Reference and Essence*. Princeton: Princeton University Press.

Salmon, N. (1982). Assertion and Incomplete Definite Descriptions. *Philosophical Studies* 42, 37–45.

Salmon, N. (1986). Reflexivity. *Notre Dame Journal of Formal Logic* 27, 401-429.

Scha, R. (1984). Distributive, Collective, and Cumulative Quantification. In J. Groenendijk et al. (eds.), *Truth, Interpretation, and Information*. Dordrecht: Foris, 485–512.

Schiffer, S. (1972). *Meaning*. Oxford: Clarendon Press.

Searle, J. (1969). *Speech Acts: An Essay in the Philosophy of Language*. Cambridge: Cambridge University Press.

Searle, J. (1975). Indirect Speech Acts. In P. Cole and J. Morgan (eds.), *Syntax and Semantics, vol. 3: Speech Acts*. New York: Academic Press, 59–82.

Searle, J. (1979). Referential and Attributive. *The Monist* 62, 140–208. (Reprinted in *Expression and Meaning*. Cambridge: Cambridge University Press, 1983, 137–161.)

Sellars, W. (1954). Presupposing. *Philosophical Review* 63, 197–215.

Sells, P. (1985). Restrictive and Non-restrictive Modification. Report No. CSLI–85–28, CSLI, Stanford University.

Sharvy, R. (1969). Things. *The Monist* 53, 488–504.

Sharvy, R. (1980). A More General Theory of Definite Descriptions. *Philosophical Review* 89, 607–624.

Smiley, T. J. (1981) The Theory of Descriptions. *Proceedings of the British Academy* 67, 321–337

Smullyan, A. F. (1947). Review of Quine's 'The Problem of Interpreting Modal Logic'. *Journal of Symbolic Logic* 12, 139–141.

Smullyan, A. F. (1948). Modality and Description. *Journal of Symbolic Logic* 13, 31–37. (Reprinted in Linsky (1971), 35–43.)

Soames, S. (1982). How Presuppositions are Inherited: A Solution to the Projection Problem. *Linguistic Inquiry* 13, 483–545.

Soames, S. (1986). Incomplete Definite Descriptions. *Notre Dame Journal of Formal Logic* 27, 349–375.

Soames, S. (1987). Review of Hornstein's *Logic as Grammar*. *Journal of Philosophy* 84, 447–455.

Soames, S. (1988). Substitutivity. In J. Thomson (ed.), *On Being and Saying: Essays for Richard Cartwright*. Cambridge, Mass.: MIT Press, 99–132.

Soames, S. (1989). Review of Gareth Evans' *The Collected Papers*. *Journal of Philosophy* 86, 141–156.

Soames, S. (forthcoming). Pronouns and Propositional Attitudes.

Sommers, F. (1982). *The Logic of Natural Language*. Oxford: Clarendon Press.

Sperber, D., and D. Wilson (1981). Irony and the Use-mention Distinction. In P. Cole (ed.), *Radical Pragmatics*. New York: Academic Press, 295–318.

Sperber, D., and D. Wilson (1986). *Relevance*. Oxford: Blackwell.

Stalnaker, R. (1972). Pragmatics. In D. Davidson and G. Harman (eds.), *Semantics of Natural Language*, Dordrecht: Reidel, 380–397.

Stich, S. (1983). *From Folk Psychology to Cognitive Science*. Cambridge, Mass.: MIT Press.

Stich, S. (1986). Are Belief Predicates Systematically Ambiguous? In R. J. Bogdan (ed.), *Belief*. Oxford: Clarendon Press, 119–147.

Strawson, P. F. (1950). On Referring. *Mind* 59, 320–344. (Reprinted in Strawson (1971), 1–27.)

Strawson, P. F. (1952). *Introduction to Logical Theory*. London: Methuen.

Strawson P. F. (1954). Reply to Mr Sellars. *Philosophical Review* 63, 216–231.

Strawson, P. F. (1959). *Individuals*. London: Methuen.

Strawson, P. F. (1964). Identifying Reference and Truth-Values. *Theoria* 30, 96–118. (Reprinted in Strawson (1971), 75–95.)

Strawson, P. F. (1971). *Logico-Linguistic Papers*. London: Methuen.

Strawson, P. F. (1972). *Subject and Predicate in Logic and Grammar*. London: Methuen.

Strawson, P. F. (1986). Direct Singular Reference: Intended Reference and Actual Reference. In L. Nagl and R. Heinrich (eds.), *Wo Steht die Analytische Philosophie Heute*. Wien: R. Oldenbourg Verlag, 75–81.

Taylor, B. (1985). *Modes of Occurrence*. Oxford: Blackwell.

Thomason, R. (1969). Modal Logic and Metaphysics. In K. Lambert (ed.), *The Logical Way of Doing Things*. New Haven: Yale University Press, 119–146.

Thomason, R. (1985). Some Issues Concerning the Interpretation of Derived and Gerundive Nominals. *Linguistics and Philosophy* 8, 73–80.

Tye, M. (1979). Brand on Event Identity. *Philosophical Studies* 35, 81–89.

Vendler, Z. (1967). Singular Terms. In *Linguistics in Philosophy*. Ithaca, NY: Cornell University Press.

Wasow, T. (1972). *Anaphoric Relations in English*. Doctoral dissertation, Massachusetts Institute of Technology. (Published as *Anaphora in Generative Grammar*. Gent: E. Story-Scientia, 1979.)

Wettstein, H. (1981). Demonstrative Reference and Definite Descriptions. *Philosophical Studies* 40, 241–257.

Whitehead, A. N., and B. Russell (1927). *Principia Mathematica*, vol. I, 2nd ed. Cambridge: Cambridge University Press.

Wiggins, D. (1975). Identity, Designation, Essentialism, and Physicalism. *Philosophia* 5, 1–30.

Wiggins, D. (1980). "Most" and "All": Some Comments on a Familiar Programme, and on the Logical Form of Quantified Sentences. In M. Platts (ed.), *Reference, Truth, and Reality*. London: Routledge and Kegan Paul, 318–346.

Wiggins, D. (1985). Verbs and Adverbs, and Some Other Modes of Grammatical Combination. *Proceedings of the Aristotelian Society* 86, 1–32.

Wilson, D. (1975). *Presupposition and Non-Truth-Conditional Semantics*. New York: Academic Press.

Wilson, D., and D. Sperber (1981). On Grice's Theory of Conversation. In P. Werth (ed.), *Conversation and Discourse*. London: Croom Helm, 155–178.

Wilson, D., and D. Sperber (1986). On Defining Relevance. In R. Grandy and R. Warner (eds.), *Philosophical Grounds of Rationality*. Oxford: Clarendon Press, 243–258.

Wilson, G. (1978). On Definite and Indefinite Descriptions. *Philosophical Review* 87, 48–76.

Wilson, G. (1984). Pronouns and Pronominal Descriptions: A New Semantical Category. *Philosophical Studies* 45, 1–30.

Wilson, N. (1959). *The Concept of Language*. Toronto: University of Toronto Press.

Wittgenstein, L. (1921) *Tractatus Logico-Philosophicus*. English tr. by D. Pears and B. McGuinness, London: Routledge and Kegan Paul, 1961.

Zalta, E. (1988). *Intensional Logic and the Metaphysics of Intensionality*. Cambridge, Mass.: MIT Press.

Index